Introduction to Forensic Psychology
Clinical and Social Psychological Perspectives

Introduction to Forensic Psychology

Clinical and Social Psychological Perspectives

Lenore E. A. Walker

and

David L. Shapiro

Nova Southeastern University, Ft. Lauderdale, Florida

KLUWER ACADEMIC / PLENUM PUBLISHERS
NEW YORK, BOSTON, DORDRECHT, LONDON, MOSCOW

Library of Congress Cataloging-in-Publication Data

Walker, Lenore E.
    Introduction to forensic psychology : clinical and social psychological perspectives / by Lenore E.A. Walker and David L. Shapiro.
    p. cm.
    Includes bibliographical references and index.
    ISBN 0-306-47908-7
    1. Forensic psychology.   2. Forensic psychology—Social aspects.   I. Shapiro, David L., 1943–   II. Title.

RA1148.W34   2004
614'.15—dc22   2003060286

ISBN: 0-306-47908-7

© 2003 Kluwer Academic/Plenum Publishers, New York
233 Spring Street, New York, New York 10013

http://www.wkap.nl

10 9 8 7 6 5 4 3 2 1

Printed in the United States of America.

This book is dedicated to
OUR STUDENTS
From whom we learn so much
As we teach

Contents

I

What is Forensic Psychology?

In this section, we will first look at the various knowledge bases in the field of psychology and how psychologists may be of assistance in understanding the legal issues by applying psychological research and clinical methods. We need to understand the U.S. Constitution and how it relates to the U.S. legal system so we provide a review of our history and how our legal system relates to other countries' legal systems around the world. While psychologists can provide informal consultation about psychology to attorneys and courts at any time they are hired to do so, when testimony is to be admitted, there are rules of evidence that must be followed. The evolution of the admissibility of psychological expertise began by admitting expert opinions in various areas of psychology until finally, psychologists as professionals were granted parity to medical doctors. More recently, all expert testimony has been regulated by changes in the rules of evidence and case law that we discuss in the final chapter of this section.

1

Introduction to Forensic Psychology

Forensic Psychology is the study of the integration of psychology and the law. It is a new blend of two old professions—psychology, which is the study of human behavior, and law, which is the study of how people rule themselves in social situations. Psychologists generally use the scientific method of induction to understand human behavior while lawyers use reason or the deductive method of inquiry to understand legal issues. Each discipline uses different methods to interpret and solve problems. We believe that using the knowledge, information, and techniques of both disciplines to better understand simple and complex problems is the best way to find 'truth'. It is like the old saying, "two heads are better than one".

This book is written from the perspective of psychologists using their knowledge, information and techniques to help attorneys and judges better solve legal problems. In order to provide the most help to the legal profession, it is important to understand the rules and practices of each discipline. The authors, who are both forensic psychologists, attempt to do that here.

TABLE 1-1. PSYCHOLOGICAL & LEGAL
METHODS OF FINDING 'TRUTH'

LEGAL 'TRUTH'
- Based on process of reason
- Uses deductive method of inquiry
- Uses an adversarial procedure
- Each side presents its best version of facts
- 'Truth' is somewhere between the two sides
- But only one side can win!

PSYCHOLOGICAL 'TRUTH'
- Based on scientific observation and testing
- Uses inductive method of inquiry
- Starts with Null Hypothesis
  Goal is to disprove it!
- Clinicians make a differential diagnosis
  Start in middle and rule out hypotheses
- 'Truth' is based on what can be measured
- Opinions are based on scientific facts

HISTORY

Although it is fairly recent, perhaps only in the last thirty years or so that psychologists have been regularly testifying in American courts, the application of science to the study of legal problems can be traced back about 100 years in Europe. In 1896, Albert von Schrenck-Notzing claims to have offered the first expert witness testimony in Munich, Germany. His testimony dealt with pretrial publicity and the impact it might have on a person's later memories. Von Schrenck-Notzing supposedly used psychological research published the previous year, 1895, about the conditions that can make testimony inaccurate to assist the court in making its decision. In 1901, William Stern published the first known journal on the psychology of forensic testimony called the *Betrage zur Psychologie der Aussage.*

Some attribute the interests in studying the criminal mind in the United States to Hugo Munsterberg, an experimental psychologist who was trained in Germany and came to Harvard University to set up a psychology laboratory in 1892 at the invitation of William James. Highly critical of the academic psychologists' lack of attention to the application of their ideas to the solution of real life problems, Munsterberg's book, *On the Witness Stand*, published in 1908 discussed forensic applications such as the impact of memory on accuracy of eye witness testimony, suggestibility of witnesses and on confessions, and the prevention of crime. In 1900, Alfred Binet, the French psychologist who developed the first standardized intelligence test, the Stanford-Binet, testified in court about the use of psychological tests with delinquents and criminals. These tests were later used in large scale for screening potential police as well as criminals and by World War II in the 1940's, were used in many different ways to classify and design treatment for soldiers. In fact, the use of scientific psychometric tests has continued to be one of the strong assets the psychologist can bring to the law. In 1911, a Belgium psychologist, Varendonck testified that child witnesses did not have the mental capacity of adults and their testimony should not be admitted in courts. That same year, a German psychologist, Carl Marbe testified about proximate cause in a civil lawsuit. He described the psychological experiments used to determine that alcohol can have a negative impact on a person's reaction time and subsequent behavior.

In the United States the introduction of expert witness testimony took a similar route. In 1921 a case called, *State v. Driver* recognized that a psychologist could be an expert on juvenile delinquency, but the court rejected that psychologist's testimony, anyhow. One of the first cases that set the standards of admitting all experts, including psychologists, called the *Frye* standard was decided in 1923. However, the admissibility of psychological testimony in courts has been a long, hard battle in the United States. This may be because of the opposition of psychiatrists, who wanted to be the only discipline to be considered experts on medical testimony about the abnormal mind, rather than permit the broader testimony psychologists could offer about the scientific understanding of normal as well as abnormal behavior. However, the courts soon realized that both medical and scientific testimony could assist the judge or jury in better making their decisions. In the Michigan case called *People v. Hawthorne* it was found that a "psychologist's ability to detect insanity could not be presumed inferior to medical man (sic)"

Cases in the 1950's and 1960's really began to define the profession's usefulness in the courts. The lead cases were in the area of civil rights where social psychology knowledge was important to help the court make its decisions. In 1954, the famous desegregation case, *Brown v. Board of Education*, determined that separation was not equal education after social psychologists Kenneth and Mamie Clark demonstrated their experiments showing that children did not treat African American and Caucasian-looking dolls in the same way. This case was also important in that the American Medical Association and the American Psychological Association passed resolutions that both groups were legitimate experts who could comment on social science. However, it must be pointed out that the values of society must be ready to accept scientific opinion. More than fifty years earlier, when the courts decided *Plessy v. Ferguson* (1896), even scientists went along with the majority opinion that segregation of the races was an acceptable policy because it was consistent with the customs and desires of people. Testimony in civil cases concerning mental status of a litigant was also decided in 1954 with a case called, *Hidden v. Mutual Life*.

Interestingly, it took another eight years, until 1962 when the U.S. District Court for the District of Columbia recognized that psychologists and not just psychiatrists have expertise in criminal responsibility cases in a decision called *Jenkins v. U.S.* While the case itself dealt with the admissibility of a psychologist's testimony, the court's ruling went beyond disciplines and gave the power to the trial court judge to determine the testifier's expertise. Prior to 1984, the Federal Criminal Code used the terms 'psychiatric examination' and 'psychiatric testimony'. In the Insanity Defense Reform Act of 1984, the wording was changed to 'psychiatric or psychological'. Together with the ruling from *Jenkins* other types of health and mental health providers were permitted to give relevant testimony if they could demonstrate their expertise in the area. A large number of cases followed that helped the courts determine a variety of constitutional issues for imprisoned criminals such as whether or not they could be involuntarily treated, either with medication or could be sent to a psychiatric hospital against their will. These will be described further in the relevant chapters.

In the late 1970's, the field of forensic psychology, as it was called when psychology and the law were combined, was sufficiently developed to petition the American Psychological Association (APA) for a division to represent psychologists who held such interests. This became the 41st division that later changed its name to the American Psychology-Law Society, Division 41 of the APA. In 1977, the division began publishing its own journal, *Law and Human Behavior* and today there are several other important journals that publish information about psychology and the law including *Psychology, Public Policy, and Law* which was recently begun. There are now several different types of international organizations whose members specialize in the various areas of psychology and the law and who meet at different times of the year. The American Board of Forensic Psychology and its American Academy of Forensic Psychology provide training workshops that lead to diplomate status and continuing education for those who are at the highest level of practice in the field. In 2001, the APA determined that Clinical Forensic Psychology is a specialty area for practice. This means that evaluation, assessment and intervention or testimony with people is the clinical branch of forensic psychology and it requires specialized training. The International Association of Applied Psychology also has a division on psychology and the law and today forensic psychologists practice in most countries of the world.

WHAT DO FORENSIC PSYCHOLOGISTS DO?

The most typical answer to the question, "Why do you want to be a forensic psychologist?" is "to learn to profile serial killers". The study of the criminal mind fascinates scientists as well as laypersons. Many people who go into policing, law, and psychology are fascinated with understanding why people do such awful things to each other. All legal systems that are based on *mens rea* or the actor's state of mind must have some way of getting into the mind of the criminal. This includes performing competency exams in a variety of areas, administering standardized psychological tests, determining if someone was insane at the time of commission of an act, and helping to decide the risk of further violence. As these are competencies learned from clinical psychology, we call psychologists who practice them, clinical forensic psychologists. However, forensic psychologists can do many more things than just provide expert testimony on criminal matters.

Psychologists can use social psychology research about the impact of social problems on individuals, help assess attitudes and detect bias when selecting lay jurors if they are used instead of judges, and submit Amicus Curiae Briefs citing research in various types of appellate cases. They can use the knowledge about persuasion techniques to assist attorneys in preparation for and conduct of a trial. They also can provide information about the reliability and validity of eyewitness identification and the stability of memories over time and in different situations. They can offer the court information about the developmental stages of a child's cognitive skills and other abilities. Or, at the other end of the life cycle, they can offer information about the decline of cognitive functions in the elderly. As in the *Brown v. Board of Education* case mentioned above, psychologists may also introduce evidence about the impact of discrimination on general or specific populations. Sometimes this information is provided informally to the court upon request, sometimes it is provided through a formal consultation relationship established, sometimes the information is in formal written reports, and sometimes it is in oral sworn testimony subject to cross-examination.

TABLE 1-2. FORENSIC PSYCHOLOGISTS & SOCIAL PSYCHOLOGY

- Apply social psychology research to study legal issues before the court
- Apply research on attitudes to overcome bias about case
- Apply knowledge about persuasion
- Apply knowledge about bias when selecting jurors
- Assess impact of attorney's presentation
- Apply psychological research to development of public policy

Using methods such as:
- Literature searches & reviews
- Community attitude & public opinion surveys
- Focus groups
- Mock trials
- Visual and graphic trial aids
- Consult and train staff
- Oral reports
- Written reports
- Prepare Amicus Curiae Briefs

Those who work in the criminal justice system may provide treatment to the many men and women who are mentally ill, have substance abuse problems, or are suffering from other mental defects and diseases. In the U.S. as well as in other countries, it is believed that over 25% of the jail and prison population have serious mental illnesses that need medication and psychotherapy treatment. Another 50% may also have alcohol and other drug problems that if go untreated may be a primary cause of recidivism and further crime. We are learning new treatment techniques for sex offenders that may help prevent them from repeating their crimes. As you will see in the chapter on interventions in forensic settings, new methods are being tried to rehabilitate criminals while they are still incarcerated. Given the enormous cost of keeping criminals in jails and prisons, we are also experimenting new treatment approaches while they are living in the community, often using electronic monitoring systems as a way of control.

As might be expected from our history, clinical forensic psychologists evaluate children and help the court decide what is in the best interests of the child, which is the legal standard in most parts of the world today. Rather than sending the child to live with one or both parents based on what they or their lawyers tell the judge, it is more common to have the input from a psychologist who can describe their parental fitness

TABLE 1-3. FORENSIC PSYCHOLOGISTS & CRIMINAL LAW

Evaluate and testify to:
- Competency to waive Miranda rights to confess
- Competency to proceed to trial
- Competency to represent oneself at trial
- Competency to enter into a plea agreement
- Sanity and insanity issues
- Other mental status issues
- Mitigation and downward departure on sentences
- Intoxication impact on mental status
- Retardation and impact on mental status
- Death penalty issues

Using methods such as:
- Standard clinical interviews & observation of clients/defendants
- Administer standardized psychological tests
- Administer other assessment instruments
- Administer neuropsychological tests
- Review other medical and psychological reports
- Review of legal documents for psychological relevance
- Integrate data with psychological research
- Create treatment plans
- Provide psychotherapy & other interventions in forensic settings

and how that matches the needs and best interests of the child. This is especially important when dealing with allegations of physical, sexual, or psychological abuse in the family. Child abuse and termination of parental rights, delinquency and prevention of youth becoming career criminals, and other areas that affect family functioning are all areas of expertise that psychologists who work with the family have developed and their knowledge may be of benefit to the court when such issues arise.

Clinical forensic psychologists also can help in the civil area of the law by assessing the ability of clients to enter into contracts voluntarily and without duress, understanding the limits of appropriate practice and malpractice, and measuring the impact of an injury on the psychological health and quality of life. Psychological impact from automobile and industrial accident injuries, exposure to toxic materials, sexual harassment on the job, airplane crashes, and other catastrophic events in life that cause injuries can be measured by using clinical psychological and neuropsychological assessment techniques that are adapted for forensic use. In addition, forensic assessment of the person's veracity can be measured by using specialized

TABLE 1-4. FORENSIC PSYCHOLOGISTS & FAMILY PSYCHOLOGY

- Assess each family member for parental fitness
- Assess each child to help determine needs & 'best interests'
- Make custody & visitation recommendations
- Make recommendations about moving to another community
- Make recommendations about adoption and foster parenting
- Help determine children with special needs
- Assess for child abuse
- Assess for woman abuse
- Create parenting plans
- Monitor parenting plans
- Determine competency for pre & post nuptial agreements
- Assess youth arrested for juvenile delinquency
- Determine effective intervention/prevention for juveniles
- Make assessments during family feuds
- Help in determining necessity for guardianship in probate cases

Using methods such as:
- Standard clinical interviews & observation of clients/defendants
- Administer standardized psychological tests
- Administer other assessment instruments
- Administer neuropsychological tests
- Review other medical and psychological reports
- Review of legal documents for psychological relevance
- Integrate data with psychological research
- Create treatment plans
- Provide psychotherapy
- Coach parents through custody evaluations
- Coach families through disputes around business and other matters

tests that detect malingering or feigning symptoms for some personal gain. The person who has been damaged by negligence or intentional harm may be awarded compensation or even punitive damages if the nexus between the act and the subsequent harm can be proven.

Forensic psychologists are often asked to assist the court in determining 'if but for that action' the person would not have the current injuries. In the American legal system a person may claim damages even if the particular act was not the first time the person was so damaged. However, if the defendant being sued was the last person to harm the plaintiff, then, like the person who pushed Humpty Dumpty off the wall and his previously cracked eggshell shattered, it is that person's responsibility. Sometimes, the court will want to apportion the damage to different contributors and psychologists may be able to assist in that task by using some of our assessment tools.

TABLE 1-5. FORENSIC PSYCHOLOGISTS & CIVIL LAW

- Assess for competency to enter into contracts
- Assess for duress in legal contracts
- Assess for psychological impact from injury from car or other accidents
- Assess for psychological impact from injury from toxic exposure
- Assess for psychological impact from injury from catastrophic event
- Assess for psychological impact from injury from negligence or malpractice
- Assess for sexual harassment
- Assess for psychological impact of discrimination of civil rights
- Assess for malpractice by other psychologists
- Assess for civil commitment when risk of danger to self or others
- Assess for neuropsychological consequences of head injury or other toxic exposure

Using methods such as:
- Standard clinical interviews & observation of clients/defendants
- Administer standardized psychological tests
- Administer other assessment instruments
- Administer neuropsychological tests
- Review other medical and psychological reports
- Review of legal documents for psychological relevance
- Integrate data with psychological research
- Consultation with others
- Create treatment plans for rehabilitation/recovery
- Provide expert witness testimony

HOW DO FORENSIC PSYCHOLOGISTS WORK?

Forensic psychologists collect information about a case by first gathering research about a particular issue raised in a case. They often use articles or books published in the literature about the scientific data in the particular area. The psychologist will review the information, critique it from a scientific perspective, give various opinions that exist, and present that information to the legal community that requested it either in written or oral form. Often psychologists write a brief report or assist an attorney in writing a legal brief that will utilize this information. Sometimes the psychologist will assist an attorney in formulating questions to ask another expert on direct or cross-examination during trial or deposition. In some cases, usually large ones involving serious financial liability, the psychologist may be asked to conduct focus groups or mock trials and determine what kind of people could judge the case in the most favorable light for them and with what various types of presentations of the evidence.

Clinical forensic psychologists will also use clinical interviews, standardized test data, and other clinical assessment techniques to learn about the individual person. They may diagnose mental illness, conduct neuropsychological examinations, or measure the impact from battered woman or rape trauma syndromes. It is common for psychologists to review other medical and psychological reports about the person's current and prior history. Histories of a person's education, work, and relationships are all important to develop a good understanding of a person's state of mind at any time. These data are then integrated with what is known about human behavior to help answer whatever legal question is at issue.

WHO HIRES A FORENSIC PSYCHOLOGIST?

Forensic psychologists work in many different settings. Clinical forensic psychologists often have a clinical therapy practice along with their forensic practice. It may be an independent practice in their own offices, group offices that are shared with others, or it may be in a separate mental health agency. It is usually not a good idea to mix therapy and a forensic evaluation for the same person as it may cause the psychologist to become biased in some way. But, sometimes it cannot be helped and in fact, will provide the court with important information that could not be obtained elsewhere. Psychologists are cautioned by the ethics code to make sure that the multiple relationship with the client does not impair the professional's objectivity and cause harm.

Attorneys often hire forensic psychologists, usually to work on behalf of their client but sometimes to assist them in preparing the case. It could be a state prosecutor or defense attorney if it is a criminal case, or a plaintiff or defense attorney, if it is a civil case. Sometimes a forensic psychologist may be hired by a large law firm, either for a certain specified number of hours or on a retainer agreement. Insurance companies may hire a forensic psychologist to help defend against a particular claim or to prevent further damage to a company, such as occurred when sexual harassment laws were initially promulgated and it became clear that a company with a good plan to deal with harassment would be given better treatment in the courts than one that continued to ignore its importance while the lawsuit was pending.

Government agencies may need to hire a forensic psychologist either to deal with a specific case or to be of assistance in formulating public policy that involves psychological issues. For example, the National Institute of Justice's forensic science policies have been formulated with the input from forensic psychologists with expertise in that particular area. Workers'

TABLE 1-6. MODEL FORENSIC PSYCHOLOGY TRAINING PROGRAM[1]

- PhD/PsyD in Clinical Psychology
- Concentration with 18 credits in forensic psychology courses
    Courses can be selected from
- Introduction to Forensic Psychology
- Forensic Assessment
- Psychology and Criminal Law
- Psychology and Family Law
- Psychology and Juvenile Justice
- Psychological Interventions in Forensic Settings
- Police Psychology
- Trial consultation and Jury Selection
- Forensic Psychology: Special Issues
- Other trauma courses
- Other assessment courses
- Forensic Practicum of 700+ hours in third year of program
    Practicum sites include rotation in:
        Mental Health Court
        Involuntary civil commitment
        Juvenile Detention Center Competency Screenings
        Drug Court
        Sex offender report reviews
        Capital crime cases
- Research in clinical forensic psychology areas
    Institute for Trauma & Victimology
    Family Violence Intervention Program
    Police Psychology
    F.B.I. Practicums
    Battered Women Syndrome
    Juvenile Justice & Innovative TeamChild program
    Neuropsychology & Forensic Psychology Issues
    PTSD & Capital Crime Cases
    Death Penalty Research
    Efficacy of Competency Restoration Programs
    Sex Predator Laws
    Trauma Reintegration Program research
- Dissertation or Directed Study in forensic area
- Optional forensic psychology internship

[1]This program is offered at Nova Southeastern University's Center for Psychological Studies located in Ft. Lauderdale, Florida where the authors are professors. See website at *www.nova.edu* for further updated information.

Compensation agencies need forensic psychological evaluations to determine disability income cases. Immigration offices may need forensic testimony to protect an immigrant who is being abused from deportation if she leaves her husband. Police and law enforcement departments hire psychologists to work with officers who need crisis counseling or assessment for fitness for duty. The FBI, for example, has a well-respected behavioral science unit, that consists of law enforcement officers and forensic psychologists. Mental health and legal agencies may hire forensic psychologists to train their staff in psychology and the law. Judges may hire forensic psychologists to assist them in preparing written opinions that they want published.

WHAT KIND OF TRAINING DOES A FORENSIC PSYCHOLOGIST NEED?

Most forensic psychologists are trained at the doctoral level. In fact, most clinical forensic training programs occur after the doctoral degree is earned in post doctoral internships and residencies or in continuing education courses. A new program is now available in some professional schools where elective credits are taken in a forensic specialization or concentration. A model program is outlined in Table 1-6.

Many master's level psychologists work as forensic psychologists without the title when they provide treatment in jails and prisons or as psychological assistants who administer and score psychological tests. Many family courts hire master's level mental health workers to assess for fitness to parent children or provide parent training classes or other types of psycho-legal interventions. In fact, the training for mental health workers in forensic settings has been in community colleges and colleges for many years now. However, the names and titles may be different from 'forensic psychologist', which is more often used for those who practice at the doctoral level. It is important to check with various colleges or university systems to see what they offer.

2

Models of Legal Systems

Although most of us studied U.S. history and the Constitution when we were in school, we rarely think about it in connection with the laws that we follow on a daily basis. Indeed, knowledge about the Constitution and its Bill of Rights is important to understand how our legal system works. This is true for any country's laws, so a quick review of how the system in the U.S. works is in order here. If you live in another country, try to substitute your country's Constitution and rules of law for those in the U.S. Obviously, those countries who use a democratic form of government will be closer to the U.S. system than those who have another form of government.

WHERE DO OUR LAWS COME FROM?

The U.S. Constitution divides our government into three different divisions—the executive, legislative and judicial branches. The legislative branch is charged with making our laws, the executive branch carries them out and the judicial branch enforces them. It was thought that the tripartite split in government would provide checks and balances to assure democracy. The executive branch may set rules that help to carry out the laws and the judicial branch may set case precedents that then are enforced by the legal system, too. However, the judicial system can be used to challenge the constitutionality of any type of law by using its trial court and appellate system. So our laws come from different areas of government and are constantly changing, with each branch providing checks and balances on the other. There is a carefully crafted set of rules that must be followed when challenging whether someone is following the law and these change too. Clearly, the law is a living process that changes with the times and will of the people.

The Constitution tells us what laws are created by Congress, what laws are created by the Senate, and what laws are left to the individual states to determine on their own. All the criminal justice codes except for those involving terrorism, kidnapping across state lines, or criminal acts committed on federally controlled lands are left to the states while those involving interstate commerce and civil rights codes are governed by the Federal system. State legislatures and courts govern most of the civil laws although some actions that are under a certain dollar amount are left to the local governments. If someone works all over the country, it is important to learn the different laws in each jurisdiction. To make matters even more confusing, different groups including the American Bar Association have put forth model laws governing different areas that are found in most jurisdictions and many states have adopted these 'Uniform Codes' as they are often called in place of their own laws. Some states adopt the entire code, language and all, while others use some but not all of the language. Obviously, the neophyte to the legal system must be vigilant in learning to distinguish one from another.

WHAT LEGAL RIGHTS DO WE HAVE?

Our legal system is based on the British Common Law system, which is used in many countries around the world. It guarantees certain basic rights called *due process* including the right to be considered innocent until proven guilty, to confront your accuser, to a speedy trial, to be treated with certain human rights, etc. Our legal system divides legal issues into criminal and civil matters. Many of the basic rights apply to the criminal justice system. The civil system deals with property issues, contracts, family matters, wills and probate matters, and the like. The two systems have different standards. To prove a case in the criminal justice system demands the highest standard of proof, 'beyond a reasonable doubt'. The civil standard of proof is either at a 'preponderance of the evidence' or 'clear and convincing evidence'. It is often said that a preponderance of the evidence means more likely than not or 51% while clear and convincing evidence is a higher standard, around 75% or so. 'Beyond a reasonable doubt' is thought to be 99% sure and criminal defense attorneys usually try to cast as much doubt as possible in their trials to help their clients. In family court the standard of proof is the 'best interests of the child' and it may require preponderance or clear and convincing evidence, depending on the type of case. For example, custody decisions are usually at the preponderance of evidence level while termination of parental rights is usually at the higher standard.

We will use these terms throughout this book as they set the level of the burden of proof that one side or the other must meet. Often logic flowing from values determines which level of proof is needed. In a decision that would be difficult if not impossible to change, the higher burden of proof is needed. The closer a verdict might deprive a person's liberty, the higher the standard that is necessary. So, in criminal cases it must be a unanimous decision of the jurors that the person is guilty beyond a reasonable doubt. But, in cases involving bad faith in fulfilling a contract, it is sufficient for the evidence to prove it was more likely than not that this occurred to a majority of the jurors.

Who has the burden of proof may also be important to understand the elements of a legal case. In the Common Law system that is used in the U.S., the state has a burden of proof in a criminal case. The defense does not have to prove that someone is not guilty because everyone, even those accused of committing a crime, is considered innocent until proven guilty. However, attorneys understand that there are many reasons that someone may appear guilty so a psychologist might be called in to testify to explain what is counter-intuitive to the average person. In civil cases, the person who brings the lawsuit usually has the burden of proof. In custody and visitation cases, the standard as we said is the best interests of the child but there are several presumptions that the law states are in the best interests of the child that have to be overcome if advocating for a different arrangement.

For example, most states presume that some form of legal and residential 'shared parental custody' is in the best interests of the child. So, if that arrangement is not appropriate for a child, it is necessary to both overcome the presumption in the law and prove what is in the child's best interests. Different states have different laws that describe how this may be done. For example, in the state of Florida, the presumption of shared parental custody is divided into two parts: legal and residential custody. The presumption is that it is best for children to have both parents make legal decisions together but it is best for them to have a primary residence where they live most of the time but also have a secondary residential parent named. To change from this standard, the burden is to show that it would be 'detrimental to the child's best interests'. The statute defines a number of ways it is possible to demonstrate what would be 'detrimental to the child's best interests'. To prove something is detrimental is more difficult than simply proving another arrangement would be in the child's best interests. We will discuss these issues further in the chapter that deals with child custody issues.

OTHER LEGAL SYSTEMS

Other legal systems are based on variations of the Napoleonic Code, Roman Law, and Dutch legal system as well as the British Common Law. In the Napoleonic tradition, for example, the accused person has the burden to prove his or her innocence rather than be presumed to be innocent. The state attorney is an inquisitor and can require the accused to answer questions. Unlike in the Common Law system where the accused has the right to remain silent and not incriminate her or him-self, in other legal systems, not responding may be tantamount to an admission of guilt. Although there are substantial differences in the various legal systems, sometimes they do not have as much impact as we might think on the way a mental health professional might work in the courts.

For example, in South Africa, the legal system is based on a combination of different legal systems including those used by the Dutch, British, and French who settled in that country. However, many of the legal standards and burdens of proof are similar to the U.S. system. Although they have different laws that regulate the determination of criminal responsibility, they still use psychologists to assist the judge in determining the 'mens rea' or state of mind of the actor at the time of the commission of the act.

MENS REA OR STATE OF MIND

The issue of 'mens rea' is another interesting one that has different definitions depending on the laws at any particular time. In criminal responsibility cases, the concept of 'insanity' is one that has been defined by lawmakers and not mental health professionals. Thus, adapting to the various definitions may be problematic for a psychologist and different mental health workers may arrive at different opinions. To further confuse the matter, in many of the U.S. states, legislators have gone back to using the M'Naughten standard to define what insanity means. This standard calls for what the person is thinking at the time of an act and not necessarily what the person is feeling or whether or not the person can control his or her behavior. Thus, a psychologist who looks at cognition or thinking, affect or feeling, and how they interact together to produce behavior may have to view the data from a different perspective when trying to determine what was in the person's mind. This is further discussed in a later chapter.

WHO DECIDES: JURIES OR JUDGES?

The U.S. is one of the few countries that still use laypersons on a jury so that a person is judged by a 'jury of his or her peers'. For example, in Israel three judges make the decision in most serious criminal cases. In Greece, three judges plus a public prosecutor and two others appointed by the court make the decision in most criminal cases. In South Africa, decisions are usually made by one judge. Judges may be elected or appointed by the ruling political party. Although some believe that appointed judges are less subjected to politics once on the bench, others see the process of getting an appointment more tainted by politics than winning an election. In Federal court the judges are appointed by the President and confirmed by the Senate. They can keep their position for the rest of their lives unless they do something that triggers the impeachment process. It is clear that judges have great power to make sure justice is done.

Although there are many benefits of the jury system, in actual practice, it is rare that someone really is judged by a jury of his or her equals or peers because the methods for selecting jurors may automatically be biased. Usually juror pools come from driver's license or voter's registration lists. Sometimes the jurisdiction where someone lives is different than the jurisdiction where the trial is held, making it less likely that an equal number of minorities will be on the jury. Many challenges to the constitutionality of a trial have claimed bias in the jury selection process, particularly those where the prosecutor asks for the death penalty. We discuss the issue of possible juror bias and ways to try to achieve a jury of a person's peers later.

DIVISIONS OF COURTS

It is also important to understand the division of the courts when working in the legal arena. The state court system is divided into three main branches: trial, appellate and supreme courts.

Trial Court

The trial court often is divided into state and local courts and these may have further divisions such as criminal, civil, family, juvenile, probate and in some cases, specialty courts. These new specialty courts are usually found in within the criminal division and provide more rehabilitation than punishment. Typically they deal with drug use, mental health issues, and domestic violence. They are often referred to as providing 'therapeutic jurisprudence' because the goal is to stop recidivism by providing access to appropriate treatment. It is common for mental health professionals to work in these courts or at least in a close consultative relationship. We will describe them more fully in a later chapter on forensic interventions.

The proceedings in trial courts go in many stages. Various pretrial issues may arise, such as admissibility or exclusion of certain evidence. These issues may be addressed in what are called pleadings. At times there may be actual courtroom argument and/or testimony on these issues while at other times judges make decisions only based on briefs and affidavits filed by the attorneys. Especially in civil cases there may be pretrial interrogatories which are questions posed to the plaintiff or defendant by opposing counsel. These are often accompanied by 'a demand for production of documents'. In most civil cases and in some criminal cases witnesses may testify at a discovery deposition to determine what they would say at trial and in the case of experts, on what their opinion is based.

In civil cases, there may be settlement negotiations and in criminal cases plea negotiations in order to avoid going to trial. If these are successful, no trial is necessary. If these maneuverings are unsuccessful, the case will go to trial. In most cases, the triers of fact will be a judge and jury.

Jury selection is a complex process that we describe later in chapter 20. It is followed by opening statements which each attorney gets to make. Usually the opening statement sets forth each side's best version of their case with promises to prove what they say in the main part of the trial that follows. In a civil case, the plaintiffs present their case first and in a criminal trial the state presents their case first because each of them has the 'burden of proof' that the elements of a case are actually met. If they are not, the defense in either case can make a motion for a directed verdict. The facts of the case must be presented through questions and answers by the attorney with witnesses that get sworn to tell the truth. Fact witnesses can only testify to what they have seen or heard while expert witnesses are also allowed to give opinions. This is what makes the expert witness so important in most trials. The defense can cross-examine witnesses following their direct testimony. The purpose of cross examination is to elicit testimony about facts that were not presented during direct testimony that may cause the finders of fact to come to a different conclusion than was intended by the direct testimony. The judge will rule on the admissibility of certain documents and testimony following preset rules of evidence.

Following the presentation of all the evidence, the attorneys each get to present a closing argument. Here the attorney will want to summarize the evidence in the light most favorable to her or his client's position. Jury instructions are proposed by the attorneys and determined by the judge. These are the questions that the jury must answer and can determine the outcome of the trial. Finally, the jury is sent to deliberate if it is a jury trial. Usually a foreperson is appointed or elected. If the jury cannot agree to a verdict, then they tell the judge they are deadlocked and ask the judge to declare a mistrial. Sometimes the judge will send them out to try again to reach a verdict with further deliberations. Sometimes the jurors ask for clarification of certain evidence and the judge and attorneys may reach an agreement as to what to tell them. Usually the parties are in the courtroom when the jury verdict is delivered. Sometimes, when the judge makes the findings of fact, he or she does so in a written opinion.

If the litigants are unhappy with the outcome and find legal reasons to file an appeal, then the execution of the verdict may be stayed while the appeal progresses. We discuss the appellate process later in this chapter.

JUVENILE COURT

In the U.S., juvenile court is an entire system that is separate from adult court. Typically it deals with youth who are alleged to have committed acts that would be considered criminal if committed by an adult but are instead called 'delinquent' because of the youth's age and maturity level. In addition, many juvenile courts deal with youth who commit what is termed, 'status offenses'. These are youth who are unmanageable for their parents and others in the community. For example, they run away from home, do not obey curfews, and are truant from school. The Department of Juvenile Justice and the Department of Social Services usually work together with the juvenile court personnel to help find ways to rehabilitate these youngsters. In many cases they are sent to residential centers where they may or may not receive educational services or mental health treatment. Sometimes these youth are provided their own lawyers but more often, the legal system deals directly with their family. Although the 'best interests of the child' standard is supposed to apply in these cases, it is often difficult to make that happen, especially in areas when the courts are overwhelmed with so many problematic youth.

In the U.S. the publicity given to a few high profile cases by the media makes it seem that youth are involved in more serious crimes even though the number of youth committing homicides and serious crime has been decreasing since the mid 1990's according to statistics promulgated by the U.S. Department Justice's Bureau of Justice Statistics (BJS). Some very high profile cases where children have killed and then were tried in adult court have raised the issue of the viability of the juvenile court system. In the Ft. Lauderdale, Florida case of Lionel Tate, a 12-year-old boy who killed a 6-year-old girl while 'play wrestling' with her, several psychologists testified for the state and the defense about Tate's mental competence and ability to comprehend what he did. Tate's defense claimed he was only trying out wrestling moves he had seen on television and had no intent to kill the six-year-old girl. The state claimed he knew or should have known that such wrestling moves were dangerous. Was it accurate to consider Tate in the same way we consider an adult just because he committed an adult crime? At what age should a youth's behavior have the full consequences accorded to an adult? These are questions that must be answered according to the standards in our legal system but the psychologists for each side disagreed with each other. The implications raised by this troubling case and others are discussed later in chapters on children's rights and juvenile laws.

REHABILITATION COURTS

It is important to raise the question of rehabilitation verses punishment at this point. Can a criminal justice system that is dedicated to deterrence of crime and justice, substitute treatment instead of punishment? This is a troubling issue and must be dealt with whenever mental health professionals work in the criminal justice system. While it is well demonstrated in science that substituting positive behaviors or removing the cause of certain behaviors will cause them to cease, and that punishment does not permanently stop bad or maladaptive behaviors (it only suppresses the unwanted behavior temporarily), there is a bias towards wanting punishment as justice and atonement for the criminal act. Even when all who are participating in a case know that the individual is mentally ill and incapable of controlling his or her behavior, it is difficult to accept that treatment might be a substitute for punishment.

Domestic Violence Court

One of the interesting areas where this has had some limited success is in the domestic violence courts. Abusers may be arrested upon probable cause that they committed a violent act against the woman but, the woman often goes down to the jail to bail him out the next morning. Battered women insist that they usually do not want their mates to go to jail; rather they want them to receive treatment to get them to stop their abusive behavior. So, advocates have designed psycho-educational programs hoping that this would promote sufficient rehabilitation. Most of these programs require that batterers spend at least one night in jail before being court-ordered into a 'batterer offender specific treatment program'. As soon as a community institutes such a pro-arrest and rehabilitation program, the numbers of arrests dramatically increase, indicating that women really will use and cooperate with the justice system if the outcome is rehabilitation rather than simply punishment. In Denver, Colorado the number of arrests for domestic violence went from approximately 3000 per year to over 10,000 the first year the domestic violence court was operational. Similar statistics were found in Miami/Dade County, Florida. Although the evaluations show that very few batterers ever actually attend or complete such a program, of those that do approximately 75% stop their physically abusive behavior while in the program. Of these, 50% continue their psychological abuse, often making the woman's life seem much worse. It is unknown how many stop their sexual abuse.

Do these programs deal with those batterers who are mentally ill in addition to abusing power to gain control over the woman? It is difficult to say. Those who have tried to measure their effectiveness suggest that the majority of batterers will reoffend within the first year of arrest. In many cases, the violence escalates over time. So, does arrest and diversion to a therapeutic court slow down or stop domestic violence? We will address that question in further depth later but first we must also look at the premise that the criminal justice system can deliver effective treatment and punishment simultaneously.

Drug Court

Drug courts on the other hand have been highly successful in getting those who have been unable to stop their use of unlawful substances into treatment programs. Again, do the treatment programs really work? Does one model work better than another? The most popular models are those based on the Alcoholics Anonymous (AA) or Narcotics Anonymous model, the cognitive-behavioral model and the controlled drinking model. There are those who are firm believers in one of these models over the others. Yet, the scientific data demonstrate that each of these models may be helpful for certain people with certain motivation although the cognitive-behavioral model seems to be the best supported by outcome data. Some in the criminal justice system claim that despite the success that some people have in controlling their drinking or drug abuse after treatment, if we send people into rehabilitation, we are being soft on crime. Yet, over 60% of the population in the jails has some form of addiction to one substance or another. Rarely do you find adequate treatment programs in jails and prisons. So, what is the answer here?

These are serious public policy questions that psychologists can help the policy-makers answer. It is important to provide the data to the courts and legislators about the success or lack of success of these programs. Often the idea to set up a treatment program is a good one but the community underfunds it, thereby making it impossible for the intervention to be successful. It is difficult to terminate an unsuccessful program as politicians are reluctant to fund a different one so it is sometimes thought that even a semi-successful program is better than nothing. Again, a partnership between the mental health professional and the courts can spot these problems before they get serious or prevent them from occurring in the first place.

APPELLATE COURTS

The Appellate Court is the court that hears cases that someone believes did not follow proper legal procedure during the trial court phase. Different states organize their courts with several judges reviewing a case and offering an opinion while other states have the entire court make the decision. In any case, one judge is usually assigned the case to read and outline for the other judges to review. This job may be assigned to a law clerk who is an attorney who works for that judge. Sometimes, when decisions raise a psychological issue, the court may request a brief from a psychologist or psychological association to help advise them on the scientific data. If they are formally submitted, it may be called an 'Amicus Curiae' brief. The American Psychological Association enters Amicus briefs into cases that members have an interest in if there are psychological data that they believe will be helpful to the court in making its decision.

SUPREME COURT

The Supreme Court is the highest court in a state (except in New York State where the trial court is called the Supreme Court). When an appellate court decision is challenged, it is submitted to the Supreme Court Justices for a decision. Their decisions only deal with issues on law and legal issues, not on the merits of the case itself. The Supreme Court has the right to accept or deny reviewing a case. This process is called accepting or denying certiorari, often shortened to 'cert'. Usually they only accept cases that they believe have legal complications requiring a decision to guide other similar cases. If a litigant is unhappy with the decision rendered by this court, then it is possible to go to the Federal Court for relief but only if they believe the legal process itself was violated. The most common challenge is to the rulings that the trial court judge made during or before the trial. It is difficult to prove that the judge made an incorrect ruling as the rules of evidence often give the judge great latitude in making decisions. Even if the judge is found to have erred, the Supreme Court still might not overturn the decision because that error is found to be insignificant to the final outcome. The expense is great and often there is little likelihood that the Federal Courts will look any more favorably on the issues than the State court did, so it is not often that cases go that far unless they deal with major policy issues.

FEDERAL COURT SYSTEM

The U.S. Federal Court System is organized in a manner similar to state courts. The trial court is the first court where the judges who are appointed by the President and confirmed by the Senate will preside. Magistrates, who are like assistant judges assigned to work with Federal Court Justices, often sort through the cases that come to the court and hear some of the pretrial motions. Federal Court Justices are appointed for life, so it is clear that they have a lot of power. They can only be removed by impeachment by Congress. One of the most famous impeachment trials was of Miami Federal court Justice Alycee Hastings who was removed from his position.

He then ran for Congress and was elected from the Southern Florida district that he continues to represent, among many of the same Members of Congress who found his behavior inappropriate as a judge.

As was mentioned earlier, certain cases go directly into Federal Courts while others come there after being adjudicated in State courts first. Federal Court has power over the entire country and so, decisions that are promulgated from there have more influence than from state court. Judges in state court often are persuaded by Federal court decisions although it is not necessary in all cases to abide by them especially if state laws rule. Civil rights cases, particularly those that arise from the various Federal laws preventing discrimination are tried in Federal court. Like the state court system, Federal court has an appellate court and then, the U.S. Supreme Court. The only recourse from a decision in the U.S. Supreme Court is for Congress to pass a new law. However, the nine Justices who sit on the U.S. Supreme court could rule the law unconstitutional keeping up the battle between jurisdictions if it so chose. This occurred several years ago over the issue of whether it was a criminal act to burn the U.S. flag. Again, Amicus Briefs are frequently filed by interested parties when the U.S. Supreme Court is considering a case that has importance for that party. In cases that deal with mental health issues, the APA as well as many other professional organizations frequently file such briefs setting forth the literature in that particular area.

ORAL VERSUS WRITTEN TESTIMONY

Psychologists who testify before the various courts in the U.S. are frequently asked to give oral testimony presented by the attorney for one side and be cross-examined by the other side. While written testimony may be accepted in legal cases in various other countries, it is more common for criminal and most civil cases to require the oral testimony so that the other side has the opportunity to question the basis on which the opinion testimony is made. Cross-examination, then, is an important part of the U.S. legal system as it can be used to make sure that an expert does not have undue influence over a particular case without careful examination of the factual basis. In some cases, such as family law, the court may accept a written report in lieu of oral testimony if there is no objection from the other side. Often the court appoints these experts and so their opinion has great weight with the court. Some psychologists believe that it is best to be appointed by the court while others believe that they can be equally fair no matter who hires them. Sometimes the admission of an expert's opinion is challenged even before cross-examination occurs. The Frye standard, decided in 1923, held that if an expert's opinion is generally accepted in the relevant scientific community and will aid the trier of fact, then the testimony must be admitted. However, more recent cases, including the Daubert case in 1993 and subsequent decisions have given the judge more power to decide if the evidence is based on a scientific foundation. The modification of the Federal Rules of Evidence in 2001 in its Rule 702 puts forth a similar requirement. Admissibility issues will be further discussed in the next chapter.

RULES OF EVIDENCE

Every state and the Federal government have legislated Rules of Evidence that govern court trials by setting forth what will and will not be considered evidence in cases. These Rules of Evidence may be modified by the legislative branch or through case law from appellate court opinions. These rules are supposed to control for admitting only the most reliable and relevant facts in a case. Generally, witnesses in a trial are permitted to testify about facts—this means only relevant information that the witness personally sees or hears. Expert witnesses, on the other hand, are also allowed to testify to their opinions about the facts of the case. Therefore, it is important to be sure that someone who offers an opinion really knows what he or she is talking about. Otherwise, it is believed that there will be biased information that is also unreliable and not credible which can confuse the judge or jury. Countries that do not use the lay person jury system, which is common in the U.S., are less concerned with confusing judges, who are supposed to be professionally trained to sort out fact from fiction.

SUMMARY

This chapter described the different types of governments and legal systems and how the laws and case precedents create the rules by which the law works. We went into depth about the U.S. system. It is important for mental health professionals to understand the laws that govern the case on which they prepare to offer their opinions of the facts. It is also important to know the different standards of proof necessary before forming an opinion.

Scientists often get confused by the standard of proof for a hypothesis to be accepted, which is usually that results will be accepted if no more than 95 to 99 out of 100 times it will occur because of the facts presented. In the law, the burden of proof is only that high in criminal cases. Most other cases accept the standard of 'more likely than not' this occurred because of the facts presented. Understanding how the mental health testimony fits into the bigger picture of the law will make the expert witness more likely to educate the triers of fact, which is the major purpose of offering expert testimony.

FRYE TEST

The first test for the admissibility of expert testimony occurred in 1923 in a case entitled *Frye vs. United States (293 F 1013, 1923)*. While this case dealt with the admissibility of the polygraph in court, it has been used in a much wider context to decide the admissibility of any proffered or proposed expert testimony. It is described as a general acceptability theory. That is, if the theory, methodology or conclusion that is being 'proffered' or offered as expert testimony is "generally accepted" within the relevant scientific field, it is deemed to meet the criteria for acceptability. Reliability, in other words, is determined by general acceptability. One of the problems with the Frye standard is that it did not define what "generally acceptable" meant. Subsequent commentary by various legal scholars has described general acceptability as referring to acceptance by "a substantial majority of the relevant scientific discipline" but once again the term "substantial majority" was not defined. In a similar manner, the "relevant scientific discipline" was not well-defined either.

Let us take a concrete example. Say you are evaluating whether a particular psychological test that purports to predict sex offender recidivism meets the Frye standard. You would have to think about who is the relevant scientific community? Does it consist of all psychologists, all clinical psychologists, all psychologists who perform sex offender evaluations or all psychologists who are familiar with that particular instrument? The testimony will be admitted depending on which scientific community is selected. In one study performed for attorneys who were trying to challenge the new sex predator civil commitment laws, a survey was done to assess how many psychologists attending a state psychological association meeting knew of or had used any of the actuarial instruments used to help predict the risk of a sex offender committing another sex crime. Although the trial court admitted the testimony anyhow, had the case gone up to the appellate level, the study may have had an impact on their decision. Nevertheless, despite these drawbacks, the Frye standard has been used by judges for many years as the criterion for the admissibility of expert testimony. It is still used today by many states.

One of the other major problems that the Frye standard encountered was because its criterion was general acceptability, there was no room for the admissibility of a well-validated but innovative or new technique. Let us assume that a particular scientist has done extensive work validating a new scientific procedure. No matter how extensive the validity studies are, under a Frye standard, unless it is well-known and well-accepted in the scientific community, it could not be admitted into evidence. A good example occurred during the trial of John Hinckley, Jr., when some of the proffered expert testimony the defense wanted admitted had to do with a neuropsychiatrist's diagnosis of Hinckley as schizophrenic based on what was then a new technique of brain imaging studies. This work was very well validated from a scientific point of view but since the idea of abnormal brain chemistry in schizophrenics was not generally accepted in the scientific community in 1981, the testimony was ruled inadmissible. Of course, had that testimony been proffered in the present day and age, where this technique is well-accepted, it would certainly be admitted into evidence.

1975 FEDERAL RULES OF EVIDENCE

In 1975, the Federal Rules of Evidence were adopted by the U.S. Federal Court system. The rules had special sections (Rules 702 through 705) to assist the court with criteria for the admissibility of expert testimony. The Federal Rules of Evidence have been incorporated into the evidence codes in many states, so that some now have either an exact replica or words closely approximating them as the basis for their own rules of evidence. These relevant sections for our discussion here dealt with what was called "scientific, technical or other specialized knowledge". These Rules of Evidence stated that if such scientific, technical or other specialized knowledge would be of assistance to the triers of fact (judges or juries) and out of the "ken" or knowledge base of the ordinary layperson, then an expert who was qualified by knowledge, skill, education, experience and training could render an opinion.

Let us look at each of the elements of this standard. First, note that it deals with broader information than merely scientific, for it talks about the possible introduction into expert testimony of technical or specialized knowledge also. This becomes a particularly critical issue when the admissibility of "social science" evidence (such as psychology) is debated. Is psychology scientific, is it technical knowledge, or is it some other kind of specialized knowledge? How this question is answered leads one to different answers regarding admissibility.

The second important phrase is that the material be "of assistance to the trier of fact". This may seem somewhat paradoxical to the reader; why would we be discussing material at all if it were not of assistance to the trier of fact? What is meant here is that the knowledge proposed by the expert witness must not be something already known by the average person.

In other words, it must add something new to the knowledge base of the layperson or provide some information to challenge misinformation that the trier of fact (judge or jury) could be expected to deduce from common sense that is really counter-intuitive to scientific findings.

A good example would be testimony regarding the battered woman syndrome which helps the layperson understand why a woman does not just leave an abusive husband. Consider a case where a woman has killed an abusive husband. Although she may have been abused for twenty years, prior to the killing, she might not have perceived herself in danger of being killed until the present situation. A judge or a lay juror could, from a common sense knowledge base, ask the question, "Why didn't the woman just leave the relationship"? Testimony regarding battered woman syndrome and the concept of learned helplessness would help explain to the trier of fact why the woman didn't "just leave". In other words, presentation of the research along with the results of the examination of this particular woman adds something to the knowledge base of the trier of fact and is therefore considered to be "of assistance" because it both addresses the common misconception of the average person who thinks it is possible to 'just leave' and provides new information that would not be readily available without the expert's opinion. An expert who is qualified by virtue of knowledge, skill, education, experience and training can then be permitted to testify. These arguments occur during the qualification of an expert witness by the judge. An attorney, who will propose or proffer an expert to the Court, will have that expert describe her or his education, training and general skills in a variety of areas. Once the judge qualifies that individual as an expert he or she can offer opinion testimony. Only the judge can decide who is an expert and who is a fact witness.

Rule 703 discusses the criteria required for the methodology upon which the expert bases his or her opinion. It indicates that the methodology used by the expert must be of the sort "reasonably relied upon by other experts in the same field". One of the problems with this aspect of the Federal Rules of Evidence is that that phrase "reasonably relied upon" was not defined leaving it to the courts to figure out if a method is scientific or not.

ULTIMATE ISSUE TESTIMONY

Another important element in this rule and subsequent cases regarding admissibility of expert testimony is a prohibition against an expert giving so-called ultimate issue testimony. In most cases, the 'ultimate issue' is defined as the actual legal conclusion that the judge or jury must come to at the end of the case. However, what actually is defined as the ultimate issue in a particular case is often variable. Some courts more narrowly restrict the testimony to avoid invading the province of the jury while others permit a wider reach towards the ultimate decision. The psychologist is usually allowed to give diagnoses, conclusions and recommendations, as well as descriptions of an individual's mental disorder but may or may not be allowed to actually testify to the causal link between that and for instance, the criminal offense, depending on how broadly or narrowly the court defines the ultimate issue.

Forensic psychologists have debated whether or not an expert witness should testify to the ultimate issue in a case in state courts where there may not be a legal rule governing its admissibility. Some contend that experts should not address such issues; that not only does it usurp the role of the trier of fact, but that it may even be unethical, for it asks the expert to draw legal and maybe even moral conclusions, which may be beyond the psychologist's expertise and for which psychologists often do not have sufficient data to answer. Others contend that the expert may well have sufficient data to offer such an opinion to the court, and should do so with the understanding that the court may not agree with it. Others note the practical issue that courts may insist that experts answer such questions; if the expert refuses, the court could turn to someone else. Still others believe that it is better to respond to the 'elements' of the issue, rather than to the issue itself; by citing, for instance, the data supportive of an inability to understand wrongfulness or an inability to conform behavior to the law without actually stating a defendant was insane at the time of the crime. This issue is more fully discussed in later chapters.

DAUBERT, KUMHO, AND RELEVANT CASE LAW

In actual practice, following the introduction of these Federal Rules of Evidence, courts used some informal combination of the Frye standard and the Federal Rules of Evidence to determine admissibility of expert testimony until 1993 when the United States Supreme Court dramatically altered the standards for admissibility of expert testimony in Federal courts when deciding a case called *Daubert*. In a case entitled *Daubert versus Merrell Dow Pharmaceuticals (509U.S. 579, 113 S. Ct. 2786, 1993)*, a case that dealt with whether a particular medication caused birth defects, the attorneys for the Plaintiff wanted to introduce expert testimony by a biochemist who reanalyzed the prior medication tests (called trials) and found that the trials that had declared the medication was safe were not done properly. The trial court ruled the testimony was inadmissible finding the reanalysis of the prior trials was 'junk science' because the biochemist had used a new methodology that was not generally acceptable and therefore failed to meet the Frye standard.

The United States Supreme Court, in a majority opinion authored by Justice Blackmun, described the Frye standard as too austere, not allowing for innovation and creativity and suggested using the Federal Rules of Evidence with some important modifications for judges to test for scientific reliability of a proposed expert's opinion. These new standards are now called the *Daubert* standards and have been adopted by a number of different states and in 2001 were incorporated into the newly revised Federal Rules of Evidence. The reasoning behind this Supreme Court decision was to give judges more guidance in how to make these difficult admissibility decisions. An important point to be noted is that Justice Blackmun restricted the analysis in the case only to scientific evidence because that was the nature of the evidence being considered in the *Daubert* case. The implication of Justice Blackmun's comment was that the criteria which he was proposing would be applicable only to scientific testimony and that technical or other specialized information could well be judged by other criteria. Nevertheless, many people misinterpreted Daubert as requiring the application of certain standards useful in judging scientific evidence to all kinds of expert testimony.

Blackmun also noted that the criteria to be outlined were suggested guidelines and were not 'dispositive'. That is, these were guidelines that the judge, as "gatekeeper," would utilize to determine the admissibility of expert scientific testimony. Some legal scholars believe that the *Daubert* decision gives judges more power to decide what expert to admit and who to keep out of the court while others see *Daubert* only as a guide to the decision making power judges always had under Frye and the Federal Rules of Evidence.

The criteria suggested by Blackmun appear to be an elaboration of the undefined "reasonable reliance" discussed in Federal Rule of Evidence 703 as follows:

1) The hypothesis to which the matter pertains is testable;
2) It has been tested;
3) The procedure has a known error rate;
4) The procedure has been published;
5) It has been peer reviewed; and,
6) It is generally accepted by the scientific community.

As noted above, there was a good deal of discussion following the handing down of this decision among mental health professionals, wondering exactly where expert psychological testimony would fall. It takes only a moment's reflection to realize that much of what clinical forensic examiners do in their evaluations may not have testable hypotheses nor known error rates. What, for instance, is the testable hypothesis in a child custody evaluation? How does one determine the "known error rate" of a clinical interview? Does it have to do with whether or not the judge or jury agrees with the proposed testimony? These are all issues that appear to separate clinical forensic evaluations from the kinds of criteria enumerated in the Daubert case if they are strictly followed rather than just used as guidelines as Blackmun suggested. In fact, a number of experimental psychologists praised the decision indicating that it would prohibit any of the more clinically-oriented material, which they regarded as "junk science." Thus, the tensions between research and applied psychologists became embroiled in legal decision-making policies.

Many courts adopted this rather narrow interpretation of *Daubert* that resulted in the exclusion of a large body of expert testimony, which could not be "scientifically validated." On the other hand, more clinically-oriented individuals were of the opinion that the narrowly construed *Daubert* criteria would keep a great deal of valuable clinical material out of consideration in the courts. If you remember, in the earlier chapters, we describe the introduction of psychology in the courts as coming about because of the helpfulness in describing what goes on in a criminal's mind. Would the very information that got psychology admitted into the courts now be rejected because of narrow interpretations of what is psychological science?

As noted earlier, how one conceptualizes psychology is a critical issue. Is psychology a science? Is it technical knowledge? Or, is it specialized knowledge? These questions were debated by psychologists in a very heated manner for a good number of years following the *Daubert* decision. In addition, several courts issued dramatically different opinions regarding how Daubert should be applied. As examples, in a case entitled *United States versus Scholl (959, F. Supp. 1189 (D. Ariz., 1997)*, the court refused to allow any testimony from a psychiatrist regarding the characteristics of a particular individual with a certain diagnosis, with the exception of the diagnostic criteria as enumerated in DSM-IV. It ruled that anything else did not meet the Daubert standard. On the other hand, a case from the Seventh Circuit, *United States versus Hall (93 F 3d 1337, 45 7th Circuit, 1996)*, suggested that social science testimony could not be judged by the same criteria as "Newtonian Science" and essentially suggested that social science testimony should be judged by a Frye standard, rather than by a Daubert standard. Suffice it to say, there was anything but unanimity, both in court rulings and among psychologists.

Further clarification appeared to come in 1999 in a case entitled *Kumho Tire versus Carmichael (526 U.S. 137, 119 S. Ct 1167, 1999)*. In this case, which dealt with the proffered expert testimony of a "tire expert," the trial court ruled as inadmissible the expert's testimony because he had not conducted any controlled scientific experiments. The expert had, on the other hand, based his opinion on thirty years of experience rather than on empirical studies. On appeal, the Court of Appeals for the Eleventh Circuit reversed the trial court, indicating that the Daubert criteria should be applicable only to scientific testimony, rather than to "experience-based testimony".

When the case reached the United States Supreme Court, however, the United States Supreme Court ruled that Daubert should be applicable to all proposed expert testimony but that it should be interpreted flexibly, and that the six criteria enumerated earlier were only guidelines and were not intended to be taken as rigidly excluding different kinds of expert testimony. In fact, the Supreme Court went on to state that the important issues were "relevance and reliability" and that it was at the discretion of the trial judge to determine what ways relevance and reliability could be determined. This essentially reopened the area for clinical forensic psychological expertise since a judge did not have to rely only on those six factors. *Kumho* was important because it made the admissibility of expert testimony far more flexible and far more at the discretion of the individual trial judge.

2000 FEDERAL RULES OF EVIDENCE

More recently, Rule 702 of the Federal Rules of Evidence was modified and adopted in December 2000. The modifications supplemented but did not replace Rule 702 with two additional criteria: (1) the testimony must be based on sufficient facts or data and (2) the testimony derives from reliable principles and methods.

The first part of the new modification is important for mental health professionals because it parallels very closely what appears in various codes of ethics: we make diagnoses, conclusions or recommendations only when there are sufficient data to back them up. The second part of the standard, which calls for the testimony to derive from reliable principles and methods, is apparently another attempt to discourage the use of invalidated or unreliable methods. To meet this part of the criteria the proposed expert witness has to demonstrate that he or she has applied the principles and methods reliably to the facts of the case. In other words, the expert must be aware of what are the appropriate scientific psychology procedures and demonstrate that he or she has reached the conclusions by using the proper procedures and has utilized them in an acceptable manner.

Clinical forensic psychologists need to show that the methods by which they have performed evaluations meet the psychological standards. This may include use of standardized tests that have research methodology with reliability and validity measures as well as standard errors written in the manuals. It may also include utilizing textbooks that describe clinical examinations using mental status exams, standard clinical interview techniques and various ways of assessing for samples of behavior. Many clinical forensic psychologists have begun using structured interviews to meet these standards. Including tests that measure over or under reporting symptoms of mental illness may be another way to demonstrate the careful methodology used before coming to an opinion.

SUMMARY

In summary, we have discussed the legal rules for admitting clinical forensic psychological testimony in the U.S. courts today. Many countries follow similar standards even if they do not have the detailed written rules that govern the rules of evidence for each state and the Federal courts. Interestingly, once the expert's testimony is admitted into court, its impact on the judge or jury has just begun. First, the attorney who requests that the expert testify must develop appropriate questions to bring out the relevant knowledge to the specific case. Psychologists cannot testify to anything that is not asked of them. Secondly, the opposing attorney has the opportunity to cross examine the expert witness to try to shake the person's credibility or even impeach him or her with contradictory materials. We discuss preparation for testimony in a later chapter. Thirdly, the judge has an opportunity to instruct the jury on the weight to give the expert's testimony when giving jury instructions. Some information that experts may base their opinion upon may not have been factually proven. Judges may also instruct juries to remember this during the expert's testimony. It is clear that forensic psychologists have many hurdles to overcome before they can present their opinions in individual cases but when we do get into court, what we say may educate judges and jurors to come to more reasoned judgments.

II

Understanding the
Criminal Mind

Clinical psychologists may perform evaluations at different several points in the criminal justice system. In this section, we will examine several important issues concerning the psychologist's role in determining competency to stand trial and criminal responsibility. Competency refers to a defendant's understanding of charges, court proceedings, and ability to assist an attorney. The psychologist will evaluate if the defendant exhibits a mental illness and if so, how that impacts on these capacities. Although there is controversy in the courts whether legal competency is a unitary construct or differs depending on the tasks that need performance, such as competency to proceed to trial, competency to waive Miranda rights, competency to waive right to treatment, etc., we present the various areas and suggestions for how to proceed.

In a similar manner, psychologists may be called upon to render an opinion on the defendant's mental state at the time of an offense. This may take the form of supporting an insanity defense, in which the attorney is asserting that because of a mental disease or defect the defendant could not appreciate the criminality of the actions or could not control his or her behavior and therefore should be excused. We present the struggle of mental health and legal professionals in trying to conform to the legislative language or case laws when the concepts are clinical psychology and do not easily fit the laws. Obviously, this results in many mentally ill inmates who are sentenced to prison rather than receive treatment in a forensic hospital. In other cases, we describe how psychologists testify to state of mind in a justification defense using the battered woman syndrome as a theory of self defense. This defense grew out of research that demonstrated the 'reasonable person' standard needed to be viewed from the battered woman's perceptions of imminent danger rather than a general perspective. In this arena, case law developed first and then battered woman syndrome self-defense legislation followed.

We introduce the methodology that a psychologist or other mental health professional should follow when performing an evaluation either for the state or the defense. Although the laws stress the cognitive abilities of the defendant, it is important to understand how emotions impact on his or her judgment and decision-making. We measure impact from personality as well as from exposure to trauma because so many who commit criminal acts have a long history of abuse in their backgrounds.

Finally, in this section we examine some of the new approaches to diversion and treatment of mentally ill defendants both within the prison system and in the community. We examine the role of police and first responders to try to divert a mentally ill person to the appropriate community treatment resources rather than jail. As that is not always successful, we look at the diversion of non-violent offenders into mental health and drug courts and domestic violence offenders into court ordered offender specific treatment programs. We conclude the section with a discussion of the limited options for mentally ill offenders in the jails and prisons today and make some suggestions for the future.

4

Criminal Responsibility

Chris is a 21-year-old man who admitted to killing his roommate in a particularly violent and bloody manner. He left his body to rot, while taking his car for a joy ride. Later, when caught, he gave many different descriptions of what happened and could offer no reasonable explanation. 'Chris' was charged with first degree murder. His lawyers tried to understand what was in his mind when he killed his roommate. The psychological evaluation of his documented history revealed that he was brain damaged at birth, had an IQ of 70 on various intelligence tests, was physically and sexually abused as a child, and had been previously hospitalized for violent and uncontrollable behavior. One psychologist who evaluated him when he was in jail found him to be so mentally impaired that he met the state's definition of insanity while another psychologist said he was malingering and should be held responsible for the murders. How can a judge and jury make decisions about what should happen to Chris in this case?

The question of what is in the 'criminal mind' has always fascinated people including those who study psychology and the law. What does someone like Chris think about when he kills an innocent person? How does he feel at the time of the murder and afterwards? Can Chris appreciate the wrongfulness of his behavior and understand the consequences? Can he control his behavior even if he does know the difference between right and wrong? Is he the same or different from us?

Criminal responsibility refers to an individual's mental state at the time of an offense. The absence of criminal responsibility is more commonly referred to as 'not guilty by reason of insanity', although mental state at the time of the offense, in fact, includes more elements than just legal insanity. It may, for instance, encompass other mental state defenses, such as diminished capacity, extreme emotional distress, imperfect self-defense, justification defenses as described in chapter 6 and other uses of *mens rea*.

In order for an individual to be convicted of a crime, the state must prove two elements—what is called the *actus reus*, or that the act itself occurred, and secondly the *mens rea*, or that a person had a mental state that resulted in the commission of the offense. Although sometimes a person may be charged with a crime even before a body is found, usually the circumstantial evidence has to be sufficient in order for the court to find what is called 'probable cause' to make the legal charge. Evidence of blood that has been cleaned can be found using chemicals such as luminal, DNA analysis, hair follicles and other technology can be used as part of the evidence for proving *actus reus* together with evidence that the defendant was at the crime scene and the victim is no longer visible. If a person assaulted another individual while in the midst of seizure activity, having no conscious recognition of her behavior, then *mens rea* could not be said to have existed. That behavior could then be excused under the law.

LEVELS OF RESPONSIBILITY FOR BEHAVIOR

Along with the concept of *mens rea* is the legal system's requirement that different mind sets be punished at different levels of responsibility. So, for instance, in Chris's case cited above, he was charged with 'first degree murder' which requires the state of mind or *mens rea* of specific intent or premeditation of the murders. If in fact, it can be proven that he did not have the requisite mind set or intent to kill the roommate but behaved in a dangerous manner and knew or should have known that the consequences of his actions would result in their deaths, then he would more properly be charged with 'second degree murder'. So, intent-to-kill calls for a higher level of responsibility than killing without the intent and would be punished at a more severe level, usually by life in prison.

In some states, if Chris could prove that the roommate had provoked him in some way or that he was suffering from extreme emotional disturbance, then he might be convicted of manslaughter, which is not considered murder. Voluntary manslaughter is an intent crime so it requires the person to know what he or she did at the time but this knowledge was influenced by his or her emotional state. Involuntary manslaughter, which is rarely used except for vehicular homicide, does not require intent, but the person was expected to know that his or her actions were reckless or dangerous. If Chris is convicted of voluntary manslaughter he still might get a lengthy prison sentence, but it would be shorter than a first or second degree murder conviction. Although manslaughter may require the mental state of intent, even if it is not the intent to kill, sometimes juries will compromise on this verdict when the elements of insanity are not completely met. In some countries, if it can be proven that the person's mental condition caused him or her to function as an 'automaton', without any thought at all, Chris' behavior may also be excused or he may be found guilty of the equivalent crime of manslaughter.

If Chris can prove that his mental retardation, behavioral disorders, and mental illness prevented him from knowing the difference between right and wrong and the consequences of his actions, then he may be excused from being held responsible for criminal behavior because of his mental state. This is called the insanity defense and the jury would issue a verdict called, 'Not Guilty by Reason of Insanity'. In most states and Federal court, this verdict would result in Chris' being sent to the state hospital's forensic division for treatment. In some states such as Colorado, the person is sent for an evaluation and if found to be sane at that time, is not hospitalized but rather, released from custody. Interestingly, in some states a forensic team in the state hospital actually performs the insanity evaluation for the prosecution and if they testify that the person is not insane but the jury comes back with an insanity verdict, then the person must be released. Although the forensic hospital is legally required to release the person when the mental illness is no longer present, this is rare when the crime is as serious as Chris'.

If Chris can prove that he killed his roommate because he feared the roommate was going to seriously harm or kill him, his actions might be considered justifiable because they were in self-defense. Battered women who kill their abusive husbands have used self-defense to justify their actions and they were found not guilty. This is further discussed in a later chapter.

HISTORICAL OVERVIEW OF THE "INSANITY DEFENSE"

The insanity defense or pleading Not Guilty By Reason of Insanity has historical roots extending back to the thirteenth century in England. Over the years there have been different ways to determine if someone should be excused for their otherwise criminal behavior. One of the earliest concepts involved the so-called "wild beast test." It was believed that an individual who had no more control over her or his behavior than a wild beast should not be held responsible for criminal behavior. Another somewhat picturesque test is called the "begat test," which indicated that if an individual were capable of procreation, then he or she should be held responsible for criminal behavior.

M'Naughten Standard to Determine 'Insanity'

The beginning of the "modern era" in terms of these concepts can be traced to 1843 in England. At that time, an individual by the name of Daniel M'Naughten (sometimes spelled M'Naghten or even McNaughten), according to the historical documents appeared to have an extensive delusional system. He attempted an assassination of a member of the British cabinet, but instead shot and killed the secretary of one of the cabinet members. Daniel M'Naughten was tried under the then existing insanity defense law, which was the wild beast test and was found Not Guilty by Reason of Insanity. It is a common misconception that M'Naughten (10 Cl. And Fin. 200 8 Eng. Rep. 718, 1843) was acquitted under the standard that bears his name rather than the wild beast standard, but the M'Naughten standard was passed into law following his acquittal. At that time, there was a huge public outcry over M'Naughten being found Not Guilty by Reason of Insanity with many people complaining that the wild beast test was too liberal and 'coddled' individuals by not making them take responsibility for their actions. The House of Lords met to debate this issue and passed a more restrictive standard for an insanity defense, which became called the M'Naughten test.

The M'Naughten standard consisted essentially of three components. It spoke of an individual of (1) unsound mind (what we would call having a mental disease or defect), who, by reason of this defect, was unable to know either (2) the nature and quality or (3) the wrongfulness of her of his or her actions.

Therefore, for an individual to be found Not Guilty by Reason of Insanity under the M'Naughten standard, she or he would have to establish some fairly extensive ramifications of the underlying mental illness (defect of reason). Not knowing the nature of the act essentially meant that she or he did not know what it was that she or he was doing. An individual, for instance, who is strangling someone but believes that she or he is squeezing a lemon rather than strangling somebody, might meet this prong of the standard. Not appreciating the quality of the act would refer to an inability to understand the consequences. In other words, an individual who might behead someone because of the belief that it would be interesting to watch that person wake up the next morning and look for his or her head, would not appreciate the quality of the act.

The second prong of M'Naughten referred to the inability to appreciate the wrongfulness of the act. In the House of Lords there was a great deal of debate whether wrongfulness referred to legally wrong or morally wrong. That is, could someone who knew that the act was legally wrong, that is, against the law, but at the same time felt that it was justified because of some delusional belief, fall under this prong of the test? The general interpretation was the broader one, that it was moral wrongfulness rather than a mere knowledge that it was against the law that was required. The defendant, therefore, can meet the insanity test if he or she demonstrates an inability to understand the fact that his or her actions offended the mores of society.

It is important to note that the M'Naughten test is mostly a cognitively-based standard. The standard spoke about *knowing* the nature and quality of the act and *knowing* the wrongfulness of the act. It did not take into account broader dimensions dealing with the person's ability to control his or her impulses at the time of the act. This is often referred to as volition because it relates to the concept of free will. There has always been a controversy over whether or not people's behavior is under their total control or if other factors interfere with their 'free will' to control themselves. M'Naughten does not deal with this issue. Despite this apparent absence of a volitional component, the M'Naughten standard became very popular. It was adopted in many countries in Western Europe and rapidly spread across the United States.

IRRESISTIBLE IMPULSE STANDARD FOR DETERMINING 'INSANITY'

It was not until the end of the nineteenth century that questions started to arise regarding the volitional component, namely the issue of impulse control. Around this period of time, several states in the U. S. adopted a so-called 'irresistible impulse' test. This added a component to the M'Naughten definitions that dealt with the strength of an impulse to do a particular act, even if the defendant "knew" that it was wrong. Varieties of disorders of impulse control, as well as the large majority of actions that were based on delusional beliefs come under this definition. In other words, even if a defendant knew the wrongfulness of her or his actions, she or he could be found Not Guilty by Reason of Insanity if she or he were acting under a delusional belief so powerful that it rendered her or his controls ineffective.

The irresistible impulse tests quickly fell out of favor because there had not been sufficient attempts to define exactly how strong an impulse had to be in order to be considered irresistible. What was the difference between an irresistible impulse and an impulse that was simply not resisted? Obviously, in the first one a person *could not* control his or her behavior while in the second the person *chose not* to do so. Informally, a number of states adopted the concept of the "policeman at the elbow test," using as the criterion whether or not someone would have committed this act had there been a police officer standing there and watching. The question, of course, is how could this be determined? In other words, unless there actually had been a police officer present at the time of the offense, it would be virtually impossible to determine whether or not the offense would have been committed had there been a police officer standing there. Merely asking a defendant during the course of the evaluation whether the presence of a police officer would have deterred him or her certainly has major problems with validity.

The irresistible impulse standard, when it existed, was used as an "add-on" to the M'Naughten criteria. That is, someone could be found Not Guilty by Reason of Insanity if he or she had a mental disorder and he or she either could not know the nature and quality of the act, the wrongfulness of the act or that he or she was irresistibly impelled to commit the act. No state that we are aware of ever adopted the irresistible impulse test on its own as its legal definition of insanity. Therefore, most states were left with a rather strict cognitive standard.

Using such a strict cognitive standard, however, leaves out a large number of mentally ill individuals, who commit acts based on emotional disorders including delusional thinking. She or he may well have known that the act was wrong but may somehow have felt that she or he needed to commit the act as part of his or her mental illness. Under a strict interpretation of this standard, there could really be no alternative except conviction for such individuals. Obviously, this would send many seriously mentally ill individuals to prison rather than the psychiatric hospital where they might be able to get some treatment for their mental disorder. In fact, prisons all over the world have so many mentally ill inmates today, that many have begun to provide treatment similar to the psychiatric hospital. We discuss these services more fully in a later chapter on psychological interventions in forensic settings.

THE DURHAM STANDARD REQUIRING CAUSATION OR PRODUCT OF MENTAL ILLNESS TEST

With the expansion of psychoanalytic theories from the consulting room into the courtroom in the 1940's and 1950's, a number of influential jurists became convinced of the need for a new and more flexible standard for assessing criminal responsibility and the use of the insanity defense. In 1954, the Chief Judge of the United States Court of Appeals, Judge David Bazelon, authored a decision called *Durham v. the United States* (214 F. 2d. 962, D.C. Circuit, 1954). Durham provided for a much broader definition of an insanity defense than had been previously used. Judge Bazelon noted in his opinion that there was a need to extend the widest possible latitude to expert evaluation and to expert testimony. The Durham standard therefore simply stated "an accused is not criminally responsible if the criminal act was the product of a mental disease or defect."

Initially, the Durham test was expected to expand the range of mental health professionals' input into the criminal justice system, and help the law account for previously ignored aspects of human behavior. Unfortunately, the Durham test had a number of assumptions that could not be validated. For instance, it was based on the premise that the concept of mental disease or defect is something that could easily be agreed upon by any group of mental health professionals. Clearly, this does not often occur. The second assumption was that the concept that the act was a product of a mental disease could be easily proven. There was an implicit assumption that once a person's mental disease or defect was determined, then it could be agreed that there was a clear causal link between that mental disorder and the person's actions. In fact, this is very rarely the case.

Different professionals use different criteria to determine whether or not a particular act is "caused by" a particular mental disorder. In actual practice, the concept of 'product of the mental disease or defect' ranged all the way from considering a person's entire life history as possible motivators for the crime to a very narrow definition which approximates the civil litigation definition of proximate cause; that is, had the mental disorder not been present, then the crime would not have been committed.

The result of the Durham standard was that large numbers of people who had serious personality disorders were being found Not Guilty by Reason of Insanity and were being sent to psychiatric hospitals to be treated. These people were not eligible for release as their personality disorders were untreatable and so they remained in the hospital, sometimes longer than if they had received a prison sentence as punishment for their crimes.

McDONALD MODIFICATION OF DURHAM WITH DEFINITION OF MENTAL ILLNESS

In an attempt to address this problem, in 1962 the United States District Court for the District of Columbia issued an opinion in a case called *McDonald v United States (312 F. 2d 844 D.C. Circuit, 1962)*. McDonald attempted to restrict the definition of mental disease or defect to any abnormal condition of the mind which substantially impaired mental or emotional processes and substantially impaired behavioral controls. In other words, under the McDonald definition, not every mental illness could rise to the level of one that could be used as the basis for an insanity defense. Only those mental illnesses that could be demonstrated either in the definition of the illness itself or from the manifestations of that illness in a particular individual to have "substantially impaired behavioral controls" could be considered as the basis for an insanity defense.

While McDonald successfully narrowed the definition of mental illness, it did not deal with whether the mental illness caused the person's behavior or 'product' (of the mental illness) as it was called in the Durham decision. In fact, the definition of product never was made by the courts which may have been what led to further narrowing of the mental health professions influence in judges' decisions about criminal responsibility. In the decade following Durham there was a growing dissatisfaction on the part of the courts about the influence of mental health professionals on judicial decisions. A psychiatrist, for instance, would render an opinion that someone's crime was the product of a mental illness without giving the court the basis for these conclusions. This prevented the court from making its own decision about the credibility of the mental health professional's statements. The trier of fact, the judge or jury, could only "rubber stamp" that conclusion rather than using the mental health professional's opinion as just one factor to reach its own opinion.

Washington Product Test and Ultimate Issue Opinion in Federal Courts

Justice Bazelon opined in the next case (*Washington*) that many judges believed that the mental health professional was usurping the role of the trier of fact. In that decision, which was *Washington v. United States (129 U.S. App. D.C. 29, 1967)*, the U.S. District Court issued an opinion stating that the mental health professional was no longer allowed to render an opinion regarding the causal connection between the mental illness and the criminal behavior. The mental health professional could only describe the development of the mental illness, the adaptation of the individual to that illness and could state whether or not the person was suffering from that mental illness at the time of the offense. However, the mental health professional would not be allowed to address the so-called "ultimate issue", namely whether or not the behavior in question was "caused" by the mental illness. That had to be a role for the judge or jury. The Bazelon opinion was only applicable to Federal Court cases and most state courts still allow mental health professionals to give an expert opinion on causation or whatever is referred to as the 'ultimate opinion' under their law.

ALI/Brawner Modifications Including Diminished Capacity Defenses

Even with the restrictions imposed by both *McDonald* and *Washington*, there was still great dissatisfaction in the courts with the Durham standard. Five years later, a new standard emerged in a 1972 case in Federal Court entitled *U.S. v. Brawner (471 F. 2d 969 D.C. Circuit, 1972)*. *Brawner* essentially incorporated a standard proposed earlier by the American Law Institute (ALI). This standard essentially consisted of three parts. First, as in earlier standards, there had to be the presence of a mental disease or defect (in this case, defined according to the criteria in McDonald). Secondly, as a result of this mental disease or defect, one of two criteria was met: (1) an inability to appreciate the wrongfulness or the criminality of one's behavior or (2) an inability to conform one's behavior to the requirements of the law.

What distinguishes this from earlier standards is that rather than it being an absolute inability to appreciate wrongfulness or an absolute inability to conform behavior, the phraseology referred to the lacking of "substantial capacity" to do so. In other words, while the basic concepts are the same as those embodied in M'Naughten and irresistible impulse, it does provide for somewhat more flexibility because of the concept of *substantial* capacity. Once again, however, what exactly constitutes substantial capacity remains undefined. As a result, there have been critics of the ALI/Brawner decision that refer to it merely as "new lyrics for an old tune", indicating that it is nothing more than M'Naughten and irresistible impulse in somewhat more modern language. There are, however, two important components in Brawner (ALI) that do not appear in earlier standards and are quite important.

The first is the statement that any mental disorder whose exclusive manifestation is repetitive criminal activity is excluded from this standard. This, of course, addresses itself to the concept of Antisocial Personality Disorder and the fact that under Durham people with this diagnosis were being found Not Guilty By Reason of Insanity, were being sent to psychiatric facilities and were basically found to be untreatable, in contrast to a mental disorder which could respond to medication and possibly to psychotherapy.

The other important contribution of ALI/Brawner was an extensive discussion of the concept of diminished capacity. In this decision, diminished capacity was regarded as some sort of condition, which could possibly include a mental disorder that resulted in a defendant's inability to form the requisite specific intent to commit a particular offense. In other words, the mental disorder did not rise to the level required in an insanity defense in which there would be a *complete* absence of criminal responsibility but merely by negating the specific intent, it would essentially make the defendant responsible for a less serious crime, sometimes referred to as a lesser included offense which did not require a mental state which encompassed intent.

For instance, if a defendant could be shown to suffer from a condition in which she or he "flies off the handle" or over-reacts to minor stimulation, such as in an Intermittent Explosive Disorder, one could argue that this individual did not intend to assault or kill someone else but that she or he suffered from a diminished mental capacity. These defenses of diminished mental capacity could be used in cases in which a particular mental state is a necessary element of the criminal charge. For example, a first-degree murder charge would require the presence not only of malice but of premeditation, also. If it could be shown through a diminished capacity defense that this crime was committed by someone who was perhaps in a

TABLE 4-1. MAJOR CASES AND THEIR SIGNIFICANCE

1. M'Naughten's Case	Origin of the right/wrong test for insanity.
2. Durham	The product case : insanity occurs when a crime is the *product* of a mental disease or defect.
3. McDonald	"legal" definition of mental disease or defect.
4. Washington	ruling that experts could not address ultimate issue of causation in insanity cases.
5. Brawner	Restatement of M'Naughten and irresistible impulse combined.
6. Jones	Court ruled that length of prison sentence is unrelated to length of treatment.
7. Foucha V. Louisiana	Cannot confine personality disorder as not guilty by reason of insanity even if still dangerous.

rage that was related to an explosive disorder, then one might argue that there was no premeditation and that therefore the person could only be convicted of second degree murder. If the same argument could demonstrate that neither premeditation nor malice existed, then the person may only be convicted of manslaughter. It should also be noted that these particular mental states are a subset of a larger group of conditions that could include such matters as addiction and substance abuse. In short, it would refer to any condition that would reduce the ability of an individual to form intent or to premeditate.

HINCKLEY AND ITS AFTERMATH

With these modifications, the Brawner standard worked relatively well until 1981, when John Hinckley stood trial for the attempted assassination of President Reagan, a Secret Service officer, Press Secretary James Brady and a District of Columbia police officer. It is well-known that John Hinckley was found Not Guilty By Reason of Insanity in Federal Court but many of the background pieces of this are not well-known.

In most state laws, the burden of proof in establishing an insanity defense is on the defense. That is, the defense must demonstrate by a preponderance of evidence (slightly more certain than not) that a given defendant met the criteria for an insanity defense. This is what is known in the law as an affirmative defense. Until the legislative reform that occurred in 1984, Federal law and the laws of some states such as Colorado presented somewhat of an anomaly. Prior to Hinckley, in Federal law, once the "threshold" was crossed and a judge ruled that there was enough evidence that an insanity defense could be raised, the burden of proof shifted to the prosecution, that is, to the government to prove 'beyond a reasonable doubt' that the defendant was sane. This became an almost impossible burden to carry when there was any kind of conflicting expert testimony. In other words, a jury would have to be totally convinced that everything that defense expert witnesses said was totally without credibility in order to find a person sane under the law because of the exceedingly high level of proof (beyond a reasonable doubt). Therefore, many legal scholars have suggested that John Hinckley's acquittal By Reason of Insanity was, in fact, an artifact of Federal law at the time of the trial, rather than really being indicative of John Hinckley's actual mental state.

Following John Hinckley's verdict, which was Not Guilty By Reason of Insanity, there was a public outcry that bore striking similarities to the public outcry following the NGRI acquittal of Daniel M'Naughten almost 140 years earlier. There were assertions that we were coddling criminals and that vast numbers of people were "getting off" by reason of insanity. In fact, several studies done immediately following the Hinckley trial revealed that many samples of the American population believed that anywhere from 45% to 75% of criminal defendants were found NGRI. This is a remarkable misperception in light of the fact that the figures remained quite consistent; only one out of one thousand criminal defendants is successfully found NGRI. What makes this misperception even more remarkable is that the vast majority of this one tenth of one percent are defendants who are so mentally disordered that the state agrees to a "stipulated" or "uncontested" insanity defense. In other words less than one third of one tenth of one percent of defendants are successfully acquitted in a contested insanity defense. Nevertheless, the public misperception led to a variety of congressional hearings, legislative proposals, and attempts at legislative reform of the insanity defense.

GUILTY BUT MENTALLY ILL LAWS

As a reaction five states abolished the insanity defense and approximately twelve states added a new possible verdict to their criminal law entitled "Guilty But Mentally Ill". Here a jury needs to make two independent findings: first, that a defendant was mentally ill and second, that the defendant committed the offense. The jury would not be called upon to state that there was a causal connection between the two. A defendant who is found Guilty But Mentally Ill would be sentenced to a fixed prison term related to the offense itself, but then would serve part of that prison term in a psychiatric facility until such time as the mental illness was declared to be in remission. Then, the defendant would be transferred back to the Division of Corrections to serve the remainder of the sentence. In practice, meaningful treatment was rarely provided and therefore, those found Guilty But Mentally Ill were kept warehoused in the mental hospital until their sentences were completed.

At this time, the U.S. Congress held hearings in the hopes of being able to reform the insanity defense. This led to a variety of position papers from different professional organizations. The American Medical Association had a rather simple position paper, which recommended abolishing the insanity defense. The American Bar Association proposed two different concepts. The first was to change the level of proof and the burden of proof in insanity cases. As will be recalled from the previous discussion, in the Federal courts (and some state courts) the burden of proof was on the government to rebut insanity beyond a reasonable doubt. This proposal from the American Bar Association suggested that the burden be placed back on the defense and that the level of proof that someone meets the insanity test be at clear and convincing evidence. The second component of the position from the American Bar Association was that the volitional prong of the ALI/Brawner standard should be eliminated. This meant that the part of the ALI/Brawner standard that required an inability to conform one's behavior to the requirements of the law should be deleted.

The American Psychiatric Association also proposed the elimination of the volitional part of ALI/Brawner because they believed that there was insufficient empirical and scientific knowledge that could address strength of impulse control. It is, of course, somewhat curious reasoning since this did imply, in restricting the insanity defense to the cognitive part, that we do, in fact, have empirical and scientific ways of measuring appreciation of wrongfulness. However, given the public misperception about the overuse of the insanity defense as discussed above, there is no way to know how much politics played a part in this decision. The second aspect of the American Psychiatric Association position was that the definition of mental illness must refer to a *severe* mental illness, which they defined as one that substantially and demonstrably impaired perception and judgment. The American Psychological Association also was approached for a position paper; but, it never did produce one, contending that research needed to be done before that question could be adequately addressed.

1984 INSANITY DEFENSE REFORM ACT

In 1984, the United States Congress passed the Insanity Defense Reform Act [18 U.S.C., 20 (a), (b)] which, in essence, embodied the major components put forward both by the American Bar Association and the American Psychiatric Association. In this Act, a defendant was considered not criminally responsible if, by reason of severe mental illness, the defendant lacked the ability to appreciate the nature and quality or the wrongfulness of the criminal act. This is, of course, a return to a very strict M'Naughten standard and, in fact, could be seen as even more narrow than the original M'Naughten, because it requires the presence of a "severe" mental illness. The Insanity Defense Reform Act also accepted the position of the American Bar Association, that insanity should be an affirmative defense, that the burden was on the defense and that the level of proof that the defendant is insane needed to be 'clear and convincing evidence'. It reiterated the prohibition against mental health professionals rendering an opinion on the ultimate legal issues in Federal Court. Interestingly the law established parity between psychologists and psychiatrists in conducting clinical forensic evaluations by specifically referring to psychiatric or psychological evaluations and testimony.

As a result of this new and highly-restrictive insanity standard in Federal court, coupled with the public misperception of insanity acquittals being on the rise, approximately two dozen states have now changed their statutes to reflect this more restrictive standard. As in the past, large numbers of mentally ill individuals are now being sentenced to prison terms, rather than receiving adequate treatment in psychiatric facilities. Studies have indicated that approximately 18% to 25% of the prison population is composed of people with severe mental illness diagnoses. These numbers are much higher if we include people who have substance abuse disorders in those who need mental health treatment. Consider the following example of an actual recent case in Federal Court:

> *The defendant had developed an extensive delusional system about his neighbor, who happened to be a federal judge. The defendant believed his delusion that the judge was sexually interested in him and when he "rebuffed" the judge's advances, the judge set out on a campaign to destroy the defendant.*

The defendant was, in fact, becoming progressively more psychotic resulting in his being fired from his job and his girlfriend ended their relationship. He became convinced that the judge had engineered his job loss and the dissolution of his relationship. He decided he had to stop the judge before the judge destroyed him. He attempted to fire bomb the judge's house. However, he waited until nightfall, dressed in black, and took a circuitous route to the judge's home to avoid detection.

Under the new law, this psychotic young man was held criminally responsible because his attempts to avoid detection indicated that he "appreciated the nature and quality and the wrongfulness of his actions." The fact that the crime was clearly motivated by a psychotic delusion was not relevant to the criteria used in the 1984 restrictive insanity defense.

LENGTH OF CONFINEMENT WHEN FOUND NOT GUILTY BY REASON OF INSANITY

Another intriguing issue is the length of time that people can be held in a state hospital when found Not Guilty By Reason of Insanity. In a 1983, Supreme Court ruling *(Jones v. U.S., 463 U.S. 354, 1983)* Jones's attorney suggested that a defendant who had been found NGRI should not remain in a mental hospital any longer than the maximum time of sentence had she or he been convicted of the same underlying offense. Michael Jones had been found NGRI of a misdemeanor charge and eight years later was still psychotic so he remained in a mental hospital. Had Michael Jones pled guilty or been convicted of his petty larceny charge, he would probably have been released within a year.

The Supreme Court ultimately ruled that there was no necessary connection between the length of his possible sentence and the length of the treatment, since one was for punishment and the other for treatment. Therefore, according to the Supreme Court, the length of time of the underlying sentence was irrelevant to the length of time of the commitment for treatment of the mental disorder. In *Jones*, the Supreme Court also spoke of the fact that there was a "continuing presumption of dangerousness" when anyone is found NGRI and therefore the burden had to be on the defendant to demonstrate that he or she was no longer mentally ill and no longer a danger to self or others.

In 1992, the U.S. Supreme Court, in a case called *Foucha v. Louisiana* (112 S.C. 1780, 1992) dealt with the issue of remission from a mental disorder in an individual who was found NGRI but who still had an underlying personality disorder that made him dangerous. The Supreme Court ruled that such an individual could not be kept within a mental hospital and would have to be released, even though regarded as potentially dangerous. Immediately, there was concern that many dangerous people would be released from mental hospitals and commit further crimes. To avoid this possibility, at least two states, California in *People v. Superior Court (Williams)(284 Cal. Rptr. 601 Cal. Court. App. 1991)* and Colorado in *Colorado v. Hilton (902 P. 24 883, 1993)* redefined Antisocial Personality Disorder to be a mental illness, which then would justify keeping such individuals in a psychiatric facility even if the mental illness went into remission. In another case, in the state of Wisconsin *(Wisconsin v. Randall, 532 N.W. 2d 94, 96 n. 2, 1995)* the state argued that their statutory scheme was distinct from Foucha as unlike Louisiana, they had a treatment program which addressed the defendant's dangerousness and therefore they could justify keeping the person in the mental hospital until the treatment program was completed.

SUMMARY

The identification of those who commit antisocial acts as either 'mad' or 'bad' has troubled the legal and mental health professions forever as we discovered in this chapter. Although only a very small percentage of those who commit these crimes are found Not Guilty by Reason of Insanity and even fewer of them are ever released from a forensic psychiatric facility, the general public believes that many more are 'getting away with murder' by using this defense. In most cases, the insanity defense fails as the burdens are so difficult to meet. Most people who have been found NGRI have been stipulated to by both defense and state rather than by a jury trial. As the definition of who is eligible to be excused for their crimes becomes broader, more criminals are sent to the psychiatric hospital rather than prison. As the definition becomes stricter, more mentally ill criminals remain in the prison system. Rarely do those who are mentally ill get appropriate treatment whether in prison or the psychiatric hospital. For those who are eventually released from prison, the risk of recidivism remains high in those individuals whose mental illness contributed to the commission of their crime. This is especially true for those who continue to experience violent delusions.

DISCUSSION QUESTIONS

1. Describe your concept of the "ideal" insanity defense—one that guarantees that mentally ill people will receive treatment, yet does not "open the floodgates" to a variety of less serious conditions.
2. Describe your thinking regarding the appropriate time for an insanity acquitee to be released from a hospital.

5

Competency to Stand Trial

In the last chapter we learned how the criminal justice system provides for someone who commits a crime without having the requisite mental state. In this chapter we shall learn about what happens to someone who is mentally ill and cannot understand their charges or the court proceedings or cannot help her or his attorney provide a defense. While this is a separate issue from mental state at the time of the offense, sometimes a person who is found to have been insane at the time of the offense had also been found incompetent to proceed to trial at an earlier time. Assessing the person's mental state at a particular time after being charged with a crime is called 'competence to stand trial' and we have developed some basic rules that must be followed so that the person is treated fairly. Remember, in the Common Law legal system the U.S. and other countries have adapted, a person must be considered innocent until proven guilty. This process cannot occur if the person cannot assist the attorney at trial.

The individual's competence to stand trial, then, is perhaps the most basic question the criminal justice system must first determine. This concept grows out of the belief that an individual cannot be tried "in absentia." In other words, a defendant is entitled to be present at his or her trial. This is understood to mean that the person has to be mentally as well as physically present. However, what constitutes mental presence can differ from one examiner to another, especially if a person is seen at different times. One well known example is Colin Ferguson.

> *Colin Ferguson, shot 19 people on the Long Island Railroad train in which he was riding because he believed white people were plotting against him. Of course, this belief was the product of a delusional disorder. His behavior during the televised trial indicated that he was responding more to his own peculiar delusional internal stimuli than to reality most but not all of the time. This is the nature of many severe mental illnesses; the illness is not always observable. Mental health professionals who were appointed by the court performed a competency evaluation and based on their findings, the judge found him competent to stand trial despite the delusional disorder. As part of his delusional disorder, he believed his attorney was also plotting against him and he petitioned the court to represent himself. The trial court ruled that he was entitled to serve as his own attorney (called pro se). It was clear that his cross-examination of witnesses, many of whom were shot by him, were observers, or were family of those killed, both caused these people great harm and did nothing to provide himself with a reasonable defense. Was he really competent to represent himself or even assist an attorney so he could receive a fair trial? Can a person with a severe mental illness such as a delusional disorder that interferes with thinking and judgment be expected to make reasonably competent decisions such as whether to choose to use insanity or some other type of defense?*

DUSKY CRITERIA

The basic criteria for competency to stand trial were elaborated in a United States Supreme Court case in 1960 entitled *Dusky v. U.S. (362 U.S. 402, 1960)*. The *Dusky* criteria for competency were essentially quite straightforward. A defendant had to have both a rational and factual understanding of the proceedings and be able to assist counsel with a reasonable degree of rational understanding in order to move forward to trial. Prior to the setting down of the *Dusky* criteria, there were no firm criteria and often a simple mental status examination had been used to determine a defendant's competency. This is inadequate because someone whose behavior is related to their mental illness may seem rational and factual one minute and psychotic the next. However, many countries still do not specify the criteria that can cause the defendant to be declared Incompetent to Proceed to Trial (ITP) relying instead on the mental health professional's opinion. Without having to meet specific criteria on which to base a psychological opinion, mental health professionals are in danger of being considered 'hired guns', offering opinions based on what the state or defense want to hear, depending upon who hires them.

In the *Dusky* criteria, factual understanding refers only to the defendant's understanding of the charges against him or her. That is, can the defendant tell the examiner what the charges against him or her are? Assessing whether the defendant has the rational understanding of his or her charges is somewhat more complex as it involves an understanding of such concepts as the role of various people in the courtroom setting (defense attorney, prosecutor, judge and jury), the different pleas available and their consequences and a general appreciation of the seriousness of the charges.

Ability to assist counsel refers to the quality of relating to one's attorney and whether or not there is evidence of any significant mental disease or intellectual or organic impairment that would interfere with effectively being able to assist one's attorney in one's own defense. For instance, if a defendant believes that defense counsel and prosecutor are part of a plot against him or her, it would appear that there should be serious doubts regarding that individual's ability to assist that attorney due to a delusional disorder. In a similar manner, if the defendant's mental illness is of such a severity that the defendant is constantly distracted by hallucinations and is unable to follow the chain of evidence, then this also would raise issues regarding the defendant's ability to assist counsel. If there were some sort of serious organic impairment, such that the defendant could not "shift mental set" and thus, constantly perseverated on one piece of information, this again would raise questions regarding ability to assist counsel.

Clearly, from the above discussion, one can see that the ability to assist counsel is one of the most difficult to evaluate in conducting a competency to stand trial examination. Many defendants possess both a factual and rational understanding, but because of their mental illnesses, have great difficulty assisting counsel in their own defense. If a defendant is found competent to stand trial, that is usually the point at which the examiner would cease having contact with that defendant, unless, of course, a sanity evaluation was also performed and there was need for further testimony regarding defendant's mental state at the time of the offense.

RESTORATION OF COMPETENCY

If the judge finds the defendant is not competent to stand trial, then another mental health professional may be asked to determine if competency can be restored and how that should be done. In some states, such as Florida, the second part is performed at the time of the first evaluation by the same mental health professional as part of the opinion about competency. In some jurisdictions the defendant is automatically committed to a state psychiatric facility and a mental health team there may opine about the possibility of restoration to competency. In many jurisdictions, the numbers of mentally ill defendants declared incompetent-to-proceed has strained the system so that those who have been charged with committing non-violent crimes and are not deemed to be a danger to themselves or others, may be released into the community and required to attend competency restoration groups there. Many of these individuals are seriously mentally ill and may never be restored to competency. Depending on the jurisdiction, the period of treatment in order to restore the individual to competency can vary rather significantly in terms of length of time. Generally, if a treatment program is successful and the defendant is restored to competency, the individual is returned to the jail and proceeds to trial. If, on the other hand, the report is that the defendant remains incompetent to stand trial, then the defendant will either remain locked up or under court supervision for further treatment, depending on his or her dangerousness. After a specified period of time, usually five to seven years, charges may be dismissed and the defendant is released back into the community. Again, if the defendant still meets the criteria for civil commitment, he or she can be remanded back to the hospital until such time the person is found no longer to be a danger to him or herself or others.

An important question to consider is whether a mentally incompetent defendant could be held indefinitely within a psychiatric facility solely because she or he is not competent to stand trial. Remember, our legal system guarantees everyone a constitutional right to a speedy trial. If, in fact, a defendant can be kept indefinitely in a mental hospital, we are essentially creating what is called a "separate class of individuals" who are not entitled to their constitutional rights because of their mental illness. These individuals were accused of committing a crime but must still be considered innocent because they had not had a trial. It was only time before the question of how long an individual may be retained in the hospital would come to the attention of the U.S. Supreme Court. The U.S. Supreme Court, as we have seen before reviews cases with issues that represent possible violations of the United States Constitution.

In 1972 that case finally came before the U.S. Supreme Court. In *Jackson v. Indiana (406 U.S. 715, 1972)*, the U.S. Supreme Court ruled that a defendant who was mentally incompetent could not be indefinitely hospitalized solely on the grounds that she or he is incompetent. The defendant could remain in the hospital only for that period of time necessary to determine whether or not she or he would regain competency within the foreseeable future. If, in fact, this can be determined, the Court will generally grant an extension of the period of treatment. If it is the hospital or clinician's opinion that the defendant is "unlikely to regain competency in the foreseeable future," the defendant should then either be committed to a secure facility in the civil system or released from confinement. That is, if this individual satisfies the criteria for involuntary commitment (danger to self or others as a result of mental illness), then that individual can be civilly committed. If, on the other hand, this individual, while perhaps psychotic, has not acted in any violent or self-destructive manner, even if the person's behavior is controlled by placement in maximum security confinement on heavy medication, then that individual must be released.

This, of course, poses some rather troubling questions for the criminal justice system in which an individual who has serious criminal charges may have to be released and never stand trial on those charges because of a mental illness. While it is rare, there are certain cases in which such individuals have, in fact, been released and have committed further criminal offenses based on the very same mental disorder which was rendering them incompetent to stand trial.

An example of this was a defendant seen by one of the authors (DS) several years ago. The defendant had an elaborate delusional system about satanic rituals and black masses. This delusional system interfered with his ability to assist counsel since he had incorporated his attorney into the delusional system. The defendant was declared incompetent to stand trial and unlikely to regain competence within the foreseeable future. Several attempts to medicate him had been unsuccessful, with the delusional system remaining intact. The defendant then informed the staff that he had "discovered" that the Catholic Church was behind all of his problems and that as soon as he left the hospital he was going to bomb churches and kill priests to "get them before they get me." The case was presented in front of the Mental Health Commission who was to decide if the defendant could be released or continue to be held in the secure hospital, emphasizing that this individual represented a danger to others because of his delusional system. Nonetheless, the Commission ruled that he had not, in fact, acted on the basis of this delusional system and therefore he did not constitute an imminent danger to self or others. He was released from the hospital. Six weeks later he slit the throat of a homeless individual whom he perceived in his delusional state to be a paid assassin from the church.

TREATMENT FOR RESTORATION TO COMPETENCY

There are different treatment models that are popular in terms of restoring an individual to competency to stand trial. The most popular method is administration of antipsychotic medication which usually will alleviate the symptoms of severely distorted psychotic thinking and allow the individual to more rationally process information needed in order to be considered competent for trial. Another method, often used in conjunction with medication, is attendance at a competency restoration group. A third method is individual psychotherapy with a specific goal to help the individual regain competency rather than simply treat his or her mental illness.

COMPETENCY RESTORATION GROUPS

Jails, out-client settings, and forensic psychiatric hospitals all utilize competency treatment groups in which the basic elements of competency to stand trial are in essence "taught" to the mentally incompetent defendant. These groups may also be utilized by mental health professionals in outpatient settings if the charges are not serious and the defendant is not found to be a danger to him or herself or others. Unfortunately, it is common for defendants in these groups to learn to state the elements of competency through pure rote memory without any true understanding. So, when asked what the prosecutor, defense attorney or judge's job is, they can name them but not really understand what it means. Typically, these defendants do not understand the adversarial nature of the court system so all the players seem likely to either help or hurt him or her. It is the job of the forensic examiner to go beneath the surface when such individuals have been in these competency restoration groups to determine whether there is a true understanding or whether the defendant is merely repeating words heard in the group.

As noted earlier, the preferred mode of treatment is with antipsychotic medication even when treatment groups are utilized. Interestingly, psychotropic medications are readily available in the jails and prisons, often used to control the growing mentally ill population. Unfortunately, the choice of drugs is usually from a formulary that is chosen primarily for cost effectiveness. The use of psychotropic medication raises problems in some courts in which judges are concerned that they are dealing with "drug-induced competency." Others believe that it is not "drug-induced competency" but rather the alleviation of the psychotic symptoms that were interfering with a defendant's competency that represents the central issue. As soon as the defendant stops taking the medication, his or her mental illness will return and competency may again be at issue. Obviously, some defendants will not want to be restored to competency so they can remain hospitalized or even out of custody while attending treatment groups until the time lapses for their prosecution. In some cases, their defense attorneys want to get the case to trial as the penalties may be less time served in jail than spent in the forensic hospital. Or, the defense attorney may be concerned that the defendant may not be able to stay off street drugs or otherwise stay out-of-trouble if placed on probation and in the community. Thus, it is important for the forensic expert to conceptualize all methods of restoration to competency without the interference of politics.

RIGHT TO REFUSE MEDICATION

The use of medication to assist a defendant in regaining competency poses some other problems as well. The defendant may, on some occasions, refuse the medication. There is, in fact, a long body of case law that supports a patient's right to refuse treatment. However, until the late 1980's, these cases dealt exclusively with civil commitment as opposed to criminal commitment patients. In 1987, the first case of right to refuse treatment of a mentally-incompetent patient with criminal charges was reviewed by the Fourth Circuit Court of Appeals. In a case entitled *Charters v. United States, (829 F. 2d 479, 4th Circuit, 1987)* the trial court initially ruled that the defendant had a right to refuse medication. This caused a great deal of consternation among not only mental health professionals who felt that their hands would be tied in terms of their treatment efforts, but also by the criminal justice system. Recall in our discussion above that under *Jackson v. Indiana*, if a defendant were unlikely to regain competency within the foreseeable future he or she would have to be civilly committed or released.

If one were to follow the *Charters* reasoning to its logical conclusion, a non-violent, psychotic defendant who refused medication would remain incompetent to stand trial. This defendant would be unlikely to regain competency but as long as he or she did not act out in a violent or self-destructive manner, he or she would not qualify for civil commitment. In fact, under *Charters* a defendant could be released from the hospital without ever having to fact trial on the criminal charges. Obviously, civil libertarians would applaud this outcome while those with a prosecutorial mind would find it objectionable. The difficulty here is the room for a competent defendant who feigns mental illness to manipulate the system. *Charters* was ultimately reversed on appeal citing deference to professional medical judgment provided that there were procedural safeguards in place.

Another intriguing issue, which went as far as the U.S. Supreme Court, dealt with a defendant's right to refuse medication during the course of a criminal trial. In a case entitled *Riggins versus Nevada* (504 U.S. 127 1992), the U.S. Supreme Court ruled that a defendant had a right to refuse medication at the time of trial unless taking the person off medication would render her or him an imminent danger to self or others. The issue of whether or not that might result in the defendant's continued incompetency was not addressed satisfactorily by this Court. One of the opinions, in fact, stated that medication might be forced on the defendant to restore her to competency only if there were no other treatment methods that could possibly restore the competency. It was clear that this particular jurist did not feel that medication was the only means of restoration to competency.

A new case heard during the 2003 U.S. Supreme Court term is *U.S. v. Sell (282 F. 3d 560, 8th Circuit, 2002).* Sell was a dentist charged with criminal fraud for misfiling Medicaid reimbursement requests. He was found incompetent to stand trial due to what was diagnosed by mental health professionals to be a delusional disorder. While awaiting trial, he allegedly attempted to tamper with government witnesses. Although the second group of charges was filed, Sell's contention is that these actions were a product of his mental illness. The doctors at the forensic psychiatric hospital where Sell is in custody sought to place him on anti-psychotic medication but Sell refused. The government's position is that newer atypical anti-psychotic medications such as Risperdal have far fewer side effects than the older traditional anti-psychotics such as Thorazine and Haldol and therefore, do not put the defendant at greater risk for incurable disorders such as tardive dyskinesia. While that is true, small amounts of antipsychotic medications may also have to be administered to eliminate the delusions and render Sell competent to stand trial.

The second prong of earlier decisions on the right of a defendant to refuse medication stated that medication could only be forced on a defendant if prescribed by and carefully supervised by appropriate medical personnel and used only to control a defendant who is displaying behavior that is dangerous to him or herself or others. In *Sell* the second group of charges could be interpreted to fit the latter prong of this decision. However, the appellate court determined that it is not appropriate to base their opinion on the second group of charges if indeed they were a product of someone already declared to be incompetent. Therefore, they only ruled based on the first group of charges which did not involve any violent or dangerous behavior on the part of Sell. The U.S. Supreme Court did not (1) distinguish between the newer atypical antipsychotic medication and the more traditional medication that is still used in many correctional facilities and hospitals as it is less expensive or (2) reverse their prior rulings that forced medication can only be used to control dangerous or violent behavior rather than just to restore competency.

IS COMPETENCY THE SAME IN ALL LEGAL SITUATIONS?

Over the course of several years, courts appear to have recognized that different tasks in court require different levels of competency. In other words, while there is one level of competency necessary to stand trial, a different level of competency, judged by other criteria, may be necessary to determine competency to confess, competency to plead guilty, or competency to represent oneself in court. However, in a rather surprising decision in 1993, the U.S. Supreme Court ruled that all competencies were the same.

In *Godinez v. Moran (509 U.S. 389 1993)*, the U.S. Supreme Court considered the case of a defendant, David Moran, who had initially pled guilty to several homicide charges but later withdrew his plea and decided to represent himself in court. The trial court had ruled that since Moran had been found competent to stand trial, he was also competent to represent himself. This is similar to what happened with Colin Ferguson, described in the beginning of this chapter.

The appellate court reversed, indicating that a higher standard should be used in order to determine competency to represent oneself. However, the U.S. Supreme Court agreed with the trial court, stating essentially that all competencies were the same. The majority opinion indicated that the decision to represent him or her self is no more complicated than the decisions that a defendant would have to make during the course of a criminal trial in assisting counsel. The Court deemed it irrelevant to consider the issue of how well that person could represent him or herself. In other words, the U.S. Supreme Court rendered the opinion that only the decisional competency (that is, the decision to represent oneself) was at issue. The functional competency (that is, how well the individual could represent him or herself) was irrelevant to the issues at hand and so, the U.S. Supreme Court ruled that the trial court was essentially correct in stating that in this case all competencies were the same.

In actual clinical practice, forensic examiners should be aware that there are different criteria to be satisfied for different kinds of competency and, in fact, representing oneself does require skills above and beyond assisting one's attorney at the time of trial, even if a consulting attorney is supplied by the court.

Colin Ferguson's trial was an excellent example of what happens when, in fact, the court treats all competencies the same. As was mentioned earlier, Ferguson terrorized and shot to death a large number of people on the Long Island Railroad. The case received a great deal of press coverage and, in fact, Colin Ferguson's ramblings during trial convinced even the most skeptical members of the lay public that he was, indeed, quite psychotic. Nevertheless, since he had been found competent to stand trial, the judge allowed him, pursuant to the U.S. Supreme Court decision in *Godinez vs. Moran*, to represent himself. What followed and was seen on live television even before Court T.V. was a bizarre demonstration of the extent of Ferguson's psychosis and delusional thinking. However, observers at the trial have stated that like many with a similar mental illness, Ferguson was able to conduct part of a cross-examination in a coherent and articulate manner but then in the middle of it, would lapse into psychotic-like behavior such as asking a police officer if he had conducted blood alcohol tests on the bullets that were found. The ability of a psychotic individual to go in and out of mental competency in a close time period is an important phenomenon for an expert to help juries and judges understand when testifying about competency.

CONDUCTING A COMPETENCY EVALUATION

As noted above, in the section dealing with restoration to competency, very often defendants appear to have learned the right 'buzz' words but really have very little understanding of the legal components needed in order to be regarded as competent to stand trial. In the course of a forensic evaluation regarding competency, the examiner must be careful to go beyond the apparent surface understanding that a defendant may have and probe for their true understanding of some of the concepts. Even if a defendant appears to be manipulating the examination and faking or malingering some symptoms, if the defendant has a mental disease or defect and cannot meet the legal criteria set by that jurisdiction, the examiner must find him or her incompetent.

While some maintain that traditional psychological testing is irrelevant to the determination of competency, others find that psychological testing can be of great assistance, not for directly answering the competency questions but for providing the clinical basis that underlies such opinions. In other words, if a defendant does not appear to understand the charges against her or him or does not appear to be able to assist counsel, the mental status examination and psychological testing can be of great value in terms of explaining what is causing the defendant's competency problems. There are a number of factors that can render someone incompetent: is it that the defendant is psychotic and has disordered thinking, is mentally retarded and developmentally disabled, shows brain damage that impairs his or her abilities, has a disease such as epilepsy that affect the central or peripheral nervous system, etc.? In other words, standardized cognitive, personality, trauma-specific, and neuropsychological tests can provide a scientific basis for the opinion in providing information regarding the clinical state that may result in the lack of competence. Of course, the exact opposite can be found as well, that the testing reveals no impairment, no psychosis and therefore nothing that could interfere with a defendant's ability to stand trial. In such cases, if a defendant may be feigning incompetence or malingering, the psychological testing can actually reveal that there is no underlying impairment which interferes with the ability to understand the charges or to assist counsel.

In addition to this traditional use of psychological testing, more specialized forensic assessment instruments have been developed to assist the examiner in these examinations. Forensic psychologist Grisso has published several such assessment tools for the forensic practitioner as described below. For instance, one of the tests currently in use is called the *MacArthur Competency Assessment Tool for Criminal Adjudication (MACCAT-CA)*. This instrument allows the examiner to evaluate, through a description of a scenario and the defendant's responses to that scenario, the defendant's cognitive abilities to understand various situations, the reasoning abilities and the capacity to appreciate the nature of the legal system. This test goes into far more depth than the traditional interview that many forensic examiners currently use. Certainly, there are some cases where a brief clinical interview will suffice, especially when there are no questions regarding the individual's competency. On the other hand, in more subtle cases, where the ability to assist counsel may be in question, it is recommended that one of the more in-depth forensic instruments be used.

OTHER COMPETENCIES

The forensic clinician may be asked to evaluate a defendant in reference to competencies other than the ability to stand trial or represent her or himself. As noted above, the criteria for each of these are, in fact, different than competency to stand trial and while the U.S. Supreme Court has ruled that legally all competencies are the same, the clinician should approach the task as if all different kinds of competencies need to be evaluated on their own merits.

Competency to Waive Miranda Rights and Give a Statement

One of the tasks which the forensic examiner may be asked to do is to evaluate whether or not the defendant understood the components of his or her civil rights, called a Miranda warning after the case that established these rights, when she or he chose to waive them and talk to the police without an attorney present. A fundamental concept in U.S. law is the defendant's right to remain silent and right not to incriminate him or herself. The test for whether a defendant 'knowingly and intelligently' properly waived her or his rights is purely a cognitive one. The examiner may do a detailed, in-depth interview to attempt to ascertain the defendant's true understanding of the concepts listed in *Miranda.* For instance, the examiner may ask the defendant what the phrase, "You have the right to remain silent" means; what the phrase, "Having the right to an attorney" means; and so forth. What is essential is that the defendant understands the right not to incriminate herself or himself. Very often, when a defendant agrees to waive his or her Miranda rights, the defendant does not know exactly what it is that she or he is doing. In some cases, the detectives doing the questioning will deliberately confuse the person using information that they have gained either from the defendant him or herself or from others.

Analysis of police interrogations is a task that the forensic psychologist may be requested to perform. The examiner, through an in-depth evaluation, can ascertain this. Consider this example:

> A defendant seen by one of the authors (DS) indicated, when asked what the right to remain silent was, that it means "You have to keep quiet." When asked why he had to keep quiet, the defendant responded, "My mother always told me that it was impolite to talk when other people were talking. Here, the police were talking, so I had to remain silent." It is clear that this individual had no recognition of the fact that the right to remain silent was for his protection against self-incrimination. A defendant, of course, need not use the words "self-incrimination" but there needs to be a basic understanding that that is the reasoning behind the right to remain silent.

Another approach to a competency evaluation, other than the in-depth clinical interview, is to utilize assessment instruments developed by Grisso regarding the comprehension of the actual Miranda rights read to the defendant by the detectives. Grisso has a series of structured interview protocols which deal with the comprehension of the usual Miranda rights and the comprehension of Miranda vocabulary. The Grisso evaluation actually describes courtroom and interrogation scenes which are presented on cards to determine the defendant's true level of understanding. These tasks are very helpful in that they tend to go beyond the surface understanding that may appear when they are asked merely what the right to remain silent means. Some forensic examiners obtain the actual Miranda forms used in their jurisdictions and carefully question the defendant to see if he or she truly understands what he or she is being asked.

COMPETENCY TO CONFESS

While the competency to waive Miranda rights and the competency to confess are clearly significantly intertwined, the competency to confess also involves an emotional component sometimes conceptualized as whether or not the defendant's will was overborne by the authorities. Here, the clinician doing forensic work can be of valuable assistance in assessing what the individual's mental state is, whether he or she is highly susceptible to influence, whether he or she may in fact be confessing to charges which he or she may not have committed, or whether there is some mental disease or defect that would make her unduly susceptible to the influence of the authorities interrogating her. This issue regarding "police coercion" is highly relevant to the admissibility and credibility of a defendant's statements. In a case entitled *Colorado v. Connelly* (479 U.S. 157 1986), the U.S. Supreme Court ruled that a psychotic defendant who gave a confession which he maintained was motivated by "the voices" could not have his statement suppressed unless it could be shown that the police somehow engaged in some misconduct or misused their influence. Certainly, the fact that the confession was motivated by auditory hallucinations would go to its credibility at the time of trial but could not, in and of itself, absent police misconduct, be used as a basis for voiding or negating the confession.

In a case seen by one of the authors (LW), the defendant had been horribly beaten by the father who had been found murdered at his girlfriend's house. The defendant, who was of limited intelligence although not retarded, had been beaten by his father until he admitted doing things that he had not done. He learned to lie in order to stop the beatings. The police played 'good cop, bad cop' with one detective playing the role his father took, threatening him and other one encouraging him to confess so he could protect him against the 'mean' detective. As might be expected, the defendant confessed and was immediately arrested. As soon as he saw his court-appointed public defender attorney, he recanted the confession. As the only evidence against the defendant was his confession to the detectives, the major legal battle was fought around the admissibility of his statement. The defense argued that the police officers exploited the defendant's weaknesses and therefore, the confession was not obtained voluntarily. LW was called to testify about her findings that the man's current psychological state was consistent with the witness reports that he had been a victim of child abuse and how that could be expected to impact on his state of mind at the time of his waiver of his civil rights when he gave the statement, making what he said in it unreliable. Eventually, the statement was admitted by the judge but under a plea arrangement, the defendant who was not in custody during the three year legal battle, accepted a manslaughter conviction with prison time suspended while he was on probation.

Another case seen by LW also demonstrates the coercive nature of the use of a polygraph examination by a recognized examiner on a battered woman who had been sexually abused by her now dead husband who was murdered by her new boyfriend. At first, the woman denied having any part in the plot to kill him. The polygrapher tried to establish rapport by being very seductive, stroking her hand and looking into her eyes for long periods of time. Although the woman was very uncomfortable being confined to a small room with this man for so many hours, he persuaded her not to leave until the examination was completed. She agreed and then he placed the wires for the machine under her blouse, stroking her gently as he did so. She did not protest but later said she was so distracted by his behavior that she could not think clearly. The results of the examination were 'inconclusive' as might be expected given the conditions under which it occurred. The examiner, who was a law enforcement officer, promised to let her leave if she would confess to her role in what happened when her husband was killed. She told all that she knew, implicating herself in the plan to kill her husband. Legal issues unsuccessfully focused on getting both the confession and the polygraph examination thrown out. Her lawyers were successful in making sure the polygraph examination was not admitted but the 5th District Federal Courts did not accept the argument that a physically and sexually abused woman was more vulnerable to not comprehend her right not to confess.

COMPETENCY TO REPRESENT ONESELF

As we previously discussed, it is rare that a defendant will petition the court to represent him or herself. In those cases where the court must make the difficult decision, the examiner will most likely be dealing with a psychotic individual. Examination of this individual needs to determine to what extent the defendant's belief that he or she can adequately represent him or herself is in fact a product of the psychotic and distorted thinking. Like in the Colin Ferguson case discussed earlier in this chapter, it is possible that even individuals with severe mental illness will have some periods of lucidity. However, it is the extent to which the individual can reasonably know that he or she can adequately be his or her own defense attorney throughout the entire legal proceedings, not just trial, that is at issue here. Rules of evidence must be followed, evidence must be gathered and presented properly, some evidence must be appropriately challenged to keep out of the trial and witnesses must be interviewed. The defendant must also be able to prepare an adequate cross-examination. These are just some of the areas that the defendant must competently deal with in order to be properly represented. In some cases, courts may appoint an attorney to assist the defendant and sit with him or her at the defense table during the trial.

COMPETENCY TO BE EXECUTED

In 1986, the U.S. Supreme Court ruled, in a case entitled *Ford v. Wainwright (477 U.S. 399, 1986)*, that a mentally incompetent defendant could not be executed. A defendant would have to be competent enough to recognize why the sentence of death is about to be carried out. This is, of course, a very minimal level of competency but even so, a mental health professional may be called upon to perform such an evaluation. There are

clearly many ethical concerns raised if a psychologist were to do such evaluations. A psychologist can raise concerns regarding the ethical principles
that call for avoiding doing harm or the potential misuse of one's data or
one's influence to cause someone to die. Essentially, the examiner would
be asked to determine whether or not the defendant's mental disorder, if it
exists, interferes with his or her capacity to understand why the sentence
of death is about to be carried out.

Many psychologists have expressed concern that performing this type
of examination would make the forensic examiner a party to the state's
machinery of death and they choose not to involve themselves in such
evaluations. Other forensic examiners feel that a finding that the person is
incompetent will save the person's life. Clearly these are moral dilemmas
for a forensic psychologist to ponder. Another troubling choice is for a
forensic mental health professional to participate as part of the treatment
efforts to restore that individual to competency for execution. It is certainly
beyond the scope of this volume to discuss the legal, philosophical, and
moral issues involved here. Suffice it to say, it is a highly controversial area
and if a psychologist chooses to involve him or herself in such evaluations,
he or she needs to carefully think through all the implications.

Some more recent cases have expanded on several of these issues.

In *Perry v. Louisiana* (498 U.S. 38, 1990) the Louisiana State Supreme
Court ruled that a psychotic inmate, who had been found incompetent to
be executed, could not be forcibly medicated in order to restore him to
competency for execution. Several years later, in *Singleton v. Norris (992
S.W. 2d 768 Arkansas Supreme Court 1999)*, the Arkansas State Supreme
Court ruled that a defendant found incompetent for execution could not
be forcibly medicated if the sole purpose of the medication were to restore
him to competency for execution. However, the court further noted that if
the primary purpose of the forcible medication was something else, such
as controlling his dangerous behavior, and the restoration to competency
for execution was merely a beneficial side effect of the treatment then the
forced medication could be justified. This could, without careful procedural
safeguards in place, result in forcibly medicating such individuals in order
to execute them, but justifying it in terms of rendering them 'No longer a
danger to self or others'.

More recently the Eighth Circuit ruled that Singleton (*Singleton v.
Norris, 319 F. 3d 1018, 8th Circuit, 2003*) could be forcibly medicated to
restore him to competency for execution because the state's interest in
carrying out a lawfully imposed sentence outweighed Singleton's liberty

interests. They based this decision on the evidence that there was no less intrusive treatment and doctors had testified that the psychotropic medication was 'medically justified'. The fact that there are now two clearly opposite views in *Perry* and *Singleton* suggests that the U.S. Supreme Court will address the issue in an upcoming term.

SUMMARY

As you can see, we have dealt with the legal and psychological complexities of a defendant's competency to stand trial in the criminal justice system. Although the legal system treats competency as a unitary construct, in fact the human mind is quite complex and someone can be competent for one task and not another depending on what mental illness or defect they demonstrate. In fact, someone can have a 'good day' and appear to comprehend more than they can on a 'bad day'. We all know people who are more competent in the mornings than later in the day because of the fatigue factor. Mental illness has variable symptoms that sometimes are more pronounced than at other times. This is especially true for those who are diagnosed with severe affective disorders such as Bipolar Depression when someone would fare differently on a competency examination given during the manic or depressed phases. So too for someone with a delusional disorder which is dependent upon when someone becomes part of his or her delusional system among other factors.

The issue of civil rights for those who are adjudicated incompetent is one that is beginning to receive attention from civil libertarians such as Michael Perlin, a civil rights attorney at New York Law School who has written and lectured extensively on mental disabilities law. The new Mental Health Courts for seriously mentally disabled people who are charged with misdemeanor crimes will also focus attention on the discrepancies between someone who is declared incompetent-to-proceed to trial and locked up for five or more years when he or she could be treated right in their community without losing their liberty. At the same time, the U.S. Supreme Court appears to be moving to a more conservative position that might reverse its previous decisions to allow the decision to use psychopharmacological restoration of competency to be between the person and his or her doctor if self destructiveness or other violence is not an issue. As we all know, these medications all have side effects and the benefits of taking them may not outweigh the dangers for different individuals.

TABLE 5-1. MAJOR CASES AND THEIR SIGNIFICANCE

Dusky v. U.S.	Defined basic criteria for competency to stand trial.
Jackson v. Indiana	Prohibited indefinite confinement of mentally incompetent patients
U.S. v. Charters	First case to discuss mentally incompetent defendant's right to refuse treatment.
Riggins v. Nevada	Right of defendant to refuse medication at the time of trial.
Godinex v. Moran	U.S.S.C. case ruling all competencies were the same.
Colorado v. Connelly	Confession that is 'coerced' by a person's mental illness is not in and of itself inadmissible. Rather, there must be evidence of police misconduct.
Ford v. Wainwright	An inmate on death row must be competent to be executed.
Perry v. Louisiana	An inmate has right to refuse medication designed to restore him or her to competence to be executed.
Singleton v. Norris	Forced medication of an inmate is permissible if for some other reason even if such medication will secondarily result in restoring his or her competence to be executed. Some other reason is defined as if medically appropriate and no less intrusive treatment is available.

DISCUSSION QUESTIONS

1. What might be the consequences of *not* forcibly medicating a patient to restore his or her competency to stand trial?
2. What might happen if a defendant successfully argues that he or she should be taken off medication at the time of the trial?
3. Would you participate in the evaluation of an individual to determine competency for execution or in the treatment program to restore competency? Why or why not?

6

Self-Defense and Syndrome Testimony

SELF-DEFENSE AS A JUSTIFICATION DEFENSE

In the preceding chapters we have discussed the psychological issues involved when assessing an individual for competency and criminal responsibility assisting the attorney in using a legal excuse defense such as insanity because of mental disease or defect like mental retardation or brain damage. In this chapter we will discuss another way for individuals to be found not guilty of a crime because their behavior was justified. Some legal scholars claim the behavior itself cannot even be labeled as criminal because the necessary *mens rea* or state of mind is not present.

The most common justification defense is self-defense or defense of others although two other types of homicides are also justified—a police officer who kills someone in the line of duty or a soldier who kills the enemy during wartime. In each of these cases, it is necessary for the individual to prove that the situation justified his or her actions. In law enforcement cases, it is usually a police commission that may hear the case and make their findings while in the military it is often a military tribunal or others with a similar responsibility. In other types of cases where self defense is used, such as when a battered woman kills her abuser in what she believes is self-defense, it is a jury of her peers who make the decision after listening to the facts. Sometimes a psychologist is called to provide expert witness testimony to explain the person's state of mind. Admissibility of this kind of psychological testimony is relatively new and has been so bitterly contested in some jurisdictions that state legislatures passed a special law creating a 'Battered Woman Syndrome Defense' rather than continue the arguing among attorneys, psychologists, and judges.

Killing another person is never desirable, but it may be considered a justifiable act if it can be proven that the killer acted in good faith and with certain elements that are specified in the law. Some believe that imposition of the death penalty for individuals who are found guilty of capital murder is a justification by the state that putting these individuals to death is for the good of the state. This could be argued as defense of others, another justifiable defense similar to self-defense and often incorporated in the same statutes.

Countries also have laws that permit killing of citizens for various reasons including violating religious norms and customs. In some Middle Eastern countries, women were killed for marrying the wrong person, having sex or babies out of wedlock, or other ways of disgracing the family, including leaving a violent husband. Rarely are the family members who kill these women prosecuted. Some cultures forced citizens to commit suicide if they commit certain behaviors or find themselves through no fault of their own in certain circumstances, such as in India where widows were expected to throw themselves on their husband's funeral pyres. At one time, so-called *dowry deaths* were not prosecuted in India and Pakistan. The parents of a man who did not like the dowry that they received from the bride's parents would kill the woman, albeit accidentally, by setting the sari she wore on fire. It is important to understand the culture as well as the laws in any community to help determine a person's state of mind when he or she commits a particular act.

SELF-DEFENSE LAWS

The laws of self-defense or defense of others are fairly standard from state to state and country to country. The basic elements are that a person must have 'a reasonable perception of imminent danger of serious bodily injury or death'. Some statutes actually define what is meant by reasonable, perception, imminent and danger. Others leave it more general and case law with its changing interpretations suffice. As we will see below, when we discuss the development of the 'Battered Woman Syndrome' to justify the use of force to defend oneself or another person, as social mores change they are reflected in what is and is not justified under the law. An act is not a crime until it is adjudicated.

Definitions of what is a reasonable perception of danger for an individual have been left mostly to individual cases rather than codified laws to define. For a psychologist, however, we probably would break down these concepts into many more different parts than legislators or courts that are less well trained in psychological constructs. For example, is a perception the same as a thought or a feeling or both? We learned in the previous chapter that insanity was defined legislatively in various ways although the current M'Naughten standard is limited to cognition or thoughts. Is it subjective, that is inside the head of the individual person knowing everything she or he knows, or is it objective, that is something anyone in the same situation would perceive as dangerous? Or is it a mixed definition of both subjective and objective standards which is what most states have now adopted.

Reasonable Perception

Does the perception of danger have to be reasonable to everyone or just the average person? If so, how do we know what an average person might think is dangerous? This is especially important in self-defense cases as the laws were originally developed using male standards because it was the responsibility of the man to defend himself, his family and his honor. Would we expect what is a reasonable perception of danger to a man be the same as for a woman? When battered woman syndrome was first introduced it became clear that men did not perceive danger in the same way as a battered woman. How should we measure reasonableness, then?

Imminent Danger

The term imminent gives us other possible interpretations. Many people believe imminent means immediate, but in fact, when going back to the records of the debates by legislators, called the legislative history, they point to the meaning as 'about to happen' rather than happening at that very instant. This permits a time period of anticipation, where an individual has time to feel scared, think there is danger, and take some action to protect her or himself. How much time can be taken is left undefined which has helped broaden the use of self-defense as a justification for those with distorted time perception from disorders such as Post-Traumatic Stress Disorder.

What would scare you so much that you would think you are about to be seriously harmed or die? Would it be the same situation that would scare your friend? Does gender matter, here? Would you be able to take some actions in certain situations and not in others? If someone had a gun pointed straight at you, would you be justified in picking up a gun and shooting that person? How do you know that person really was going to shoot you? These are the questions that jurors will ask and forensic examiners must try to provide answers to when trying to measure someone's reasonable perception of imminent danger of serious bodily injury or death. If a juror had knowledge that someone with a certain psychological syndrome perceived danger differently from other people that might make it easier for the juror to determine what is and is not self-defense for that person or persons. In this case, the different perception of danger has to do with timing; the battered woman perceives danger faster when there are specific cues present that have accompanied actual danger previously. It is not that the syndrome causes the battered woman to have a mental illness that excuses her actions but rather, she is able to accurately perceive danger with fewer cues than might others who have not developed the syndrome. This is where expert witness testimony by a mental health professional can be helpful to a juror.

In fact, that is how self-defense is said to have been codified into law. In the days when the U.S. was being settled and there were few rules to govern behavior, one of the earliest rules was that a man could defend himself or his property, which was usually but not always, limited to his home, his women and his children. If another man challenged him to a fight, he had no choice but to respond and defend himself. These social customs went back as far as history records them and not just in the U.S. Usually the weapons chosen had to be the same for each and it was assumed that each had around the same level of skill in using that particular weapon. The most typical example of a self-defense argument is a barroom fight where two drunks beat each other up until one ends up dead. Old Western movies like High Noon with Gary Cooper or those of the Knights of the Round Table in the Middle Ages, glorified these men while they fought to their death to defend their honor or property.

Laws still exist today, in some Western U.S. states such as California, Colorado, Wyoming, Montana, Arizona, and others that permit someone to shoot and kill another person if the shooter has a reasonable perception or belief that the person who was killed was going to harm him or herself or his or her property. In this case, the reasonable perception has to be proven by the dead person's behavior—usually if the person enters the shooter's property without permission and does something that triggers the shooter's reasonable belief of harm. If these conditions exist, then the law states the shooter is not even supposed to be charged or prosecuted because he or she did not commit a crime. What they did was automatically justified. This law was demonstrated in a Clint Eastwood movie some years ago when he goaded a man to come onto his property without his permission and 'make my day'. Since that movie popularized the concept, these laws have been termed the 'make my day laws'.

What about justification when a woman kills her partner after being terrified that she or her children will be seriously harmed or killed? How can the woman's reasonable belief in facing imminent danger be demonstrated if she kills her partner before the current incident reaches the lethal stage? Most battered women act to protect themselves and their children before or after an acute battering incident. They know that during the acute battering incident, the batterer's rage might be too much for them to stop. For many battered woman who have developed battered woman syndrome, each new battering incident results in their re-experiencing fragments of earlier incidents together with the current one. The combination of the current incident and memory of prior incidents results in an accumulation of fear well beyond what would be expected from the actual behavior observed. Thus, evidence of the presence of battered woman syndrome has been admitted into testimony as a short cut to describe what would be the expected state of mind of the battered woman at a particular time.

SYNDROME TESTIMONY

A syndrome is simply a collection of psychological symptoms that occur in a pattern and are usually found together in a particular disease or disorder. It is popular to give a syndrome a name and then everyone who knows about the syndrome can understand what to expect if it occurs. Use of a syndrome to explain how a person's state of mind might be impacted if they have those symptoms can be very helpful in meeting some of the general concepts in the law and the syndrome can explain many counter-intuitive scientific facts that challenge well known myths and beliefs. Knowledge about a syndrome may be useful in identification and assessment of thoughts and emotions that are thought to accompany certain observable behaviors. Some syndromes have been studied using scientific methods while others are simply convenient names given to phenomenon that are not very well understood. It is important to differentiate those that have some scientific reliability and validity from those that do not have research to back them up.

SYNDROMES AS SUBCATEGORIES OF PTSD

Syndromes that are subcategories of Post-Traumatic Stress Disorder (PTSD) such as Battered Woman Syndrome, Battered Child Syndrome, Child Abuse Accommodation Syndrome, Rape Trauma Syndrome, and Viet Nam & Gulf War Combat (and possibly Iraq War) Syndromes have been successfully used in various legal settings. The pattern of symptoms expected in someone who has been diagnosed with PTSD may help to explain the concept of imminency as perception of time may be expected to be distorted and reasonable perception of danger as a major characteristic of PTSD includes the experience of intrusive memories of past trauma that is triggered by the current event, obviously raising the person's level of fear from cumulative rather than just this present trauma. Other syndromes without research such as Premenstrual Stress Syndrome, Parental Alienation Syndrome, Psychological Munchausen-by-Proxy Syndrome, and Urban Stress Syndrome have been introduced in some cases but cannot meet the scientific challenges when they occur. Indiscriminate use of syndrome testimony to infer that certain thoughts and emotions must have occurred in a person's mind at the time of an act or as a result of certain situations is not appropriate and may raise ethical concerns that conclusions are based on inadequate data sources. It is always a risk to use observable behavior as proof of the existence in someone's mind of that which is not observable. But, if we know that in a particular syndrome such as PTSD certain behaviors usually occur in a pattern, this gives us more confidence in our opinion.

If our scientific experiments demonstrate that a syndrome or particular pattern of symptoms are more likely than not to occur under certain circumstances, then it is clearly acceptable. But, what about clinical findings? When we talk about feelings and cognitions, we are in the clinical psychology realm and need to look at the commonalities found by treating psychotherapists outside of laboratory studies. Psychologists themselves argue about the credibility of clinical versus empirical findings so it is not surprising that the legal world finds them questionable. What level of confidence do we need to reach before we can state a syndrome exists beyond a reasonable doubt (the criminal law standard), clear and convincing evidence (the standard in juvenile parental termination and other civil cases) or more likely than not (the preponderance standard most often used in civil and family law cases)? Can you base testimony on one person's clinical cases that might give rise to some common symptoms seen? Two therapists' cases? Three? Fifty? Of course not. However, if we had a representative number of cases from therapists in a defined sample, then we might be able to make generalized statements to everyone in that sample. As scientists we must be careful not to base our conclusions on data that do not meet our standards. This means acceptance of standard and structured clinical interviews, results of standardized tests that give us good samples of behavior, and our carefully crafted observations may also meet the scientific tests of reliability and validity even if we have not calculated an error rate as the original *Daubert* criteria on admissibility suggested.

When we do go too far, it leaves us vulnerable to criticisms of people such as Alan Dershowitz, the famous appellate attorney from Harvard who wrote about the *Abuse Excuse* in his book of the same name or Margaret Hagen who criticized all expert witness testimony in her book, *Whores of the Court*. They both took the most extreme examples and based a whole theoretical argument on them, rather than attempting to look at the issue more broadly. Hagen, an experimental psychologist with obvious disdain for clinicians, bases her argument on admissibility of testimony that she believes unjustifiably accused her brother of a sexual abuse charge against his child. We will discuss this issue in the later chapter on child abuse. Dershowitz, on the other hand, approached his argument from the legal field without seeming to understand the differences between the scientific underpinnings of some types of syndrome testimony and the lack of science in other similarly labeled phenomena. This emphasizes the need for some consistency in the mental health field when we take our findings and use them in another setting, such as courts of law.

How would someone judge whether or not a syndrome has credibility? There are different scientific methods to choose to test hypotheses and form conclusions based on scientific facts. Each type of test requires a different experimental design depending upon what kind of relationship is being tested. Advances in statistical techniques that can analyze for different inferences permit the use of quasi-experimental designs that gets psychologists into the field and out of the laboratory setting. Adequate sampling techniques will determine the generalizability of findings from one group to others. For example, when a random assigned group is impossible to achieve (such as when studying battered women), it is possible to stratify the sample so the results will still be generalizable to the groups in the stratification. Although telephone surveys are an efficient way to collect epidemiological data, the sample will not be representative of those who do not have telephones. In addition, family members may not want to reveal abuse data or other embarrassing information if others are nearby and able to listen to what is being said.

These are some of the important factors to consider when researchers or clinical psychologists are presenting scientific or clinical data in the courtroom. Laboratory research does give you better control over the variables to be studied but it is less helpful if the variables occur in a context outside of the laboratory that cannot be replicated. It may yield better scientific results to control variables measured in field or in other studies that include variables-in-context by using sophisticated statistics that can hold one or more variables constant while manipulating others. Clinical research may give less reliable group data as it is difficult to generalize from one sample to another, but it yields more reliable data about the individual and the context in which the individual's thoughts, emotions, and behavior interact to produce a particular state of mind at the time of an incident. Anecdotal studies may be less reliable in generalizing outside of the context in which they are collected but can give us ways to generate hypotheses that can then be measured with more reliable techniques.

BATTERED WOMAN SYNDROME

Let's take a look at the example of Battered Woman Syndrome that has been used to broaden what actions are permissible to defend oneself or others as an example. Since the late 1970's, the pattern of symptoms that constitute what is typically called Battered Woman Syndrome has been used to help judges and juries determine whether a battered woman is justified in killing her abusive partner by meeting the criteria for self defense or defense of others such as her children. The case law developed first, as opposed to statutory changes, as many attorneys believed that the self defense laws could adequately handle cases needing this type of testimony. However, the admissibility issues became an obstacle in some jurisdictions and by the early 1990's legislators in those states began to codify what became known as the 'battered woman syndrome self-defense' into law.

This created problems for some feminist psychologists and advocates who believed that the battered woman syndrome itself did not account for enough of the impact on different women who killed in self-defense. In particular, the criticisms focused on the need to better understand the larger social context in which woman abuse occurs. All women experience discrimination from sexism that still exists in various forms in all societies. It is dangerous to consider that a diagnosis of mental illness is what impacts on their state of mind when it is a justified perception of imminent danger that motivates them to protect themselves and their children or other loved ones. Although this is a compelling argument, the courts were more ready to accept the argument that a different state of mind existed in women who killed than in those who were battered but were able to terminate the relationship in other ways. Clinical experience does tell us that the violence and abuse does not stop when the relationship terminates, especially if there are children involved. This is further discussed in later chapters on family law, custody, and child abuse.

HISTORY OF THE CASE LAW

Do battered women as a group perceive danger differently from other people? Is what is reasonable for a battered woman the same as for a person, a man or another woman? Is there something about the impact from domestic violence that creates a particular state of mind that impacts on a person's reasonable perception of imminent danger? What is considered dangerous for a battered woman? Does every battered woman have the same experience? Obviously not. Can we identify whether or not people who have been battered have a particular mind set that leads them to believe that they are in danger of serious bodily harm or death even when the abuser is sleeping or has stopped the beating and walked out of the house? Are there certain characteristics to the dynamics of a domestic violence relationship identified by research that can guide our hypotheses about the state of mind of someone experiencing it? Does a psychologist have anything special to teach jurors or judges about domestic violence that the average layperson could not understand on his or her own? These were questions that had to be answered before an expert's testimony could be admitted into evidence.

INEZ GARCIA

In the 1970's a San Jose, California woman, Inez Garcia, was raped and beaten by two men, known to be involved with drugs, who lived in her neighborhood. When they left her lying on the street, they threatened to kill her if she told anyone what they had done. They warned her that they knew exactly how to find her. Garcia was hurt and had many conflicting emotions that bubbled up inside of her. Led by her fear of their threats, Garcia went home, found a shotgun and set out to find these men to stop them from hurting her again. When she found one of the men she shot and killed him. Garcia was charged and prosecuted for the rapist's murder. Using insanity as a defense, the Garcia jury found her guilty of second degree murder. She appealed her conviction on legal grounds and won a new trial. In the second trial, her attorneys used a self-defense strategy, emphasizing that a reasonable perception of imminent danger for someone whose assailant knew where she lived, had just physically and sexually assaulted her, and threatened to find and kill her later, had to be defined as constant fear and terror. This new jury found her not guilty.

JOAN LITTLE

Emboldened by the admissibility and success of the self-defense argument in Garcia, Joan Little's attorneys decided to use the same strategy in her case. Little stabbed to death the warden with an ice pick in the jail where she was being held on other non-related charges after he started molesting her. She grabbed an ice pick from his hand at the time. Testimony of Little's fear that of this man's aggressive behavior proved helpful in convincing the jury that she was justified in stabbing him to keep him from harming her. As she was in custody and therefore he knew where he could find her even if she got away this time, she used the argument that there was no escape from this man.

YVONNE WANROW

In 1977, a Washington State woman named Yvonne Wanrow shot and killed a neighborhood man as he disobeyed her orders to stay away and entered her home where she was alone babysitting young children. Wanrow believed that this man had molested other children and feared that he would overpower her and harm the children sleeping in the house. When the man entered the house, she was sitting in a chair with a shotgun at her side. Her leg was in a cast as it was healing from a broken bone. As the man came forward, despite her shouts to leave the house immediately, Wanrow shot and killed him. In her first trial, she was found guilty of murder. She appealed the case claiming she should have been able to claim self-defense even though she was armed with a shotgun and the man had no weapons other than the parts of his body he used to commit violence. In an opinion reflecting the changing social mores of the times, the Washington State Supreme Court stated that a woman could use a self-defense argument and receive the jury instruction even if she used a weapon with an unarmed man because of what the Court labeled 'the long and unfortunate history of discrimination against women' so they were never trained as men were to use parts of their bodies to defend themselves.

All three of these cases involved self-defense against a non-related person but they broadened the definition of self-defense so it could be used by battered women who killed their abusive partners. First, they were women and used deadly force in an anticipatory manner, although Garcia admittedly was raped and beaten first. However, she had already escaped to the albeit temporary protection of her home and she was the one who got the gun, went out, and looked for the men before they had a chance to come back and made good their threats. Secondly, they defined the term 'imminent' in a way that was different from its typical use, between two men in a barroom fight where the odds were more evenly matched. Even in Wanrow, they defined what was a 'reasonable woman's perception' as different from a 'reasonable person's perception' of danger and redefined equal force to include the presence of a separate weapon for a woman even if a man doesn't have one. Wanrow also defined as acceptable self-defense for a woman what some legal scholars have termed 'anticipatory' or 'imperfect self-defense'—she shot and killed the man when he entered her home and didn't wait to see if he would or would not molest the children or harm her.

The next important case more directly relevant to battered woman syndrome where the man lives in the same house as the woman was Beverly Ibn-Tamas.

Beverly Ibn-Tamas

Beverly Ibn-Tamas was married to a neurosurgeon who was highly respected in their Washington, D.C. community. They lived on what was called the Gold Coast in a lovely home with their two-year-old daughter. Ibn-Tamas had battered her on several occasions previously but this time, pregnant with her second child she feared for both her and her unborn son's safety. He came swinging at her as she fled down the stairs and ran into the room where she knew a gun was kept in a cabinet. Grabbing the gun, she described crouching in fear, waiting for her husband to come and make good his threats to kill her as he was shouting while running after her. He came screaming into the room where she was hiding and in her terror, she shot him one time in the forehead. Although she was a nurse and should have known the bullet would be fatal from where it landed, she was angry that the police took her to the homicide division. She, like many battered women, believed that her husband was omnipotent and would not die.

She was charged with murder and at her first trial, the jury found her guilty of second degree murder without any testimony about their stormy relationship. At that time, in 1977, testimony was only permitted about the incident that caused his death—not past incidents that led up to her fearfulness. As we saw earlier, this is a problem as it is expected that fragment memories of prior battering incidents as well as the current incident will raise the level of fear in the woman's mind. The appellate courts granted her a new trial and her attorneys tried again to present evidence that she was acting in self defense. The judge did not permit the expert testimony stating it did not meet the Frye standard in effect at that time because there was no evidence of general acceptability of battered woman syndrome as a mental disorder by the psychological or medical community. Before he reached his decision, the judge requested testimony from the expert (LW) outside the presence of the jury. This is called a 'proffer'. The judge was impressed with the expert's proffered testimony and when Ibn-Tamas was again found guilty of second degree murder, he sentenced her to only two years in prison. She had already served part of that sentence and within several months she was released and went home to raise her two children. Interestingly, LW had contact with the daughter, now an adult, who read an account of this case in another book LW published (*Terrifying Love: Why Battered Women Kill and How Society Responds*) and told of the loving home her mother created afterwards including preserving the memory of the positive aspects of her father for both children.

Interestingly, the appellate courts held on to this case for over six years, issuing their final opinion in 1983, ultimately supporting the court's exclusion of the testimony for very narrow reasons. In between, however, *Ibn-Tamas* set the admissibility standard in a 1979 ruling that there needed to be a three-pronged basis for permitting this novel testimony. First, it had to be proven that the information was 'beyond the ken of the average juror', which legal scholars had thought would be the most difficult prong to meet. However, the *Ibn-Tamas* court ruled that the proffer did meet that criterion since there were so many myths that the layperson had about battered women, especially why they didn't leave the relationship when they were abused.

The second prong was that the expert who was to offer testimony had to be 'properly qualified' in his or her profession. As the court had not acquired sufficient information from the proposed *Ibn-Tamas* expert in the proffer, that question was sent back to the trial court to answer and the judge found the expert was so qualified without taking further testimony. Third, 'the testimony had to be accepted by the scientific community' which was part of the original *Frye* standards. In this case, *Ibn-Tamas's* attorneys did not put on the witness stand other psychologists to answer that question as occurred in the Joyce Hawthorne and Gladys Kelly cases pending around the same time. The trial court judge used the fact that the PTSD or BWS diagnosis was not in the DSM-III at the time and ruled it inadmissible. In the two later cases, *Kelly* and *Hawthorne*, the American Psychological Association submitted an Amicus Curiae brief reviewing the psychological literature and offering its opinion that the psychology community accepted the reliability and validity of what was known about battered women at that time. This was in 1981 and there was not that much research but what was there was pretty consistent. Others have since used those Amici briefs when the issue of scientific community acceptance was raised.

OTHER RELEVANT CASES

Following the interim decision of the Court that BWS was admissible because it was beyond the knowledge of the average juror, other appellate courts also ruled to admit the psychological testimony of the expert in different cases. Some of the early cases were in Florida (*Hawthorne*), Missouri (*Martin*), New Jersey (*Kelly*), Ohio (*Kelly*), Washington State (*Allery*), and Wyoming (*Burhle*).

Joyce Hawthorne

Joyce Hawthorne had three trials that were overturned by the appellate courts, each time ruling on a different issue. In the first, the court found that exclusion of evidence of her husband's abuse beyond the last three weeks of his life must be admitted for a jury to understand her belief that she and her children were in danger. In the second *Hawthorne Opinion*, the court ruled that psychological testimony should be admitted but following the insanity statute instructions, the state had the opportunity to have the defendant examined by an expert of their own choosing. In addition, the Court also ruled that testimony by the daughter that she had told her mother of her father's incest just a short time prior to the homicide was also admissible as its probative value was more important than its prejudicial value.

In the third Hawthorne trial, the expert's testimony was still not admitted and the *Third Hawthorne Opinion* reversed her conviction of manslaughter (she had been convicted of first degree murder in the first trial, second degree murder in the second trial and manslaughter in the third trial) and remanded it back to the trial court again, ordering expert testimony to be admitted if there was a fourth trial. Instead, the judge who had kept the first three trials passed the case to a new judge who dismissed it stating that nine years after Aubrey Hawthorne's death, a fourth trial would be cruel and inhuman punishment. In fact, Joyce Hawthorne had been released on bond during this time and was able to raise her five children even with her uncertain legal status.

Another important issue that was raised but not settled in the *Hawthorne* case that lasted until 1986 was whether a person using self-defense had a 'duty to retreat' or demonstrate a 'cooling off period' before using deadly force. Florida statutes (as well in other jurisdictions) had a 'man's home is his castle' doctrine which suggested that a man did not have the duty to retreat in his own home. In 1999, this issue was finally settled in Florida by reversing the *Weiand* decision where the trial court had excluded a jury instruction on self-defense because the defendant was held to this duty in a marital relationship where in a non-related self-defense homicide no such duty was required.

Gladys Kelly

In the New Jersey *Kelly* case, occurring as the *Ibn-Tamas* and *Hawthorne* cases were winding their way through the courts, the facts were very different from the other two cases. In *Kelly* the defendant and her abusive partner were no longer living together when she stabbed him to death. Gladys Kelly went to find her partner at another home, they got into an argument about child support money he owed her, and after they left that house and were on the street, she stabbed him with a pair of scissors to prevent him from further hurting her. Neither thought the wound was serious at the time, but later, when he had a heart attack and died on the emergency room gurney while in treatment at the local hospital, it was learned that the stab wound pierced the lining around his heart. She was charged with second degree murder and the trial court would not permit expert testimony about self-defense since she was the one who went to look for him so she could not have had a 'reasonable perception of imminent danger'.

In one of the most important decisions in this arena, the *Kelly* opinion explained that a reasonable perception of danger for a battered woman is different from a reasonable woman or a reasonable person. In addition, the court reaffirmed treating battered women as a special class because the New Jersey legislature (like most other states) intended that they be special when they passed the domestic violence protection legislation that gave them legal protections including the right to obtain protective orders 'ex-parte' without the alleged abuser present. Like the *Wanrow* court, *Kelly* reaffirmed the woman's right to arm herself with a weapon to defend against the man who used parts of his body to inflict harm against her. Interestingly, Kelly did get a new trial with testimony about battered woman syndrome and self-defense but the jury still found her guilty of manslaughter. However, this time her sentence was only five years in prison. Unlike Joyce Hawthorne, Gladys Kelly, a poor Black woman, spent the time awaiting her appeal and new trial in prison. By the time her second trial was over, she had already served over half of her time.

Several other cases warrant study here to fully understand the development of this expansion of self defense or as some believe, the new syndrome testimony defenses. Two of these cases come from Washington State, *Wanrow* which we discussed earlier and *Allery*.

Gladys Allery

In 1984, just as Joyce Hawthorne was getting her third trial and Gladys Kelly was getting her second trial, the *Allery* case was decided in Washington State. Allery, a battered woman was not permitted by the trial court judge to get public funds to pay for a psychological evaluation to see if she had developed battered woman syndrome that impacted on her state of mind at the time she killed her abuser. She appealed her conviction and in a very progressive opinion, the Washington State Supreme Court found that every defendant was entitled to a psychological evaluation under the U.S. Supreme Court decision in *Ake v. Oklahoma*, which required the state to fund such an evaluation if a defendant was indigent and others with their own financial resources were permitted to have such an evaluation. Therefore, the Allery court ruled, it would constitute malpractice if an attorney did not make sure the defendant got such an evaluation if domestic violence was raised to determine if a battered woman syndrome was appropriate to use as part of the defense.

Attorneys all over the country took note of this decision and fearing they might not be providing the best defense for their battered women clients, they began requesting psychological evaluations to see if there was evidence of battered woman syndrome and if so, did it impact on the defendant's state of mind at the time they killed their abusers. As these cases were being litigated, it became clear that the average person did not understand that many of the psychological symptoms that were typical for a battered woman to display, such as re-experiencing the fear of prior battering incidents during the incident where she defends herself, raises her level of danger, and constitutes self-defense for a battered woman even if it occurs before there are lethal-type blows delivered in the present incident. In addition, women who had been beaten into submission, sometimes for years prior to the final incident, had great difficulty talking about the abuse and their feelings on the witness stand. A psychologist could fill in the gaps and help the jury understand what was in the woman's mind at the time she took action.

Edith Burhle

However, not all attempts to admit what became known as battered woman syndrome self defense testimony were successful. In the state of *Wyoming* in an early case known as *Burhle*, tried in the late 1970's, the court ruled that the testimony was not admissible and refused to give a self defense instruction. Edith Burhle went to the motel room where her abusive husband was staying and while she was standing outside and he was inside the room, they argued for over one hour about his refusal to give her money. When he finally got up and walked towards Edith, she mistook the reflection of the light on something silver for a gun and thinking he was about to shoot her, she shot and killed him first. As we shall see later, hypervigilance to cues of danger is an automatic protective response made without any thought when the autonomic nervous system is stimulated by fear. In those days, unlike the *Kelly* case later, it was simply impossible to persuade the judge to overcome the objections that the facts showing that Edith went to where her husband was staying (although she stated it was at his demand if she wanted the money), the length of time she stood there arguing and could have left at any time (although she stated that she believed he would have followed and shot her if she left) and her arming herself with a shotgun (she said she knew he always carried several guns with him) did not negate her fear of imminent danger as a battered woman.

Helen Martin

In Missouri, in the *Martin* case, Helen Martin admitted being manipulated by some of her husband's gangster enemies into letting one into her home with the intentions of killing him, because of her fear that he would keep good his threats to kill her and their five-year-old daughter. However, the court decided that she could not use self defense because a third-party killed her husband and did not admit expert testimony as to her state of mind at the time. Despite her testimony that she had changed her mind and told the killer not to do it, the jury found her guilty of conspiracy to commit murder and sentenced her to 50 years in prison. After approximately 15 years, Helen Martin was freed by a special clemency rule. She and her now adult daughter, who was five at the time her mother was sent to prison, spent several years afterwards helping other battered women gain clemency and making sure Missouri legislators passed a special statute so others could get expert testimony admitted at their trials.

Donna Yaklish

Even Colorado, which was one of the first states to admit battered woman syndrome testimony to support self-defense, ruled that a woman had to commit the killing herself and not hire someone else to do it. In deciding Donna Yaklish's appeal, Appellate Court Justice Sandra Rothenberg, a strong feminist jurist wrote the opinion stating that while it was possible to make an argument that a sleeping man could cause a woman to believe she was in imminent danger, the hiring of another person to kill an abuser carries the self defense argument too far. In *Yaklish* it was the state that filed the appeal stating that the trial court erred by permitting expert witness testimony on battered woman syndrome to support Yaklish's claims that she hired two boys to kill her abusive police detective husband because she was afraid he would make good his threats to kill her as she believed he had killed his first wife. The Court's ruling effectively prevented other battered women from using such testimony if they were charged with conspiracy to commit murder.

CLEMENCY FOR BATTERED WOMEN

By the late 1990's, it seemed clear that a new defense had been created over the objections of state prosecutors who vehemently argued that women were getting away with murder. However, those who truly understood the complexity of how women got trapped in these abusive relationships, usually by men who stalked them, and were willing to die themselves in order to control and possess the women, were beginning to use expert testimony to win convictions in simple and felony assault cases where women were too fearful to testify against the man. Stopping a batterer at an early level often helped prevent escalation of the violence to lethal levels.

Battered women advocates were successful in persuading governors in various states to develop clemency commissions to review the cases of battered women who killed their partners in what appeared to be self defense but did not get to put on testimony in their defense or even get a trial, as had happened to so many women serving long sentences in their prison. As in any new defense, it was unequally applied in different jurisdictions so these inequities began to be addressed. It also became clear that poor women and African American women were more likely to be convicted and sent to prison for longer periods of time than less marginalized women with resources. Governor Celeste in Ohio and Governor Schaeffer in Maryland, where new laws had to be created before battered women got a fair trial, granted clemency to large groups of battered women. Despite the fear of many prosecutors, none of them have been reported to have used violence since their release. The same good record is true for women released in other states with clemency programs such as Florida, Colorado, and Illinois. Many other battered women are still waiting favorable findings from other clemency or parole commissions or governors themselves.

APPLICATION TO OTHER DEFENSES

Lorena Bobbitt

Once the success of the battered woman syndrome defense was well established in women who killed their abusers in self-defense, its use began to be broadened in the courts. For example, when a woman committed an assault against the man, the facts indicated that it often was in anticipatory defense of his further harm to her. The famous case of Lorena Bobbitt was a good example of how battered woman syndrome would have explained how the repeated sexual violence committed by her husband towards her created the state of mind that caused her to believe he would rape her again when she cut off his penis. Like other battered women who killed out of desperation that they would be further harmed, so too did one of the authors (D.S.) find that Lorena Bobbitt had a reasonable belief that she was in imminent danger of being seriously bodily harmed or killed by John Wayne Bobbitt who was not necessarily finished assaulting her that night given his prior behavior. Unfortunately, she had to use a temporary insanity defense rather than self defense due to the peculiarity of the laws which did not permit the presentation of battered woman syndrome testimony in the state of Virginia at the time her case was tried.

DURESS CASES

Another logical extension was to use the same testimony about how the syndrome impacted on the battered woman's state of mind so as to create such fear and terror that she committed other criminal acts under the duress and coercion of the batterer. The most common duress defense is used in cases where the woman is a co-defendant in both property crimes and drug offenses. In some of these cases, the man does not participate in the actual criminal act himself, but rather, intimidates bullies and terrorizes the woman into doing it for him. This is commonly seen in women, often called 'mules', who bring drugs in from other countries. They are the lowest paid workers in the chain of drug suppliers and most do it both for the promise of more money than they can earn in a lifetime as well as terror that the man will beat them up or even kill them. They are shocked when they are arrested and most were so unfamiliar with the drug world that they had no idea of the consequences that they risked. In many of these cases, especially in Federal court where the self defense statute calls for the perception of danger to be directly related to death in some way, the battered woman syndrome is more likely used at sentencing in order to reduce the mandatory sentence guideline by using a downward departure of one or two levels and cutting average sentences by several years.

OTHER BATTERED WOMAN SYNDROME TESTIMONY

Battered women use the evidence of battered woman syndrome in cases other than criminal charges. They may use the psychological evaluation to demonstrate the nexus between their current psychological damages and the expected damages from a domestic violence relationship in a personal injury 'tort' case, described later or to demonstrate lack of competency in signing various kinds of contracts, especially prenuptial agreements in family law or wills, trusts, and other financial documents in a civil case. These cases are popular in some jurisdictions, such as New Jersey where a special type of lawsuit may be filed in family court, called a *Tevis* claim. In many cases, the damages part is folded into a divorce settlement and the claim never goes to trial. In an Idaho case, *Curtis v. Curtis*, Sandra Curtis won over one million dollars from her former live-in boyfriend of 10 years when she proved that the abuse had caused her to develop 'battered woman syndrome' despite the fact that they had not been legally married.

ADAPTATION OF BATTERED WOMAN SYNDROME TO OTHER SYNDROMES

Battered woman syndrome has been adapted to other subcategories of Post-Traumatic Stress Disorder syndromes to demonstrate that children who are abused, sexual assault victims, girls or boys who have been sexually assaulted, or women who have been sexually exploited also have a high risk of developing a state of mind that is similar to the effects of battered woman syndrome. Thus, their actions may well be a product of fear that makes them have a reasonable perception of imminent danger even if someone who had not been abused does not perceive danger or at least doesn't see it as imminent, yet. We will discuss these defenses further when we deal with juvenile crime in later chapters. It may be important to differentiate those cases where there is repeated versus a single traumatic incident, those where there is a special love relationship between the abuser and his victim such as in battered women or child abuse, and those where there is another type of relationship bond, such as exploitation by authority figures or those with special religious roles. PTSD from natural disasters usually doesn't have the same impact on victims although many of the features of the emotional reactions are similar.

RAPE TRAUMA SYNDROME

Rape trauma syndrome is another syndrome that produces an identifiable pattern of psychological symptoms that impact on someone's state of mind in a predictable way. This could be used as a similar defense when defending someone like Inez Garcia or Yvonne Wanrow who commit a homicide. However, the courts have ruled that it cannot be used by the prosecution to prove that a crime did occur. This makes some sense as most sexual assaults do not occur in front of anyone else, so if it were admitted, the testimony would have to be used to prove that it was beyond a reasonable doubt that the woman was raped by the man being prosecuted. Although it is possible to measure the psychological impact from a sexual assault or rape, and it is possible to say that a woman's psychological state of mind is consistent with rape trauma syndrome, it is not possible to say without any hesitation that it was this particular defendant who sexually assaulted her.

However, in cases where the man admits to having sex with the woman, but claims she consented, the presence of Rape Trauma Syndrome symptoms can help bolster the woman's credibility. In some cases, it is not possible to meet the criminal standard of beyond a reasonable doubt but the psychologist may be able to state that the data do support that it is more likely than not that she believed it was not consensual. This testimony may be used in civil tort cases especially when liability is assessed against a third party for failure to protect against the foreseeable possibility of a sexual assault occurring (like not fixing a broken parking lot gate or not checking the criminal record of a school janitor). Testimony that confirms psychological harm might also be used in cases where a person in authority sexually exploits another person like in the civil lawsuits against the church where clergy who were known child abusers were placed in another parish without notification.

SUMMARY

In summary, the development of the self defense strategy to justify a battered woman's desperate fear when she kills her husband is used as a way to introduce the concepts of self defense and justification defenses. The use of a syndrome, such as Battered Woman Syndrome is described to give the reader an understanding of the scientific basis or lack of it when attempting to introduce syndrome testimony to justify actions. How syndromes can be studied and the process by which it can become part of the law is demonstrated by using Battered Woman Syndrome as an illustration.

7

Clinical Assessment in Forensic Settings

ATTORNEY:	Doctor, in your opinion, is this defendant mentally ill?
PSYCHOLOGIST:	Yes
ATTORNEY:	Doctor, would it change your opinion if I showed you this letter that the client wrote stating he was going to 'play crazy' for the doctor?

If you were the psychologist here and you only had a clinical interview to support your opinion, you may have some credibility problems no matter how you answer this question. However, if you had standardized test results, your answer might be something like this:

PSYCHOLOGIST:	No, that would not change my opinion because my opinion is based not only on my clinical interview but also on the results of the standardized tests that I administered.
ATTORNEY:	But, doctor, can't all these tests be faked?

PSYCHOLOGIST: It is always possible but there are scales that con-
                   trol for validity in several of the tests that I admin-
                   istered. I also administered tests that are designed
                   specifically to assess for someone who is trying to
                   look more crazy than they actually are.

If you also reviewed forensic documents concerning the actual facts of
the crime you could also respond to the cross-examination like this:

ATTORNEY: Well, doctor how do you know that he didn't be-
                   come this way after the crime from held in jail. After
                   all, jails aren't nice places, are they?

PSYCHOLOGIST: I was able to compare other peoples reports of the
                   client's behavior both before and during the crime
                   with the current test results and my interview. I
                   found the client's behavior to be consistent across
                   all these data sources.

The above cross-examination is typical of what a forensic expert witness can expect to face when testifying to the conclusions about a person's
behavior being consistent with what is expected for someone with a particular type of mental illness. If you only used a standard clinical evaluation as
your data source, which may be appropriate in an initial clinical interview
to develop a treatment plan, a forensic examiner is at a disadvantage. If you
also administered several clinical tests to assess for mental illness, the forensic examiner can more effectively deal with the obvious question of the
client's inconsistent behavior, such as outright lying or pretending to feign
psychopathology. However, if you also review documents such as police reports and witness statements that describe the client's behavior at the time
of the incident, then you can make statements that support your opinion.
The more data sources you have, the more credible is the forensic opinion.

There are two major differences between a clinical and forensic assessment. First is the different interpretation of the data gathered through
traditional clinical means. Administration of the clinical interview, history taking, mental status, and psychological testing would be the same
whether for a clinical or forensic evaluation. Second, is the need for more
than one data source. This may include witness statements and other discovery in a criminal case, other reports about the person's health in a civil
personal injury case, police records in an abuse case, or collateral interviews in a custody evaluation. In clinical settings these assessments are
used for developing a diagnosis and treatment plans. In forensic settings,
the evaluator must interpret the clinical material not just for diagnosis and

treatment purposes, but also as a way of generating hypotheses relevant to important forensic issues in the case itself. The clinical data are important but do not represent all that is needed for a forensic assessment. They are, in essence, only a jumping off point and clinicians unfamiliar with forensic procedures may make many errors when they try to over-generalize from these clinical data to legal or forensic conclusions. It is here that the forensic clinician must address the other forensic issue—the integration of multiple data sources. While the use of several data sources is important in clinical settings, it is even more critical in a forensic evaluation.

The first part of this chapter will deal with the forensic methodology involved in interview and history, and the second part with the use of psychological testing in forensic cases.

CLINICAL FORENSIC ASSESSMENT

The goal of forensic assessment is to come to a professional opinion within a reasonable degree of psychological certainty, which is the legal standard. This means that your opinion is more likely than not to be accurate rather than the higher standards psychologists use for rejecting the null hypothesis in research. The final forensic conclusion must represent an integration of multiple data sources representing analysis of the consistencies across these data sources and explanations of where there were inconsistencies. If there are inconsistencies, which frequently occur, these may qualify rather than invalidate your professional opinion. A fair and ethical opinion will report any data that may indicate such reservations. However, once on the witness stand, you are only required to answer questions posed to you by each attorney. Here trial strategy is important to develop with the attorney with whom you work.

Conceptually, it is necessary to use this integration and consistency model because in forensic evaluations the answers to legal questions usually require data other than that obtained in a clinical interview. These parameters will be detailed in the other chapters outlining procedures for evaluations in each type of legal proceeding in this book. However, there are some general procedures that will be presented here.

COMPETENCY TO STAND TRIAL

While the primary focus is on how the defendant appears at the time the forensic examiner performs the evaluation, some dimensions require the necessity for input from sources other than the clinical interview. The clinician may well be able to determine the defendant's ability to understand the charges, court proceedings, and important people in the court process, but ability to assist counsel and susceptibility to deterioration may require input from others. For example, an interview with the attorney to determine how the defendant relates to her or him, and a review of psychiatric records could be helpful. Learning if the defendant has been placed on medication and analysis of what it is, its effects, its possible side effects, and the consequences of changing or stopping the medication are all relevant issues. As noted in the chapter on competency, defendants have the right to refuse medication at the time of trial if they choose. Were this to occur, a careful review of the mental state of the individual when not on medication, coupled with a consideration of the stress of trial proceedings would be an important addition to an opinion about the defendant's current competence.

In reviewing psychiatric records it is important to note typical behaviors when the defendant is actively psychotic compared to those times when the illness is in remission. If the defendant is in jail, a careful review of behavioral observations made by staff can be helpful in determining the validity or lack of validity of certain symptoms the defendant may be presenting. A case examined several years ago by one of the authors (DS) revealed that a defendant, who appeared to have severe cognitive impairments, such that he had difficulty answering the simplest questions, in fact was the "champion chess player" on the ward. Clearly, the concentration necessary to play chess was inconsistent with the severe cognitive impairment observed on the clinical tests.

CRIMINAL RESPONSIBILITY

In the evaluation of criminal responsibility, the necessity for integration of data outside of the clinical evaluation becomes even more critical, because we are dealing with the defendant's mental state at the time of an offense, not her or his current mental state. Without careful consideration of other sources of data, the clinician has difficulty knowing whether the mental state at the time of the evaluation is the same as, or different from, the mental state at the time of the offense. The defendant may have been mentally intact at the time of the offense but deteriorated by the time of the evaluation, perhaps due to the stress of being incarcerated. On the other hand, a defendant may have been overtly psychotic at the time of the offense and have reconstituted, or gone into remission, by the time of the evaluation.

Defendants in remission may attempt to reconstruct their behavior to appear non-pathological, to make it more acceptable. The clinical evaluator is trained to accept the client's descriptions of an event as therapists work with a client's perceptions of events. The forensic evaluator should not accept automatically the defendant's description of his or her mental state at the time of the offense as necessarily accurate. In general, a criminal responsibility evaluation requires a careful review of police reports, witness statements, hospital, employment, and school records, and interviews with family, friends, witnesses, and police officers. In some forensic evaluations it is necessary for the examiner to interview some of these people personally while in others a review of an investigator's interview, a statement or a sworn deposition will suffice. An integration of all of these sources of data will help the psychologist determine the defendant's state of mind at the time of the offense to a reasonable degree of psychological certainty, and whether it was different from the defendant's mental state at the time of the forensic evaluation.

Police reports and witness statements may provide the best contemporaneous evidence of behavior at the time of an offense. While these lay witnesses are generally not mental health professionals, they can often provide descriptions of behavior that can assist in the reconstruction of a mental state. In one case seen by DS, the defendant was charged with an apparently unprovoked assault on a police officer, after the officer had seen him shoplifting a jar of peanut butter. Upon interview, the officer recalled that as he approached the defendant, the defendant's eyes "rolled back in his head" and "his body got all stiff." The behavioral description made it clear that the apparently unprovoked attack was in fact the random striking out seen at times during a seizure. Subsequent neurological evaluation confirmed the diagnosis.

It is also possible that the reports of police officers and detectives who do not record the events in a timely or clear manner will not be helpful. Confusion at a crime scene can interfere with the reports as can other factors described in the later chapter on eyewitness testimony. Battered women, rape victims and others with PTSD may not tell the police all that influenced their behavior for a variety of reasons including shame and embarrassment. They may also have difficulty separating out what actually occurred from fragments of other similar trauma events that were being reexperienced in their mind at that time. So, caution is advised in the weight given to those reports.

For example, in one case seen by LW, the defendant kept describing her husband throwing a telephone at her that broke. However, no broken telephone was found at the scene. During the evaluation it was discovered that he had thrown the telephone in another similar battering incident that occurred shortly before this one. It could be inferred that the current incident triggered memories of the previous one so she was responding to both at the time of the incident. This information can be helpful in supporting a self-defense hypothesis and testimony to its accurate context can make her statement more credible to the jury.

PERSONAL INJURY

In a personal injury lawsuit the integration of multiple sources of data is critical. The legal standard is whether the accident or injury was the proximate cause of the current condition. Proximate cause is sometimes described as a 'but for' test: but for the accident or injury (i.e., had it not occurred), the current mental/emotional condition would not exist at all or in the intensity noted. Obviously, this question cannot be answered without a careful consideration of the plaintiff's prior condition and subsequent behavior since the time of the accident or injury. The prior condition is usually determined by review of records and interviews with family, friends, and employers. This is important to establish a baseline of what was the plaintiff's pre-existing condition.

Even if the plaintiff had a pre-existing psychiatric condition, it does not eliminate the possibility of recovery in a tort action. In the next chapter we describe what lawyers call the 'egg shell theory' of personal injury tort claims. This is often explained by using the nursery rhyme involving 'Humpty Dumpty' who was a cracked egg when he sat on the wall, but if someone pushed him, then they must take responsibility for all the damages, not just the subsequent ones. Others state the theory as 'you take your plaintiffs as you find them', meaning if the defendant injured the person beyond what his or her condition was before, then the defendant is responsible for the person's current condition. However, often personal injury cases are settled by apportioning the amount of money to be recovered according to prior and current condition. In any case, the clinician must determine how much worse the current condition is, or in what way the accident or injury exacerbated the prior condition.

A review of records since the time of the accident or injury is also important, because it will help provide substantiation or lack of substantiation for the deficits the plaintiff is claiming. If, for instance, she or he is claiming severe anxiety or depression, but a therapist's notes reveal that the symptoms are mild, this can be important information. If a plaintiff claims that she or he is experiencing a phobic reaction since the injury such that she or he avoids certain areas, but an investigation reveals frequenting of such areas, this is highly relevant data. It should also be noted that sometimes a plaintiff will seize upon an accident or injury to justify symptoms she or he has been experiencing for many years, and not consciously acknowledge that the symptoms have pre-existed the accident or injury. Careful history gathered from outside sources will help illustrate this.

DS examined a young man whose car had been in a minor motor vehicle accident, when a postal service truck had hit him from the rear, while stopped at a red light. The impact was at approximately 5 miles per hour and caused only minor dents to the plaintiff's car. He was claiming that, in addition to Post-Traumatic Stress Disorder, he was suffering organic impairment which resulted in a marked decline in his grades in college. A review of academic transcripts revealed no drop in his grade point average.

It is also necessary to integrate the data with what mental health professionals know about the expected behavior of someone with similar experiences or diagnosis. For example, LW had a case where a sexually abused woman began a clandestine sexual relationship with a co-worker while her husband claimed that she was refusing to have sex with him as part of the damages. The insurance company that was representing the party being sued discovered their relationship after putting her under video surveillance, not unusual in highly contested cases. Testimony included a discussion of the behavior known to occur in rape victims which sometimes includes sexual acting-out or experimenting to see if they still can function normally.

CHILD CUSTODY EVALUATIONS

As a final example, let us consider child custody evaluations. It is well known that parents in a contested custody situation will be "putting their best foot forward." Reliance on the clinical interview and psychological testing alone will give an incomplete picture. Again, careful history taking, structuring parental interactions with the child, interviewing friends and family, and obtaining outside records such as school, medical, and treatment records, can be very important in helping to provide a more complete picture. If there has been an allegation of child abuse, a careful review of social service records is critical; even here, the records may not be available or complete. If there are allegations of domestic violence, once again, record review is critical, along with a careful consideration of the research literature that details the effects on children of witnessing domestic violence.

COMPREHENSIVE FORENSIC ASSESSMENT MODEL

The following is a suggested comprehensive forensic evaluation model which provides the general parameters that are necessary to include in a report of a comprehensive forensic assessment in criminal and personal injury settings. A similar outline to be utilized in custody evaluations can be found in Chapter 13. The exact order of this outline need not be followed strictly and it may be adapted to different circumstances.

Clarify Purpose and Parameters of Exam and Obtain Informed Consent

As early as possible, there has to be a clear statement reflecting the defendant's or plaintiff's informed consent to the evaluation, and his or her understanding of the conditions under which the results of the evaluation will not be kept confidential. While this may seem self-evident to the examiner, it may not be clear to the defendant or plaintiff. People who have had experience with a psychologist previously may assume this interview will be confidential, too. The fact that this is a different kind of evaluation needs to be clearly explained. The details of the informed consent will vary depending on the jurisdiction, and depending on the nature of the examination, but generally it should contain a statement of who the examiner is, who retained the examiner, what the purpose of the evaluation is, confidentiality issues as noted above, and the person or persons to whom the results of the evaluation will be released. The examiner needs to indicate, in some manner, that the person being examined is competent to understand the above dimensions and consented to the examination. If there are questions regarding competency to participate, the attorney or judge should be notified before proceeding.

Gather Basic Demographics

The examiner should begin gathering basic demographic data along with the reason for the referral. In criminal cases, the referral question usually refers to the legal issue at hand (e.g., competency, criminal responsibility, mitigation). In civil cases, especially in personal injury settings, the referral usually has to do with the extent of psychological or neuropsychological impairment and whether that impairment can be related to the accident or injury. The psychologist must consider the different facets of the plaintiff's claims in order to relate the findings to the referral question. Some parts of relationship to the injury, what is legally referred to as "proximate cause" may or may not be within the psychologist's expertise. In those cases, the psychologist can only render an opinion on how the cause of the injury related to the psychological findings. For instance, let us assume that the legal action has to do with some allegedly improper medical treatment. Not being a medical doctor, the psychologist cannot testify to whether or not that treatment was improper. But, the psychologist could testify to the probability that such treatment could reasonably lead to the psychological condition we found in our assessment. Of course, if the issue had to do with allegedly harmful effects of some kind of psychotherapy, then the expert could respond to the entire proximate cause issue as well.

REVIEW DOCUMENTS

As mentioned earlier, one of the distinctions between a clinical and forensic evaluation is the review of various documents. These documents will need to be listed in the report and comparisons will need to be made of the various samples of behavior revealed about the defendant or plaintiff. In criminal cases, these will usually be police reports, witness statements, transcripts of interrogations, transcripts of pre-trial hearings, as well as motions filed by both sides regarding certain legal issues and whether certain testimony will or will not be admitted. In civil cases, one should review what are called the "pleadings," which lists the allegations regarding the causation of the injury and the nature and extent of the injury in addition to the documents reviewed in criminal cases.

It is also helpful to keep a careful log of all other people interviewed. In doing the comprehensive assessments described earlier, it is important to look for consistency across data sources. If the attorney permits, given time and money available, it is often helpful to interview as many people as possible to gain insight, from a layperson's perspective, just how that individual functioned on a day-to-day basis. In a criminal case, of course, we want as much information as possible about functioning at the time of the offense. As noted earlier, interviewing arresting officers and witnesses can be very valuable here. In civil cases, we want to pay particular attention to differences in functioning, pre and post injury.

Details of the Incident

In a forensic evaluation, it is important to obtain a detailed accounting of the crime or injury both from official documents and from the examinee. Careful attention should be paid to similarities and discrepancies in any different accounts. Especially in criminal cases, the defendant may, upon advice of counsel, not want to discuss the offense. This may also occur if the evaluation is part of an independent 'medical' or 'psychological' evaluation that defendants are usually entitled to request from the court. This should be noted in the report. The degree of disclosure necessary varies with the reason for the referral. If the examination is for competency alone, then the defendant does not need to discuss the incident. He or she only needs to understand the charges and the legal process. If the examination is for criminal responsibility, then the need for the defendant to describe his or her actions, thoughts, and feelings at the time of the offense becomes much more important. In personal injury cases, it is important to obtain the plaintiff's accounting of the incident and his or her perceptions of how his or her daily functioning has been affected by the injuries experienced.

Gather Relevant Histories

Once the sources of information and referral questions are understood, it is important to begin reviewing the information gathered in the history-taking part of the evaluation and compare it to the reports that were reviewed by others. Some examiners like to begin with a summary of any medical or psychiatric records since the time of the crime or injury while others prefer to begin with their own assessment and then compare it to the reports of other medical and psychological findings. In a criminal case, this is helpful because it may give some insights into the defendant's behavior around the time of the offense and the severity of symptoms if any are present. In a personal injury situation, of course, it gives additional sources of data to evaluate degree of impairment in daily functioning.

Mental Status Evaluation

A detailed mental status examination should be performed, paying attention to speech, affect, and any evidence of serious psychopathology. If the plaintiff or defendant is responding to internal stimuli then his or her reality testing may be poor impacting the credibility of the information obtained in the interview itself. If there is a history of head injuries or other neurological symptoms, it may be important to assess for neuropsychological injuries also.

Childhood, Social, Educational, and Work Histories

A detailed social history is important to obtain from the plaintiff or defendant. This should include early childhood history, nature of family relationships (including possible abuse), and history of any serious illnesses or injuries. A similar history should be taken for early school years, adolescence, young adulthood, and adulthood—varying—of course, with the age of the client. There should be questions detailing nature of peer interactions, romantic relationships, degree of academic success or failure, and nature and duration of employment including military service and possible citations for misconduct or psychiatric problems. All of these can provide information relating to deficits or mental illnesses pre-existing the crime or injury. Sexual and marital history should be obtained as well as the issues that may have led to divorce or separation.

Alcohol and Other Drug Use

A history of alcohol and other drug abuse is critical because it impacts on many different areas of the evaluation. It is important to learn if there is a family history of substance abuse. The plaintiff's or defendant's drug-of-choice or polysubstance abuse should be ascertained including when the abuse started, how long it lasted, and whether there has been any treatment for it. This is particularly important for a variety of reasons. It can give insight into possible dependence or addiction, and substance abuse can lead to organic impairment or to the presence of certain psychiatric symptoms. If a client presents such symptoms during mental status examination, it is important to determine whether or not they are related to alcohol and other drug use. A history of substance abuse can also have a major impact on the legal issues involved. For example, if a person claims to be suffering serious depression from an injury, but also has a history of substance abuse that can cause depression, this issue would need to be factored into an assessment. If a defendant in a criminal action appears to have been suffering from a drug induced psychosis, it is important to know whether the drug exacerbated a pre-existing psychosis. There appears to be a high incidence of those who were exposed to drugs and alcohol while a fetus who have committed major crimes so it is important to attempt to assess for fetal alcohol syndrome and other similar effects.

PRIOR CRIMINAL HISTORY

In criminal cases it is important to obtain a criminal history, both from official records and from the defendant. This will provide an ability to assess patterns of behavior and whether or not punishment appears to have deterred subsequent criminal activity, an important diagnostic consideration. This information may also be important if asked to give an opinion on adjustment in a prison population or even, a risk of reoffense if placed on probation.

SUMMARIES OF OTHER DATA

The examiner may choose to write separate sections on the different histories, especially if issues are identified that are relevant to the nature of the legal questions and hypotheses that have been developed. For example, any history of learning disabilities and the impact of such disability on behavior could be important in better understanding the person's current mental state. Others prefer to put all the histories in chronological order rather than separate the information into the different categories. This is a matter of personal preference and should be determined by what makes the report most readable and conveys the best picture obtained of the individual evaluated. Consultations from other professionals and the opinions obtained from them should be detailed in this section, too.

FINDINGS

In this section it is important for the forensic examiner to state his or her own opinions, integrating the relevant histories, the clinical and test findings from the current evaluation, what the literature says about the particular issues being assessed, and how it all answers the legal questions asked in the referral. The examiner's opinions must be linked to the sources of data from which they are obtained.

Psychological Test Results

The results of psychological testing should be presented, with a focus on their relevance to the legal issues at hand. Not all findings need to be discussed, only the relevant ones. There is some degree of subjectivity in determining what is relevant, but certainly the following should be considered as a bare minimum. There should always be a statement regarding the validity of the test results since it is important to acknowledge the precautions taken to account for self-interest in the favorable outcome of any forensic evaluation. Although, psychologists are often cross examined specifically about the possibility of a client's malingering, the issue in a forensic examination is much broader as both clients and attorneys sometimes have a lot depending upon the results of this examination.

Psychological tests can measure current cognitive functioning, critical judgment, degree of impulse control, and the various intellectual skills that are necessary to understand concepts that are important for legal responsibility. The degree to which a person's current performance on a test is related to his or her capacity to perform intellectually can also be inferred. Comparisons of his or her performance with others at the same age or developmental level can be made when standardized tests are used. If the cognitive abilities were assessed at an earlier time, the examiner can compare the current performance with the previous test results. If impairment on the cognitive test is noted, it may be important to refer for further testing to find out what is causing the impairment. This could be due to neuropsychological deficits or emotional problems or other unknown factors.

Personality tests are usually administered in addition to cognitive tests. It is typical to use several different measures in order to assess for any pathology using a variety of data sources. For example, an objective measure might ask for just one answer to a true or false question or permit several forced-choices such as in a Likkert scale where numbers might range from 1 to 5 in levels of severity. It is called an objective test because the examiner does not have any flexibility in how to score the answer. However, there may not be one right or wrong answer in those tests that have created scales made up of groups of answers. Again, a person's responses can be compared to others on whom the test has been standardized or with his or her own previous responses, if available.

Projective tests have more flexibility in the range of possible responses and how they are scored and interpreted. They are very useful in those clients who are trying to present a particular image of themselves as there are no right or wrong answers nor does social desirability play as important a role, particularly in naïve clients. Comparisons of test results from projective and objective tests give a better understanding of the plaintiff or defendant's total personality and how it may have impacted on the legal questions. Many of these test results also conform to the diagnostic categories that are used in clinical and legal evaluations so they can be used as checks and balances with each other and the clinical interview findings.

There are now standardized tests that assess the psychological impact from trauma. These can be useful if psychological problems are being attributed to one or more traumatic incidents. Some of the test results give specific data about the precise areas of functioning that have been significantly impacted and like the cognitive and personality tests, can permit the comparison of one person's responses with others on whom the test has been standardized. Others measure the criteria that must be met to make a PTSD diagnosis.

There are many other kinds of assessment instruments that are not standardized but assist in the collection of more objective information or at least gather data in a systematic way to avoid leaving out important components of the evaluation. Actuarial instruments are now being used to assist in assessing risk of violence. These actuarials are based on statistical probabilities and can be useful as guidelines if the population on which they will be used is similar enough in demographic and cultural and ethnic backgrounds. Often forensic evaluations must make sense of a lot of information so the use of structured interviews, actuarial instruments, assessment instruments of specific cognitive, affective or behavioral domains in a particular client may help organize the important data.

INTEGRATION OF RESULTS

The integration of the results from the entire evaluation includes the degree of cognitive impairment, the extent of serious psychopathology, the degree of impulse control, and the capacity for stress tolerance that may have been found. These areas are of particular legal relevance. Opinions about the acuteness or chronicity of the condition should be made if possible. If neuropsychological assessment has been done, the nature of impairment and its similarity to or differences from pre-existing impairments should be detailed. Once again, bear in mind that the test results do not answer the actual legal question, but need to be integrated with other data.

SUMMARY AND RECOMMENDATIONS

In the final section of the evaluation, a summary and recommendations for further evaluation, if any, should be made. Careful attention again needs

TABLE 7-1. SUMMARY OF STEPS IN A FORENSIC EVALUATION AND REPORT

I.   Informed Consent
I.   Reason for Referral and Legal Questions
II.   Basic Demographic Data
III. Procedure
      – Documents Reviewed
      – People Interviewed
IV.   Statements of Facts
      – Charges in Criminal Case
      – Details of Injury in Personal Injury
V.   Plaintiff's or Defendant's Description of the Facts
VI.   Relevant histories
      – Medical and/or psychiatric records since time of crime or injury
      – Social History
      – Vocational History
      – Sexual and Marital History
      – Educational History
      – Military History (if any)
      – Drug/Alcohol Abuse History
      – Criminal History (if any)
      – Psychiatric History
      – Neurological History
      – Consultations
VII. Findings
      – Mental Status Examination Results
      – Compare current clinical findings with previous reports
      – Results of Psychological Testing
      – Integration of all of psychological findings with literature and other data sources
X.   Summary and Final Recommendations

to be paid to the legal issues, and how the psychological issues impact on them. It may be appropriate to repeat the examiner's psychological opinions relevant to the legal questions here.

THE USE OF CLINICAL PSYCHOLOGICAL TESTS IN FORENSIC SETTINGS

There are differences of opinion among forensic psychologists about the usefulness of traditional clinical psychological tests in a forensic setting. Some maintain that the tests may be misleading since they were designed to measure constructs that are unrelated to legal criteria.

Others maintain that the tests provide valuable insights about the very dimensions that *are* important to evaluate legal criteria in court related proceedings. Others maintain that only test instruments that have been specifically validated in forensic populations should be used. The latter would invalidate most of the clinical psychological tests currently in use.

Our approach takes into account the above arguments but still finds clinical psychological tests important if used properly in forensic settings. We have stressed, throughout this volume, the necessity for the forensic psychologist to integrate multiple data sources, to look at each source as generating hypotheses that will be subject to verification or disconfirmation from other data sources. Traditional psychological tests can assist in both the formulation of these hypotheses and in their confirmation. This helps the clinician avoid overgeneralization from one or more data sources by providing different samples of behavior. Traditional psychological tests also provide important insights into, but not explanations for legal constructs. In other words, for example, if we were to conclude that a defendant was incompetent to stand trial, because of an inability to assist counsel, psychological tests may tell us *why* this particular defendant may have such difficulty; e.g., the individual tests in a range of I.Q. scores consistent with mental retardation, such that she or he does not have the capability of understanding the concepts that the lawyer is trying to explain. This is different from saying that the defendant is incompetent to stand trial merely because she or he is mentally retarded. Another variation may involve a defendant that demonstrates, on neuropsychological testing, significant perseveration which may make it difficult for that defendant to follow the chain of evidence presented at trial. The important issue is to demonstrate how the inferences and scores derived from testing are relevant to the underlying legal constructs.

It is important to remember that a standardized psychological test can only be compared to its norms if it is administered correctly according to the standardized instructions. This includes filling out the forms accurately and completely and administering all items on the test. Attorneys may consult with other psychologists to check that the test was administered correctly and the scoring is accurate. It can be embarrassing and damaging to a forensic expert's credibility if any errors are pointed out during cross examination. In some cases, judges have not allowed testimony about a test that is not administered, scored or interpreted appropriately. If an unauthorized administration of a test is used, it must be carefully defended, usually because of additional information that cannot be obtained elsewhere or as a way of adapting the test to an unusual context or individual.

SPECIFIC FORENSIC TESTS

A number of tests have been constructed by forensic psychologists to assist in the assessment of questions that are specific to forensic settings. Some of the more popular ones will be discussed below:

TESTS OF MALINGERING

The issue of malingering or deliberate deception is highly relevant in a variety of forensic contexts. In criminal contexts, a defendant may have motivation to successfully fakes a mental disorder in order to be found incompetent to stand trial or not guilty by reason of insanity. In a personal injury context, a plaintiff may have motivation to successfully feign a mental disorder in order to recover substantial compensation. On the other hand, patients attempting to obtain release from a psychiatric hospital may engage in 'negative' malingering or denial of psychopathology that does in fact exist. Similarly, in child custody evaluations, it is expected that parents seeking custody will want to deny psychopathology even though that might not be the ruling factor in the final decision. Within the past ten years, a variety of instruments for the assessment of malingering have been developed. A few examples will be discussed.

The SIRS (Structured Interview of Reported Symptoms) consists of a series of scales which assess Inconsistent Symptoms, Blatant Symptoms, Exaggeration of Symptoms, Improbable Symptoms, and others. Decision rules are provided for the probability that a particular pattern is consistent with malingering.

Tests such as the TOMM (Test of Memory Malingering) use a forced choice format in which patients are asked to recall a series of very simple pictures. Norms are provided for patients with genuine memory impairment, as well as for those with normal memory, and those who have something to gain by feigning memory deficits.

The Validity Indicator Profile (VIP) also uses a forced-choice format to illustrate malingering on cognitive tasks. It produces interpretations of valid, irrelevant, careless, and malingered performance.

Forensic Assessment Instruments

In recent years, a variety of instruments have been developed to measure specific functional legal capacities. Unlike the traditional psychological tests described above, these instruments are developed around certain legal standards. Some examples follow.

The F.R.I. (Function of Rights in Interrogation) (Grisso, 1997) consists of a series of sketches outlining police interrogation of a defendant, consultation with an attorney, and participation in a courtroom proceeding. Structured questions are asked, with specific probes, to elicit a defendant's understanding of the ability to waive Miranda rights. Companion instruments are the C.M.R. (Comprehension of Miranda Rights), CMR-R (Comprehension of Miranda Rights–Recognition), and CMV (Comprehension of Miranda Vocabulary).

The MAC-CAT-CA (Macarthur Competency Assessment Tool-Criminal Adjudication) presents a series of scenarios and structured interviews, with scoring criteria to assess three different areas of functioning relevant to competency to stand trial adjudications: understanding, reasoning, and appreciating. This instrument demonstrates the degree of impairment, if any, in each of these domains and provides a much finer discrimination of various legal capacities relevant to competency than does a clinical interview. This test has been further discussed in chapter 5 on competency to stand trial.

The Rogers Criminal Responsibility Assessment Scales (RCRAS) are a series of scales developed essentially to code the information necessary for a determination of criminal responsibility. The scales include an assessment of malingering, a determination of the presence or absence of a mental disorder, and an assessment of the degree of impairment demonstrated at the time of an offense.

Violence Assessment Instruments

The problem of assessing the potential for future violent behavior will be more fully discussed in Chapter 10 on involuntary commitment and assessment of violence. At this point, we should just note that there is an ongoing controversy between those that advocate purely actuarial assessments based on static factors and those that advocate a clinical approach. A compromise approach is sometimes referred to as the "guided clinical"; in this approach, a structured interview, based on dimensions identified by the research, is utilized.

ASSESSMENTS IN CAPITAL SENTENCING

Psychologists who work on death penalty cases must conduct a comprehensive forensic assessment as outlined in the model noted above. In addition, testimony in capital cases must present to the jury the presence of what are called aggravating and mitigating circumstances. Most states have statutory and non-statutory aggravators and mitigators. Statutory aggravators are specified by the law, such as the defendant having committed another homicide during a different felony, the homicide of a police officer, or committing action during a crime that are designated as "heinous, atrocious, and cruel." Statutory mitigators are also specified by the law and include factors such as the youthful age of the defendant, his or her having a more minor role in the crime if others were involved, substantial impairment of cognitive or emotional processes and extreme emotional distress. These last two mitigators often permit the introduction of testimony about the person's mental health history. Non-statutory aggravators and mitigators refer to anything else in the person's history that may be relevant and probative.

Juries in capital cases are asked to weigh aggravators against mitigators. In theory, if aggravators outweigh mitigators, the jury is more likely to recommend the death penalty. If mitigators outweigh aggravators, then it is more likely they will recommend that the defendant spend the rest of his or her life in prison without the possibility of parole.

EXPERT WITNESS TESTIMONY

Once the comprehensive assessment is completed, the question arises just how the assessment is to be used. The expert must always bear in mind that his or her role is to assist, not determine, the judicial process. Not all the material that emerges in an assessment can be utilized by the attorney, and, in fact, some of it may undermine a given legal strategy. Therefore, one should always consult with an attorney orally and share the results of an evaluation fully before putting anything into writing or agreeing to testify. In fact, it is preferable for the psychologist to accept a forensic case in two parts; first, to do an objective and comprehensive forensic evaluation and second, to testify as an expert witness. The comprehensive forensic evaluation includes an oral report of the results to the attorney. The attorney in consultation with the client and psychologist will determine whether and to what extent the findings may be utilized. This is always a strategic decision because once the name of an expert is revealed as a potential expert witness all the material and data upon which that expert's opinion is based is subject to legal discovery.

SUMMARY

The forensic assessment of a criminal defendant or a plaintiff or defendant in a civil personal injury lawsuit is a complex process that takes a great deal of time and expertise to complete. A variety of sources of information must be utilized in forming a professional opinion that can withstand the rigors of the rules of evidence and the cross examination process. Clinical assessments are insufficient for forensic purposes but clinical assessment instruments can be used if they are supplemented by review of documents and forensic assessment techniques and interpretation. It is important to know what are the legal questions that the clinical forensic psychological evaluation must answer before deciding what data sources to consult. A comprehensive forensic assessment model can be adapted to different forensic situations that give rise to these legal questions.

DISCUSSION QUESTIONS

1. A defendant, from a foreign country, commits a brutal triple homicide. Clinical interview and psychological testing reveal no evidence of a mental disorder. What additional sources of information would you want to consult and why?
2. A plaintiff has suffered a serious fall and has become severely depressed. She presents with a prior history of depression and treatment with E.C.T. What sources of data would you want to consult in order to do your evaluation?

8

Psychological Interventions in Forensic Settings

Tom is an inmate in the state prison system. He has been diagnosed as suffering from PTSD. One day, he refused to come out of his cell for recreation. Officers sprayed him with mace and forcibly dragged him out. When he returned to his cell, he slashed his wrists seriously enough that it required 10 sutures to close the wound. Tom requested a transfer to the mental health unit. The request was denied because the prison staff regarded his behavior as manipulative and not genuinely suicidal.

If you were the staff psychologist in the prison, what would you do? What if your only choices were to refer him to the mental health unit or place him on lockdown? Is his behavior a product of his mental illness or a desire to manipulate the system? These are some of the dilemmas faced on a daily basis by psychologists who work in correctional settings.

INTRODUCTION

In previous chapters, we have discussed the various mental health issues that can arise after a defendant is charged with a criminal offense

(e.g., is he or she competent to proceed to trial, was he or she lacking criminal responsibility due to a mental disease or defect). In this chapter we will
discuss some of the ways the criminal justice system intervenes in these
prisoners' lives. The above vignette about Tom unfortunately is a common
response by prison staff, many of whom do not appreciate the desperation
of a mentally ill inmate. Some question the ability of prison officials to ever
adequately understand or provide for the needs of the mentally ill, stating
that the goals of the prison system are to punish the offender and protect
society rather than rehabilitate and reform. Yet, look at the statistics of who
ends up in prison; certainly those from the underbelly of society, lending
support to the classical thinkers who believe that crime is based on 'weak'
genes or other failures of strong will to avoid temptation as juxtaposed
to the reformers who want to treat them more kindly given their backgrounds filled with abuse and despair. Prisons have the largest population
of adult illiterates suggesting that both education and psychological treatment might reduce recidivism and produce better citizens when offenders
return to society.

We will begin by looking at some of the characteristics that define
the mentally ill population in the criminal justice system. Then, we will
review some of the issues facing 'first responders' who include police, fire,
and other rescue workers, describe ways of identifying the mentally ill in
the jails after arrest, review the movement towards specialty courts and
diversion programs, and then describe some of the typical albeit scarce
treatment programs in jails and prisons today. In theory, of course, the
issues we have raised before (competency and insanity evaluations) should
target those individuals with severe mental illness and divert them from
the criminal justice system. In practice, too many people who are mentally
ill have slipped into the system. Unfortunately, with the new sentencing
guidelines that give judges very little flexibility in how much time to give
in a sentence, those who slip in may be there for many years before anyone
even notices them. There are so many mentally ill in pre-trial detention
facilities (jails) and post conviction places of confinement (prisons) that
they have, de facto, become the new mental hospitals of the 21st century.

IDENTIFYING MENTAL DISABILITIES IN INMATES

Over the past twenty years, there has been a steady increase in the
percentage of inmates with serious mental illness. In 1980, less than one
percent of prisoners had diagnosable mental illnesses. In 1999, it was estimated that it increased to between 16 and 24 percent of inmates. Today

the numbers of inmates who have been diagnosed and/or treated with a mental illness is even higher. The U.S. Department of Justice (DOJ), who works within Departments of Corrections (DOC) in each state and the U.S. Department of Health and Human Services (DHHS) where the Substance Abuse & Mental Health Administration (SAMHSA) is located have been authorized by Congress to fund joint programs to deal with this large and still growing population. The reasons for this dramatic increase are not well known. Some maintain that it is as a result of a 'get tough on crime' attitude, prevalent in the last 20 years, in which the mentally ill get 'swept up' along with other people charged and convicted of crimes. Others point to the drastic restrictions placed on the insanity defense by federal and state laws as resulting in more mentally ill people convicted and sentenced to correctional facilities. Some have suggested that in the 1960's and 1970's there was more concern about treatment issues and deinstitutionalization resulting in a new class of homeless mentally ill people who previously had been cared for in state mental hospitals. In fact, the fastest growing 'homes' in the U.S. building industry has been said to be new prisons that are far more expensive to build and maintain than a long-term care facility for the chronically mentally disabled. These people now face a more punitive attitude landing them in jail and prison. There has not been any one answer or any controlled research that has clearly pointed out the reasons for this dramatic increase.

If we add to the percentage of mentally ill inmates those with co-occurring problems with substance abuse, the jail and prison percentages jump to somewhere between 50 and 60 percent of inmates in need of therapeutic services. However, drug treatment is available at less than one third of correctional institutions. Even Alcoholics Anonymous and Narcotics Anonymous groups that are volunteer-run are difficult for inmates to attend, usually because of space and management problems. Then, add to this mix the large numbers of prisoners who have been abused in the past, some studies estimate over 80% of men and 90% of women, and have untreated PTSD symptoms, it is almost the entire population who needs services. If we also count the numbers who cannot read or write, (and in some facilities this includes those who cannot speak English), we are doing inmates a disservice not to provide educational and therapeutic programs all day long. It is also important to remember that in the past 20 years, there has been a 200% + increase in the male prison population and a 300% + increase in the female prison population, so overcrowding is a problem despite all the new prisons that have been built.

The legal issues regarding treatment within correctional facilities are also, at present, very confusing as they are unclear and contradictory. For example, in 1998, a state court in Pennsylvania ruled that the Americans with Disabilities Act (ADA) also applied to inmates in prison. As we discuss in Chapter 18 on discrimination law, the ADA specifies that institutions must make "reasonable accommodations" to address a person's disability. However, the Pennsylvania court decision did *not* address whether or not this would apply to mental illness, although other employment case decisions do mandate the ADA's applicability to make accommodations for severe mental illness if it does not interfere with the individual's ability to do a particular job. Since it is a stretch to call the inmate's role in an institution 'work' it is difficult to understand how to apply the law other than in public accommodations areas. If it did apply, then what would "reasonable accommodations" in a correctional facility mean? Would it mean a separate unit in which the mentally ill would live, would it mean group or individual psychotherapy, or having the right medication and not a formulary available? What diagnosis, if any, would be considered a disability? All of these questions have yet to be answered.

A further legal problem regarding treatment in correctional settings is that the bar is set too high to force officials to meet the inmates' needs. The standard for what is called 'a right to treatment' lawsuit states that the institution must be proven to have been 'deliberately indifferent' to an inmate's treatment needs. If such a standard cannot be met, the defendant (i.e., the state or federal prison) could be granted a summary judgment and the case would never go to trial. For instance, a state could demonstrate that they performed a psychological assessment and determined that the inmate was not in need of treatment. The mere fact that they performed an assessment would demonstrate that they were not 'deliberately indifferent'. The burden would then be on the inmate as plaintiff to show that the assessment was so deviant from accepted professional standards or that it was not performed in good faith, that it did indeed constitute deliberate indifference. Clearly, then, the odds would be "stacked against" the inmate. The American Civil Liberties Union (ACLU) has filed a number of class action lawsuits against prisons and jails to force them to upgrade conditions for prisoners but most of them are settled with only minor changes occurring except for those corrections made in the most egregious areas of violation.

TRAINING POLICE AND FIRST RESPONDERS

The first contact an individual usually has with someone who represents the criminal justice system is what we now call a 'first responder', that is someone who is trained to make a crisis or emergency call. This includes police and law enforcement officers, fire rescue workers, emergency medical technicians (EMT), trained Red Cross and other crisis workers, and other community volunteers. First responders are trained to recognize serious mental illness and learn how to respond to them so the person's symptoms are not exacerbated and they can be diverted out of the criminal justice to the health system for intervention if it is needed. In the past, it was not unusual for untrained police officers to approach someone who was responding to his or her internal world and unaware of their mental condition, frightened them, provoking a violent reaction. This person then would be arrested for their original misconduct and for an assault on a law enforcement officer, which in many jurisdictions is a felony. These new charges will make the person ineligible for mental health courts that only deal with misdemeanors. We describe a typical scenario in Chapter 16 on delinquency where the youth was injured, but sometimes it is the police officer who can be badly hurt, too. Obviously, training police and first responders to identify behaviors that are consistent with certain mental illnesses can avoid many of these scenarios.

Communities that have developed a coordinated response train the first responder to first try to ascertain if the individual is safe. That usually means, does the person have a place to stay? Can he or she meet the basic needs? Does the person have enough food and money to live? Does the person seem to be medically stable? Is the person on any medication and has she or he taken it? Is the person high or intoxicated and needing care? Is the person suffering from dementia rather than another diagnosable illness? Is the person living in an Assisted Living Facility (ALF) or other care facility? Is the person dangerous to her or himself or others? Depending on the first responder's answers to these questions, the person can be linked to the proper community resources rather than being taken to jail. Unfortunately, many communities do not have other resources except perhaps a hospital which is just a temporary stabilization facility. Obviously, medically unstable people should be taken to the hospital or urgent care center rather than to jail. Some communities are linking police computers with names of citizens who are under care for mental illness. While this may be an invasion of their privacy, it may also prevent inappropriate arrests and get the person necessary psychological or medical care quickly. Another solution is to have the person wear a medical tag that specifies the medications and types of treatment the person needs. However, many mentally ill or homeless people are bothered by these bracelets or necklaces and 'lose' them.

Table 8-1. Effective Qualities of a First Responder to Crisis

Effective crisis workers have the following characteristics:
1. Successful resolution of their own life experiences
2. Professional skills such as attentiveness, listening, congruence, ability to be supportive, think analytically, and problem solving skills such as assessment and ability to make appropriate referrals.
3. Stability and poise
4. Creativity and flexibility
5. Energy
6. Quick mental reflexes
7. Multicultural competencies

Crisis Intervention Programs

Police and other first responders are being trained in providing immediate crisis intervention to those who have experienced some kind of critical incident or trauma. Critical incidents can cause psychological crisis. Critical incidents could be homicides, rapes, robberies, assaults, serious accidents, acts of terrorism and natural disasters. They are usually specific incidents that are time-limited and may involve loss or threat to personal goals or well-being. Often the usual coping mechanism fail individuals exposed to critical incidents. Experiencing a critical incident could be a turning point in someone's life. Although it is experienced by direct or primary victims, a critical incident can also cause trauma to witnesses to these painful incidents, which can produce secondary victims.

Research suggested that there are certain qualities that make for effective crisis workers. Effective crisis workers usually have been able to successfully resolve their own problems, have skills such as the ability to listen carefully, be supportive, attentive, analyze and help solve problems, and make referrals. They have lots of energy, quick mental reflexes, are pretty stable themselves, demonstrate flexibility, and are creative. They can relate well to people of all ethnocultural groups and demonstrate compassion. These characteristics are outlined in Table 8-1.

Critical Incident Stress Management

A popular technique used by police and other first responders is called critical incident stress management. It is a step-by-step approach that encourages the intervention with victims of a crisis whether it is a single incident or a large scale tragedy. The first responders are trained in

TABLE 8-2. STAGES OF CRISIS RESOLUTION

Basic Crisis Theory and Intervention
1. Identify grief responses to loss, which can be tangible or intangible such as loss of quality of life, different internal feelings, or self-image.
2. Assess impediments, if any, to attaining life goals.
3. Recognize and correct temporary distortions produced by crisis such as those in the cognitive, affective, and behavioral domains.
4. Help the client reorganize and resolve the crisis.
5. Assess for residual effects even after the crisis is resolved.

Six-Step Crisis Model
1. Defining the problem.
2. Ensuring client safety.
3. Providing support.
4. Examining alternatives.
5. Making plans.
6. Obtaining commitment.

listening skills and trained to both help the victim to talk about their feelings and reflect them back. Offering consolation and comfort may include providing a blanket or cup of hot coffee and just sitting with the person to help them stabilize. During the rescue efforts at the former World Trade Center in New York City or the Pentagon in Washington, D.C., many psychologists who were trained as first responders were surprised to find that during the initial period after a crisis people were more likely to be comforted by sharing hot chocolate and cookies rather than talking. They needed time to absorb the shock and gain some perspective on the situation. Many communities took this opportunity to train their own first responders and sent them to New York City to relieve those who had been on the front lines. Typical interventions used in critical incident stress management are presented in Table 8-2.

Debriefing

An important part of critical incident stress management and crisis intervention is the ability of the first responders to prevent their own secondary victimization responses by participating in debriefing sessions. Psychologists working with first responders found that they were more likely to develop the same symptoms as their clients just from listening to the horrible stories without taking care of their own mental health needs. In addition to coming to work with a positive attitude

TABLE 8-3. CRITICAL INCIDENT STRESS MANAGEMENT

CORE ELEMENTS OF CISM include:
1. Pre-crisis preparation (individuals and organizations).
2. Large scale mobilization and demobilization procedures for large scale disasters.
3. Individual acute crisis counseling available.
4. Small group discussions for the acute phase that are brief are the primary means of dissemination of information and discussion of feelings.
5. Small group discussions that are longer including Critical Incident Stress Debriefing (CISD) which is a trademark of this intervention especially with crisis workers to prevent further emotional harm to them.
6. Family crisis intervention techniques when entire families are involved.
7. Follow up procedures and referral for long-term therapy where needed.

and having their own problems under some control, it was found that crisis workers needed to talk to each other about what they were hearing and seeing. Most first responders now use the same kind of group psychological debriefing techniques that intentionally were developed to assist crisis workers in lowering their own reactions to job stress. The goals are similar to other forms of crisis intervention which is to prevent maladaptive responses to critical acts and stabilize, restore feelings of mastery, and develop support networks. It is based on the goals of immediacy, proximity, and expectancy. First responders are expected to participate in debriefing sessions at regular intervals immediately after their work, so that they can share the horror and other feelings they may have experienced together. If the first responder has his or her own personal problems it may make it more difficult to recover their own resiliency after intervening in crisis situations. Debriefing usually follows a step-by-step approach and a model is presented in Table 8-3.

Hostage Negotiation

Hostage negotiation is a particular crisis that may find a trained police officer working together with a psychologist and other first responders. Usually law enforcement officers are taught to take charge and act quickly with authority. However, the principles of hostage negotiation run counter to those strategies. The negotiator must overcome the urge to 'act' while using words to defuse a critical life and death situation. Negotiators must use active listening skills to successfully resolve a crisis. These skills include: emotional labeling, paraphrasing, reflective mirroring, effective pauses (silence), minimal encouragers, 'I' messages, and open-ended questions. These techniques help stall for time, lower subject's expectations, and help the subject feel powerful and in control.

By utilizing these techniques, it is hoped that the subject will begin to realize that he or she is not in control, nor does he or she have all the power. This may give the subject more motivation to initiate 'give and take' bargaining. Through the use of active listening skills, the negotiator is able to bring the subject from an emotional, irrational state to a rational, goal-directed state. The success of crisis negotiation allows for the building of trust and rapport while encouraging a peaceful surrender. The FBI has one of the most successful training programs for law enforcement and first responders to learn how to become a hostage negotiator. Psychology and criminal justice students find their courses helpful adjuncts to their other skills.

DIVERSION FROM JAIL AFTER ARREST

If the mentally ill person is not diverted before arrest, many communities attempt to get them out of jail as soon as possible after the arrest. This may involve training the jail staff to screen when they are placed in holding cells, similar to the attempts to remove alcoholics and send them directly to detoxification centers to dry out. In some communities, the local mental health center reviews the names of those arrested before they make a first appearance in court and these individuals can be diverted into new specialty courts such as mental health court, drug court, or domestic violence court. In other communities, the cases are sent to judges who are knowledgeable about mentally ill people. In Broward County (Ft. Lauderdale), Florida we send our practicum students into Magistrates Court each morning to screen all those arrested for misdemeanors and felonies for mental illness prior to their making a first appearance. The psychology intern can then testify before the magistrate recommending that the individual be diverted into one of the specialty courts available. Obviously, these are voluntary programs so if the individual refuses treatment, then he or she will remain in jail and go through the usual procedures until his or her case is resolved. In these cases, the psychology intern will notify the attorney who is selected to represent the person (usually in the public defenders office) and the jail authorities so that appropriate intervention can begin as soon as possible. In the Broward County Detention Center this usually means that the inmate can be placed on medication, sent to the medical or psychiatric unit or kept in general population. The person can also be transferred to the crisis hospital unit for stabilization if he or she is deemed dangerous to him or herself or others. The attorney can request competency and sanity evaluations quickly, often preserving evidence that might not have been available without this speedy response.

MENTAL HEALTH COURTS

Broward County was the first community in the U.S. to set aside a therapeutic court that is dedicated to working with the seriously mentally ill who are arrested, usually for non-violent misdemeanor crimes such as shoplifting, loitering, intoxication in a public case, minor theft and robbery, and the like. Many of these people are also homeless, poor, without family contacts, without resources, and floridly psychotic at the time of their arrest. They have previous diagnoses of schizophrenia, paranoia, bipolar and major depressive disorders, they may have neuropsychological disorders, and they may be HIV positive or have other disorders. Most of them have experienced abuse at one or more points in their lives. A day in this courtroom will seem like spending time in a psychiatric ward in a hospital with all the attending drama and chaos. In one corner, the psychology interns and social workers are gathering more information from the defendants, in the back families and friends are conferencing with attorneys, social workers, and case managers, and the judge and her court staff are hearing cases in front of the bar. When each case is called an array of support staff are available to assist the judge and the client in making referral decisions.

Broward County designed this new therapeutic court after several high publicity cases where poor mentally ill defendants fell through the 'cracks' and spent long periods of time incarcerated in jail awaiting hearings on minor charges. In many of our urban cities the jails are overflowing because defendants cannot pay even the lowest charges to be released on bail. If they are also homeless, they will have to remain in jail despite eligibility for pretrial release. In Florida it is possible to hold a defendant for up to 21 days without a formal charge—and an extra week might be granted if the prosecutor requests it. (Under the new homeland protection legislation passed after the 9-11 terrorist acts, suspected terrorists can be held indefinitely, often without being able to meet with their attorneys.) Determining that it would better serve the community interests to rehabilitate by mental health treatment rather than incarcerate and punish these defendants, a judge with considerable training in mental health treatment was assigned to this special court along with representatives from the local mental health community. Students from the doctoral psychology program studying forensic psychology also were available in the court to assist the judge in making appropriate referrals.

Diversion to mental health courts is controversial in some ways. For example, there is a conflict between the individual's rights to liberty and rights to obtain adequate treatment for a problem. Once the referral is made, the defendant usually is brought to mental health court that convenes later that day. There may be difficulty if the defendant would be eligible to bond out or the sentence on the charges is fulfilled by the time-served in jail prior to the first appearance. A conflict between the therapeutic jurisprudence goal for the defendant to obtain treatment and the court's goal to discharge the case can occur and it is usually the defendant's right to make the final decision. Sometimes the defendant is so psychotic and dangerous to him or herself that he or she must be sent for involuntary hospitalization to be stabilized. This occurs most frequently when someone either forgets or intentionally does not take his or her medication and then gets into trouble and is arrested for some minor infraction. Other times psychotic individuals are not dangerous but still may need treatment but can't be expected to make their own decisions. There are patient advocate groups that monitor how mental health courts are functioning to protect the rights of the mentally ill not to be forced or coerced into treatment that they do not need or want.

Treatment is provided by others in the community although it is clear that the resources for treating the seriously mentally ill are quite limited. The seriously mentally ill usually need intensive case management to coordinate their many different needs. For example, they usually need medication to manage their illness but first, they need comprehensive psychological and neuropsychological evaluations to see what medications might be the most useful in reducing symptomology. In many cases, if the right combination of medication is found, the individual is able to stop substance abuse if it is related to controlling their symptoms. If they continue to substance abuse, then a separate drug program might be recommended. Housing is often a big issue for this population, so case managers need to be familiar with obtaining federal, state, and local housing grants for them. Often they are eligible for disability and medical benefits and need assistance in obtaining them. Day treatment centers are also an important option, especially for women who are at high risk for further abuse either at home or on the streets. Many of these women have young children who are being cared for by relatives or are in the custody of the child protective services. It is important to provide intervention so that these women can better parent their children and prevent the cycle that is so often seen in the criminal justice system. Model programs are described in Chapter 13 where we discuss children who are in the child protection system.

Approximately 25% of the caseload in mental health court are women which is an overrepresentation in the criminal justice system where women are less than 10% of the total population. In Broward County, approximately 20% have had between one to nine prior arrests for misdemeanor and 10% have had prior felony arrests. Approximately one-third have had between one to nine prior hospitalizations for mental health problems while almost one-quarter reported no prior mental health treatment. The most common diagnoses were schizophrenia, bipolar disorder, major depression, and schizoaffective disorder. These data are similar to reports in programs in other states. In fact, one study showed that 70% of women who were convicted for a felony were first arrested for prostitution. Over half of those women were sexually abused as a child. Most were also battered by a male partner. If correctly identified and encouraged to participate in intervention programs, perhaps we could have averted their later criminal behavior.

In 2002, the U.S. Congress passed legislation to authorize 100 new mental health courts across the country. Although funds were authorized to accompany this legislation, they have not yet been released to communities, either to fund the court or the expansion of community services that must accompany them. As helpful as mental health courts are, however, the process will only work if clients are motivated to voluntarily attend community programs once they are stabilized. In Broward County the psychology interns report that for every client who accepts a referral into mental health court, approximately four defendants refuse the services. Therefore, other ways of helping these individuals must also be found.

Drug Courts

Drug courts that would handle those with misdemeanor and sometimes felony charges provided they were just using and not selling drugs were among the first therapeutic courts established in the U.S. As in mental health court, defendants are offered treatment rather than jail time for drug offenses if they agree. However, once they agree, they are usually more closely monitored with random drug testing. Usually, those with alcohol and other drug addictions are sent into local outpatient treatment programs with close supervision by the court. Case managers or probation workers who have been trained in alcohol and drug treatment are assigned to these courts, the judges usually volunteer for duty there, and in some cases there are psychologists and social workers who are available for further evaluation and referrals. Understanding that alcohol and drug treatment is difficult and often has many reversals before the individual is finally off all substances, these courts are patient with relapses and continue to hold the case provided the defendant goes back into treatment. Abstinence and continuation in an Alcoholics Anonymous type of model is the typical treatment protocol that the courts usually recommend. Some courts try different and innovative treatments, such as acupuncture. Others have tried a controversial controlled drinking approach where abstinence is not required as long as the individual carefully controls the amount and use of the substance as she or he is taught.

In some cases, special legislation, such as the Marchman Act in Florida, is activated, which provides for involuntary hospitalization of the defendant. If the arrest includes more than possession of alcohol or other drugs, then it is rare that drug court referral will be made. This is especially true if there is any violence involved in the charge or if selling drugs is involved. Sometimes it is difficult to make this assessment quickly, especially if there is possession of a large quantity of drugs that seems like it will be sold rather than used personally. Once in drug court, the defendant's records are available to the judge and attorneys, who all act in concert rather than being adversarial, with the goal being to help the defendant to become drug-free. Obviously, the goal of the court is to keep the defendant from reoffending. Thus, careful supervision of the defendant is required with frequent appearances scheduled before the court for monitoring of his or her progress. Usually the social workers or case managers from the drug treatment program are also present at these follow-up court times.

DOMESTIC VIOLENCE COURT

The third type of specialty court that we will discuss here is the domestic violence court. Here both defendants and victims are seen with defendants being deferred into psychoeducational types of 'offender specific treatment' and victims provided with an advocate who helps describe the court process and the community resources available to victims of domestic violence. Special victim advocates can assist the victim in obtaining an order of protection in most jurisdictions today. Some jurisdictions do not have a special court that hears domestic violence cases but have made the process of obtaining a civil order of protection easier and less costly.

This provides some additional safety from law enforcement officers should the accused offender be released prior to the criminal case being heard.

Law enforcement officers have been trained to deal with domestic violence disputes in different ways. Today, law enforcement officers usually are made aware of the special danger that can occur when responding to a domestic violence call while they are in training and at the Police Academy. Sometimes the abuser is still battering the victim when the officer gets to the house or other location. Other times, things calm down immediately and the officer has difficulty in figuring out who is the perpetrator. In some cases, the man quiets down and is quite responsive to the officer while the woman is still agitated and angry, sometimes even screaming and yelling at the officer. In these cases, it is tempting to arrest them both, especially if the man as well as the woman has physical marks on his body evidencing the woman's aggression against him, too. Although it is difficult to sort out who is the aggressor, and if the wounds are defensive rather than offensive ones, most of the time, it is the man not the woman who is the perpetrator. Even when the woman is arrested by mistake, she often pleads guilty just to get released in time to prevent her children from going into foster care. Although she is the victim and not the aggressor, she will agree to attend the offender-specific intervention program. These facts usually come out in the treatment programs and present a challenge for the system.

The typical model is to arrest the perpetrator, usually the man, for domestic violence if the law enforcement officer has 'probable cause' to make that arrest. This means that the law enforcement officer believes that domestic violence did occur and that the person arrested was the perpetrator. It is on that officer's sworn statement that the arrest goes forward. No longer does a victim have to sign a complaint which, of course, makes it less dangerous for her but also prevents her from being able to 'drop the charges' which was so common in domestic violence cases prior to the new 'pro-arrest' laws.

Once the arrest is made, in the model suggested, the perpetrator is placed in detention to wait for the next regularly scheduled domestic violence court session. In most jurisdictions, this is later in the day, usually around 12 to 24 hours after the arrest. On weekends, it might be longer as domestic violence arrests have been taken off the bonding schedule. Research has shown that the wait in jail is a helpful deterrent for some perpetrators, particularly those who have never had contact with the criminal justice system previously. Once before the judge, the perpetrator has the option of pleading guilty or no-contest (which is treated as a guilty plea) and agreeing to go into a special 'offender-specific treatment program'.

Like the drug court treatment, the domestic violence treatment program is cognitive-behavioral with an emphasis on changing attitudes and behaviors towards women, especially this woman. Often the treatment program is offered by the local battered woman's shelter but in another location so that the perpetrators and victims are not forced to see each other, either intentionally or accidentally.

The court monitors the defendant's progress in the treatment program through the use of special probation officers who have direct contact with the counselors who run the treatment program. The research suggests that approximately 25% of the batterers who attend a treatment program (and some research suggests that less than 10% of all batterers ever get to attend the program) will stop their physical and psychological abuse of the victim, 50% will stop their physical abuse but continue their psychological abuse, and 25% continue to physically and psychologically abuse the victim even while attending the treatment program. There are no data on the cessation of sexual abuse unless the offender is also sent to a special sex offenders program, which is rare in domestic violence cases. However, there may also be concomitant treatment in drug court programs if alcohol or other drugs were found at the domestic violence site.

These treatment programs are unique in several ways. First, there is no promise of confidentiality nor does the defendant have 'privilege' which is accorded to others who seek mental health treatment. This means that the treatment provider must communicate information about the treatment to the court, usually on a regular basis. Most important is regular attendance at the program since it is still difficult to measure whether or not the actual program is successful in changing attitudes, values, thoughts, feelings, and behavior other than reoffenses. Secondly, the treatment provider may not be well trained in other issues besides domestic violence or drug abuse. Unlike psychologists and other doctoral level mental health professionals who are trained in the broad spectrum of human behavior, both abnormal and normal, these providers who are not well paid, are trained in the specific program to be administered. If the individual is unique in any way, the program may not be tailored to fit, perhaps making it inappropriate for that particular defendant. Thirdly, the treatment program, which is often a psychoeducational model, may not be able to deal with any mental illness or other problem that the defendant demonstrates and thus, is insufficient to stop all violent behavior. Even so, there is a lot of support for these domestic violence offender specific treatment programs, especially from victims who believe that the batterer may well stop his violent behavior once he is in a special treatment program. Unfortunately, this does not appear to be the case, but it may well be important to try in order for victims to be willing to take the next steps in order to insure their safety and that of their children.

INTERVENTIONS IN JAILS AND PRISONS

As noted earlier, there has been a dramatic increase in the percentage of inmates with serious mental disorders. There are a variety of treatment approaches utilized in jails and prisons including medication, crisis intervention and suicide precautions, drug treatment, anger management and domestic violence prevention, sex offender programs and special programs for women. There are voluntary groups that prisoners can attend including those with a religious focus, AA and NA types of groups, and family integration groups for those inmates about to be released. Education programs are commonly offered in jails and prisons including vocational training and programs leading to the Graduate Equivalent Diploma (GED) and college level courses. As education programs become more available on the internet, computer assisted education may become even more popular in prisons.

MEDICATION

The most common treatment in jail or prison is the provision of medication for the amelioration of severe symptoms such as hallucinations, delusions, and extreme agitation. One of the most challenging issues here is to provide enough training for the correctional staff, so that they can recognize the symptoms of a mental illness in an inmate's behavior, and not respond to that inmate in a way that will further exacerbate the problem. One of the authors (D.S.) recalls giving a lecture to a group of correctional officers on identifying symptoms of mental disorder in inmates. One of the officers responded that it was all very interesting, but with the inmates for whom he was responsible, "I will respond to force with force!" While management of large groups of known offenders may be a daunting task, the old adage, 'violence begets more violence' is true in prisons, especially when prisoners are stripped of all dignity and power to regulate their daily activities of living. Medication is often misused by the staff as a way of keeping everyone calm and under control but also by the inmates to just vegetate and do their time. However, let's look at the proper use of psychopharmacology first.

In addition to the use of both traditional and newer atypical antipsychotic medications, doctors in institutions have begun prescribing antidepressants and mood stabilizers, which appear, in some circumstances, to assist in the control of disruptive behavior. The newer atypical psychotic medications such as Resperdal, Seraquil and Zyprexa have fewer side effects such as movement disorders called 'tardive dyskinesia' and do not make people feel as groggy or sleepy when taking them. However, they are very expensive as they are new and not available in generic forms. Some psychiatrists use them in combination with small amounts of the older antipsychotic medications such as Haldol and Thorazine to get maximum relief of delusions and hallucinations, which can produce some of the more violent behavior. There is a high incidence of bipolar affective disorders where people move back and forth between manic and depressive symptoms. People with bipolar disorder may lose the ability to form good cognitive judgments when cycling back and forth into these moods and commit crimes that they might not have done otherwise. Mood stabilizers and anticonvulsant drugs may be helpful here along with some of the new selective and non-selective serotonin reuptake inhibitors. Medications such as Prozac and Zoloft are popular on prison formularies as they are available in generic form and, therefore, less expensive. Some recent neuropsychobiological research has also pointed to the fact that some (but not all) antisocial individuals seem to have deficits in certain neurotransmitters in the brain (e.g., serotonin, norepinephrine, and dopamine). Some physicians are considering treating these individuals with such medications as Prozac or Wellbutrin which serve to regulate the reuptake of these different neurotransmitters in the brain.

A particularly troubling problem exists when an inmate who is in need of medication refuses to take it. Are the legal rights of an inmate the same as a defendant who is awaiting trial? In 1990, the United States Supreme Court considered the case of an inmate in the Washington State prison system (*Harper v. Washington* discussed in Chapter 10). Harper had taken antipsychotic medication for six years, but then refused any further medication stating the side effects could be permanent such as in tardive dyskinesia. The U.S. Supreme Court stated that the inmate did have a 'protected liberty' interest in avoiding the unwanted administration of antipsychotic drugs, but tried to balance this against the state's interest in the prisoner's medical status. The court ruled that if treatment was in the inmate's best interests, and there was a genuine mental disorder, then medication could be administered over his objections. This was to be distinguished from the use of medication for purposes of control or prison security. Certain procedural safeguards were put in place. Determination to override the inmate's refusal of medication was to be made by a committee within the prison. The inmate was not entitled to a full jurisdictional review which is what Harper requested. These procedural safeguards were just reaffirmed in *U.S. v. Sell*. Obviously the right to refuse treatment as we discussed in Chapter 5 when competency restoration is at issue under certain circumstances does not apply to those who are already adjudicated guilty of a crime.

CRISIS INTERVENTION PROGRAMS IN PRISONS

Crisis intervention programs exist in most correctional institutions because of the high potential for destructive and self-destructive activities of inmates. Crisis intervention techniques such as those for first responders that are outlined earlier in the chapter are commonly used inside jails and prisons when a crisis occurs. The most common crisis is when an inmate attempts to or successfully commits suicide. Suicide is the third leading cause of death in prisons, following behind natural causes which is #1 and AIDS which is #2. The prison rate of suicide is twice the general population rate, and the jail rate is nine times the general population rate. In jails, suicide and suicide attempts occur most frequently within the first month of incarceration. The most popular method is hanging which usually occurs when the inmate is alone or the cellmate is sleeping. Self-mutilation is also common, but it is often treated as manipulative and punished by isolation as we described in Tom's case when this chapter began. If, of course, it was not manipulative, but an expression of profound depression or a desperate cry for help, such punishment would be highly inappropriate, ineffective and counterproductive.

A need for careful assessment by well-trained professionals is critical. Suicide prevention programs can identify the potentially suicidal inmate ahead of time, e.g., at the time of arrest (prior to jail) or at the time of classification (prior to being committed to a prison facility). As noted earlier, staff must be well trained, must monitor the potentially suicidal inmate, must establish special housing units for them, and must refer them to trained mental health professionals for assessment and treatment. The correctional staff and mental health staff must be in continual communication about the status of the inmate. There needs to be a coordinated plan, made in advance, regarding the handling of a suicide attempt in progress, as well as administrative procedures for reporting and notification to appropriate authorities and family members. Fifteen-minute observations are standard, sometimes using closed circuit TV.

In practice, these procedures are rarely followed especially with the introduction of medical contracts to private for profit health service agencies who are supervised by people different from the regular prison staff. Inmates are constantly being referred for medical or psychiatric treatment, long waiting lists develop, and by the time an inmate is seen, he or she is returned to general population as quickly as possible. Here, turf issues sometimes become predominant with each assigning responsibility and ultimate blame to the other agency. It gets even more complicated when private prisons are managed by profit-making companies whose ability to provide competent medical services are at a level similar to managed health care companies run by business people rather than those with medical knowledge. In some cases, untrained staff have been given suicide check lists with little or no training in how to obtain the information or what it might mean.

Inmates who receive disturbing news while incarcerated may also decompensate and become suicidal. Rarely will the staff be told about this and unless careful attention is paid to the signs of decompensation, it will go unnoticed unless the inmate requests special attention or does something dramatic. It is even more unusual for medical and housing staff to confer about an inmate's need for protection from him or herself or others. The small local jails where a defendant is usually well known to local officials are being replaced by 'state of the art' centralized detention facilities which tend to be technologically sophisticated but lacking in personal warmth and attention. The panic and confusion experienced by a mentally ill person is intensified in such a setting frequently leading to acts of desperation such as suicide attempts.

SPECIAL PROGRAMS FOR ABUSE SURVIVORS

Recognizing that many inmates have had histories of abuse and trauma, especially female inmates, some mental health professionals have suggested a need for "Survivor Therapy" programs, designed by one author (LW). While a number of battered women shelters have such treatment programs, correctional institutions have not yet incorporated many of these programs based on feminist and trauma theories. Given the large numbers of abuse survivors in prisons, it would be prudent for these programs to be found in all prisons especially for those women who will be released after short sentences. There have been some attempts at psychoeducational programs that help prisoners about to be reintegrated into society deal with difficult past relationships but most of the leaders are not trained therapists and cannot deal with the re-exposure to trauma situations and memories that can trigger PTSD responses.

The survivor therapy model calls for five stages of treatment:

1. Label the abuse, describe the details and assess for the psychological impact.
2. Develop a crisis intervention plan to deal with safety issues.
3. Begin intervention for effects of PTSD including high levels of hyperarousal, avoidance, and intrusive memories.
4. Integrate trauma treatment with other psychological issues in the person's life.
5. Work towards termination by focusing on valuing own qualities and building new interpersonal relationships.

SPECIAL PROGRAMS FOR WOMEN PRISONERS

Jean Harris, the former principal of the fashionable girls' preparatory school in Virginia, shot and killed her lover, Dr. Herman Tarnover, the author of the successful Scarsdale diet program. Obviously it was a big media scandal. Tried and convicted of manslaughter, she was incarcerated at Bedford Hills Reformatory for Women in Westchester, New York. She writes about her experience there in *They Always Called us Ladies*, decrying the lack of consistent programs for women in that prison and others today. For example, she states that almost 10% of the women incarcerated are pregnant. In previous times, babies born to incarcerated women were permitted to remain with their mothers for up to two years. Today that is rarely done, although infants can stay for short periods of time to encourage emotional bonding so critical to their own development. Large numbers of women are single mothers and most of their children are placed in foster care while they are in prison. Placement of prisons outside the urban areas where most of the prisoners lived makes it almost impossible for mothers to remain emotionally and physically connected to their children while doing time.

One of the authors (LW) has visited battered women in prisons in many different states and around the world. The conditions vary from state to state with those who have women managers trained in psychology providing the best programs, including individual therapy where possible. Legislators are reluctant to fund mental health and psychosocial support programs in prisons fearing they will look like they are soft on crime in their home districts. However, the women need support, care, and the opportunity to rebuild their ability to connect with a variety of different individuals. Some call this 'self-esteem' but in fact, it encompasses a whole set of social skills that many women raised in chaotic and abusive environments either never developed or no longer have available to them. The cottage atmosphere popular in the middle of the last century, still observable in some prison sites, served women better than the stark modern buildings where doors are monitored electronically and hallways separating one area from another seem to go on for miles with twists and turns that even breadcrumbs sprinkled on the floor wouldn't permit an easy return. Women with problems are either sent into medical units or placed in isolation, which is terrifying for most women who prefer to be with others than alone. PTSD symptoms from abuse experiences are constantly with the women, often filling their thoughts as they reexperienced parts of past events whenever they feel threatened anew.

Sex Offender Relapse Prevention Programs

Programs for convicted sex offenders exist in a number of correctional facilities. They usually follow what is described as a "relapse prevention model." These are often done in a group format, with the inmate given homework assignments to recognize the various stages of relapse prevention—stopping the behavior before it happens. The model is based on teaching the person the several different components to committing an offense so it can be prevented or stopped at an early stage. The steps used in the model are as follows:

1. *Abstinence*: Agreeing not to commit any offenses and not to think about or plan to commit any offenses.
2. *SUDs*: Seemingly Unimportant Decisions—Identify everyday decisions that appear reasonable, but can create problems because they may place the individual in a situation that may result in re-offense, e.g., agreeing to baby-sit a child when a neighbor has an emergency.
3. *Dangerous Situation*: Know what are the situations where the person has the *opportunity* to re-offend.
4. *Lapse*: Behaviors or fantasies that bring the person close to committing an offense.
5. *Giving Up*: The person believes that he or she has violated one of the other principles so therefore, since there is no turning back, the person may as well commit the offense.
6. *Offense*: Committing an actual re-offense.

The treatment program teaches cognitive exercises that the inmate can use to change her/his behavior at each stage. This is done both with hypothetical situations and with the inmate's actual criminal behavior. In other words, the inmate is asked to detail what he/she could have done differently at each stage. Texts and workbooks using this model are available commercially.

ANGER MANAGEMENT PROGRAMS

Anger management programs have also been used in a variety of correctional settings. The first few sessions concentrate on educating the inmates about anger and its components while the remainder of the sessions concentrate on building skills to better handle angry feelings. Early sessions center around what causes anger (e.g., stress, frustration, fear), looking at maladaptive responses to anger, and how anger can be helpful. This is followed by learning intervention techniques to keep anger from getting out of control (e.g., Progressive Muscle Relaxation, anger logs detailing conditions before the anger is felt and consequences of acting-out). This stage is similar to the behavior modification technique called reciprocal inhibition; the relaxation will inhibit the angry response. Subsequent sessions focus on communication skills, both verbal and non-verbal assertiveness training (learning the difference between assertive and aggressive), problem solving, and role-playing.

OTHER TREATMENT APPROACHES

Other programs, somewhat more general, focus on development of the cognitive skills to solve problems, rather than responding impulsively to the situation. By identifying the problem when it first occurs, an escalation of the problem is avoided. The therapist helps the inmate identify areas in which the inmate has not handled a situation appropriately or wished that she or he had handled it differently. The therapist and client develop a hierarchy of problems to be solved, and focus on alternative strategies to the way the situation was previously handled.

More recently, some correctional programs have started looking at a treatment technique called Dialectical Behavior Therapy. This approach was originally developed by Linehan for the treatment of borderline personality disorder. The technique is used to address the client's experiencing one emotion and expressing a different one. The client becomes aware of the emotional conflict and is assisted in balancing the emotion. Inmates are taught skill modules. The first is core mindfulness which includes developing a balance between thinking driven by logic and thinking driven by emotion. Interpersonal effectiveness is the second skill module. Inmates are taught to reduce their distorted sense of entitlement and become more respectful of and sensitive to the rights of others. The third module is emotional regulation, learning to identify and label emotions appropriately, increase emotional attachment, and increase empathy for others. The fourth module, distress tolerance, teaches the inmate to learn and accept distress through the recognition that it is a fact of life.

All inmates go through the skill training modules twice, and then have to apply Dialectical Behavior Therapy to the crime they committed by completing a Behavior Chain Analysis. The inmate must give a non-judgmental description of the crime, review the consequences for the victim, and describe the crime through the eyes of the victim. The inmate then creates a relapse prevention plan using the skills acquired and examines what, if anything, can be done to correct the consequences.

Notably absent from this review of treatment techniques has been the psychodynamic model. This model, derived from psychoanalytic theory, postulates that antisocial behavior represents the acting out of unconscious conflicts. In theory, if the therapist can help the inmate to bring these conflicts into consciousness, the inmate can deal with them rationally, and no longer needs to act them out. In practice, this approach has not been effective. The reasons for its lack of effectiveness are not well known, but some theorists point to the inability of inmates with serious personality disorders to form the therapeutic alliance necessary for effective treatment. Others observe that the antisocial behavior itself is so gratifying to the inmate that the motivation to change is not really there.

Another approach that was strongly endorsed earlier, in the 1960's and 1970's, was the therapeutic community begun by psychiatrist Maxwell Jones from the Tavistock Institute in London. The entire "community," i.e., a ward or cellblock, was designed to be a therapeutic milieu. Staff would be trained to observe and intervene in all day-to-day interactions where beneficial interventions could be made, not just in a structured therapy session. Patients or inmates would be trained to respond in a therapeutic manner to one another on a daily basis. With the general shift to a less therapeutic and more punitive orientation, such programs are rarely seen these days.

Many states do have provisions for short-term, crisis-oriented mental health treatment if an inmate becomes mentally ill while serving a sentence. Some of these units are within the prison complex and others transfer the inmate to a correctional mental health center, a facility that serves all of the prison facilities in a given state. Unfortunately, these facilities are usually understaffed and overcrowded, resulting in a pressure to return inmates to their original setting. In one setting in which one of the authors (DS) worked, staff would diagnose 40% of their patients as malingering and return them to their original prisons. Considering the fact that most research on malingering suggests that between 15% and 25% of an inmate population are malingering, this figure of 40% seems somewhat inflated.

Finally, recent research on psychopathy (Hare, 1993) point out that these individuals, who constitute perhaps 15% of inmate populations, may actually experience pain differently from others. Due to defects in their brain structure, psychopaths will seek out stimulation, even painful stimulation. Clearly, repeat punishment with such an individual would be ineffective. Yochelson and Samerow in their work *The Criminal Personality* propose a different approach that might be more in line with the treatment approaches more acceptable in the corrections field today. They identified a number of "errors in thinking" utilized by antisocial individuals to justify and rationalize their behaviors. Their treatment focused on confronting inmates with their thinking errors and resocializing them into more adaptive ways of thinking. As there are few successful treatment programs for psychopathic individuals today, the prisons are an ideal place to begin testing some new models.

Public health models for dealing with large scale epidemics of diseases may have some promise in the prisons today if there were sufficient public support. As public health models point out, jails and prisons represent an opportunity for tertiary prevention as inmates are isolated from the community for a period of time and rarely turn down an opportunity to attend activities, especially if they are credited to reduce prison time. Public health models also describe primary and secondary prevention strategies. Primary prevention models try to utilize education and the identification of high-risk populations to build in protective factors. Secondary prevention is designed to intervene when the symptoms have developed, but are still in their early stages. Through outpatient therapy and various other therapeutic activities, the attempt is to contain or prevent the 'disease' from spreading. Again, funding for these primary and secondary prevention programs is often very difficult to obtain.

LIMITATIONS TO TRADITIONAL TREATMENT

Even if ongoing treatment programs existed in correctional facilities, many limitations exist. The very basic issue of "Who is the Client" has been debated for several decades. In a correctional setting, the therapist cannot promise the inmate confidentiality because correctional authorities can have access to records on a 'need to know basis'. Privacy does not exist in a prison. While therapists are generally aware of limits to confidentiality, e.g., for suicidal and homicidal threats and child abuse, they often do not know how to grapple with the fact that an administrator can view the record at her/his discretion. This raises, of course, a related issue: how much material can be entered into the chart and in what kind of detail? If an inmate, for instance, is experiencing angry fantasies about another inmate or an officer, should this be entered into the chart? If it is, someone can gain access to it, treat it as a threat, put the inmate in confinement, and destroy the therapeutic relationship. If the therapist chooses to keep the material private, and the inmate does in fact act out, the therapist is in the difficult position of concealing information that led to a security breach. Some institutions utilize a therapist/administrator split in which the therapist maintains the confidentiality, but the unit administrator need not be bound by this. In practice, this does not work out very well when the situation is a critical one. If the therapist tells the inmate at the outset of treatment that material revealed by the inmate is not confidential, will that have a "chilling effect" on therapy and result in the inmate holding back material. The issue of the impact of punishment on a mentally ill person is one that has created much debate with mental health advocates pointing out the strong possibility that solitary confinement or other punishment may exacerbate the prisoner's decompensation and create even more illness and behavior problems. This becomes especially problematic because parole boards frequently look at the extent of the inmate's cooperation with treatment programs as one of their criteria for parole so inmates who enter treatment might be signing up for more punishment when revealing their innermost thoughts.

SUMMARY

In summary, this chapter has looked at the issues of intervention in the criminal justice system first by keeping mentally ill individuals from being arrested for non-violent, misdemeanor acts, secondly, to divert them into community treatment programs where possible, and thirdly, to develop and implement treatment programs in jails and prisons as the mentally ill offender is there. Specialty courts that practice therapeutic or restorative justice were described here as one way to divert those who need treatment rather than incarceration. In jails and prisons, medication is often the first line of intervention in most jails and prisons today. While defendants awaiting trial do have a legal right to refuse or demand medication or other treatment, inmates already convicted and sentenced to prison do not generally have such rights. Many institutions have limited availability in group support programs with voluntary inmates as the leaders and in psychoeducational programs with educators as the leaders. Some have specific treatment programs that deal with special issues. We have described some model programs that have been adapted to prison conditions. In general, however, individual psychotherapy is not available in prisons and given the cost and other administrative issues, it may not become available despite arguments in its favor. The double bind that agreeing to treatment puts some prisoners in who reveal their thoughts and fantasies or actually become so agitated during treatment that they act out and then get written up or punished for it, is a real problem even when therapy is available. However, it is clear that the mentally ill are in prison and do need intervention to prevent their further deterioraton.

III

Can Psychologists Measure
Pain and Suffering?

The concept of psychological pain and suffering accompanying a physical injury has been part of the law forever. However, defining and quantifying what is actually meant by such pain and suffering has become the work of the clinical forensic psychologist. This section provides the information a psychologist needs to understand the civil law and the information a lawyer needs to understand what a psychologist can provide to assist in answering the questions raised by his or her particular case.

In personal injury cases, a psychologist may be able to measure changes in the way the person thinks, feels and acts from reviewing a myriad of documents detailing before and after behavior and extrapolating the current clinical functioning to estimating the damages, if any. In other cases, the psychologist's function is to draw the nexus between the act and the injury. This occurs in civil rights cases also. In some cases, the mental health professional can examine the defendant to a civil lawsuit and try to help determine if he or she had the requisite state of mind to intentionally, recklessly, or negligently create the actions that are said to have led to the injury and damages.

Another area in civil law is the involuntary hospitalization and treatment of someone whose behavior is said to be dangerous to himself, herself, or others. Here the psychologist is being asked to assess future dangerousness, always a difficult prospect. Involuntary civil commitment of those who do not commit criminal actions deprives them of their liberty, a precious commodity in our democratic society. We discuss some of the new research that led to the development of actuarials now used in assessment of risk of violence and their integration with clinical findings. This is especially important in the assessment for capital sentencing determinations as those convicted of a crime that a jury could elect the death penalty are permitted to introduce mitigating factors including the low risk of reoffending with another crime of violence. We also discuss the new laws that permit the civil commitment of sex predators after they have served their prison sentences. Here we also entertain discussion about the role of psychologists and other mental health professionals who are hired to evaluate sex predators who are predicted to still be dangerous to send them to a treatment center where there is no effective treatment that can guarantee that they will not reoffend. Obviously, this means that these sex offenders will be committed indefinitely so we raise the question about the feasibility of lengthening the mandatory sentences for sex offenders and keeping them in prison instead.

Civil Law and Personal Injury

Dr. Jones is a psychologist in the independent practice of psychology who had been treating Herman Smith, a 38-year-old Caucasian man, because of violent outbursts of anger since a pipe fell on his head and injured him the previous year. During the therapy process, Dr. Jones has consulted with a neurologist, neuropsychologist, and psychiatrist. During one therapy session, Mr. Smith tells Dr. Jones that he feels he is being tormented by several people and he doesn't know if he can control his impulses to assault them. Dr. Jones attempts to involuntarily hospitalize Mr. Smith but the hospital refuses to admit him. As the only medical insurance that Mr. Smith had was Workers Compensation, they refused to pay for the hospitalization. Shortly after, Mr. Smith commits suicide. His family files a malpractice lawsuit against Dr. Jones for failure to assess Mr. Smith's suicidal potential and failure to take appropriate strategies to prevent the suicide. If you were a psychologist retained by the family's attorney, how would you perform your assessment?

INTRODUCTION

Forensic experts often perform psychological evaluations in various stages in civil personal injury cases. In these cases, the State has not brought criminal charges against an individual. Rather, an individual (or group), who is called the Plaintiff(s) files suit against another individual (or group) who is called the defendant(s) alleging that the defendant(s) breached some duty or obligation to him or her (them) and that, as a result of that breach of duty, some harm or injury has occurred. The plaintiff will file with the court 'pleadings' or a list of 'causes of action', which are allegations of what the defendant(s) did to (or failed to do for) the plaintiff. The defense will usually file motions trying to dismiss the claims based on both legal and substantative reasons. Sometimes the defense will file for 'summary judgment' to dismiss the lawsuit if it contends that there is no legal basis for the claim or claims. If summary judgment is not granted, then the long process of civil litigation begins.

The plaintiff or plaintiffs will sue for damages. These damages may be physical, mental, emotional and economic. If there are no damages, then even if the defendant is liable for a bad act, the lawsuit cannot go forward. The remedy to a civil tort or malpractice action is a sum of money. Once the plaintiff puts her or his mental or emotional state at issue in the litigation, this gives the defense the opportunity to hire their own experts and conduct their own examinations. Quite frequently, then, in these cases, there will be psychological evaluations done both by a plaintiff's expert and a defendant's expert, with each expert reviewing the work and conclusions of the other. If psychological testing is performed by either side, the psychologist is obligated by statute to turn over the raw test results to the psychologist on the other side. This avoids the plaintiff having to retake psychological tests especially since retaking certain tests within a certain period of time can skew the results.

ROLES OF THE EXPERT

The mental health professional may play important roles in civil litigation both in the realm of 'liability' and in the realm of 'damages'. Liability refers to whether the plaintiff has a right to recover under the applicable law. Damages refer to the amount of money necessary to compensate the plaintiff for injuries suffered at the hands of the defendant. Expert testimony may be necessary to define what the relevant standard of care might be. As an example, let us look at Mr. Smith's family who are suing his psychologist (defendant), Dr. Jones, for failing to protect him from his own suicide. This would be an allegation of substandard psychological services against Dr. Jones. In this case, the expert will have to start with a review of Dr. Jones chart notes. Here is where making notes in a chart or file is of critical importance; not for the specifics of what is discussed but to see if Mr. Smith's committing suicide occurred as a result of some alleged substandard psychological services. Expert testimony may be utilized to establish what the appropriate standard for those psychological services ought to be. If it is found that there was a deviation from a standard of care, and that deviation caused the plaintiff's harm or injury (this is what is called the 'nexus', the 'proximate cause' or the 'but for' that is essential in a civil case, the mental health professional may then be called in to evaluate the extent of the injury and what kind of treatment would be necessary to restore the plaintiff to the previous level of functioning.

The wrong that one party commits against another is called a tort and is the basis for the civil lawsuit. It is legally improper conduct that causes harm to someone else. There are four basic elements of a tort, and all four are necessary to prove liability. They include 1) the duty, 2) a breach of the duty, 3) proximate cause, and 4) harm.

ELEMENTS OF A TORT

A tort action in the civil law has several parts. The first element is what is called a duty, legally owed by a defendant to a plaintiff. Legal duties to others occur when there is a special relationship (like a professional would have to a client) or the person is a member of a protected class (like a child, the elderly or someone who is mentally challenged). Sometimes the court declares a group to be a special class for a particular issue, like all cigarette smokers in the recent tobacco lawsuits. To expand on the example discussed above, a psychologist who is treating a patient in psychotherapy has an obligation to do a reasonably competent assessment of that individual in order to determine the appropriate treatment modality. An important point is that the 'reasonableness' should *not* be inferred retrospectively, if for example, the treatment has an unfavorable outcome. "Reasonable" refers to standards or guidelines in place at the time the treatment is rendered, not an after the fact judgment in which the harm was known. For example, a psychologist assessing a patient for psychotherapy needs to rule out any possible physical basis for her or his presenting complaints, e.g., anxiety or depression, by a referral to or consultation with a physician. Assuming that the patient became ill or died from a physical condition that was also causing the psychological problems, the duty is defined not by the fact that there was an unfortunate outcome, but rather by the fact that the standards of the profession require a comprehensive assessment, ruling out possible physical causes of the symptoms.

The second element is the dereliction or breach of the duty owed. This may be seen as either an act of omission or an act of commission. In other words, the defendant did something that she or he shouldn't have done, or did not do something that she or he should have done. As noted above, the mental health professional may be called upon to render an opinion on the standard of care and also whether the particular behavior constituted a breach of the standard of care. Usually a standard of care is decided based on local or national customs for particular business or professional actions.

The third element is causation. The plaintiff must establish that the injury would not have occurred but for the above mentioned dereliction or breach of the duty. If there were multiple causes, the dereliction or breach had to have been a *substantial* factor in the causation of the plaintiff's condition and the harm was a foreseeable risk of the defendant's actions. Expert testimony will most frequently address causation, because forensic experts are expected to render an opinion on whether the particular behavior in question could reasonably lead to the particular kind of injury the plaintiff has sustained.

Causation can become very complex when there are multiple causes of the plaintiff's injuries. In some cases, the injuries may be attributed ("apportioned" in legal terms) to more than one cause. The defendant may then only be liable for a certain percentage of the plaintiff's problems. If there is a pre-existing injury or impairment that contributed to an unfortunate outcome, the defendant may be liable only for the additional damages caused by his or her conduct. Finally, there may be cases where multiple defendants might share in the liability for a plaintiff's injuries.

Harm or injury, the fourth element, must be demonstrated by a significant impairment in the plaintiff's functioning. Theoretically, an injury, which does not result in a substantial impairment of functioning, would not be able to be utilized as the basis for civil liability. Here the role of the forensic expert is a complex one, for there needs to be multiple determinations: (a) Is there an injury? (b) Is the injury significant enough to cause substantial impairment? and (c) Is the plaintiff's current emotional state significantly different from her or his preexisting adjustment? If the answer to (c) is "no," then one cannot argue that there are compensable damages, because there has to be some degree of deterioration from premorbid functioning.

In civil rights claims filed in federal court for discrimination or sexual harassment, there does not have to be a showing of damages once the pattern of discrimination has been successfully demonstrated as the damage is the violation of the person's civil rights. Sometimes the plaintiff chooses to demonstrate damages even in federal court cases to prove how egregious the defendant's behavior was in order to request the jury award punitive damages to punish the defendant above the compensatory damages that pay for lost wages, lost opportunities, medical and other bills and future losses. Often forensic accountants work together with attorneys and psychologists to estimate the total cost of damages to be compensated.

MODELS OF RECOVERY FOR COMPENSABLE DAMAGES

When is a claim for emotional damages compensable? Until recently, it was rare to be able to file a personal tort for emotional damages alone. Now, states have generally recognized four different models for recovery of emotional injuries. These will be presented in decreasing order of difficulty for a plaintiff to establish.

The first rule is called the *physical injury or impact rule*. Here, recovery for emotional injuries is allowed only if the emotional injury is the result of a physical injury. This restriction occurred because lawmakers feared there would be a flood of litigation if the law allowed emotional injury to be a basis for litigation by itself. It led, however, to its own set of excesses, with plaintiff's 'stretching' the concept of physical injury in order to justify a claim for emotional damages.

One of the earliest recorded cases is a good example. In *Christy Brothers Circus v. Turnage (144 S.E. 680, 1928)*, a plaintiff developed PTSD after some circus horses stampeded towards the bleachers where she was sitting. Because she had to claim physical injury too, the plaintiff asserted damages from fecal matter that one of the closest horses sprayed on her when it defecated. Then, she also claimed emotional damages which were the major injury she experienced. Nevertheless, there are many cases in which genuine emotional injury can be tied to real physical injury, and a mental health professional may be utilized to explain to a judge or jury just what the connection might be.

The second rule is called the *zone of danger* rule. Here, recovery for emotional injuries is permitted without any direct physical impact: However, the plaintiff must be within the 'zone of danger', that is, even though there is no direct physical impact, there might well have been. Under this rule, recovery is permitted if the plaintiff is also threatened with physical harm due to the defendant's negligence. For example, two people were crossing a street when a motorist ran a red light. The motorist struck and killed one of the pedestrians but the other jumped out of harm's way. The pedestrian who survived filed a lawsuit for emotional injury, alleging that she or he was in the zone of danger. While the expert may not play a direct role in the zone of danger determination, she or he could give valuable testimony regarding the person's *perception* that she or he was in the zone of danger. Testimony might be given regarding how situations of extreme stress might alter a person's perception of the potential for harm or injury.

The third rule is called the *'bystander proximity'* rule. Here, recovery for emotional damages is permitted, even if the plaintiff is not in the zone of danger, if the plaintiff was (1) physically near the scene of the accident, (2) actually observing the accident, and was (3) closely related to the victim. For example, let us take the example noted above, in which the motorist runs a red light, strikes one pedestrian, and almost hits another. Let us assume that the mother of the person who was struck and killed observed the accident from her home, which was twenty feet from the accident scene. The mother could recover for emotional injuries, even though she herself was neither struck, nor in the zone of danger, because she suffered the trauma of seeing her child killed. A forensic expert could clearly testify as to the impact the witnessing of her own child being killed could have on an individual.

A new approach to this rule has recently provided additional areas for psychological input. Several courts have now extended the concept of 'closely related to the victim' to people who have strong emotional ties to the victim, even though they may not be family members. This is similar to the concept of 'transferred intent' when a person is unintentionally harmed when the intent was to assault another person. A forensic expert could help reconstruct whether the nature of the relationship between the individuals had been close enough to fall under this part of the statute.

The fourth rule is referred to as the *'full recovery'* rule. This allows recovery for the infliction of serious emotional distress brought about by certain highly stressful circumstances. These are the cases in which the stress is so intense that it would cause serious emotional disturbance in anyone, even theoretically, an individual who has NO pre-existing mental or emotional problems. Examples of this would be domestic violence, sexual assault, being a witness to a brutal crime, etc. A mental health professional's role here might have three aspects. First, the expert could describe what the complainant's current mental and emotional state is. Secondly, she or he could explain what the impact of the mental distress brought about by this particular set of circumstances might be on a 'normally constituted reasonable person.'

Thirdly, if the individual had some mental or emotional difficulties that pre-existed the trauma, the expert could render an opinion on how the trauma affected an individual who may have already been fragile. This, in and of itself, could become a challenging legal issue because the defense would assert that the plaintiff already had mental and emotional problems and the distress she or he is now experiencing could not be attributed to the circumstances in question. The plaintiff would assert that the trauma exacerbated the pre-existing problems, caused deterioration, or caused regression from a previous level of coping ability. The skillful forensic expert would, through careful history taking and review of previous records, determine what the pre-existing mental or emotional state had been, and render an opinion on how the stressful event affected that pre-existing state.

THE NATURE OF TORT ACTIONS

The law recognizes three kinds of tort actions: intentional, reckless, and negligent. Most lawsuits file for all three counts. In some jurisdictions, these types of torts are broken down even further such as actually permitting a separate claim for infliction of emotional distress.

INTENTIONAL TORT

An intentional tort is one that is knowingly and purposefully done. An intentional tort occurs when the defendant deliberately commits an act that then causes harm or where the harm should have been reasonably foreseeable. This means the defendant must have a certain state of mind needed to commit the intentional action. It is not necessary to prove that the defendant intended to harm the plaintiff; the intent is to behave in a particular manner. The current litigation brought against tobacco companies are pled as intentional torts because the plaintiffs believed the defendants deliberately used a formula with dangerous substances in their preparation of cigarettes and other tobacco. They claimed that the defendants knew that the health risks were recognizably foreseeable and deliberately covered up this scientific knowledge to continue their profits.

Often, the legal issue in the latter prong is what the defendant knew or should have known. In other words, if the defendant knew or should have known that her or his actions would cause harm to the plaintiff, but the defendant performed the actions anyway, the law would consider this an intentional tort. The most frequent intentional tort action against mental health professionals is sexual misconduct with a client. The defendant, who engages in a sexual relationship with a client, knows (or should know) that these actions will harm the client. There is abundant professional literature addressing the harm that can occur and the behavior is forbidden by codes of ethics. The most common intentional torts are assault, battery, and false imprisonment.

When a plaintiff is claiming intentional infliction of emotional distress, she or he must also demonstrate that the breach of the duty by the defendant was 'extreme and outrageous' using a preponderance of evidence as the legal standard. These terms refer to whether the behavior in question violated the general sense of decency within the community. Certainly, having a sexual relationship with a therapy client meets this prong of the test for the prevailing community standard. A person seeks help from a therapist for personal problems, the therapy relationship is predicated on trust, there is a power differential between the therapist and the client in favor of the therapist who misuses his (or her though this is rare) power and manipulates the client into a sexual relationship which clearly violates standards of community decency. In these cases whether or not the client consents is irrelevant; the power difference makes consent a moot issue. Finally, the plaintiff must demonstrate that, as a result of the breach of duty, she or he suffered from extreme emotional distress. The distress has to be of such intensity that it would cause damage to the 'reasonable or normally constituted individual'.

There are several areas that could be considered intentional torts. These include assault or stalking cases (intentional causing fear or offensive contact), sex crimes, or battery cases (actual infliction of harmful or offensive bodily contact), stalking, false imprisonment, and infliction of mental distress. Intentional or negligent torts (described below) may also include wrongful death in murder or manslaughter cases, often when family members do not want the person who caused their loved one's death to inherit or enrich themselves from the family member's death. In cases where a battered woman's family believes that her husband killed her, but the prosecutor did not believe there was sufficient evidence to obtain a conviction, they can file a wrongful death case as a civil tort or even in probate court to prevent the batterer from inheriting the battered woman's share of property. It is important to remember that the standard of proof in a criminal case is 'beyond a reasonable doubt' while the civil standard is usually 'a preponderance of evidence' or more likely than not that what was claimed actually happened.

The famous civil case against O.J. Simpson filed by Ron Goldman's father and sister and Nicole Brown's parents on behalf of her children is a good example of going to another court and filing for civil damages. The plaintiffs claimed that O.J. intentionally placed Nicole in danger, not that he killed her. This was consistent with California law at the time. California has certain protections in the tort law that limits the amount of damages so that someone does not become a 'pauper'. Obviously the state has an interest in making sure it doesn't have to support an individual because someone else got all his or her property. Like many wealthy men, O.J. had most of his property and his retirement pension from the N.F.L. protected. His defense was not as vigorous as was his criminal defense where his liberty was at issue. The civil jury, picked from a different jurisdiction (Santa Monica) than the criminal jury (downtown Los Angeles) was less inclined to believe that O.J. didn't cause Nicole or Ron Goldman to be in harm's way. In this case the plaintiff's burden of proof was different, too as it was 'more likely than not' or 51% likely.

In claims of intentional infliction of emotional distress, the expert again may play several roles. As noted before, assessment of the emotional state of the plaintiff is usually required in order for the tort to go forward. Testimony regarding the standard of care is another area. Here the expert is asked to identify the nexus of harm; that the standard of care was breached and the harm was caused by that breach. A final area arises if the defendant is claiming some degree of impairment her or himself. The expert may be asked to render an opinion whether the defendant suffered from emotional problems or cognitive limitations, such that she or he did not have the capacity to foresee the harm that her or his behavior could cause.

Defenses to intentional torts include self defense, defense of others, defense of property, consent, necessity, and authority of law. Many of these defenses can be used against reckless and negligent claims, also. Let's look at them more closely. Self defense, as we saw in Chapter 6 on syndrome testimony, includes the reasonable perception of imminent danger. But, as we have seen in this chapter, we have to prove some other elements in addition to determining if an act is in self defense in the civil arena. Most states require that the force with which a person defends him or herself must be in proportion to the actual danger. If it is exaggerated in any way, then it may be considered 'imperfect' self defense. If there is a fight where both parties live or work, and have a legal right to be there, then if there is no duty to retreat in the law in that jurisdiction, that could also be a part of self defense.

Closely allied to self defense is the defense of others. This usually occurs where a child or someone else is in danger and someone gets hurt while trying to protect or defend the other person. In some of the western states, a defense of property may be another reason why someone took an aggressive action against someone who that person reasonably believed was going to damage the property. The old western movies used to portray these kinds of gunfights. Clint Eastwood popularized it when he dared someone to 'make my day' so he could fight back in the movies. In some states, such as Colorado, the so-called 'make my day' law actually prevents the prosecution of a criminal case but it still can be used as a defense to a tort claim. A necessity defense may be used when a person knows that they have to take some action that might inflict harm on another person, but it is the lesser of two evils. So, a person who pushes someone out of the way who then breaks his or her leg could not be sued for an intentional tort if he or she was protected from being hit and possibly killed by a large object that was falling from a window. Finally, a police officer might use the authority given by the law as a defense to shooting a robbery subject.

RECKLESS TORT

A 'reckless tort' refers to the conscious disregard of a known risk. In order for such a claim to prevail, the plaintiff would first have to establish that the risk was known at a particular point in time. For example, if a certain drug is being prescribed which is *later* found to be harmful, then a physician prescribing that drug at some time in the past cannot be said to have acted recklessly since the harmful side effects were not known at the time the treatment was being rendered. Tardive dyskinesia is an incurable disabling neurological movement disorder leaving a person without the control of his or her muscles. It is linked to the long term use of antipsychotic medicine, mostly Haldol and Thorazine. It was not a known side effect of these drugs at the time original dosages were prescribed. In the early 1970's, there were several class action lawsuits filed against state hospitals that were dismissed on the grounds that the risk of tardive dyskinesia was not known at the time it was originally prescribed. However, lawsuits filed against the hospitals in the 1980's when the risk of tardive dyskinesia was already known were successful.

The second element that the plaintiff would have to establish is that the defendant ignored or failed to pay attention to that risk. Defendants often use the evidence of signed informed consent to establish that she or he considered the risks and discussed them with the plaintiff. In some cases, this suffices to dismiss a claim of recklessness in the absence of evidence that the plaintiff was coerced or mentally incompetent at the time of signing. However, in some cases where the risk is both unnecessary and great, even a signed consent form might not protect the defendant. To avoid medical malpractice cases, for example, doctors should get patients to sign informed consent forms after explaining both risks and benefits of a particular procedure. However, if the defendant used a medication known to have more side effects than another drug that was available, and the patient was seriously harmed, a signed consent form would probably not be relevant. Doctors, like other service professionals, have a fiduciary responsibility to the person who pays for their services and they are responsible for making competent medical decisions, not the patient. In such cases, the role of the mental health professional would be to assess the extent of damages, render an opinion on whether or not the condition was caused by the behavior of the defendant, and whether or not the plaintiff was competent to render informed consent to the treatment.

NEGLIGENT TORT

The third kind of tort is referred to as negligence. Negligence does not require the level of evidence necessary for a claim of an intentional tort (deliberate wrongdoing) or reckless tort (conscious disregard of a known risk). Rather, to show negligence it is necessary to demonstrate that harm or injury came to the plaintiff (who had a special relationship with the defendant or is in a protected class) as a result of a deviation from the standard of care. Either the defendant failed to do something that she or he should have done, or did something that she or he should not have done. It is negligent if the defendant should have seen the causal connection between his or her act and the subsequent injury. This is called foreseeability. Professional liability insurance (malpractice insurance) primarily covers these kinds of issues, excluding for the most part, intentional and reckless torts. Negligence does not rely on the defendant's intent, but rather on the defendant's behavior.

For example, in a malpractice action against a mental health professional, the plaintiff (usually the patient or former patient) will assert that the clinician, by virtue of the professional relationship, had a duty to exercise the skill and care of the average or relatively prudent practitioner (sometimes called the standard of care). The plaintiff will further assert that the clinician in some way breached that duty by doing something he or she should not have done, or not doing something he or she should have done, and that it was that breach of duty (deviation from the standard of care) that was responsible for the harm or injury experienced by the plaintiff. In many negligence cases a separate count might also be claimed for infliction of emotional distress. No physical injury is needed for this claim but the act that allegedly caused the emotional distress has to be 'extreme outrageous conduct'. In claims that are filed by men who were sexually abused by priests, one of the claims is usually intentional or negligent infliction of emotional distress as it is difficult to argue that sexually abusing an alter boy is not extreme outrageous conduct.

In such cases, the expert will play one or both of the following roles. First, as in the other kinds of tort actions, the clinician will be asked to render an opinion regarding the plaintiff's mental or emotional condition and whether or not it was caused by the defendant's alleged wrongdoing. Sometimes the psychologist is hired by the plaintiff and sometimes by the defendant because in tort cases, a defendant is permitted to hire his or her own expert to give an 'independent medical or psychological opinion'. This is permitted to give the defense a chance to rebut the charges with a neutral or fair examiner rather than one who was hand picked by the plaintiff. Sometimes the independent expert is known to work for insurance companies who have insured the practitioner from liability and damages (professional liability insurance) and as such, the expert may not be as independent as the law suggests since he or she might have just as much self-interest in delivering a favorable opinion to assure repeat business. Secondly, unlike the other two areas discussed, clinicians may also be asked to render an opinion on what the standard of care might have been and whether the defendant's actions or lack of action constituted a deviation from that standard of care.

With these basic parameters in mind, let us briefly look at some areas in which expert testimony may be requested.

TYPES OF COMPLAINTS

WRONGFUL DEATH

In what are called wrongful death complaints, the plaintiff is alleging that the actions or inactions of someone let to the death of someone else. Someone who murdered another person could be sued in a civil court because murder is considered an intentional crime. Or, it could be someone who is convicted of manslaughter, as manslaughter also is usually an intentional act. In one case in which LW was involved, an 80-year-old man shot and killed his wife in what some might have termed a 'mercy killing' because of her debilitating illness. The state attorney declined to prosecute the man. However, his wife's children from a previous marriage sued him in probate court in order to prevent him from inheriting his share of their mother's property. The court found that he was guilty of manslaughter and gave the children all of their mother's estate.

The person doesn't have to intend to kill, but has to have an intent to act which results in harm. In malpractice cases, a psychiatrist may be held liable for failing to protect an intended victim of the danger his or her client was planning if there is an obligation to protect third parties. In a famous California case, *Tarasoff v. Regents of the University of the State of California*, mental health professionals were originally found to have a duty to warn intended victims. Several states broadened that duty to warn to a duty to protect. Obviously, it is difficult to protect a third party if a therapist is only treating a client once a week for a 45-minutes therapy session. Even if the client is hospitalized, the doctor is rarely in charge of how long before discharge, which usually is within a very short period of time.

DEFAMATION LAWSUITS

In defamation suits, the plaintiff is asserting that the defendant harmed the reputation of the plaintiff by publicizing through writing (libel) or orally (slander), material about the plaintiff that the defendant knew to be untrue. Defamation and slander lawsuits are very difficult to prove, especially if the person is a public figure as there is a higher standard to meet there.

EMPLOYMENT CASES

Employment litigation covers a wide area of injuries in the workplace that are not covered by workers compensation. Personal injury litigation always requires the attribution of fault, as distinct from workers compensation, which is a no fault system. A company which provides workers compensation insurance to its employees will pay to any worker injured on the job a certain amount. This does not prevent the worker from filing a separate tort action, which, in fact, happens quite frequently.

Some examples of employment litigation are wrongful discharge, discrimination (sexual, age related, or racial) and retaliation against a worker. We discuss civil rights cases later and in chapter 16 on violence in the workplace and Chapter 18 on discrimination law.

Product Liability Cases

If a company promises to produce a product that has a particular function and it malfunctions, harming the user, that user can sue the manufacturer for abrogating their fiduciary responsibilities by failure to produce a safe product. For example, in one case that LW was involved, a manufacturer constructed a crib for a baby that had slats in which a baby could get his or her head caught. In addition, there was a decoration made out of string that could unravel and the child could choke him or herself on it. In fact, in this case the child did manage to both strangle herself with the string after she got her head caught in the slats. She then failed to develop normally probably from anoxia due to the strangling incident. The manufacturer was found liable for making a product that they knew or should have known was dangerous for the age group for which it was intended. LW testified as to the psychological damages while a medical expert testified to the medical and neurological damages. There have been many product liability cases over the years including those that involve health hazards, cars that explode on impact, faulty tires that blow out at normal speeds, and the like.

Third Party Failure to Protect Cases

Similar to product liability cases, third party failure to protect cases often arise when one party promises, or has a fiduciary duty, to protect a class of people and doesn't do so. These cases became popular after singer Connie Francis was raped in a motel that had broken locks on the windows. A rapist climbed in the window and assaulted her. The motel was found liable as they failed to fix the broken locks. Other cases followed where buildings that promised security failed to provide adequate protection. In these cases, it was important to prove that the defendants knew or should have known that there was danger or failed to properly warn potential victims that the security system was broken or fix it in a timely manner. For example, in a recent case, a residential home development advertised that it provided security with gates to the parking lot that could only be opened with a special keycard. Only residents had such keycards. However, a gate to the back entrance had been broken for months and despite reports to management, it was not fixed. Three women were beaten and sexually assaulted by someone who got in through the broken gate. They sued the apartment complex and won a substantial award at trial.

In another case, a child was sexually assaulted by a day care worker. The school system was sued for failure to properly hire or supervise the employee. In another lawsuit against both the school board and the owner of a commercial building where the school board rented space, a woman who was sexually assaulted and beaten successfully sued them for failure to protect because they had prior reports of a suspicious person who tried to harm others and they failed to take precautions or warn students.

OTHER TYPES OF COMPLAINTS

There are a number of other types of personal injury complaints on which forensic psychologists might consult here. Some include automobile accidents and road rage, medical malpractice cases, personal injury complaints against husbands for domestic violence, sexual abuse claims against adults in authority positions, among others. Most of these cases are handled in similar ways; first liability has to be established, and then damages must be assessed together with the proximate cause.

DAMAGES

The issue of damages in a personal injury action is almost always a complex one, because, as noted earlier, the plaintiff will try to establish a significant deterioration in functioning, while the defendant will try to say that the impairment, if any, is no different from some pre-existing condition. The law recognizes the "egg shell theory," that one takes the plaintiff where you find her or him, even if she or he is impaired prior to the accident or injury. The question is how much different or how much worse than the pre-existing level of impairment is this individual currently? The degree of impairment at the present time, "subtracting out" the pre-existing impairment in functioning, is equivalent to the impairment caused by the accident or injury. This makes for a fine theoretical formula, but in actual cases, the distinctions become highly problematic. Let us say, for instance, that a person who has experienced periods of depression throughout her or his life, suffers an accident or injury which also causes depression. How does one "parcel out" what the pre-existing depression is? In theory, it is the difference in the degree of impairment, but often the plaintiff may not even recognize her or his previous condition as one which is diagnosable and believes (honestly, but mistakenly), that *all* of his or her current problems are a function of the accident or injury. If there have been prior mental health evaluations, especially if psychological test scores are available, one can determine, with some degree of objectivity, just how much different the condition is. Ultimately, however, the final test is always how the individual functions now, compared to how she or he functioned before.

TYPES OF DAMAGES

Finally, in looking at personal injury actions, the law recognizes a variety of damages. The least serious of these is called a nominal damage. The damage is "in name only" and is awarded in cases in which there is no real loss or injury, and the trier of fact is awarding a minimal amount to indicate some wrongdoing, even without true injury. These are the cases in which the jury may award the plaintiff one dollar, a symbolic indication.

Compensatory damages are so named because they represent a compensation for some loss suffered by the plaintiff. These are further broken down into general damages (sometimes called the pain and suffering award) and the special damages (sometimes called actual damages, such as lost pay and medical bills). General damages may include loss of consortium (loss of the companionship of a family member) and hedonic damages (loss of the ability to enjoy life). Due to the fact that some general damages were regarded as astronomical, some states voted to artificially "cap" general damages at a particular dollar amount. Special damages may include future damages (inability to work in the future or inability to work at an occupation that is at a level of skill commensurate with the plaintiff's earlier occupation), and consequential damages (future damages that may come about due to the "weakened" state of the plaintiff.

In addition, exemplary or punitive damages may be "added on" to the compensatory damages essentially to punish or make an example of the defendant who has engaged in outrageous conduct. Often, the punitive is seen as a 'treble damage', i.e., is three times the amount of the compensatory damage. In order to obtain punitive damages, a plaintiff would have to demonstrate that the wrongful behavior of the defendant was intentional or willful, wanton, and reckless.

Before leaving the topic of damages, we need to look at an area in which the forensic expert may play an important and helpful role to an attorney: the assessment of contributory negligence, which exists when the plaintiff's own behavior is a proximate cause of her or his own injury. Let us look at a case, as an example, in which a patient of a therapist makes a serious suicide attempt and subsequently files a lawsuit alleging that the therapist's substandard care was the proximate cause of the suicide attempt. The therapist may argue, as a defense, that there was contributory negligence that the patient failed to take the prescribed medication or in some other way failed to follow the prescribed treatment plan. An expert retained by the defense could demonstrate, by reviewing the therapist's treatment plan and progress notes, whether and/or to what extent, the patient failed to follow the treatment plan. Why the matter of contributory negligence is quite important is illustrated by the fact that most states have laws that will 'subtract' from an award the degree of damage that a judge or jury feels that the plaintiff is responsible for. Some states, on the other hand, have an even stricter standard where if contributory negligence is found at all, it totally eliminates the plaintiff from recovering any damages. This is one of the reasons risk management suggests keeping very detailed notes that reflect whether or not the client/patient is in fact following the prescribed treatment plan.

METHODOLOGY

The methodology to be followed in personal injury examinations is detailed earlier in the chapter on clinical assessment. Let us, however, make some additional comments here. We can always assess, quite accurately, what a person's mental and emotional state currently is from our psychological and neuropsychological assessments. We can also compare this performance to group norms that have been established for people of similar ages and educations. Some of the indices on our psychological testing address themselves to whether the impairment we are seeing is more likely a current, as opposed to long-term condition. For instance, on the MMPI-2, several scales refer to the stability of the profile, whether it is likely to be changeable over time. Another scale measures state (as opposed to trait) indicators of anxiety. The Rorschach has indices that allow one to compare current capacity for stress tolerance to long-term characterological coping abilities. The WAIS-III has some subtests which appear stable over time and others which are more susceptible to situational components.

However, even with the results of all these scales in front of us, we must recall the caution not to over generalize from them. We compare the test results to outside, more objective indices of impairment, and contrasts to pre-existing levels of impairment. These data come from interviews with family, friends, coworkers, and employers or employees. The expert must review hospital records, not only the current records relating to the accident or injury, but also prior records of other accidents or injuries to evaluate similarities and differences in the sequelae. Review of employment records pre- and post-accident or injury can reveal whether there is in fact a difference in functioning and, if so, the extent of the difference. Review of school records may reveal whether or not certain cognitive deficits being attributed to an accident or injury were, in fact, there before the accident or injury occurred. In addition, the forensic expert needs to understand the types of emotional conditions that commonly follow injuries, common co-morbid conditions, and what the prognosis for resolution of the condition is; the expert need always qualify these impressions if the normative data concerning the plaintiff is significantly different from the normative population on which the assessment instruments were standardized.

In summary, what we are doing, once again, is integrating multiple sources of data. Any one data source should be looked at as a way of generating hypotheses, to be confirmed or disconfirmed by other data sources.

SUMMARY OF IMPORTANT CONCEPTS

1. **Cause of Action:** what defendant did or failed to do to (or for) the plaintiff?
2. **Summary Judgment:** statement by defendant that there is no legal basis for the plaintiff's claim.
3. **Standard of Care:** level of practice of the average or relatively prudent professional.
4. **Tort:** civil wrong committed by one party against another.
5. **Proximate Cause:** *But for* test to assess for the *nexus*.
6. **Physical Impact Rule:** emotional injury directly linked to physical injury.
7. **Zone of Danger:** emotional injury occurs to someone who was in area where they *could have* been injured, but were not actually physically injured.

8. **Bystander Proximity Rule:** recovery for emotional injury allowed, even if plaintiff not in zone of danger, was close to the zone, observed the accident, and was closely related to the victim.
9. **Full Recovery Rule:** recovery for infliction of severe emotional distress, if a normally constituted reasonable person would be so affected by the trauma.
10. **Intentional Tort:** one that is knowingly and purposefully done.
11. **Reckless Tort:** one that occurs due to the conscious disregard of a known risk.
12. **Negligent Tort:** one that occurs due to deviation from standard of care or carelessness, not taking appropriate precautions.
13. **Nominal Damage:** damage "in name only."
14. **Compensatory Damage:** award based on loss.
15. **Punitive Damage:** additional damage added on as a "punishment."

DISCUSSION QUESTIONS

1. Do you believe recovery for emotional damages should require a causal link to physical damage?
2. How does one actually determine a "zone of danger."
3. How closely related to a victim does a plaintiff have to be to recover under a theory of bystander proximity.
4. How would you define the concept of "a normally constituted reasonable person?"

10

Involuntary Commitment and Other Civil Liberties

Andrew Goldstein pushed a young woman, Kendra Webdale, to her death in a New York City subway station in January 1999. In the two years preceding this attack, Goldstein had been voluntarily hospitalized in psychiatric hospitals 13 times, but had been frequently discharged after 3–4 days. Psychiatric hospital administrators make decisions whether to admit a patient for long term care, if the patient requests it (and can afford it), to refer him or her to another treatment facility, or if the patient does not want to remain in treatment voluntarily, to determine whether the patient meets the criteria for involuntary hospitalization which requires a mentally ill person to be a danger to him or herself or others. Despite the fact that in the two years prior to Kendra's death, Goldstein had assaulted at lease 13 people, including treatment staff at several of the hospitals, he was NOT seen as meeting the criteria for involuntary commitment.

Civil libertarians and patient's rights advocates consistently argue against involuntary civil commitment because of the significant deprivation of liberties involved. Where does one draw the line, balancing individual liberties against protection of society? Did the public hospital system in New York City discharge Goldstein after four days because of concern for his civil rights? Or, did they have a long waiting list and prefer to provide treatment for more compliant, less violent individuals? Did it see Goldstein's violence as a product of his mental illness or rather, as a personality disorder that could not be treated? These questions have no easy answers. Under what circumstances should people be hospitalized against their will if they have not committed a crime? Today it is agreed by most states that anyone who has a mental illness and is dangerous to him or herself or others, including being unable to care for him or herself would fit the definition. But, assessment and implementation of this standard is variable; many factors impacting upon it, not the least of which is the availability of resources. This chapter will look at some of the legal history behind involuntary commitment as well as some issues involved in the assessment of violent behavior.

HISTORY

Mental health professionals these days are aware of the presence of involuntary commitment laws, but most are not aware that prior to the early 1970's, there was no uniform body of case law that dealt with commitment or set forth the constitutional protections against involuntary detention. Prior to the 1970's civil commitment laws were very informal; relatives could bring family members in for hospitalization with few, if any court or judicial determinations regarding procedure. Involuntary psychiatric hospitalization was seen as having a benevolent purpose and for that reason it was felt that no due process protections were necessary. Courts basically adopted a "hands off" attitude. The basis for the commitment was vague and indefinite (such as "need for treatment"); there were no attorneys present to represent the rights of the person being hospitalized, there were frequently no formal hearings, and there was no assessment of the need for treatment, of the efficacy of treatment, or of whether or not the patient desired the treatment. It was merely assumed that since it was not in the patient's 'best interests' to be mentally ill, there was no need for these protections and safeguards.

This informal, hands-off attitude toward the rights of the mentally ill changed in the 1970's. A general sensitivity to the rights of the mentally ill began to emerge, advocacy organizations such as the National Alliance for the Mentally Ill (NAMI) gave voice to families of the mentally ill, and courts began to re-evaluate the hands-off attitude. The media exposed the deplorable conditions in a variety of institutions where treatment wasn't even an option and some courts and civil liberties attorneys looked seriously at the need to protect the mentally ill.

DANGER TO SELF AND OTHERS

A 1972 Wisconsin case entitled *Lessard v. Schmidt* was the first case in which procedural protections in civil commitment proceedings were extensively discussed. These rights included being represented by an attorney, the privilege against self-incrimination, and the need for an evaluation to determine if the person met the criteria for a finding that someone was 'a danger to self or others'. Dangerousness was defined in terms of a recent overt act, or an attempt or threat to do harm to oneself or others. The history of how the law defined dangerousness and how it related to whether or not an individual could be involuntarily held in a mental hospital can be found in Table 10-1.

DEFINING DANGEROUSNESS

At about the same time that *Lessard* was being decided in the civil courts, a case in the criminal courts had a major impact on laws regarding involuntary commitments. *Jackson v. Indiana*, the U.S. Supreme Court case

TABLE 10-1. LEGAL CASES ASSERTING RIGHTS ABOUT INVOLUNTARY COMMITMENT

1. *1974 Lessard v. Schmidt*: Case defines dangerousness as a recent overt act and determines it as the criterion for involuntary commitment.
2. *1974 Donaldson v. O'Connor*: State cannot confine non-dangerous mentally ill individual.
3. *1979 Addington v. Texas*: Case defined clear and convincing evidence as the standard for involuntary commitment.
4. *1993 Heller v. Doe*: Not unconstitutional to have different levels of proof for civil commitment of mentally ill and mentally retarded.
5. *1966 Rouse v. Cameron*: First case spelling out right to treatment of involuntarily committed patient.
6. *1972 Wyatt v. Stickney*: Extension of right to treatment.
7. *1982 Youngberg v. Romeo*: Extended right to treatment to developmentally disabled.
8. *1982 Rennie v. Klein*: Right to refuse treatment case.
9. *1980 Rogers v. Okin*: Right to refuse treatment case.
10. *1990 Washington v. Harper*: Right to refuse treatment case.
11. *1997 Kansas v. Hendricks*: Sex predator case.
12. *2002 Crane v. Kansas*: Sex predator case.

that was also discussed in Chapter 5 under criminal competency, dealt with the issue of whether a defendant who was so severely mentally ill that she or he would never regain competency could be confined indefinitely in a mental hospital. The *Jackson* court ruled that such indefinite confinement was unconstitutional and required due process protections such as the nature and length of the commitment be related in some logical way to the reason for confinement. In other words, the treatment program must be tailored to a diagnosis and treatment plan including a specific purpose and specified period of time, a far cry from the "hands off" approach described above.

In 1975, in *Donaldson v. O'Connor*, the U.S. Supreme Court ruled, in a case involving a patient named Kenneth Donaldson, that people with a mental illness had a 'right to liberty'. The presence of mental illness, in other words, was not enough to hospitalize someone against her or his will. There had to be a finding of dangerousness, and the danger had to be causally related to the mental illness. However, the requirement that dangerousness be premised on a recent overt act, as suggested in *Lessard*, was far from a unanimous view. Some states rejected the 'recent overt act' standard as placing too great a burden on the state. Many mental health professionals feared that this requirement would be too restrictive, and that under such a doctrine, substantial numbers of patients with serious mental disorders would go untreated. A particularly compelling argument against this approach stated that using dangerousness as a criterion for involuntary commitment was 'false and misleading' and not at all progressive. Advocates suggested discarding dangerousness as a criterion for commitment entirely, and suggested using the following:

1. A reliable diagnosis of a severe mental illness.
2. The immediate prognosis involves major distress.
3. Treatment for the illness is available.
4. The illness impairs the person's ability to accept the treatment voluntarily.
5. A reasonable person would not reject the treatment.

While no states actually adopted these suggestions as a viable alternative to 'dangerousness', several of these concepts have become incorporated into state civil commitment law, most notably that the observation that the mental illness can prevent the individual from voluntarily seeking the treatment.

Other recent court decisions also pointed to some of the difficulties involved in using the general concept of dangerousness as a criterion for involuntarily commitment and proposed a variety of other criteria. Some courts made it clear that they had no intention of utilizing 'recent overt acts' as the criterion for dangerousness, but rather that they must consider the nature of the mental illness and the pattern of associated behavior. One is able to use the patient's prior criminal history, as it relates to the mental disorder, in determining the criteria for commitment. That is, if the mental illness which the individual suffers from is, by history, associated with particular kinds of antisocial acting out, then the prior criminal history can indeed be used to justify involuntary commitment. This represents a significant departure from earlier thinking which embraced a rather narrow definition of dangerousness as 'recent overt acts'.

Assessment of Dangerousness

In several cases, patients were denied motions for discharge from hospitals citing that their record of prior criminal activity indicated a high probability of return to a life of violent crime. That is, the likelihood of their injuring others in the future was based on the patient's past criminal activity. This is precisely the argument used in the new sex predator civil commitment laws that have been passed in many states. Mental health professionals are instructed to use actuarial assessment instruments that give a score that supposedly can predict the likelihood of the prisoner committing another violent or sexual act upon release. If the score is too high, then the inmate may be eligible to be involuntarily committed in a forensic hospital for treatment until such time as the individual is no longer deemed dangerous. As there still is no known effective treatment for some disorders involving violence, it seems disingenuous at the least to suggest that there might be some way for these civilly committed people to be released. Why not just keep them in prison with others who are dangerous?

> George Cook was a 38-year-old man who was admitted to the hospital after he threw a lamp at his wife. During the evaluation, George noted that he had previously wounded her with a pump shotgun. He also gleefully told the interviewer that he fully intended to kill her, cut her body into four parts, and put them at the four corners of where they lived. The hospital sought to obtain civil commitment from the court. The civil rights attorney representing George prevailed by arguing that the current assault did not cause serious harm and the previous act was not recent enough to be of concern. Citing from psychological literature the poor ability of mental health professionals in predicting future dangerousness, George's attorney won his freedom.

Two years later, George successfully murdered his wife. Could this homicide have been prevented? Had George been involuntarily committed, could he have received treatment that would have prevented him from killing his wife?

LEAST RESTRICTIVE ALTERNATIVE

Other recent cases have dealt with situations in which a patient's delusional system caused the individual to feel persecuted so a finding of dangerousness was warranted because of the possibility that the patient would act out in misguided self-defense. Once again, the courts have reasoned that a number of factors had to be balanced, including how likely it was that the individual would come in contact with situations that would stimulate the paranoid system. As these arguments progressed, a concept referred to as the 'least restrictive alternative' began to emerge. This concept stated that given the severity of the person's mental illness and his or her potential to harm self or others, there is no less restrictive alternative than involuntary hospitalization that would result in the alleviation of the symptoms and the safety of society. Full time involuntary hospitalization was seen as a last resort. Eighty percent of states have now adopted some variation of this concept.

GRAVELY DISABLED

Another issue discussed frequently in these cases was active vs. passive danger, and the concept of being 'gravely disabled'. Active danger, of course, referred to someone acting violently toward others or toward themselves. Passive danger (grave disability) might refer, for instance, to an individual with a delusional belief that her or his food is poisoned so the person refuses to eat, placing her or him in danger of starving to death. Would this be regarded as a danger to self substantial enough to justify civil commitment? Some states have maintained that the concept of 'gravely disabled' is unconstitutionally vague, while other states maintain it as one of the bases for involuntary commitment. Currently, most states allow an 'emergency hold' for a brief period of time (usually 72 hours), at which time a more formal assessment of potential for violence and need for treatment occurs. This is also used as a period of time to stabilize mentally ill people so they can go back to their previous level of functioning if no other treatment is available. Usually it involves involuntary administration of medication given intraparentally.

LEVEL OF PROOF FOR CIVIL COMMITMENT

Until 1979 the standards—that is, the level of proof required for civil commitment—varied from state to state. Depending on the state, the degree of proof needed could be varied from preponderance of evidence (slightly more certain than not), clear and convincing (around 75% likelihood), or beyond a reasonable doubt (around 99% likelihood). A case which reached the U.S. Supreme Court (*Addington vs. Texas*), addressed this very issue.

The trial judge had initially instructed the jury that the state's burden was to prove each of the required standards for civil commitment by clear and convincing evidence. On appeal, an intermediate appellate court reversed this, stating that the proper standard was 'beyond a reasonable doubt' which as we have seen in earlier chapters is the standard of proof needed in criminal cases. The Texas Supreme Court, however, issued an opinion which required a standard of preponderance of evidence, a lower standard than either of the other two. The matter was then appealed to the U.S. Supreme Court, which, in April of 1979, ruled that the proper standard for civil commitment should be 'clear and convincing evidence'. Obviously, this ruling was basically a middle ground between the two extremes and, in fact, a decision that was in line with the initial court recommendation.

PURPOSE OF CONFINEMENT

A very important collateral issue was raised by the American Psychiatric Association in an amicus curiae brief submitted in *Addington*, which argued that the level of due process protection should be measured by the 'state's purpose in confinement'. That is, since the purpose of confinement for civil commitment should be treatment and not punishment, the American Psychiatric Association argued that there ought to be a less demanding standard than in criminal trials. The U.S. Supreme Court rejected that argument stating that commitment to a mental institution deserves the same due process protection as other types of confinement. The court concluded that commitment for any purpose constituted a significant deprivation of liberty and therefore, it required due process protection. It should be noted that the U.S. Supreme Court sets a basal level that satisfies the constitution; any state can set a higher standard. Do you think a more liberal or a more conservative court might change this standard?

More recently, the U.S. Supreme Court considered a case (*Heller v. Doe*) that challenged the *Addington* opinion. In Kentucky the state did, in fact, set a higher standard than required by *Addington* for the commitment of the mentally ill. Kentucky's involuntary commitment statute required the 'beyond a reasonable doubt' standard for the involuntary commitment of the mentally ill. However, the lower standard of 'clear and convincing evidence' was used to commit those who were mentally retarded. The challenge was to the constitutionality of this division between mental retardation and mental illness in terms of criteria for commitment. The U.S. Supreme Court upheld the constitutionality of the commitment scheme, essentially agreeing with the points made by the State of Kentucky in their defense. They argued first that a lower standard was permissible because mental retardation was easier to diagnose than mental illness, making error less likely. Therefore the confinement of this population required less constitutional protection. Secondly, the argument was that since retardation was permanent and not changeable, predictions of dangerousness could be more accurate for mentally retarded patients. As you might suspect from your other studies, there is no empirical evidence to back up this statement; it is purely a conjecture based on a mistaken understanding of mental retardation. Remarkably, the state did not cite any literature to back up their argument. Finally, the state argued and the court agreed that mentally retarded patients receive less intrusive treatment than do mentally ill patients and therefore do not need the same level of constitutional protections.

OUTPATIENT COMMITMENT

In an attempt to deal with some of the concerns regarding the deprivation of rights in involuntary commitment proceedings, some states have adopted the concept of outpatient commitment. A court can require a patient to attend outpatient treatment. While this sounds benign, in practice, many problems arise. The voluntary nature of the treatment is questionable, because in most circumstances, there are mechanisms for forcible medication, if the patient does not follow the treatment regimen. Further, failure to adhere to the treatment program may, in many cases, result in criminal contempt findings: the mental health center will notify the court of the patient's failure to adhere to the treatment program, the court will find the patient in contempt and commit the patient to an inpatient setting. It is also possible that many communities do not have treatment programs needed by some individuals. Sometimes there is a long waiting list if there are limited resources available. If the person has to travel great distances to obtain special treatment, this can place an undue burden on the person and her or his family. This has created divisiveness between the two different government entities; the court who gives the order and the state mental health agency that is responsible for its implementation. It is not unusual for people to get caught in the middle and not receive the necessary services.

RIGHT TO TREATMENT

Another issue which is taken for granted these days—the right to treatment once a patient is involuntarily committed—was not always present. Significant case law in this area began in the 1960's with a case called *Rouse v. Cameron (1966)*. This case spoke of a statutory right to treatment. If a patient was involuntarily committed to a hospital (deprived of liberty), the state had to provide the means by which the patient could leave that involuntarily state (i.e., provide treatment). Denial of treatment was regarded as a denial of due process, and the purpose of involuntary hospitalization was regarded as treatment, not punishment. The hospital had to be able to demonstrate that it made a bonafide effort at providing treatment, though, interestingly, the court did not make any statements about what the nature of the treatment had to be.

The next major right to treatment case originated in the state of Alabama (*Wyatt v. Stickney, 1972*) and took the reasoning a step beyond the *Rouse* case. The court in this case described the right to treatment for involuntarily committed patients as a constitutional right (though, interestingly enough, the U.S. Supreme Court has never ruled that it is a constitutional right). The *Wyatt* court reiterated that the purpose of involuntary hospitalization was treatment, but went beyond *Rouse* in that it described three fundamental conditions for effective treatment: (1) a humane psychological and physical environment (the court actually discussed how large patients' rooms needed to be), (2) a sufficient number of qualified staff (the court discussed staff/patient ratios) and, (3) individualized treatment plans.

In 1982, a case entitled *Youngberg v. Romeo* extended the right to treatment to the developmentally disabled population. The decision spoke of the fact that these patients were entitled to reasonable care and safety, freedom from bodily restraint, and reasonable training. Previously, there had been various scandals reported in the state institutions for the developmentally disabled and severely mentally retarded that alarmed the nation, especially the television reports by a then young lawyer, Geraldo Rivera, who exposed horrible conditions at *Willowbrook*, an institution in Staten

Island, New York. While this was seen as a generally positive move, some advocates of patients' rights were concerned about repetitive language in *Youngberg* that discussed deference to a 'professional judgment standard' which was very vague. Liability could be found only if there were a substantial departure from professional judgment. One of the justifications for this was the observation that effective training of the severely retarded might not even be possible. Justice Burger, in fact, went so far as to say that the state did not have a duty to provide treatment and reiterated that there was no constitutional right to treatment.

THE RIGHT TO REFUSE TREATMENT

In contrast to the lack of a constitutional basis for the right to treatment, the right to refuse treatment cases cite privacy concerns and the right to be free of unwarranted intrusions into one's body. Two early cases were *Rennie v. Klein (1982)* and *Rogers v. Okin (1980)*. Both cases recognized a constitutional right to refuse treatment, and that that right could be overridden only if there were a substantial deterioration in a patient's condition that made her or him a danger to self or others. The primary difference between the two cases involved the manner of resolution of the issues. *Rennie* followed an informal, within-hospital model. That is, the patient (or patient's advocate) informally met with representatives of the hospital and tried to work out a program. The *Rogers* model is more formal, in which the patient is entitled to a full judicial hearing to address the issues in open court. Subsequent to the *Rogers* decision, several other cases considered, in addition to danger to self or others, the issue of whether the patient was competent to make a treatment decision in her or his own best interests. In other words, if the finding was made that a patient was not competent to make a treatment decision, then their right to refuse treatment could be overridden.

In *Washington v. Harper*, a case we discussed in Chapter 8 also, an inmate in the Department of Corrections contended that his civil rights were being violated because he was forced to take medication against his will and he did not have a full judicial hearing, as was required in *Rogers*. The U.S. Supreme Court's ruling basically affirmed that the informal model that existed within the prison (like in *Rennie*) was sufficient, provided a variety of procedural protections were in place.

In addition to the right to refuse treatment raising many conflicting legal issues, it has also engendered a great deal of debate in the mental health community. Some who oppose the right to refuse treatment argue that exercising this right requires a seriously mentally ill individual who is under additional stress because of involuntary hospitalization to make a major decision in a relatively short period of time. The decision is, of course, a major one, because a refusal of treatment may adversely impact the patient's life for quite some time. Even psychiatrists, who are accustomed to making such decisions routinely, admit to difficulties in accurately identifying patients truly in need of treatment. Therefore, to ask a patient who has never made such a decision before to do so, while struggling with a mental illness, may simply be demanding too much. On the other hand, patient advocacy groups insist that the mentally ill can usually make these decisions and it is the right of an individual to remain mentally ill and without treatment. This is usually because treatment often involves taking medication that could have serious and incurable side effects. However, the newer atypical psychotic medications and new combinations of medications requiring lower doses do have fewer side effects.

Opponents of the right to refuse treatment also feel that most refusals of treatment are not likely to be based on rational or reasonable grounds, though this of course is one of the issues to be decided in each individual case. One of the unfortunate consequences of right to refuse treatment lawsuits is that many patients will be hospitalized without being treated. These are the patients who are severely mentally ill, who are too dangerous to be discharged, and yet who continually refuse treatment.

A short-term benefit of medication, especially antipsychotic medication, is the ability to calm down agitated and potentially violent individuals, consequently giving staff the tools to protect the patient and others. This raises staff morale and makes it easier to provide needed treatment to everyone. When patients are adequately medicated, the staff feel less anxious and more willing to interact closely with the patients; this interaction itself can lead to important therapeutic gains. Additionally, without medication, the length of a patient's illness could be much longer than in a treatment program with adjunctive medication.

Advocates of the right to refuse treatment point out that involuntary treatment is generally much less effective than the same treatment voluntarily received. Patients can sabotage the effects of medication, much as they can resist psychotherapy. The question as always is whether the potential benefits are worth the risks? The concept of the least restrictive alternative, which has been applied in the issue of choice of custodial setting, has been extended to the choice of treatment in recent court decisions. Alternative, less intrusive treatment methods must be tried before more intrusive techniques can be justified.

The question of exactly what is or is not intrusive is, of course, subject to much debate. Generally, psychotherapy is regarded as a less intrusive type of treatment, but one has to consider various forms of behavior modification as potentially intrusive as well. There have been some constitutional challenges, for instance, to aversive therapy. Even if psychotherapy may be a less intrusive form of treatment, how can one perform psychotherapy effectively with a protesting patient? If a patient insists that there is nothing wrong with him or her, no therapeutic alliance can be formed and the treatment is doomed to fail. Many of the court decisions point out that the most effective treatment involves both medication and psychotherapy, and that medication cannot be used as a substitute for therapy. Some mental health professionals believe that medication can be successful only within the framework of a good treatment plan; only in the context of a trust relationship achieved through psychotherapy can medicine be employed in a manner beneficial to the patient. While this is true if patients must regulate their medication themselves, it can have positive effects when administered in a hospital setting. Advocates state, however, that while medication may calm some patients, this fact cannot be used as a rationale to drug all patients. Individualization and individual treatment plans must be central issues.

SEXUALLY VIOLENT PREDATOR LAWS

One of the most controversial areas in the forensic field today is the involuntary commitment of so-called 'sex predators'. A relatively new legal phenomenon today, the sex predator laws actually have an historical background in an earlier set of laws referred to as sexual psychopath laws. These laws had their origin in the 1930's and had been adopted by twenty-six states as an alternative to incarceration. That is, if a given offender were found to fit the statutory definition of a 'sexual psychopath', the offender would be committed to a psychiatric hospital for treatment rather than to a correctional facility for punishment. Sexual psychopath laws were based on the assumption, largely grounded in the psychoanalytic movement, that mental health professionals knew how to effectively treat this condition. However, the laws did allow for indeterminate commitment, that is, treatment until such time as the individual was no longer a sexual psychopath. As these laws were subjected to scrutiny, it was noted that the defendants committed under them had relatively poor treatment success. By the 1970's, most of these laws were abolished as they were too vague and didn't reduce the recidivism rate amongst sex offenders.

Laws mandating treatment of those found to be criminal sex predators made a resurgence in the early 1990's, but these laws required treatment after they completed their prison sentences by civil commitment to a forensic treatment facility. The State of Washington, in 1991, was the first state to pass a sexual predator law and currently approximately twenty states have legislated similar laws, with another five states having them under consideration. The major difference between the current laws and the earlier sexual psychopath laws is that the commitment to the psychiatric facility for treatment occurs *after* the period of incarceration rather than as an alternative to incarceration. That is, the evaluation to determine whether or not someone is a 'sexual predator' does not occur until such time as the inmate is being considered for release from a correctional facility. This is different from the typical civil involuntary commitment statutes as there cannot be a finding of immediate dangerousness due to the fact that the defendants have been incarcerated for a period of time. Therefore, the determination is one of future dangerousness, a prediction that has little research to support any risk factors for sexual re-offending other than the previous criminal act for which the individual was already punished.

In 1994, the State of Kansas passed its sexual predator law modeled largely on Washington's. Leroy Hendricks, who was committed under that sexual predator law, challenged its constitutionality, stating that the law violated several constitutional protections, such as double jeopardy and ex-post-facto punishment. In 1997, in *Kansas v. Hendricks*, the U.S. Supreme Court ruled that the Kansas sexual predator laws (and by implication all other sexual predator laws that were similar) did not, in fact, constitute double jeopardy because the second commitment was for treatment rather than for punishment, even though, in the same opinion, the Court acknowledged that there was a lack of effective treatment for sexually predatory behavior.

LEGAL DEFINITIONS OF A SEX PREDATOR

Most laws define a 'sexual predator' as an individual who suffers from a mental abnormality or personality disorder that predisposed the individual to commit predatory acts of sexual violence. This definition poses some serious difficulties for the psychologist. First, one has to ask the question of what exactly is a mental abnormality? It does not exist in the DSM-IV, nor in any psychiatric or psychological textbook. In short, mental abnormality is a legislative construct which is used to confine those designated as sexual predators. The term, in fact, is so broad that virtually any human psychiatric or psychological condition can fit into it.

The second issue regards the second aspect of the definition, "a personality disorder that predisposes someone to predatory acts of sexual violence." There is, in fact, no such personality disorder listed in the DSM-IV. Predatory acts of sexual violence are not listed as a characteristic of anything that is described as a personality disorder. It appears that the legal definition permits confinement for mental disorders that would not otherwise result in civil commitment, such as personality disorders, substance abuse disorders, and the various paraphilias listed in the DSM, which under these new laws are sufficient to justify involuntary commitment as a sexual predator.

Most recently, the U.S. Supreme Court considered another case from the State of Kansas (*Crane v. Kansas, 2002*). In this case, the court made it clear that it was concerned with the lack of clarity described above in terms of the definition of sexual predator. The court suggested that in order for someone to be classified as a sexual predator, the evaluation would have to draw a causal nexus between the inmate's personality structure and the inability to control sexual acting out. The court suggested that if such a causal nexus could not be drawn, the offender would be handled more appropriately in the criminal justice system rather than in a psychiatric setting.

The third aspect that is still being litigated is the issue originally raised in *Hendricks* that committing someone for involuntary treatment is double jeopardy as it is further punishment. Although, the U.S. Supreme Court in *Hendricks* found that commitment for treatment is not punishment, there are other cases that are pending demonstrating that there is no effective treatment offered in the current facilities. For example, in *Young v. Weston*, a Washington case, Young demonstrated that he is actually incarcerated indefinitely in the forensic sex predator center and not receiving any treatment at all. The U.S. Supreme Court in 2002 sent the case back to Washington State to demonstrate to the court that treatment was actually taking place. As the issue of whether there really is effective treatment for sex predators is still controversial, this issue will continue to be important. Unfortunately, there is a high rate of recidivism among predatory sex offenders, especially those who are pedophiles and commit sex acts with children. This raises the issue of public safety concerns and who should be responsible for protection of society—the criminal justice or the civil mental health system.

ASSESSMENT OF VIOLENT BEHAVIOR

Much of what we have reviewed in this chapter so far has to do with the assessment of future violence. It had long been assumed that mental health professionals had the ability to predict future dangerous or violent behavior and their findings were routinely used in such areas as civil commitment (is this individual a danger to self or others?), parole decisions (what is the likelihood of criminal behavior if this inmate is released from custody?), and even capital sentencing decisions (will this individual pose a threat to society in the foreseeable future?). Clearly, these predictions could have major and serious consequences for an individual's life, all the way from being released from prison, to perhaps being executed.

It was not until research in the late 1970's that mental health professionals began to question these assumptions. A number of researchers, most notably psychologist and attorney John Monahan, challenged the ability of mental health professionals to make such predictions. Monahan demonstrated that mental health professionals were incorrect in these positive predictions of future violence two out of three times. That is, they were accurate in their predictions of future dangerousness only one in three times. This, of course, raised some very troubling questions. For instance, if there are two chances out of three that an individual may in fact *not* be dangerous, but a mental health professional declares that he or she is, then the state may use that rather shaky evidence to justify the imposition of a lifetime of civil commitment or even a death sentence.

Monahan's research launched a series of major initiatives to identify the various risk factors that needed to be considered in these assessments. The focus on risk factors, in fact, represented a major conceptual and methodological shift from earlier work. The early work spoke of 'dangerousness' as if it were a unitary phenomenon, and the judgment call was a dichotomous one: that is, the individual being evaluated either was or was not dangerous. The subsequent work was far more sophisticated, recognizing that we could not approach 'dangerousness' with a single focus, and the potential for violence was a function both of certain risk factors and of the context within which a given individual would find her or himself. Therefore, it was recommended that mental health professionals use rather a statement of relative probabilities, given the confluence of various risk factors, further refined by certain contextual variables.

MacArthur Foundation Study

One of the major research efforts was coordinated by Monahan under the auspices of the MacArthur Foundation. It identified three major deficiencies in the early work on prediction of dangerousness. The MacArthur group recognized that the early work suffered from what they described as impoverished predictor and outcome variables. Essentially, they found predictions of dangerousness were based on impressions derived largely from clinical interviews, most often in a limited time period. It did not take into account demographic, sociological, biological, or contextual factors nor did it include data from unreported violent behavior that didn't come to the attention of the criminal justice system such as most domestic violence incidents. The new research was designed to take all of these other variables into account, and was therefore far more comprehensive in terms of the numbers of variables studied. Therefore, consideration of risk factors, within a probability model that utilized contextual variables made it possible to consider recommendation of intervention or management strategies to reduce or minimize the risk (e.g., drug or alcohol treatment, domestic violence restraining orders, etc.). The previous dichotomous model, i.e., dangerous or not, did not allow for such flexibility.

One of the most controversial areas in risk assessment had to do with the relationship of mental illness and violent behavior. The media have always been quick to relate the two, speaking of a violent mental patient or a 'homicidal lunatic' when a particularly heinous crime has been committed. Early research suggested no relationship between mental illness and violence. In other words, the base rate of violent behavior in hospitalized psychiatric patients was no higher than in the general population. In the population of all psychiatric patients, this was probably true: the large majority of psychiatric patients did not act in a violent manner. However, more sophisticated research during the 1980's led to an understanding that certain groups of psychiatric patients, those with particular patterns of disturbance, did present a higher risk of violent behavior. Monahan described this as a modest but significant relationship.

For example, it was demonstrated that paranoid individuals were at higher risk for violent behavior, because, due to their paranoid ideation, such patients felt a need to take a preemptive strike (get them before they get you). Most notable as a risk factor in those with paranoid ideation was what came to be called 'thought-control override'. This particular type of paranoid thinking was characterized by a patient's feeling that her or his thoughts were being controlled by outside forces and that he or she was powerless against the outside forces. Notably, other common delusional beliefs (e.g., the patient's body looks different, the patient has a fatal disease, people who say they are someone well known to the individual are really imposters) did *not* show any notable correlation with violent behavior. Also, those paranoid individuals who were 'confirmation seekers', in other words, those who would find 'confirmation' for their thought-control override delusional beliefs, in seemingly innocuous phenomena, were seen as being at higher risk for violent behavior. Substance abuse, especially when it was paired with non-compliance with psychiatric treatment (the client was self-medicating with drugs or alcohol) was also found to be a significant risk factor.

Finally, psychopathy was found to be a significant risk factor. While according to the current diagnostic nomenclature (DSM-IV), this would be classified as a subtype of antisocial personality disorder and not a major mental illness, its strong relationship with violent behavior cannot be overlooked. The construct of psychopathy, as conceptualized by Hare in the early 1990's consists of two major factors; one deals with impulsivity, irresponsibility, and antisocial behavior, and the other deals with callousness, lack of empathy, manipulativeness, and egocentricity.

Utilizing this risk assessment approach to assessing risk of future violent behavior essentially means studying individuals, seeing how many risk factors she or he has in common with violent individuals, and then making a probability statement about the likelihood of violence in a given individual, given a particular context. Current research from the MacArthur Foundation has yielded well over thirty risk factors that need to be considered in a risk assessment model. It should be noted that while, overall, certain statements about accuracy of violence predictions are only slightly better than chance, in any given individual, that accuracy may be higher, if for example, some prominent risk factors are present.

This point is important, because it allows for case specific phenomena which may be omitted when one looks purely at actuarial data. The findings from the MacArthur research make it clear that it is important to consider the risk assessment of violence from a multitude of perspectives. Some authors note that the early efforts were hampered by looking at the phenomenon of violence from *just* a psychological, or *just* a sociological perspective, failing to note that we need to study violence from multiple perspectives: psychological, sociological, biological, demographic, and contextual. In the following, we will briefly describe some of the major variables.

Demographic Variables

Demographic variables refer, of course, to static dimensions. Such variables as age, sex, and socioeconomic status would be included here. On a purely statistical basis, violence tends to occur more frequently in younger individuals (ages 15–24), males more often than females, and those in lower socioeconomic groups. Although race was originally thought to be a factor with greater frequency of violence among Blacks than Whites, when the studies were controlled for socioeconomic status, the racial variable washed out. It isn't clear, however, if violence occurs more frequently in people who are poor or if they are more likely to be arrested or otherwise come to the attention of the authorities so they are more likely to be counted.

Under psychological variables, violence is more likely to occur if someone has one of the major diagnoses that we discussed earlier. This includes paranoid disorders, substance abuse, and psychopathy, as well as as affective disorders and schizophrenia. Compliance with treatment is another risk factor, especially among those who tend to self-medicate with drugs and alcohol. Some authors, such as J. Reid Meloy, have studied a range of 'attachment pathologies' such as erotomania. Meloy and others also have studied borderline and narcissistic personality disorders but they are so frequently confused with other disorders, it is difficult to separate the violence from the mental disorder here. Impulsivity and aggression are other dimensions.

The sociological or sociocultural variables include a variety of factors as well. Has violence been taught within the family as an acceptable way of resolving disputes? Does the peer group have values that support or inhibit violent reactions to problems? Is there evidence of economic instability such as a higher rate of violence among those who are unemployed or under the threat of losing a job? What has been the attitude toward or skill in using lethal weapons such as firearms? Meloy observes that many clinicians fail to inquire into an individual's history with weapons. He has developed a structured interview called the Weapons History Assessment Method (WHAM). This interview elicits not only possession of, and skill in, using weapons, but also, the degree of a person's emotional investment in her or his weapons. The available victim pool is also considered—considering the person's history of violence, who are the likely targets of that violence and how large is that pool?

Under the heading of contextual variables, we look at the similarity or dissimilarity of future contexts to the context in which violence had occurred in the past. This becomes one of the most critical variables to assess when using the risk assessment model described above, because we look at whether we can reduce the likelihood of violence by changing the context; placing an individual in an environment less likely to result in violent behavior.

Finally, we need to consider biological variables, specifically those having to do with central nervous system impairment. Many studies have demonstrated increased incidence of violence, especially impulsive or affective (as opposed to predatory), among those who have sustained head injuries. Careful neuropsychological history taking, coupled with neuropsychological testing and possible neurological examination should be performed in those individuals with a documented history of head trauma.

With these broad headings in mind, let us now look at different approaches to the assessment of violence. These usually fall into four categories—actuarial, adjusted actuarial, clinical, and guided clinical. Each category will be discussed briefly with some illustrations of instruments used.

ACTUARIAL APPROACH

The purely actuarial approach to the assessment of violence maintains that static variables, those which can be gleaned from a file or chart review, are superior in their predictive power to clinical variables and that clinical input would, in fact, detract from the accuracy of the actuarial. Perhaps the best known of these is the Violence Risk Appraisal Guide (VRAG). This is an actuarial instrument, developed retrospectively, based on the post release community adjudiment of 618 male offenders referred for pre-trial or pre-sentence assessment following a violent offense. It was used to postdict violent recidivism. The items on the VRAG, differentially weighted were: (1) lived with both biological parents until age 16, (2) elementary school maladjustment, (3) history of alcohol problems, (4) marital status, (5) history of non-violent offenses, (6) previous failures on conditional release, (7) age at index offense, (8) victim injury, (9) victim sex, (10) personality disorder diagnosis, (11) diagnosis of schizophrenia (negative weight), (12) score on PCL-R. Some commentators have observed that, since the last three variables require clinical processes to make the diagnoses, the VRAG is not purely actuarial. Others contend that these variables come from file review and do not require clinical input. In short, the VRAG, like other actuarial instruments, gathers static data and puts that data into a statistical predictive equation. The data or variables are derived empirically. Error rates and validity data are limited to the populations on which the equation was derived, and the recidivism estimates are typically for a specific time period.

Adjusted Actuarial

One of the major objections to this approach emerges from those who point out that it does not consider case specific dynamic data so a person can never change their original score as you can't change static variables. To deal with this objection, some examiners utilize what they call an adjusted actuarial risk assessment: they consider non-equation related variables considered relevant to the particular case. The actuarial formula is sometimes called the anchor of a judgment which can be 'clinically adjusted' after the individual clinician reviews other factors. Of course, clinical adjustment contradicts the basic theory of actuarial assessment which maintained that clinical procedures actually detract from the predictive validity of the assessments. In actual practice, the process is still highly subjective and politicized; those who are perceived as dangerous by the clinician will have their actuarial assessments adjusted upward, but rarely downward. In other words, if the actuarial assessment yields a high enough likelihood of recidivism, then clinical adjustment downward is not used, even if there are case specific factors which would argue for their inclusion. If the actuarial assessment is not high enough, then clinicians tend to use clinical adjustment in order to prevent the individual's release.

Clinical Risk Assessment

Clinical risk assessment is the one traditionally and historically used by mental health professionals. The clinician, based on her or his own style gathers and integrates interview, history, and test data, compares it to relevant literature and diagnostic manuals, and reaches a conclusion, opinion, or clinical impression. While clinical assessment is a flexible approach that takes account of the case specific information that the actuarial approach does not, it suffers from the problems noted above, including the examination approaches are idiosyncratic, limiting reliability and validity, that accurate predictions are less likely than when using actuarial approaches, and that risk rates cannot be specified with any degree of precision.

Guided Clinical

The final approach is called Guided Clinical. In this approach, certain variables that have been demonstrated empirically to be relevant to the assessment of violence are used to "structure" the interview and guide the areas of inquiry utilized by the examiner. The examiner gathers test data, interview information and history, according to the structured format, and renders an opinion on the probability of future violence. Some examples of the Guided Clinical Assessment are the HCR-20 and the Assessment Scale for Potential Violence (ASPV) created by psychologist Jack Annon.

An example of the HCR-20 as a guided clinical assessment is presented in Box 10-1.

Box 10-1   HCR-20 ITEMS

The HCR-20 consists of twenty areas of inquiry, designated as Historical (H), Clinical (C) and Risk (R) variables. Again, it is noted that each of the areas is predetermined by variables empirically derived from the literature and demonstrated to be risk factors. The variables on the HCR-20 are:

Historical Variables
1. Previous Violence
2. Age at Time of First Violence
3. Relationship Instability
4. Employment Problems
5. Substance Abuse
6. Major Mental Illness
7. Psychopathy
8. Early Maladjustment
9. Personality Disorder
10. Prior Supervision Failure

Clinical Variables
1. Negative Attitudes
2. Active Symptoms of Mental Illness
3. Impulsivity
4. Unresponsive to Treatment
5. Lack of Insight

Risk Variables
1. Unfeasible Plans
2. Presence of Destabilizers
3. Absence of Personal Support
4. Noncompliance with Remediation
5. Presence of Stress

Based on the impressions gained, the examiner rates the risk as low, moderate, or high. Each dimension is scored as 0 (absent), 1 (partially or possibly present), or 2 (definitely present). The individual's clinical style does not detract from the accuracy of the assessment, because the relevant variables have been empirically derived.

The construct of psychopathy, which appears in several of these instruments, consists of "a constellation of affective, interpersonal, and behavioral characteristics, including egocentricity; impulsivity; irresponsibility; shallow emotions; lack of empathy, guilt, or remorse; pathological lying; manipulativeness; and the persistent violation of social norms and expectations" (Hare, 1998, p. 188). Psychopathy is assessed most validly and reliably with the PCL-R (Psychopathy, Checklist Revised), an instrument constructed by Hare. It is a 20-item clinical rating scale based upon data gathered from a semi-structured interview and review of records and reports. Items are scored (0) (not present), (1) may be present, (2) definitely present. Those with scores greater than 30 are considered consistent with a diagnosis of psychopathy.

SEXUAL RECIDIVISM ASSESSMENTS

There are some parallel developments in the attempts to assess the potential for sexual offense recidivism, though the research is by no means as extensive as the violence assessment research.

Some of the actuarial instruments are the SORAG (Sex Offender Risk Assessment Guide), the RRASOR (Rapid Risk Assessment of Sex Offender Recidivism), the STATIC 99, and the MNSOST and MNSOST-R (Minnesota Sex Offender Screening Tool and its revised version). These are all based, as noted earlier, on Static variables that can be derived from a chart review, requiring no clinical input. As in the critique of earlier actuarial instruments, clinicians raise the issue of whether purely actuarial assessments should be used when making statements about individuals. An instrument parallel to the HCR-20, is the SVR-20 (Sexual Violence Risk). Like the HCR-20, this is a "guided clinical interview"; the dimensions covered are those demonstrated by the research to be relevant to sex offender recidivism.

SUMMARY

This chapter has focused on the involuntary commitment of individuals who are violent towards themselves and/or others, which is the definition of dangerousness used in most civil commitment laws. The arguments for a high threshold using great precision in assessing dangerousness and risk of future violence were discussed including a focus on the advocacy for the civil rights of the mentally ill by libertarians and the advocacy for treatment for the mentally ill even if it is involuntary at first. In a society

TABLE 10-2. MAJOR ISSUES IN THE ASSESSMENT OF VIOLENCE

1. Shift from predicting danger to risk assessment
2. Deficits in early work:
   a. Impoverished predictor variables
   b. Impoverished criterion variables
   c. Failure to consider intervention effects
3. Importance of context
4. Importance of base rates
5. Mental illness and violent behavior: evolution from no perceived relationship to a relation between certain symptom patterns and violence.
6. Importance of psychopathy as a risk factor
7. Difference of actuarial and case specific data
8. Multidimensional approach to assessment of violence
9. Approaches to assessment
   a. Actuarial
   b. Adjusted Actuarial
   c. Clinical
   d. Guided Clinical

where treatment is available, it is difficult for those who want people to function at their highest capacity to do nothing to help people reach their potential. However, it is important to understand that individuals do have a right to make choices that govern their lives without interference from the government. Research into the prediction of dangerousness and future violence by mental health professionals has been discussed and examples of new methodologies presented. The use of actuarials to predict risk factors associated with physical and sexual violence is described with a warning about the need to use caution when interpreting even the newest assessment instruments. Table 10-2 attempts to summarize the major points in this chapter.

DISCUSSION QUESTIONS

1. Given the limited state of knowledge in the area, is it ethical to offer assessments of the potential for future violent behavior?
2. How would one evaluate the potential for violent behavior in a psychotic inpatient who is seeking to be released from a hospital?
3. Which approach or approaches do you think are most valuable for the assessment of violence?

IV

Family Law and Fitness to Parent

Perhaps the area of the law that most people are exposed to today is that of family law. The divorce rate in the U.S. indicates that over 50% of first marriages and over 60% of second and further marriages will terminate in divorce. In fact, the average marriage lasts approximately six years according to census statistics, although there are two major patterns with one group of marriages terminating within the first two years and the other group lasting twenty years or more. Other countries are also finding increases in the number of divorces and new family combinations that result. Family membership is being redefined as children must learn to relate to parents and stepparents in a new way, and integrate siblings and stepsiblings, new grandparents, and relatives from extended family combinations.

Mental health professionals are often called upon to work with families in trouble before they settle into dysfunctional patterns that are difficult, if not impossible, to change. Marital and family therapy systems have proliferated without much attention to scientifically testing whether the assumptions upon which they are based actually are true. Many believe that by the time a couple gets to the therapist's office the negativity is so profound that positive change is unlikely to occur. This is especially true with the limitations placed on types and length of treatment by managed health care companies and governmental agencies. So few people around the world have any help other than friends to get through the complexities of life.

Families are considered important to the preservation of the individual, the culture, and the state. Most people want to live in a family, whether in some kind of relationship with their own families-of-origin, or in self-designed relationships or families-of-choice. Most religions have provisions that regulate marriage, procreation, and the rituals in which families engage. Marriage is a legal and economic contract that details its member's obligations and responsibilities. Marriage guarantees at least minimum standards for its members, especially children and those with special needs. This is especially true in cultures where it is impossible to remain unmarried. For example, in some cultures an unmarried woman is still forced into prostitution to support herself and her children or be killed if she disgraces the family in any way.

The civil law becomes involved in regulating marriage and the family because of the state's compelling interest in preserving the status quo as well as the special rights accorded to family members. Family law regulates who can get married and what types of contracts people can enter into when they are married. For example, a psychologist may be asked to evaluate if a person entered a marriage under duress or if he or she signed a prenuptial or antenuptial agreement under duress. If he or she did not have the requisite mental capacity at the time of entering into these and other contractual arrangements, then it is possible the marriage or agreement will be voided. If the family is dissolving, then the psychologist may be asked to perform an evaluation to determine who has access to the children and under what conditions. This might be an entire traditional custody and visitation evaluation or it might just be an examination of one parent's fitness to parent a child. If the family is expanding or reconstituting, the impact on the children might be explored by a mental health professional.

The criminal law becomes involved when family members abuse each other, especially when children, women, and the elderly are abused, usually by men who want more than their share of power in the relationship. Here, testimony in criminal court may provide guidance for the judge to determine if diversion into an intervention program might be appropriate. Psychologists may also be asked to design and implement such treatment programs that were discussed in the prior section. A separate juvenile court provides protection for children through a system where the state takes custody of children or elderly adults who need protection. This child protection system works closely with the criminal justice system in providing penalties for abusers. However, mental health professionals may also be involved in designing and implementing services for children who have been abused including those who are in the foster care system. Psychologists also may assist the courts in training and supervising court appointed guardians and conservators for the protection of those who have special needs.

Finally, we include a chapter on a new and fascinating area of the law, which is called 'reproductive rights'. Once again, psychological data are presented to inform legislators and other policy-makers as well as courts to deal with such issues as a woman's right to choose to have a child, an adolescent's competence to make decisions about whether or not to have an abortion, lesbians' and gay men's abilities to raise a child, and new legal questions about who owns the fertilized gametes when couples using the new reproductive technologies to get pregnant decide to terminate their marriage.

11

Marriage and Divorce

WHAT IS A FAMILY?

Marriage between two people is one of the oldest social institutions in the world. So why do we need to legally regulate marriage? The answer is simple—marriage is a contract, albeit a special one, between two people that covers many aspects of their lives together. Most countries in the world like each state in the U.S. define a marriage as taking place between a man and a woman. But, we know that there are many family arrangements where people live in a marriage-like home without a formal marriage ceremony. This includes same gender couples as well as friendship groups often called 'families-of-choice'. Sometimes the law covers them and sometimes it does not.

When a marriage is over, the legal contract needs to be dissolved. In many states the legal contract is only what has been put on paper and filed with the proper authorities. In other areas, living together, buying property together, or having a child together creates a legal contract and obligations that follow must be legally terminated even if nothing was formally registered anywhere. Unfortunately, the legal issues surrounding marriage and divorce are not quite so simple. Complexity is added by the emotions that are attached to marriage and family values—from religion, social mores, and psychological attachment issues. In this chapter, we will attempt to explore the legal issues impacting on marriage, the family, and its dissolution. However, it is important to keep in mind that it is the emotional complexity that makes the implementation of these legal rules difficult.

The U.S. Constitution guarantees the right of privacy to every citizen, including the right to marry and raise a family. In fact, there are laws that are supposed to maintain order and protect family members both from themselves, as well as from undue influence of the state. The state has a compelling interest in keeping the family together, primarily because it is believed that families are the best institution for protecting its members, particularly children. If nothing goes wrong with the marriage then it is unlikely that any family members will have contact with the courts. The family resolves most legal issues by itself. But, if the couple develops irreconcilable differences and chooses to divorce, then the state has laws that govern that dissolution and continued protection of the children. If there are other domestic disputes, the courts can settle them, also. If relationships within the family need clarification or definition, such as who is related to whom and what, if any, responsibility does that incur, then the courts may get involved. If the members of the family fail to protect each other, then the law may step in to assure minimum life standards.

Take the following cases that illustrate some of the complexities that can occur:

Julie turned 90 and celebrated her birthday with several friends and Laura, the person who took care of her for the past two years. Although she has two grown sons, they do not come to visit her very much as they have their own lives to live. Julie wasn't angry at her boys for failing to come to her birthday party. She understood and besides, it was Laura to whom she turned whenever she needed anything. The two women formed a close bond and Julie decided that she wanted to leave her entire estate to Laura rather than her children. She reasoned that her sons were very successful and didn't need her money while Laura could make good use of her limited savings.

Bill and Christina were married for over ten years. They had tried to have a child of their own but were unable to do so. After several failed attempts, they decided to adopt a child. They sought legal advice to decide what method they should use to obtain a child.

Mitchell is a 12-year-old boy who was picked up by the police for stealing a car. He had bruises on his body when he was placed in the detention center. Upon interview, he admitted his stepfather had beaten him. What should happen to him?

Donald Jones is a 70-year-old man who has built a prosperous business over the years. He wants to slow down and let his sons run the business for him. But, one of his sons wants to sell the business while the other one wants to keep running it. How can this dilemma be solved?

Lisa signed a prenuptial agreement prior to getting married to Luis. Although Luis disclosed that he had over $2 million in assets, the agreement called for him to give her $50,000 if he died or they were divorced. Lisa didn't think it was fair, but Luis assured her that he would give her much more money and the agreement didn't matter anyhow, he told her. He needed her to sign it to please his accountants. He sent her to an attorney who had done work for him previously just to rest her fears. The attorney noticed that Luis didn't list everything on his financial disclosure statement, but when he called Luis to suggest he correct the papers, Luis got angry and hung up the phone. Luis also threatened to call off the wedding if Lisa didn't sign it and reminded her about the 'trouble' she would be in if he was embarrassed by having to call off the wedding. Lisa remembered the violent fight they had the previous week when she asked him to let her parents stay at their house. The wedding was only five days away when she finally signed the papers. Is this a valid agreement?

Jennifer was 15 years old when she and her 18-year-old boyfriend, Andy ran away to another state and got married. They lived together for 13 years and had three children. Andy came home one day and told Jennifer he wanted a divorce. Jennifer's parents had given them money to purchase their first house where they lived while Jennifer worked to put Andy through college. Now he was earning much more money than she could earn as she never even finished high school. Should Jennifer file for a divorce or an annulment?

HOW LAW REGULATES FAMILIES

The law gives people the right to marry and to divorce. It defines a person's status to determine if marriage is possible. People must be over a certain age (usually over the age of 18 without parental permission), single, not a close blood relative (to prevent incest), without certain diseases, and honest in revealing important information such as financial status and assets brought into the marriage. They cannot be two people of the same gender nor can they have a marriage among three or more people even if they live together as family-by-choice. If the specific requirements are not met, then the marriage might not be legal. This can affect laws to inherit and share property as we shall see later in this chapter. Family law also grants members the special privilege to raise their own biological, adopted, and foster children. Family law can maintain order in families, by policing them, protecting them, and defining various familial and legal relationships. Although there is a belief, particularly in the U.S., that families have a privacy right to close their doors to outside scrutiny, domestic disputes often get settled in courts of law, sometimes airing 'dirty laundry' to everyone.

The changing role of the family in people's lives may be seen through the evolving family laws in different cultures. In those cultures where the family system is a strong and fundamental part of life, there may be more permissiveness in family litigation, especially in the ease in which a family can be dissolved by divorce because it will not threaten the family as an institution. However, there are other areas of family life besides divorce that are also impacted by family law.

In the U.S. today, family members can sue each other for breaches of these implied or specified contracts especially since the interspousal immunity tort has been removed in most jurisdictions, permitting husbands and wives to testify against each other. Previously, if one person did not want revealed something they did or told the spouse, then such testimony could be prevented. However, this rule often worked against women more than men by preventing them from testifying about abuse or financial mistreatment. Children can sue parents for divorce, control of a family business, and harm from abuse. Inability to mutually decide access to children during a divorce is perhaps one of the areas where forensic mental health professionals most frequently are asked to give the court their opinion. This area is specifically dealt with in Chapter 12.

The legal basis for the rights that the state maintains in family law doctrine comes from Roman and British Common Law doctrine of **Parens Patriae**, or the state as protector and trustee for those unable to protect themselves. A list of the important case laws that help determine our current family laws can be found in Table 11-1.

Usually the threshold to trigger the doctrine of *Parens Patriae* or to involve the state through civil family court occurs when the family cannot take care of its own business, perhaps because some disruption or unsolvable dispute has occurred. The most common unsolvable disruption in an intact family is when abuse of children, women, or the elderly is alleged. Although families typically have special rights under the law such as the right of privileged communication and privacy, when this threshold is crossed, then the court may appoint lawyers and mental health professionals to become involved, similar to what is done when criminal charges are filed. In fact, since the early 1980's, family abuse may be filed as both criminal and juvenile cases. Juvenile court, as we will see in a later chapter,

TABLE 11-1. CASE LAW ESTABLISHING FAMILY LAWS IN THE U.S.

Reynolds v. U.S. (1978)
 – Declared polygamy illegal.
Meyer v Nebraska (1923)
 – Case established the right of an individual to marry, have a home
 and raise his or her own children.
Pierce v. Society of Sisters (1925)
 – Declared husband and wife 'being of one body'
Popham v. Duncan (1930)
 – Declared marriage is a contract for life and can only be terminated
 by the court after a formal hearing.
Skinner v. Oklahoma (1942)
 – Case affirmed that marriage is between one man and one woman
 and includes the right to procreate so the state can't order
 sterilization
Griswold v. State of Connecticut (1965)
 – Affirmed right of marital couples to be free from government
 interference in a case concerning the right to use contraceptives
 using the 14th Amendment to uphold privacy laws.
Carey v. Population Services International (1972)
 Challenged the right of a family to use contraceptives
Planned Parenthood v. Danforth 1976
 – Established the family's right to engage in family planning

is a rehabilitative court where family unity is the goal. The criminal court deals with punishment and is unconcerned about family reunification even if rehabilitation is provided.

As was mentioned earlier, at one time, family members were not permitted by law to testify against each other. This made it almost impossible for the state to prosecute crimes such as child abuse or woman battering. Nor could women or children file civil lawsuits for damages from such abuse. However, 'the interspousal tort immunity', which is what that rule was called, has been removed in most jurisdictions making it possible for wives or husbands to disclose what went on inside their homes no matter what the other partner desires.

ROLES FOR MENTAL HEALTH PROFESSIONALS

Forensic psychologists and mental health professionals can help courts answer many legal questions that are difficult to answer because of the nature of the family. The cases given earlier demonstrate several situations where an expert opinion may be helpful. In Lisa's case, an expert may render an opinion that the prenuptial agreement was signed under duress. The expert may evaluate a parent's fitness for adoption in Bill's and Christina's case, or determine appropriate interventions in a case of alleged child abuse as in Mitchell's case. Experts may also render opinions about mental competence in cases involving contested wills should Julie's sons decide they instead of Laura should inherit Julie's estate. They can help resolve cases involving disputes about family businesses, as in the case of Donald, sometimes by referring the family for therapy. In addition, expert opinions may be sought in custody and visitation arrangements, designing treatment plans for juveniles, and assessing allegations of domestic violence.

PSYCHOLOGICAL EVALUATOR

To assist the court or finder of fact in these cases, mental health professionals may perform psychological evaluations, administer, score and interpret standardized psychological tests, and prepare oral and written reports. They may also be required to testify under oath in deposition and at trial. Treating therapists may have their records subpoenaed or they may be called into court to provide either factual or opinion testimony. Certain care must be taken not to violate a client's confidentiality when responding to these legal demands. If the family is the client, then, by law, each member retains his or her own privilege of confidentiality. Consultation with the client's attorney or the client may resolve the issue while at other times the therapist must hire an independent attorney to represent the legal duty not to violate the client's privilege or other ethical standards and legal rules. Caution is especially needed for family therapists who see various parties who may later be involved in adversarial litigation against each other. We discuss the ways to respond to legal summons in Chapter 22.

EXPERT WITNESS

Although some forensic psychologists suggest that treating therapists should only be fact witnesses, it is the judge's prerogative to decide if the witness has sufficient expertise to give an opinion. Sometimes an attorney just wants to establish the fact that a client attended therapy sessions on particular dates. That could be considered factual testimony. However, testifying to a mental health diagnosis that is based on clinical or empirical data is an opinion and not a fact, so if that question is to be asked of the therapist, then he or she must be qualified as an expert. The difference between a fact and an expert witness is that the expert can give his or her opinion about what the facts mean whereas a fact witness must stay with what he or she hears or observes.

Forensic Evaluator

Another more common role for the mental health professional in family law is as a forensic evaluator to assist the court or jury in understanding the state of mind or amount of psychological damage in a particular client. Mental health professionals may offer different opinions in the area of criminal responsibility for child abuse, if a marriage is valid or a prenuptial agreement was signed under duress, what custodial arrangement is in the best interests of the child, if a person is fit to parent an adopted child, or whether a particular event that occurred is the proximate cause of the current mental health status of the client. Interesting debates occur among forensic mental health experts about who is their client (the attorney, the court, or the client), what level of psychological knowledge is necessary before testimony should be admitted on a particular topic, or if testimony on the ultimate opinion should be given in these areas. In the end, it is the judge who decides the answers to these issues so it often differs from court to court.

Consultant

Another area that is fertile ground for mental health professionals is to be hired in a family law case as a consultant. If a professional has a particular expertise that can assist the attorney in trial strategy, case conceptualization or even client management, there is need for the consultative services of an expert who may never get to testify. In hotly contested custody cases, reviewing another professional's test data where simple mathematical errors might change the interpretation, critical review of a written report, preparation of deposition questions or those used in direct and cross-examination of other experts, and commentary on sufficiency of the data base upon which an expert opinion relies, are all examples where a consultant might be helpful. Sitting with an attorney at counsel table during a personal injury trial in family court may also provide another opportunity for a non-testifying expert to offer consultation. In many jurisdictions, mental health professionals and lawyers are collaborating on various joint projects so that their ability to communicate with each other becomes enhanced. As in any case, it is critical for an expert to be

up-to-date on the family laws and psychological knowledge in this area
before accepting a referral.

LEVELS OF PROOF IN FAMILY LAW CASES

In criminal cases, we discussed the need for the total evidence presented to reach the usual level of proof which is 'beyond a reasonable
doubt' in the judge or jurors' minds. In family law, which is usually part of
the civil court division (in large cities it may be its own division), the level
of proof is usually 'a preponderance of evidence' which, as we have discussed previously, is equivalent to 51% or the 'more likely than not' test. In
some special cases such as termination of parental rights the level of proof
is higher, at the 'clear and convincing evidence' level, which is around 75%.

Most states settle these disputes using a judge as the trier of the facts,
although a few states, such as Georgia, may have jury trials in family
matters. New Jersey has case law that now bifurcates a family law case
so that the dissolution of marriage issues are tried before a judge, but if
there is a claim of personal injury (called a *Tevis* claim), usually made by a
battered woman for injuries sustained from the batterer, then that can be
tried before a jury. Interestingly, in claims that involve domestic violence,
New Jersey case law (*Giovine v. Giovine*) has determined that the tort action
is a continuing one from the date of the first abuse incident until the last one
claimed. This is a modification of the usual civil law rule that limits how
far back in the past a claim of injury can go, which is usually two to four
years depending on the type of claim. The rule modification also permits
the different incidents to be tried together as a continuing tort, recognizing
that the psychological injuries are cumulative rather than separate for each
battering incident.

TOLLING OF THE STATUTE

In some states, there is case law that permits the tolling of the statute of
limitations on cases in which children can file lawsuits against parents for
personal injury from physical and sexual abuse. Tolling the statute means
that the time limitation, usually two to four year statute of limitations, in
bringing forth a lawsuit is waived, recognizing that in some cases part of
the psychological damage from abuse includes repressing all or some of the
information so it is not in the victim's conscious memory some or all of the

time. In addition to family members, this has become an important issue in many cases being filed against authority figures, such as priests who have allegedly sexually abused children who are now adults. In some states, the tolling of the civil statute begins from the time that the person 'knows' that she or he has been harmed while in other states, lawsuits alleging damages from child abuse must be filed within a certain time after reaching age 18. As might be expected, these cases have been extremely difficult to prove and therapists who have helped clients recover these memories sufficiently so that they become emotionally capable of going forward with a claim, have been under legal scrutiny to be sure that they have not implanted such suggestions in their client's minds.

RECOVERED MEMORIES

Courts have often been confused by the scientific debate among experimental and clinical psychologists about what kind of evidence is sufficient to make a psychological statement about recovered memories. In one noteworthy so-called 'recovered memory case', a California case, *in re Ramona*, that was in the courts through much of the 1990's, psychologists who testified for both sides disagreed with each other about the validity of the memories that were said to be recovered after therapy using sodium amytal, the so-called 'truth serum'. Although a psychiatrist administered the drug during therapy, psychologists were concerned about the allegations that memories of abuse could be planted in the client's memory by a therapist. Most of the cases that ended up in the courts actually involved inadequately trained therapists, usually below the doctoral level of most psychologists. However, the APA was concerned about the scientific integrity of this area of practice and formed a task force to study the issue with both experimental and clinical psychologists represented.

Experimentalists charged that laboratory research demonstrated that children's memories were so malleable that implanted suggestions of events that did not happen could be recalled as real events. Clinicians demonstrated the large numbers of therapy patients who regained memories of early abuse in their therapists' offices, since the early days of Freud and Breuer. The politics of the situation interfered with the scientific evaluation and the experimentalists could not come to a common conclusion with the clinicians. Each side issued a report that was published and subsequent commentaries keep the issue alive. Newer brain research, such as is reported in Chapter 6 on syndrome testimony, indicates that there may well be two different sites for memory; cognitive memory which is what experimental psychologists are studying and emotional memory which is stored in the midbrain structures and is not easily accessed through cognitive processes. Psychotherapy, often called the 'talking cure' may be the best way to translate the emotional memories into storage in the cognitive area of the cerebrum.

Let us now turn to the history of how psychology helped develop laws governing the family.

HISTORICAL CASE LAWS ON MARRIAGE AND INDIVIDUAL RIGHTS

Some of the early U.S. cases give a picture into the use of the law and psychology to resolve family issues.

RIGHT TO MARRY AND PROCREATE LAWS

Reynolds v. U.S. (1898) is an early case that outlawed polygamy in the U.S. and defined marriage as permissible between one man and one woman.

Meyer v. Nebraska (1923) established that it is the right of an individual to marry, have a home and bring up children.

Skinner v. Oklahoma (1942) reaffirmed that marriage is the basic right of one man and one woman and it included the right to procreate without interference from the state. In this case the state wanted to order sterilization of Skinner. The rationale the court used to affirm Skinner's rights, was that marriage and procreation was basic to survival.

DOES MARRIAGE TAKE AWAY OTHER INDIVIDUAL RIGHTS?

Pierce v. Society of Sisters (1925) declared that a husband and wife are of 'one body'. With such a declaration, it becomes easy to understand how interspousal tort immunity laws came about. It also made it possible for there to be abuse of individual rights such as the right to hold property in one's own name—the man's name, the right to obtain credit in one's own name—the man's name, and other areas that gave men civil rights that really belonged to women. The new women's rights movement fought for and won back women's rights to own property and credit in their own names as recently as in the 1970's. Until the return of individual rights under the marital contract, it was not possible for a woman to file a lawsuit against herself or another entity that included the woman as a part of it, for damages under civil statutes.

In 1930, a case called *Popham v. Duncan (1930)* claimed that marriage is a contract for life and could not be signed away except by court order after a formal hearing. This ruling made it imperative for a couple to go to the family court for a divorce decree when they wanted their marriage to terminate. Even those who lived under common-law marriages were required to get a divorce decree. It also gave courts power to review prenuptial and antenuptial agreements, as individuals were not permitted to contract away the courts' right to rule when marriage contracts were to be terminated.

Marriage as a Contract

When people enter into marriage they are entering into a special contract that gives them certain rights without having to demand them. Distribution of property amongst family members is one such area governed by the marriage contract. For example, a will is a document that fulfills the intentions of how to distribute a person's property at the time of the person's death. Usually there are witnesses to the making of a will and each state has specific laws that govern the procedure. Marital partners are automatic heirs to a certain percentage of the partner's assets whether or not there is a will, usually one-third to one-half, if there are surviving children. Another way to distribute property is to create a trust that specifies who gets one's assets. There are various kinds of trusts, some of which can be changed and others that are irrevocable. A spouse may be disinherited under a trust more easily than under a will but a trustee who may not follow the deceased person's wishes must manage the assets in the trust.

Spouses can also make health care surrogate decisions for a partner even if the partner has not officially designated them. This can be very important when a person becomes mentally incapacitated by illness, accident, or age as in the case of Sharon Kowalsky described below. A marital partner can terminate life support systems or demand heroic efforts as it is assumed under the law that the partner knows what the other partner would want done. Obviously this is not always true and self-interests may rule the ultimate decision. However, the state presumes that until or unless the marriage contract is terminated, the marital partner has the best interests of the family at heart.

RESTRICTIONS TO MARRIAGE

To be declared a valid marriage, the parties must have obtained a valid marriage license. In some states, such as Florida, the marriage license must be signed in front of a county court or county clerk's office. In some states, the marriage license is only valid if also signed by someone who is legally designated and approved while in other states, such as Colorado, almost anyone can apply for the right to marry a couple. Although most states require someone to be over the age of 18 to marry, those who are over 16 may marry with the signed consent of parents or guardians unless they have been emancipated. In some states, an underage couple can marry if they are the parents of a child or are expecting one!

On the other hand, family law also restricted who could marry simply for social reasons. Some of these laws are quite outdated, make no sense, and/or no longer represent the social mores. For example, Florida laws prohibited marriage if someone was related by consanguinity (blood) such as a father, mother, aunt, uncle, sister, or brother. Incest was defined as 'sex with a person so nearly related that marriage is prohibited'. However, you can marry your brother or sister if you were adopted and not biologically related. A stepfather can marry his stepdaughter even if she is below the age of 15 to avoid child abuse charges, especially if she is pregnant. But, a lesbian or gay couple still cannot marry in most places in the world.

RACIAL ISSUES

Many states have had laws prohibiting cohabitation and marriage between Black and White persons. For example, in Florida, Blacks who lived together were declared as having established a common law marriage while Whites were required to follow the registration laws. It wasn't until 1969 that the Florida legislature repealed these laws although in 1968, all common law marriages were outlawed. On the other hand, states such as Colorado have extremely liberal common law marriage laws where if a couple co-mingled assets and held themselves out to be married even for only one day, they could be considered legally married. While most U.S. states have repealed laws that prohibited interracial marriages, social ostracism is still very possible. It follows that interracial adoptions are much more controversial than adoptions within the same race and culture.

Lesbians and Gay Males

Lesbians and gay males also have faced and continue to experience discrimination in all areas of family law. Their experiences often invalidated and discounted them as people, especially since they do not have the same legal rights as heterosexuals. Since lesbians and gay males cannot legally marry their domestic partners, they do not have the rights and privileges accorded to married couples. They do not have automatic legal protection if child custody issues arise, cannot legally obtain financial support if their partnership breaks up, and cannot adopt the children they raise. They have little real protection against domestic violence, rarely can obtain health benefits from their partner's workplace, may have difficulties with immigration, may have tax disadvantages, and may not be able to inherit in the same way as would a married partner. In some jurisdictions that have passed domestic partnership laws, some of these rights are returned to these individuals. In the 19 states that still have sodomy laws, same-sex partners are prevented from having legal sex with each other even if they consent as adults.

Gay males and lesbians also face discrimination in housing, public accommodations and employment in all but the 9 states and 200 municipalities in the U.S. where they are granted the same civil rights as other people. An example was Amendment 2 in Colorado in the 1990's, which, if upheld, would have denied equal protection to gays and lesbians. The law was challenged in state court where the judge declared it unconstitutional. However, the conservative Attorney General of the state filed appeals right up to the U.S. Supreme Court. The APA along with many other professional associations filed Amicus Curiae briefs presenting scientific data indicating that homosexuals were not deviant nor mentally ill and deserved their full civil rights. The U.S. Supreme Court case, *Romer v. Evans (1996)*, supported the trial court and eventually overturned the legislation.

The consequences for discrimination can take its toll in ways that may not always be predicted. Take, for example, the case of Sharon Kowalsky and Karen Thompson, two lesbians who had lived together openly as domestic partners prior to Sharon's total incapacitation. Sharon's parents placed her in a nursing home despite Karen's desire to take her to their home and care for her there. Karen fought a ten-year battle until the courts finally gave her sufficient standing to bring Sharon home. Had they been legally married, Karen would not have had to seek legal redress to do what marital partners do naturally.

Despite the social disapproval, somewhere between 6 to 7 $1/2$ million children live with one or more lesbian or gay male parents. Over 25% of the parents were previously married to the child(s) other parent, others may have had the child as a single parent, while others may have had the children together with their domestic partners. If the domestic relationship terminates, the non-biological parents will have no legal recourse to continue to remain a part of the children's lives unless they have found one of the few places that permits adoption by lesbian and gay male partners.

Lesbians or gay males may even lose custody in a divorce if challenged, despite psychological research that demonstrates no adverse effects on children raised by homosexual parents. Even if they obtain visitation rights, they may not be permitted to have their children stay overnight should their domestic partner share the same home. Courts may even take children away from the mothers who have raised them and place them with biological fathers who have not been active in their lives or grandparents with whom they have never lived for fear that exposure to homosexual parents will cause them to become lesbian or gay themselves. However, research (and common sense) demonstrates that this is not true; after all, most lesbians and gays grew up in heterosexual families. Children lose access to the love and affection from a parent, grandparents, and other family members by these unwise and psychologically unsound decisions.

Prenuptial and Antenuptial Agreements

Psychosocial Prenuptial Agreements

Thinking about a prenuptial agreement is a good exercise for a couple to do prior to getting married. Kaslow in her *Handbook on Forensic Family Psychology* discussed two kinds of prenuptial agreements; psychosocial and legal. To make up a written or oral psychosocial agreement, the couple should think and talk to each other about at least five basic areas:

1. expectations such as loyalty, fidelity, children, security, and accountability;
2. emotional and physical needs such as closeness, power, and styles of communication;
3. external issues that might impact on their happiness such as families of origin, former in-laws and partners, and friends;

4. attitudes and values about important things like who keeps the home, savings, spending, contributing money to the relationship; and

5. sexuality.

As these are all important issues to the psychological health of the individuals as well as the couple, it may be wise to have a mental health professional or counselor present as the couple discusses their individual ideas and try to come to compromise. It is unlikely that each person in the relationship will agree on each of the items. However, it is important to learn if the differences can be tolerated or if they will destroy the relationship, either at this time or later on when the disagreement must be resolved. Many religious counselors insist on meeting with a couple prior to their religious marital ceremony and use some or all of these issues as a point of discussion. In some cases, it might be a good idea to write down the resolution of the issue, particularly if coming to compromise took some time and emotional energy.

Legal Prenuptial and Antenuptial Agreements

Now, let's go back to the vignette in the beginning of this chapter about Luis and Lisa and the question about whether the prenuptial agreement that Lisa signed was valid or not. Do you think that they honestly talked about the points mentioned above in the psychosocial prenuptial agreement? Obviously not or Luis would not be putting such an agreement in front of Lisa five days prior to the wedding, threatening to cancel the marriage if she did not sign it. In many states, the threat to cancel the wedding would itself constitute duress or coercion. For example, in Florida, the law states that only prenuptial agreements signed a minimum of 9 days prior to the marriage would be valid, so Luis' agreement wouldn't be valid even if Lisa did sign it.

There are guidelines for prenuptial agreements that were promulgated in the *Premarital Agreements Acts of 1983* by the National Conference of Commissioners on Uniform State Laws. Antenuptial agreements are similar but they are contracts entered into after marriage occurs. Ante and prenuptial agreements usually cover financial issues during the marriage and distribution of property afterwards, whether it terminates by death or divorce. They can also cover ownership and use of property during the marriage and sometimes afterwards, such as permitting a widow or widower to remain living in the marital home after the death of a spouse even if the home is owned by another person. Ante- and prenuptial agreements often cover alimony or past child support payments, but cannot govern future child support. There must be adequate disclosure by both parties as to their assets and the terms must be fair, reasonable and adequate. However, in addition to having the right elements to be held as a valid contract, an ante- or prenuptial agreement must also be signed by a mentally competent person who knowingly signs the contract with adequate comprehension of intent and content and freedom from duress or coercion. It can be declared as unconscionable if these elements are not met and the challenger may be able to prove fraud, duress, undue influence, misrepresentation, and withholding information. This is where the forensic expert may offer an opinion on the state of mind of the signer to offer a court in rendering a judgment should there later be a challenge.

Formal prenuptial agreements are most frequently used by couples who marry when older, often after a previous marriage ends, and one or both have property they wish to keep separate. Since the divorce rate is over 50% in the U.S. and remarriage rate is over 75%, a prenuptial agreement is something that many entering into a marriage should consider. In some cases, an ante- or pre-nuptial agreement is demanded by one party who brings much more property to the marriage than the other or who has an interest in family wealth that family members agree is not supposed to be shared with marital partners. It is an attempt to protect from a distribution of property that is unfair in a 'court of equity', as family court is often called.

Some case law helps to define how the courts have interpreted ante and pre-nuptial agreements that have been challenged. For example, in a 1980 California case, *Pablano v. Pablano*, the court found that it was fraud and duress to make a woman sign a prenuptial agreement by threatening to call off the wedding and send her home in disgrace. In 1979 a D.C. court in *Norris v. Norris* found that a prenuptial agreement was invalid because the man coerced the woman into signing the agreement one hour before the wedding. In a more recent 1995 California case, *Sieg v. Sieg*, the court extended the timeliness challenge to the fact that one witness did not properly sign the document until after the wedding ceremony and declared the agreement invalid.

Lack of proper legal representation for both sides was found to be a reason to invalidate other prenuptial agreements such as in a 1996 Nevada case, *Cook v. Cook*, where the court found that the husband had threatened the wife if she got her own attorney. In addition, he did not adequately disclose the value of his law practice, failed to give her an income, and held her liable for taxes! In a 1997 New York case, *Dobi v. Matisoff* the court held the original agreement invalid because statutory requirements were not met even though the new antenuptial agreement that was drawn up by the wife's attorney did not claim fraud and gave the wife more favorable terms. These cases were also based on language that stressed the fiduciary responsibility of a husband to a wife requiring proper disclosure of assets. It is no accident that so many challenges are brought by wives against agreements they signed when marrying their husbands as more men have property when entering into marriage than do women.

DISSOLUTION OF MARRIAGE

Marriages can be legally terminated in a variety of ways. The most common way is to dissolve the marriage through death, annulment, or divorce, although sometimes a marriage can be voided if it can be proven that it was between two parties who were forbidden to marry by law. The division of property can be affected by how the marriage is dissolved so this sometimes becomes contested. For example, if a marriage is annulled or voided, it is as if legally the marriage never occurred. Thus, any appreciation on property may not be shared equitably by the parties as it would if a divorce occurs. The most common areas in which mental health professionals become involved is when there is a question about the competency of one of the parties to have entered into the marital contract in the first place. This may occur if the person was below the minimum age, if there was duress and coercion, if there was fraud such as failure to disclose some important facts, or if there was presence of a psychological problem that would cause incapacity. A voidable marriage may return the parties to the legal status as if no marriage ever occurred, not only placing property distribution but also access to children in a legal quagmire.

Although divorce laws vary from state to state, and country to country, there are several major principles that seem to follow no matter what legal system is used. Provisions are usually made for property division, spousal support, and parental responsibility for access to and support of children. Property decisions rarely can be changed after the divorce decree is final while child custody and support decisions are more flexible and can be reopened as the 'best interests of the child' changes. As was mentioned earlier, when the law considered the married couple as 'one body' that controlling body was usually the man. This followed from the laws that initially gave inheritance rights to men. Later, the laws changed so women and children could inherit equally or according to parental wishes.

In the 1970's the laws in the U.S. changed so that women could obtain their fair share of property division in cases of divorce. The United Nations Decades for Women initiatives beginning in the mid 1970's helped change divorce rules around the world so that in many countries, unless forbidden by religion, women and men could both obtain divorces and a share of the marital property and access to children. Until then, divorces were difficult to obtain and usually only granted if one party could prove the other party was committing wrongful acts such as 'adultery' or 'physical or mental cruelty'. Property was usually in the husband's name, so it remained his, while wives, who were unlikely to work outside of the home, were granted 'alimony' which usually lasted for the rest of their lives or until they remarried. Under the new laws, property was divided with a 'presumption' of a fifty–fifty split. However, if one person came to the marriage with more assets than the other, and contributed those assets to the marital property, then he or she could remove them from the total, prior to its equal distribution. This was called 'equitable distribution' of property and the courts could decide who deserved what amounts, based on contribution to work both inside and outside the home in a marriage. The default position or legal presumption, then, is an equal split of marital assets although initial contributions, gifts or inheritances to one party are often removed from the total before the distribution is halved.

Division of the pensions of those who worked outside of the home, increase in property values during the marriage and military service benefits are among other contested areas that have been resolved by statute and case law. For example, Congress, under the leadership of former Congresswoman Patricia Schroeder passed laws in the 1980's that a non-employed spouse is entitled to part of the other person's contributions to social security benefits if married over ten years (cf. Civil Service Retirement Spouses Equity Act in 1984). Military wives are entitled to a portion of their husband's pensions after ten years of marriage also (Uniform Services Former Spouses Protection Act in 1990). This was an attempt to equalize benefits for those partners who choose a traditional marriage arrangement where one partner gives up his or her career in order to assist the other partner's career development. In countries where social benefits are not obtained through employer benefits, these inequities are not necessary to address. In a few states, all marital assets are considered 'community property' and are presumed to be distributed to each party equally no matter who contributed what to obtain the property. However, even in these states, case law has modified the original intent to split the assets equally, so today more of an equitable distribution concept applies there, too.

Spousal support is also determined at the time of the dissolution of a marriage. Remember, in the U.S., marriage and the family is the institution that is expected to support its members—financially, as well as emotionally. However, it is rare for anyone to receive unlimited alimony after the introduction of no-fault divorce laws in the 1970's. This places women who have chosen to follow the traditional marriage role at a major disadvantage. These women are stay-at-home wives and moms who supported their spouse's ability to pursue a career by taking care of all the 'stuff' that goes into maintaining a particular lifestyle. Sometimes, these women work at jobs to earn enough money to support a husband while he gets an education and then, once he starts to earn a good income, and it is her turn to be supported by him, he decides to leave her and the children to start his new life. In these cases, courts may award time-limited maintenance to give the woman a chance to get educated or trained to support herself. Is this fair? Those who support women's rights believe that each person must be responsible for supporting him or herself unless there is a reason that he or she cannot do so. However, there are those who suggest that the divorce reform act did not benefit all women in the way it was intended.

Most notable are the women who have slipped below the poverty level after divorce. Statistics indicate that the largest number of women and children on the welfare roles are those who are divorced and trying to raise their children. Even if adequate child support and maintenance are awarded after divorce, large numbers of working parents do not pay their share in a timely manner. Prosecutors offices around the country have been set up with various ways to collect support from them, but one trip to the courthouse on whatever day 'deadbeat dads', as they are often called, come in makes it clear that we have not yet figured out a good way to solve this important societal problem. There are some who suggest that the entire philosophy (that marriage and the family is the best way to support the individuals who live within them), is outdated and needs overhaul. Models of other countries, such as Sweden or the Netherlands, where the state assumes the responsibility of support of those who cannot support themselves, indicate that there are other models to be considered.

UNIFORM FAMILY LAW MODELS

Although the laws dealing with marriage and the family are different from state to state, there has been an attempt to develop common principles that could be used by state legislatures and higher courts to make and enforce the laws more uniformly. The American Law Institute (ALI), which we discussed earlier in Chapter 4 on criminal responsibility, in connection with the insanity laws, has also attempted to put together a document, called the 'Principles of the Law of Family Dissolution'. This document suggests the principles that lawyers believe are important to pay attention to when developing family laws.

Actual model statutes have been suggested by the Uniform Law Commission with the Uniform Interstate Family Support Act, Uniform Child Custody Jurisdiction Act, and Uniform Premarital Agreement Act. These documents are available for state legislators to use when creating their own laws and many simply adopt the entire model statute or take language from it as necessary.

Obviously, given the mobility of the people around the world, it is important to have the laws as uniform as possible from state to state and country to country or people will move simply because of a particular unique provision that fits that person's needs. In some cases, such as those where battered women were afraid for their own and their children's safety, there needed to be protection when a woman fled the state or country with a child for protection. Until Congress passed an exception from the Federal Kidnapping statute, these women were prosecuted under the law. One of the most celebrated cases was that of Elizabeth Morgan, who went to jail for contempt of court because she refused to tell the judge the whereabouts of her daughter, who she believed was being sexually abused by the child's father. A well-educated and quiet spoken doctor, she claimed she would rather sit in jail than place her child back in that dangerous situation. Eventually, she was released by an Act of Congress, but not until she had spent over two years in jail for her defiance of the law. We will discuss protective moms more fully in the next chapter.

Some Federal and International domestic laws that affect marriage and the family are listed in Table 11-2. As is clear, most of these laws attempt to protect family members from lack of support or to protect children from being kidnapped and taken into other countries where one parent might have dual citizenship and out of the legal reach of the United States. The Family and Medical Leave Act passed by Congress in 1993 gives both men and women the right to take time off work to take care of family members

TABLE 11-2. INTERNATIONAL & U.S. MODELS FOR DISSOLUTION OF MARRIAGE LAWS

American Law Institute (ALI) Model Law Project
 – Principles of the Law of Family Dissolution
Uniform Law Commission Draft Statutes
 – Uniform Interstate Family Support Act
 – Uniform Child Custody Jurisdiction Act
 – Uniform Premarital Agreement Act
Actual U.S. Laws
 – Uniform Marriage & Divorce Act of 1979
 – Uniform Child Custody Jurisdiction Act of 1979
 – Civil Services Retirement Spouses Equity Act of 1984
 – Uniform Services Former Spouses Protection Act of 1990
 – Child Support Recovery Act of 1992
 – International Parental Kidnapping Crime Act of 1993
 – Family and Medical Leave Act of 1993
Hague Conference on Private International Laws
 – Hague International Child Abduction Convention of 1980
 – Hague Convention on Protection of Children & Cooperation in Respect
 of Intercountry Adoption of 1993.
 – Hague Convention on the Protection of Minors (revision of 1961 laws)

who are ill or when a new baby is born without the fear of losing their jobs. Again, remember that since all of American social benefits accrue through employment, if someone is terminated because of the need to take a temporary leave of absence to fulfill family responsibilities, then that person would lose all the employee benefits. This law was designed to make it clear that employers, even to their own business' detriment, must adhere to the family values that prevail.

PSYCHOLOGICAL EVALUATION FOR DURESS

As is evident from the discussions in this chapter, one of the major roles of the forensic examiner in family law is to measure the state of mind when an individual enters into the contract of marriage itself or ante- and prenuptial agreements. The standard of proof is usually a preponderance of the evidence or more likely than not that this person was coerced or under duress when he or she implicitly agreed to or signed or the relevant contract. How can a mental health professional measure duress or coercion, especially some time after the fact, which is when we are usually asked to render our opinion? The answer is found in the language of the laws: first assess if there was physical or mental duress, coercion, undue influence, fraud, misrepresentation, and withholding information. Then, measure how that may have impacted upon the person's state of mind at the point in time in question.

A good clinical interview with carefully detailed histories concerning the individual's level of fears then and fearfulness now; presence of physical, sexual, or psychological abuse; fraudulent promises; threats to harm the person or loved ones including children; withholding accurate information about assets; promises to have children with no intention to follow through; and harassment or threats to withdraw love, affection, and the marriage itself are all direct evidence of what the courts have declared to be unconscionable behavior. But, is that enough to constitute psychological duress?

In some cases it would be but in other cases it is difficult to measure based only on the client's descriptions and other supportive evidence is required.

Let's look at domestic violence as a claim to duress.

> In a case that one author (LW) was involved, the woman was about to marry her husband when he suddenly demanded that she sign a prenuptial agreement. Not only did he threaten to call off the wedding after all the guests were invited but he insisted she see the attorney he picked rather than one she might choose. When she protested, he punched her in her head and stomach several times causing bruising. The woman became terrified especially as he had previously told her that he arranged for his last wife to crash her car and die when she didn't obey him. Over the years there were many more incidents of physical abuse, some of which were witnessed by others or the bruises were treated by doctors. Psychological testing demonstrated that this woman's ordinarily good judgment and intelligence was interfered with by strong emotions, especially high arousal and avoidance symptoms that are consistent with Battered Woman Syndrome, a subcategory of Post-Traumatic Stress Disorder. Assessment of the impact from trauma suggests that she is still suffering from the effects of domestic violence. An inference can be made that the psychological data support her claim of duress.

In other cases the presence of domestic violence may be more difficult to prove. For example, if this man did not physically abuse the woman seriously enough to necessitate medical attention, which provided supporting records, it would be more difficult to demonstrate duress. Psychological abuse, particularly unrelenting harassment to do what the man wants, is a typical strategy to force a woman to do something like signing an ante- or prenuptial agreement without benefit of impartial legal counsel. However, it is difficult to demonstrate that the current psychological condition is as a result of the relentless harassment that may have taken place many years earlier. Demonstrating current susceptibility to duress or documenting a pattern of decisions made using bad judgment when under threat or duress in an otherwise competent person sometimes can meet the legal standard of duress. Some psychological threats can also rise to the threshold without demonstrating other domestic violence acts such as threatening to expose pictures to children and friends explicitly demonstrating a woman having sex with a lover during an extramarital affair. Again, like in the use of psychological tests together with a structured clinical interview and any relevant documents like are described in the earlier Chapter 7 on assessment of criminal responsibility, but in this case using documents of any evidence of duress all go to proving the individual's state of mind at an earlier time period that may overturn a contract in family as well as other areas of law.

SUMMARY

In summary, the law can regulate almost every area of family life as the state has a compelling interest in keeping the family together. This is due to the presumption that the family is the best institution to care for its members by providing food, shelter, and financial and emotional support to its members. Obviously, the high numbers of family abuse cases dramatically exposes the fallacy of this legal presumption but nonetheless, the law still prevails when there is no challenge such as filing domestic violence or child abuse charges against an alleged abuser. Still, marriage is a contract and the laws do support the various functions in family life— support, access to property, succession of property and businesses after death, and access to children while alive. Families may keep their business private unless members are unable to solve a problem that triggers the threshold for state interference. Legislated laws and case laws impact on various areas of family law. Legal groups have set forth various models for rules to regulate both the preservation of and dissolution of the marriage and the family. In the next chapters, we will deal separately with abuse of family members and child custody, visitation, and removal to another jurisdiction.

12

Access to, and Protection of, Children

SOLOMON'S CHOICE

Ever since history has been recorded, the issue of who gets access to the baby has captivated the interest of the courts. In King Solomon's day the custody battle was between two women who claimed to be the child's mother. Solomon gave the child to the mother who was most willing to give him up to the other woman in order that he might live. Today, it is more likely to be a battle between divorcing parents who claim ownership of the child. Rarely is a judge as courageous as was King Solomon, preferring instead to split the baby in half. Sometimes the battleground is drawn between the state and the biological parent. The state has the right to enter into a dispute only when it is necessary to protect the child. In most cases, where parents cannot decide custody and arrangements for each to have access to the child by themselves, family court will intervene and require a psychologist or other mental health professionals to assist in making the final decision which almost always is a recommendation that both parents stop fighting and learn to share. Rarely will the state, through its social service agencies as described in the next chapter, act by itself unless the lethal danger to the child is unmistakable. Even in some of the most horrendous abuse cases, the state is hesitant to interfere with parental rights.

As we saw in the last chapter, family law supports the constitutional right of the individual to privacy unless some behavior triggers intervention. Even so, modern technology has made for some interesting legal cases. One example is where birth parents fight with adoptive parents over custody of a child when a surrogate mother wants her birth child returned. Or, another case is when a husband's sperm fertilizes his wife's ovum in a petrie dish and the fertilized gametes are then frozen, awaiting the right time to be implanted, but the couple decides to divorce first. How to decide who legally owns the fertilized embryos is described in Chapter 14 on reproductive rights and health. In the case where a lesbian couple use artificial insemination to have their baby together and then dissolve their relationship, who gets custody or access to their child? Scientists suggest that we are very close to producing a true genetic clone of human DNA. When that occurs, who is the custodial parent of one's own genetic clone? We discuss these types of cases further in the chapter on reproductive rights but some of the principles about parental fitness and access to children described here may have some relevance should such issues arise under these newer circumstances.

CUSTODY AND VISITATION DISPUTES

Child custody and visitation disputes most commonly occur as a result of divorce and are litigated in family court when the parties are unable to resolve the issues on their own. In the U.S. and most countries, that means a judge gets to make or ratify the final decision. Although it is said that more than 90% of decisions about access to children are worked out between the parents themselves, the less than 10% of the custody determinations that must be settled by a family court judge take up an enormous amount of court time and cost the parents outrageous sums of money in fees to lawyers and mental health professionals who conduct evaluations to assist judges in making these difficult decisions. Some surveys, especially those that were done in connection with the states' gender discrimination task forces in the 1990's, suggest that over 85 out of 100 of the less than 10% of custody decisions left to the court involve allegations of abuse, with courts judging in the favor of the allegedly abusive father in around three-quarters of those cases. Yet, the custody evaluation guidelines promulgated by the American Psychological Association, for example, do not even address abuse issues that must be investigated and are silent on the issue of children's harm from exposure to an abusive home.

The advocates for therapeutic family law suggest that interdisciplinary groups of professionals using a rehabilitative model can resolve many of these bitter custody disputes. This rehabilitation model, however, frequently fails to deal with the identification and resolution of violent and abusive behavior threatened or displayed by at least one of the parties. Even mediation, which was embraced by many as a possible solution to the custody quagmire in the courts, cannot be effective when one party refuses to give up power and control over the other and is willing to use the children as a pawn in this battle. It is simply impossible to negotiate fairly with a batterer who is willing to use violence to get his (or her) way.

Let's look at the common issues raised in custody disputes. First, we must determine if the law itself is inadequate to resolve the emotional complexities that occur when access to a child is changed because the divorcing birth parents now live in two different homes and have separate lives? Second, are the modern social conditions so confusing that it is impossible to set up appropriate rules to satisfy each person's needs? Third, how can the mental health professionals and the legal community involved in family law be more sensitive to the changing family structure and the development of newer models to better assess and accommodate children's needs as well as those of their mothers and fathers? Although we treated the family as a unit in the last chapter, here we will look at each person's needs separately to see if they can be fairly resolved in different family structures.

Custody Laws and Legal Presumptions

In the U.S., the *Uniform Child Custody Act of 1979* has been adopted (sometimes in part or modified) by most states as part of the rules to follow when deciding with whom and where a child will reside and what kind of contact, if any, the child will have with the other parent after a dissolution of the parent's marriage. Although the standard to be used in making the decision is *'in the best interests of the child'* in fact, there are no clear guidelines as to how to measure what is truly in the child's best interests and no undisputed scientific data as to what conditions constitute such an ideal environment for all children. Thus, rather than using psychological data when they are available, mental health professionals, attorneys, judges, and parents instead often use common sense wisdom, personal experiences, religious ideology, and folklore when making these complex decisions.

The *Uniform Marriage and Divorce Act* (1979) cites five major criteria that judges shall consider when making a custody decision including 1) the parents' wishes regarding custody; 2) the child's wishes regarding custody; 3) the interaction and interrelationship of the child with the parents, siblings, or others who significantly impact on the child's best interests; 4) the child's adjustment to home, school, and community; and 5) the mental and physical health of all involved. As these criteria are only to be used as guidelines, they are subject to various interpretations and different courts will give each criterion a different weight, which, as we stated earlier, often depends on the court's own beliefs rather than any substantiated knowledge.

It is critical for a forensic examiner to understand the law in a particular jurisdiction so as to provide the data that may meet the legal burdens of proof, if possible. The legislative and case laws are not the only areas that govern the behavior of the forensic examiner in family law cases. There are many details that can be found in the rules of evidence and presumptions of law that are described further below. In some jurisdictions it is necessary for psychologists to put their opinions in writing or give sworn testimony in front of both parties before the court will even pay attention to it. The ethical issues that can be raised when an examiner who is not trained in child development or in the impact from trauma and abuse makes a custody finding are enormous and discussed in a later chapter.

What is a Legal Presumption?

A legal presumption in family law means that the law assumes something to be the best way to meet the legal standard. It places an automatic assumption as the way that is the best and most preferred way. If you don't agree, then the burden of proof is placed on you, as the person who disagrees, to overcome the particular presumption. This is called a rebuttable presumption. Obviously, it is more difficult to prove that something is not the best way than to accept the legal presumption. Often the law itself tells you how to overcome that presumption but not always. Even when the standard is stated, it is often in such a general way as to leave room for a variety of interpretations. There are at least three presumptions in most family laws that a good forensic evaluator must pay attention to when conducting a custody or parental fitness evaluation. They are (1) the presumption that joint or shared parental custody is in the best interests of the child unless rebutted or proven otherwise; (2) the presumption that the parent who is more friendly to the other parent will act in the best interests of the child; and (3) the presumption that exposure to domestic violence or child abuse will have long-term negative consequences for the child and therefore, should rebut the presumption of joint or shared custody.

PRESUMPTION OF JOINT OR SHARED CUSTODY. The presumption of joint or shared custody is the major one that must be dealt with in most disputes that involve access to children. The law assumes, without sufficient scientific evidence as we will later see, that the burden of proof for what is in the child's best interests has been met with a joint custody arrangement. If another custody arrangement is desired, then the person who requests it must prove why it is better than joint custody for the child's best interests. However in some states, such as Florida, the presumption of shared parental responsibility, as joint custody is called in the law, can only be overcome by proving that it is detrimental to the child. Detrimental to the child is a higher standard to prove than something else that is in the best interests of the child.

Interestingly, Florida law presumes that it is in the best interests of the child to live in one house rather than be transferred back and forth to two different homes, called 'rotating custody', which is popular in many other states. But the law also presumes that it is in the child's best interests to have both parents involved in important decision-making such as education, medical care, religious upbringing and values, financial support, and social networks. Therefore, the Florida law provides for designation of a primary and secondary residential parent while specifying joint legal decision-making. Even so, many custody evaluators still recommend splitting the residential custody of the child equally without any data to support why it would be detrimental to the child to have a primary and secondary residence and the courts accept such a recommendation and make it part of their findings usually having the child spend one week in one parent's home and the next week in the other parent's home, without requiring that the burden of proof be met that this is a better arrangement than the child having a primary residence.

In Pennsylvania, for example, there are significant financial consequences for the parent who has less than 50% of residential time with a child. Obviously, if a parent is looking for ways to reduce his or her financial support responsibilities to the other parent, fighting for more custodial time will make a major difference over time. Although it is difficult to argue that the parent with 51% of the custodial responsibilities is really taking on more of a financial burden personally than the parent with 49% of shared parenting time, and as such deserves more money than if custody is split equally at 50/50, in fact the parent with 49% time will have to pay more money to the other parent. It is common for one parent to give in to the other parent's request for time division, without really understanding the financial consequences. The burden becomes even higher if that parent wants to go back to court to change the arrangement originally agreed to. In some states, such as Colorado, you can only go back to reopen a custody or visitation decision after two years from the last review, unless, of course, there is an emergency situation that arises during that time period.

In other states, such as New Jersey, it may be necessary to prove 'irreparable harm' to the child when overcoming this presumption. Again, proving something is bad and harmful before proving that something else is better, is much more difficult. In many courts, even when the parent admits abuse, it may be almost impossible to prove a concept such as shared parental custody is bad and causes irreparable harm to a child when the judge believes that it is good for a child to be shared by the two people who allegedly love him or her. In reality, many are discouraged from even trying to prove what seems impossible, especially if serious harm from physical or sexual abuse or emotional maltreatment cannot be clearly proven. Without financial resources to put together a long and sustained legal battle, these cases cannot be won and millions of children from poor or even middle income homes go unprotected and without their needs being adequately met.

FRIENDLY PARENT PRESUMPTION. Another presumption in the law found in a growing number of states is termed the 'friendly parent' provision. Here it is assumed that the parent who is more friendly to the other parent will be a better custodial or residential parent for the child. However, when custody or visitation is being determined, one parent may still be angry about the impending divorce and unable to work constructively with the other parent. These normal feelings of anger and betrayal often recede over time and may not get in the way of the relationship between the other parent and the child unless that parent is behaving in ways that interfere with the rebuilding of the relationship with the child him or herself. In cases where one parent has misused power and control during the marriage, it is rare that this personality style will change after the divorce and cooperation for the sake of the children cannot be assumed.

This presumption works against a protective parent who has reason to believe the child is at risk for harm when in the responsibility and care of the other parent. It is difficult to understand why a battered woman would be expected to be friendly to the man who has abused and hurt her, especially if the law has not been able to protect her. In many of these cases, the mother is protective of her child, understanding that it is the disorder of power and control that causes the man's abusive behavior. So, if the child disobeys the father, the mother believes that the child will more likely be harmed, especially if she is not there to intervene and calm down the father. Whether or not this actually will happen is difficult to predict, but past behavior is the best measure of future behavior so, it seems reasonable for the mom to believe the risks to her and the child are higher than if the father were a non-abusive person. Despite the strongly held belief that love is enough to protect the child, the friendly parent statute applied to most of the cases that end up in litigation can be expected to actually work against the best interests of the child. Since it is estimated that well over half of the custody disputes that come to the courts for resolution involve allegations of abuse, it seems that the assumptions behind the friendly parent presumption are wrong to use in contested disputes.

JOINT CUSTODY IS INAPPROPRIATE IF ONE PARENT IS ABUSIVE. A third presumption that is important to understand is the assumption that joint or shared parental custody is inappropriate if one parent is abusive towards the other parent or the child. This presumption actually is supported by empirical and clinical data. It is only necessary to prove that abuse has occurred to trigger the provisions for the court to consider it as one factor in making the custody and visitation decisions. This is one reason why it is so important for battered women to obtain domestic violence injunctions where a judge makes a 'finding of fact' that domestic violence or child abuse has occurred. Once that legal fact is in place, it is no longer the responsibility of the family court judge to challenge the other judge's factual findings, but rather, it does require the family court judge to look at custody from a different lens using a different standard.

In most states this presumption has been adopted only as a cautionary rule for the judge—e.g., as in Colorado, the court must consider domestic violence before rendering a decision but it could still decide based on the evidence presented to award custody or unsupervised visitation to the abuser. Obviously, in parenting evaluations, it is important to consider past or current domestic violence and child abuse in making recommendations about the parent's risk for violence and ability to adequately protect and take care of the child. This is a 'rebuttable presumption' in that someone who has been judged to be a domestic abuser may have gone for treatment and if he or she can prove that he or she is no longer a risk for committing abuse, then joint or sole custody may be awarded.

The American Bar Association has introduced a suggested amendment to the Uniform Child Custody Guidelines and similar legislation has been introduced in Congress to make a finding of family or domestic violence an automatic but rebuttable presumption to the various types of joint custody presumptions in the legislature. Several states have already added this language to their access to children laws. The National Council of Juvenile and Family Court Judges passed Model Code #401 on Child Custody, which states:

> In every proceeding where there is a dispute as to the custody of a child, a determination by the court that domestic or family violence has occurred raises a rebuttable presumption that it is detrimental to the child and not in the best interests of the child to be placed in sole custody, joint legal custody, or joint physical custody with the perpetrator of the violence. (1994).

Interestingly, with the introduction of the presumption of no-joint custody if there is domestic violence in many states, there has been a rise in the number of cases using unsubstantiated diagnoses such as Parental Alienation Syndrome and Psychological Munchausen-by-Proxy as a defense. More will be discussed later about how behaviors that alienated children from their allegedly abusive parent can be misinterpreted and misused by mental health clinicians who are not trained in the assessment and treatment of domestic violence disorders. California now requires a minimum of 12 hours of continuing education training in domestic violence disorders (including child abuse) for anyone who is court-appointed to perform a custody evaluation. New York State requires two hours of training in child abuse. Florida requires one hour of training in domestic violence every two years, documented when the professional license is renewed. Many other states require at least some continuing education in both spouse abuse and child abuse for all licensed professionals when they renew their professional licenses.

RULES OF EVIDENCE

As we have seen in earlier chapters, courts have many different rules of evidence that govern what can and cannot be admitted in a case for a judge's consideration. For example, evidence that is obtained illegally may not be admitted even if it is the best evidence to demonstrate abuse.

In a case by one author (LW), a tape recording was made of a domestic violence incident where the father hurt both the mother and the child, who was trying to protect his mother. The tape recorder that was in the mother's handbag was voice-activated by their screams. The father denied knowing the mother had the tape recorder present during the incident. The judge ruled that the father had the right to privacy in his home and that the tape was made illegally without warning to the father. In effect, the court determined that the rules of evidence took precedence over the rights of the child and mother to protect themselves by documenting the father's abusive behavior. Had the mother notified the police and told them that she would record the father's abusive behavior or had it been permitted on a no-contact or no-violence restraining or protective order, the taped evidence might have been admitted. Other judges might have used their discretion to admit such testimony using the protection of the child as the ruling interest. This requires a 'lesser of two evils' type of decision. Tape recording telephone calls are permitted in many states provided the caller is notified that the call may be recorded. If a caller speaks into a recording machine to leave a message that is usually considered evidence that he or she was aware of the recording. I suggest that those in litigation get answer machines on their telephones to document any verbal abuse or threats. Surprisingly, the knowledge of an answer machine does not seem to stop the abuser from making horrible and embarrassing comments.

HISTORY OF THE LAW

Sometimes when we find ourselves in an incomprehensible systems quagmire, as in mandatory joint physical custody and forced visitation with an abusive parent, it is helpful to look back at history and see how we got to this point. Prior to the 19th century, children were seen as property and as we learned in the previous chapter, that meant they belonged to the man as did all property in a marriage. However, the role of raising young children was the responsibility of the woman as it was believed that men did not have the ability to parent them. When the child got older and could be of help to the man in earning a living, especially if the child was a boy, fathers were more likely to be awarded custody. This arrangement was critical for survival; if a child was still nursing, then the mother could feed and support him or her but once the child was seen as a separate person, then it was the responsibility of the father to feed and support the child. If the mother died or disappeared or there was the unlikely possibility of a divorce, then the father kept any child who was not nursing. Older children usually took physical care of the younger ones. This was known as the doctrine of 'Patria Protestas'.

By 1839, in the *British Balfour Act*, this arrangement was codified and children were kept with the mother until age 7 and then sent to the custody of their father to be raised after that time. This became known as the 'tender years doctrine' and remains as law today in many different countries around the world. Unless the mother was found unfit by reason of adultery, alcoholism, or mental illness, it was presumed that she was the best person to raise the young child. Freud's influence on society during the latter half of the 19th and early 20th century reinforced this presumption by stressing that the emotional nurturance needed by children was better provided by mothers.

MORE RECENT PRACTICES

Not until the middle of the 20th century, when the new women's liberation movement gained strength was this presumption challenged by both women and men. Women understood that if they were truly to have choices about what they did in their lives, they would have to be free from or at least share the child-raising responsibilities. As men began taking more responsibility for their own emotional nurturance and became less reliant on women to nurture them, they realized that they missed emotional nurturance from their own fathers and wanted to provide that kind of emotional support to their own children. Unfortunately, in many cases their wishes far exceeded their skills. The scientific data on parenting show that although men in general are perfectly capable of adequately parenting children, if they do not have formal or informal training in actual parenting skills, custody with a father is not automatically 'in the best interests of the child'.

As divorce reform was being legislated, making women legally equal to men in property distribution, the custody standard changed from the tender years doctrine to the best interests of the child. The idea of joint custody became popular and by 1979, without any scientific data to demonstrate the emotional consequences, the Uniform Child Custody models supported a move to the presumption of sharing the child when parents divorce. Interestingly, it was thought that this change would be more likely to keep fathers in their children's lives, including continuation of their financial support, rather than the dismal picture of abandonment that commonly took place after divorce when mothers were awarded custody. This did not happen and the issue of awarding and collecting child support payments is still one that plagues men, women, and children. In fact, some believe that many men use joint custody as a way to reduce any financial obligation they might have to support the child. The data show that while some fathers are more likely to remain in the child's life after divorce since these new laws were passed, these were not the cases that utilized the courts to make custody decisions for them. Rather, the most bitter and seemingly never-ending custody disputes were more likely to occur in what was then called, 'high conflict' families.

High Conflict Cases

Judith Wallerstein, a California psychologist wrote a book based on a small sample of parents with high conflict divorces. From her initial sample, she indicated that it was emotionally better for the child to be shared in a custodial arrangement than to have one parent abandon the child. However, 20 years later, after much more research, Wallerstein and her colleagues no longer uniformly support joint custody. Their work indicates that it depends on the age, developmental and other special needs, and gender of the child, as well as the parenting style of each parent, and the ability of the parents to get along with each other to put the child's needs ahead of their own. Further, children who are exposed to abuse have different needs from their parents and have different needs than those who lived in homes with simple conflict or dysfunction. In cases where the child him or herself also experiences abuse from a parent, it may be necessary for there to be supervised visitation or no contact at all with the abuser for a period of time.

There are numerous possible arrangements so that children can have some kind of access to a parent if it is considered appropriate and these recommendations are specified later in this chapter. Nonetheless, the courts and many mental health professionals automatically equate the 'best interests of the child' with joint or shared parental custody, not even considering the various limitations this may have for the child's future physical and mental health.

CURRENT LAW

Access to a parental fitness, custody evaluation or visitation recommendations including permission by one parent to remove a child from the current home and school and move to another locale are initially made or approved by the court once a divorce is filed. These decisions can be changed as the child's needs change or there are other changes in circumstances. However, there is a higher standard that must be met to change a custody order once it is issued and in some jurisdictions the courts will not entertain a change more than one time in two years unless there is an emergency to provide stability for the child.

These decisions may also be necessary if a child is placed in foster care because of abuse, as is further discussed in the next chapter, or offered for adoption. As mentioned in the beginning of this chapter, mental health professionals also may be asked to perform evaluations when the court has to decide who owns a fetus, a fertilized embryo, or a child born through an artificial insemination donor or surrogate mother. In each of these cases, the standard of the best interests of the child governs so the evaluation must cover similar areas—parental fitness, exploration of the child's needs both developmentally and individually, ability of a fit parent to provide for these needs, and recommendations for access. Specific issues that are raised in foster care and adoption cases are further discussed in the following chapter dealing with issues that arise when the state takes custody of a minor.

PROCEDURES FOR PARENTAL FITNESS AND CUSTODY EVALUATIONS

Here is a suggested outline of the procedure that is summarized in Table 12-1:

1. Prepare yourself for the type of case that you will be evaluating by reviewing the legislated and case laws that govern. Remember that you will have to evaluate one or two parties in a parental fitness or visitation examination—mother or father and perhaps the child, if possible. You will have to evaluate at least three parties in a custody evaluation—mother, father, and child. It is also possible that step-parents, grandparents, and other close family or friends who spend considerable time with the child will be evaluated or at least interviewed. If there is a nanny, then she or he may be evaluated. If an examiner is not qualified or trained to evaluate one or more parties, it may be necessary to bring in a co-examiner such as someone who is trained in child development and interviewing techniques with young children.
2. Before starting any formal evaluation, it is important to provide the clients with informed consent including the evaluator's obligation to report suspected child abuse. Issues about the fees involved and who is responsible for them must also be resolved prior to the evaluation. Many evaluators believe that it is best to get the estimated fees paid prior to beginning an evaluation so that neither party can use money as a way to unduly influence the examiner. Usually all fees are collected before a report is issued although sometimes court timelines make this difficult.

TABLE 12-1. SUMMARY OF CUSTODY & PARENTAL FITNESS EVALUATION STEPS

1. Prepare for the evaluation of the case reviewing the issues before the court
2. Disclose to the parties your requirements and obtain informed consent and a clear understanding of how and when your fees will be paid if you are an independent practitioner.
3. Review documents obtained from the court or the attorneys involved
4. Collect assessment data from questionnaires sent to parents
5. Interview one or both parent's individually to set parameter of evaluation
6. Interview one or more children alone and in sibling combinations
7. Perform a parental interaction examination of each child with each parent or parent-like participant
8. Interview each parent and parent-like participant in depth
9. Interview collaterals for information relevant to parental fitness including school performance, behavioral observations and character references.
10. Administer psychological tests and custody evaluation instruments, if used, to each child and parent individually
11. Review additional materials including abuse reports, medical reports etc
12. Prepare data to be communicated to the parents, attorneys and court.
13. Make recommendations based on data.
14. Prepare to give sworn testimony in court.

3. Review documents and allegations contained in prior evaluations, if possible, including any abuse reports. Often when abuse is alleged there have been other evaluations that have not addressed the abuse issue. While some evaluators do not want to be 'biased' by other's reports, it may be important to know what was and was not done and what issues remain contested so that appropriate assessment methods will be used. In some states, such as California, the law states that an evaluator must review law enforcement and child protective agency investigations as a required part of a custody evaluation. This is a good idea even if it is not required by law.

4. Send assessment questionnaires to the parents (and teachers if the child is in school) and request that they be mailed back if no other information about developmental milestones, history and other pertinent information is available.

5. Interview one or both parents, without the child present, to gather other relevant information including any particular ways the parent has used to make the child comfortable in accepting the parents' separation. If abuse has been reported or suspected, find out how the parent helped the child feel comfortable in reporting

what has allegedly occurred. If the referral comes from one parent's attorney, it is also important to learn what the allegations are from the reporting parent and what evidence has been put forward to substantiate the claims. It is also important to learn if the information-gathering procedure to date introduced bias so that the same procedure can be avoided or other unbiased data can be collected. This interview can be conducted on the telephone but if so, another more formal face-to-face interview will need to be conducted with that parent after the child(ren) have been evaluated to see if and how the parent can best meet child's needs.

6. Interview the child or children first, alone with both a structured and unstructured interview and together if there is more than one child. Note that it is best for the evaluator to be familiar with the literature on suggestibility in order that the interview is conducted in a manner so as to not ask the child leading questions.

In a structured interview you will need to obtain information about the child's developmental performance based on age expectations. It is especially important to obtain the child's knowledge of vocabulary and language to assess whether the abuse report is possibly coached or the child's own report. Can the young child count, does he or she understand sexual parts of the body, does the child know colors, shapes, textures especially if there were allegations of ejaculation? Does the child's report make sense? How does the child view each parent's ability to support him or her? How does the child understand discipline from each parent?

In an unstructured interview, it is important to watch the child's spontaneous play looking for developmental milestones and personality issues. What kind of toys or games does the child like to play? Can the child make decisions easily? What kind of drawings does the child make? Only when rapport is established and the child feels safe and comfortable that the interviewer understands what he or she is interested in and saying will disclosure occur. This takes time and patience and cannot be hurried due to time pressures.

It is possible that several visits will be needed including a home visit. If videotaping is done, this might save the child from additional interviews by others especially if disclosure occurs. If not, it may be used as evidence that the abuse didn't occur which would be a mistake and leave the child unprotected. Thus, videotaping is a controversial procedure that should be used carefully.

7. Perform parental interaction interviews to collect behavioral observation data with the child and both parents individually, each for about one hour. If more than one child is involved, do each separately and then all together to assess if a parent can manage different developmental ages together. If one parent is insisting on joint or shared custody and there are no abuse allegations, it may be appropriate to have both parents together with one or more children, although this can get too chaotic if there are too many people involved to make adequate judgments. However, the chaos might also tell you that joint custody is not a good solution for one or more of the children involved either.

   The parental interaction part may be one of the most important parts of the evaluation as it operationalizes what each parent has said about the child during the interviews. Often parents know the right things to say but really haven't spent enough time with a child to know how to apply the principles. In addition to the formal interaction interview described below, it may be helpful to try to observe the different family structures in a more naturalistic setting such as having lunch together. This gives a good idea of the additional interactions that can occur with cranky or hungry children and parents or simply how mealtimes can be managed.

   For the parental interaction examination, ask each parent to bring toys or games that they can use to interact with the child for approximately 30 minutes. It is often a sign of the parent's expectations of the child just to see what they choose to bring. If it is something that they have not played with before you can observe how the parent teaches the child to do something new. It is also helpful to ask the parent to bring something that he or she knows the child likes to do together, again to demonstrate the parent's knowledge of the child's interests and skills. Finally, it is helpful to ask the parent to do something with the child that involves something new that the evaluator brings. Here it is possible to evaluate for creativity, spontaneity, flexibility, and commonality of interests while observing them interacting together. If you are looking for evidence that a parent is trainable in parenting classes or making a decision about recommending therapeutic, supervised, or monitored visitation, it may also be helpful to join in the interaction and assess the parent's and child's reactions to a third party.

8. Interview each parent next, without the child present, unless sufficient information has been obtained to understand how the parent

can meet the child's needs based on the additional information collected from your interviews with the child and parental interaction observations. This is not a difficult part of the evaluation if both parents have the ability to be an adequate or even great parent for this child, despite their different styles. Even if you can't judge who would be the better parent for a particular child, you can assume no harm will be done as both parents will care for and nurture the child. Look for positive parenting behaviors such as empathy and awareness of the child, predictability, non-intrusiveness, emotional availability, ability to trust and be intimate, and ability to adapt to new situations and multiple demands. Also look for negative parenting behaviors such as self-centeredness and self-focus (other than around protective behaviors), depression, anti-social behavior and attitudes, inconsistency with behavior towards siblings or new stepchildren, domestic violence and child abuse, and other mental illness.

If there are abuse allegations, interview the alleged abuser by beginning with gentle questioning about the allegations after some rapport is established. You must obtain informed consent and be clear in disclosing that you will have to make a formal child abuse report if this hasn't already been done and you have some reason to suspect that the child has been abused. Obviously, this procedure makes it difficult for someone to be honest because of the possible repercussions. However, if you have admissions from the child, you will have to make a child abuse report anyhow, and it is usually appropriate to share the fact that the child is saying that the parent did whatever is alleged. Be careful not to disclose the child's language or facts that would compromise the child's safety. If the interview is videotaped, it may be used as evidence in other legal proceedings.

9. Interview collateral witnesses to each parent's parenting ability. These usually include anyone significant in the child's life such as a new spouse or live-in partner, grandparents, friends with and without same-age children, religious advisors, teachers, doctors, therapists, and babysitters or nanny's. The goal is to understand that person's knowledge and interaction with the child, any observations of parenting abilities of each parent, any evidence of abusive behavior, or other concerns. These interviews are frequently done via telephone unless the person will have direct caretaking responsibilities for the child and then an interaction visit might be appropriate.

10. Psychological testing of both parents and the child will often provide additional data to support a custody or visitation recommendation. This area is quite controversial as it is common for psychologists to assess for clinical disorders without relating how they might prevent a parent from acting in the best interests of the child. It is critical to base the findings and recommendations on a variety of data sources, so it is important to assess for mental stability and parenting ability using objective measures as well as interview data, clinical impressions, and observations of others. Most of the newer tests that purport to assess for information specific to custody evaluations do not have carefully standardized procedures that permit basing a custody determination on them. However, they may be useful as a part of a total evaluation provided other data sources are used and comparisons for consistency or inconsistency are made and explained. Some of the psychological tests that can be used are listed in Table 12-2.

11. Review additional documents including court papers to determine if your data can answer the court's questions and make appropriate recommendations based on the data obtained. If abuse allegations are made, then any witness statements, police reports, doctor's or hospital notes, court transcripts such as testimony for an order of protection and the judge's findings, and other evidence of abuse should be reviewed.

12. Communicate your findings to the attorneys, parents, and court in a timely manner in oral and written reports as required. Issues that arise during these evaluations often cause the psychologist to be concerned about the safety and mental health of one or more parties. It is important to know the mandatory abuse reporting law in your state to make sure that you do not violate any legal obligations you might have to protect children, the elderly, or adults in those states where reporting is required. Even if you believe the allegations do not rise to the level of a mandated report, put the findings in your report. Remember, if you find that more likely than not there has been domestic violence, the judge will have to take it into account when making final decisions. Document all phone conversations with interested parties especially attorneys. Most states have specific requirements for written reports in this area. These requirements may include the time by which the report must be submitted (often a certain amount of time prior to

TABLE 12-2. TYPICAL TESTS USED IN CUSTODY AND PARENTAL FITNESS
EVALUATIONS

Psychological Health of Adults
  Cognitive Assessment
    WAIS-III—Weschler Adult Intelligence Scale-Third Edition
  Personality Assessment
    MMPI-2—Minnesota Multiphasic Personality Inventory-Second
    Edition
    PAI—Personality Assessment Inventory
    RORSCHACH Ink Blot Test
    TAT—Thematic Apperception Test
    MCMI-III & MCMI for Custody—Millon Clinical Multiaxial
    Inventories
    House-Tree-Person Figure Drawings
  Trauma
    TSI—Trauma Symptom Inventory
    DAPS—Detailed Assessment of Posttraumatic Stress
    MDS—Dissociation
Psychological Health of Children
  Cognitive
    WISC-III—Weschler Intelligence Scale for Children—Third Edition
  Personality
    MMPI-A—Minnesota Multiphasic Personality Inventory for Adolescents
    MCMI-A—Millon Clinical Multiaxial Inventory for Adolescents
    School-Related Achievement & Learning Disabilities Tests
      WRAT—Wide Range Achievement Test
    Child Behavior Checklists
      Achenbach Child Behavior Check List
  Trauma
    TSCC—Traumatic Stress Checklist for Children
    (two versions—with and without sexual abuse questions)
Violence Risk Assessment
  MacArthur Variables
  HCR-20—Historical (10) Clinical (5) Risk (5) Factors (total 20 factors)
  PCL-R—Psychopathy Check List—Revised
  V-RAG—Violence Risk Assessment Guide
  SO-RAG—Sex Offender Risk Assessment Guide
  CAP—Child Abuse Potential
Custody Assessment Instruments
  Achenbach Child Behavior Checklist (CBCL)
  Bricklin Scales
  ASPECT
  CAP-2, PSI

a scheduled court hearing), format of written report, rules to whom to send the report (i.e., in some jurisdictions all attorneys and the court must get the report at the same time).

13. Make recommendations about access to the child that are detailed and give specific changes needed as the child's developmental needs change. For example, while it may be appropriate for each parent to attend sporting and school events on a schedule when a child is ten years old, by the time that child becomes an adolescent, spending time with friends is more important and there is need for a different kind of parental supervision.

14. Be prepared to give sworn testimony by carefully reviewing your entire file prior to being called as an expert. Review every page in the file and make sure it is reflective of the work you have done on the case. Review the findings and the data on which are based. Go over the raw test data to be familiar with the results. Make sure your documents are separated in files that are easy to find because of labels or other identifying features.

CHALLENGING PARENTAL FITNESS AND CUSTODY EVALUATIONS

It is not uncommon for one or both parents to challenge the custody report and its recommendations. Sometimes the challenge is to decisions that are based on inaccurate information. Other times the recommendations are not congruent with information on which they should be based. If one or both parents find that the recommendations of a parental fitness or custody evaluation are inappropriate and unworkable, they can be challenged. While it is always best to try to persuade the original evaluator as to why the recommendations should be different, sometimes that is simply impossible for a variety of reasons. In those cases, a second evaluation may be requested and the court may be asked to order all parties to cooperate. If that does not happen, then an additional parental fitness examination may be obtained by one party to contest the findings of the other evaluation. If the evaluation appears to violate the standards of care that are set down by law or professional guidelines, then hiring a consultant to critique the methodology is an option. If the evaluation appears to be insensitive to the needs of the child, then it may be appropriate to place the child in therapy with someone who is well respected by the court and understands the relevant disputed issues, such as need for protection from an abusive parent.

Therapists do not always want to get involved in legal disputes, so it is important to check this out first.

Coaching a frightened parent through the myriad of legal issues that evolve in a custody or access dispute is critical. Many lawsuits are fought over whether or not one parent can remove the child to another state. The parent who must remain in the location for business or personal reasons can learn how to keep contact with a child even if this does occur. Technology makes connection possible even when parents live in different countries, today. Finally, parents who feel that the system is not responding to their needs can take political action. This is occurring within various organizations formed to support fathers' rights or protective moms' rights. Unfortunately, many of these advocacy groups get co-opted by abusive parents who use the group for their own personal vendettas.

ALLEGATIONS OF ALIENATION

The most common allegations that are offered to explain why a child does not want to live with or spend time with a parent is that the other parent has engaged in a campaign to alienate that parent. In some cases this may be true, but it is far more rare than the courts or evaluators want to believe. Sometimes behaviors that appear to alienate a child occur but they can be easily confused with other reasons including wanting to protect the child from perceived harm. Obviously, these allegations are raised most often when domestic violence or child abuse is alleged by the other parent. Courts and evaluators are often at a loss to know who to believe; the child whose behavior clearly demonstrates distrust and harm from the allegedly abusive parent, the mother who has been abused and believes that the child must be protected from the father's controlling maltreatment, and the father who believes that the mother is implanting ideas of alienation through her behavior. Often times the court chooses one parent over another based on personal preference or a behavior demonstrated by a parent that is inconsequential to the potential harm to the child.

For example, it is common for a battered woman to use manipulation tactics that she hopes will protect her child. Sometimes these are seen by the court as so manipulative that it angers the judge and the mother is punished by taking the child away from her and giving the child to the other parent. Another common example is when the child and the abusive parent are placed together in a supervised setting, the child's play with the father is interpreted as evidence that there was no abuse rather than understanding the nature of family violence; victims can both love and fear the abuser depending on the context of the situation. Mothers, who are usually the ones accused of 'parental alienation syndrome' are often in a catch-22 situation; if they report suspected abuse, they are considered an alienating parent and if they do not report it, they are considered failing to protect their child. It is important to understand that there are no data to support the existence of a parental alienation syndrome that was merely a descriptive label invented by the late psychiatrist, Richard Gardner without any empirical evidence.

There are many ways to protect a child from physically, sexually, and psychologically abusive behavior by a parent even if it does not rise to the level of a child protective services intervention. First, psychologist Leslie Drozd suggests understanding alienation symptoms that a child might demonstrate on an attachment continuum that begins with equal attachments between both parents on one end of the continuum and alienation and estrangement on the other end. Drozd defines 'equal attachments' as part of normal infant development for infants, children, and teens although there may be times when one parent is more relied upon as a caretaker than the other. 'Affinity', the second point on the continuum, is a normal stage where the attachment to a parent depends on gender, interests, and ability to spend time with the child. 'Alignment' is another point on the continuum, where a child is more likely to attach to a particular parent as a normal response to maltreatment or mental illness. Here, the child may like to be with the other parent, provided he or she feels protected but is still aligned with the non-abusive parent. 'Alienation' is the fourth point on this scale where children respond to a parent where there is general dysfunction, alcoholism or drug abuse, extreme overprotective behaviors, abuse, and serious mental illness. 'Estrangement', the final anchor on the continuum, is when the child does not want anything to do with a parent who has been abusive, neglectful, or in other ways harmed the child. Sometimes the child goes through a few of the earlier points on the continuum before reaching the alienation or estrangement stage witnessed by the court.

CUSTODY AND ACCESS RECOMMENDATIONS

Custody arrangements can be as creative as the evaluator or parents suggest. They can permit access with a range of no visitation for a period of time, therapeutic supervision, supervised visitation, monitored visitation, co-parenting, parallel, or alternate parenting. They can include both parents sharing the child's home on alternating time periods, each parent providing a primary residential home for a child in the same school district or neighborhood, or parents living in new homes with space for the children when they visit. Some parents divide the number of waking and sleeping hours in a child's day and insist on sharing them equally while others let the child decide where to go and at what times. Holidays and such special days as birthdays, Mother's Day, and Father's Day need to be alternated unless parents learn to get along with each other. If something disrupts the schedule, it needs to be resumed as quickly as possible to give children the predictability they need. Children are remarkably resilient but they need love, constancy and predictability, empathy, and understanding to overcome many of the natural feelings of anger and betrayal that all family members feel when a marriage dissolves.

Parents can begin new lives and integrate their children into them. This is especially popular if there are children from the new partner's previous relationship or the new relationship that also get integrated. These new family networks are similar to kinship networks that exist in many non-Western cultures. While it is important to give the children time to adjust to each other, it is also important to treat them all as equally as possible to avoid jealousies that can be worse than normal sibling rivalries. Marriage counselors suggest that the most common reason for second marriages to dissolve are poor relationships with children from prior marriages. Perhaps the greatest challenge is to learn how to talk and listen to a child without burdening them with parental problems.

EMPOWERING CHILDREN

Courts and evaluators need to understand the impact of maltreatment of children as more important than punishing a parent who offends the court by some particular behavior. Children who have lived in homes where they have not had any power to make some decisions for themselves, even if only to pick out what clothes to wear to school or what to drink with dinner, need to begin to feel empowered if they are to grow up mentally healthy and physically strong. Custody and access recommendations need to take into account children's preferences, if they can express them, or at least attempt to give them power to make some of their own decisions. For example, a child who is required to visit a parent on a weekend when he or she has a special party or other activity to attend, should have the right to negotiate with the parent so he or she can attend the party. A child who spends time with a parent who has bi-polar disorder and starts to go into a manic state, should be able to call the other parent and go back to that home. If a parent gets drunk or abusive, the child should have an escape plan to stay out of harm's way. If it is affordable, I suggest teaching children how to use the computer and email to keep in touch with the non-residential parent. A cell phone is a necessity for teens to carry and use freely, so they can maintain contact with their peers. Digital cameras to send pictures back and forth is another way to keep up the attachment when physical presence is not possible. Parents who cannot communicate with each other should send faxes with reasonable instructions, like any medication or special needs for the child, when switching homes. It is most important to remember that children often blame themselves when parents separate so they must be reassured that it is the parents who are getting a divorce; not them.

SUMMARY

In summary, this chapter attempts to take us through the often murky and unpleasant world of a child custody or parental fitness challenge. Some of the most bitter battles are fought by parents over children without realizing the tremendous emotional damage that the battle itself does to the child. While children are resilient in most cases, those who have been exposed to homes where one parent displays an excess of power and control whether or not it leads to actual physical violence, where there is alcohol and drug abuse by one or both parents, and where there is serious mental illness resulting in child maltreatment have special needs. We have tried to discuss the performance of a custody evaluation with the assumption that abuse may be one of the allegations to be assessed.

The legal standards, levels of proof, and rebuttable presumptions that govern the courts when they make the decisions about access to children have been described. Obviously, it is always better if parents can come to joint decisions putting their own needs aside for the good of their children. While joint or shared custody is considered in the best interests of the child, in fact, there are no research data to support that it is really the best arrangement for most children, especially if the parents cannot agree. Self interest including financial interests and personal preferences may enter into disagreements about custody and access. If a custody evaluation, that includes interviewing all parties, is impossible due to non-cooperation or other factors, then a parental fitness evaluation can still be presented to help the court make these difficult decisions. Sometimes creativity in access arrangements is necessary to foster the attachments between a child and a parent. The bottom line, however, is to always keep the child's safety and needs as the priority in making such decisions.

13

Protection of Abused Children, the Mentally and Physically Challenged, and the Elderly

The Miami Herald headlines screamed that five-year-old Reyla Wilson was missing and no one had seen her for almost two years. Where is she? How can the Florida Department of Children and Families have lost a foster child in its custody? In New Jersey the Newark Star Ledger also had screaming headlines, accusing the New Jersey Department of Children, Youth, and Families of failing to protect two little boys in its care, each killed by a caretaker. In city after city, the headlines tell the story of children who are killed by family members. Isn't the child protective services system supposed to prevent this from happening?

INTRODUCTION

The duty to protect children and others who cannot protect themselves is delegated to each state's child and family protective services agency that is part of the U.S. Department of Health and Human Services. An entirely separate legal system that has its own state and Federal laws governs the operation of this protection system. The system is supposed to protect citizens who cannot protect themselves from harm. This is generally defined as children, the elderly, and those who because of mental incompetence (often defined as intellectually limited, neurologically impaired, or mentally ill) cannot care for themselves. In this chapter, we will attempt to explain the system, review definitions that vary from state to state and under Federal law, and discuss its benefits and drawbacks. One of the cornerstones of the protection system is the mandated reporting laws that require mental health professionals along with others specified in the statutes to report any suspicion that those covered by the laws are being harmed. The precise definitions are discussed here. As might be imagined, these reporting statutes also have their benefits and limitations. To make it even more complicated, the protection system must interact with the criminal justice system and the family law systems when there are cases that are filed in these divisions, also. In some districts, there has been a movement towards a Unified Family Court where all three divisions can come together and dispose of cases within the same family.

In a quick overview, the child and family protection system deals directly with investigating reports of child abuse, abuse of the elderly, and harm to others who cannot protect themselves and providing them with appropriate services. It also deals with prevention of further harm by overseeing a system of foster care and homes for children, adults and the elderly usually called Assisted Living Facilities or ALF's. The foster care system where children and sometimes adults are placed is divided into family or kinship care and approved foster homes. As many of these children's parents or relatives continue to be unable to care for them, this leads to adoptions, so adoptions are also placed in this division of the legal system. Finally, many of these individuals need treatment to overcome the effects of the trauma, so the regulation of residential treatment centers is also assigned to this court.

As might be expected, the numbers of cases overwhelms the system. In 2001, over 3 million referrals concerning the welfare of approximately 5 million children were reported to CPS agencies across the country as suspected of being abused or neglected. In over one-quarter of those reports, the investigation found a child to be at risk, or already abused and maltreated. The National Clearinghouse on Child Abuse and Neglect Information serves as a resource for national data on child maltreatment reports and publishes the National Child Abuse and Neglect Data System (NCANDS) and National Incidence Study of Child Abuse and Neglect (NIS) at regular intervals. These are updated regularly and are available at their website. Half a million of these abused children were placed in the foster care system because their parents were unable to care for them. In addition, more than one-quarter of other children whose child maltreatment reports were unfounded also received services from their local CPS agency.

States also must provide services for children who have special needs. To fulfill this mandate, the social services systems interact with the school systems on behalf of these children. When they are out of school, the state has the responsibility of providing adult vocational training programs, day care centers, and residential facilities in addition to the ALF's mentioned earlier. In most states, protection of the elderly comes under the same department's care and protection, although probate court, which determines competency to care for one's basic needs may also become involved when abuse reports are made. To further complicate the picture, if abuse is determined to have occurred towards anyone in this system's care, the state may also file criminal charges against the abusive parent or caretaker, adding a third legal proceeding with yet a different standard of proof required.

DEFINITIONS

CHILD MALTREATMENT

As we have seen in other chapters where definitions of an act are based on law, each state and the Federal government have slightly different definitions. In some cases, there will be laws passed by Congress that suggest states follow a particular definition, but these usually are only guidelines to be sure all the elements are covered. 'Child maltreatment' is the term used to cover all forms of physical abuse, sexual abuse and exploitation, neglect, abandonment medical neglect (usually not if caused by poverty or religious beliefs), psychological and verbal abuse, corporal punishment and intentional or unintentional committing, causing or permitting actual or threats of harm to a child. In 2001, almost 1 million children were found to have been maltreated. More girls (52%) than boys (48%) were reportedly abused. Half the victims were white with one-quarter African American, 15% Hispanic, 2% American Indian/Alaskan Natives and 1% Asian American. Both the 2000 and 2001 rates of abuse (approximately 12.4 per 1000 children in the population) are lower than the 1998 rate. Overall the rate of abuse is inversely related to the age of the child with children from ages birth to 3 representing 28% of the victims. These statistics have remained fairly constant for the past five years.

Physical Abuse

Physical abuse of a child is defined as inflicting physical injury on a child by hitting, kicking, punching, beating, throwing, biting, burning, starving or otherwise harming a child. The injury may be a result of one severe incident or cumulative from several injuries. The trauma can be minor, with bruises and abrasions, or major, with injury to internal organs such as the spleen or liver and head trauma. As might be expected, most children who die from child abuse are under the age of six and have suffered severe injuries to their head and internal organs. Physical abuse of a child also includes bizarre forms of abuse including locking a child in a room or closet for days or weeks at a time, forcing participation in satanic cult type of rituals, tying a child up to restrict all movement for long periods of time, and forcing the child to drink so much water that his or her electrolytes are disrupted. Physical abuse also includes use of torture such as electrical stimulation with cattle prods, confinement in a coffin, and forcing the child to walk for long distances in the cold until the child drops from exhaustion. Almost one-fifth (19%) of the child abuse cases reported in 2001 involved physical abuse. Approximately 1300 children died of child abuse in 2001 with the youngest children being the most vulnerable. Almost one-half the deaths were children under the age of one year and 85% of the children who died were under the age of six.

Sexual Abuse and Exploitation

Sexual abuse includes a very broad range of behaviors that range from exposure of the genital area, to inappropriate touching or fondling with or without clothes, and forcing or coercing the child to perform sex acts (whether or not the child 'wanted' to participate), including digital, manual, oral or penis–vagina penetration. Sexual exploitation includes the above, prostitution, electronically recording and selling pictures of the child commercially, Internet child pornography, or other ways of sexually interacting with a child and others. Parents and caretakers are the most frequent child sex abusers. Although there are some treatment programs for abusers, rarely are they successful unless they have relapse prevention components that include no contact with children. We will discuss this further later in the chapter.

While incest between fathers and daughters or sons is the most frequently reported form of child sexual abuse, others in a position of authority have also abused and exploited children. This includes athletic coaches, teachers, and religious leaders. The recent headlines concerning the large numbers of altar boys who were sexually abused by priests in the Catholic Church is an example of how a hierarchical network of priests could and did cover up this abuse, sending priests known to have committed child sexual abuse to another community where they had access to many more children unbeknownst to the parents. Children may be abused in groups or individually, in homes, cars, churches, schools, swimming pools, locker rooms, or anywhere that children are found. They may also be forced into ritual and satanic abuse or other bizarre activities that sound unbelievable but have been known to occur. We shall discuss the damage that occurs when children are sexually abused later. Ten percent (10%) of children who were reported as abused in 2001 were found to have been sexually abused.

Emotional or Psychological Abuse

Emotional abuse is defined as acts or omissions that caused, created, or threatened to cause serious emotional, cognitive, behavioral, or mental disorders in a child. These acts or omissions are usually made by parents, relatives, or caretakers. It includes a number of behaviors on a continuum from belittling a child, cursing and name calling, making damaging derogatory comments, scapegoating, and humiliating, to isolating, screaming, raging, and rejecting the child. Emotional abuse cases accounted for 7% of the cases reported.

Child Neglect

Child neglect is not providing for the child's basic needs. Usually, not providing something the child needs because of poverty is not considered child abuse, although it may harm the child. There are different types of neglect including physical, educational, emotional, and medical neglect. More mothers are found guilty of child neglect than of physical or sexual

abuse of the child. Neglect cases accounted for more than one-half of the child abuse cases reported in the U.S. in 2001.

ABUSE OF THE ELDERLY

Although there are different statutes that protect the elderly from abuse and neglect, the illegal acts are similar to those listed above for child abuse. In the elderly, the most frequent abusers are caretakers and adults responsible for the care of elderly parents and grandparents. However, if we looked more closely at physical abuse cases we would find a preponderance of elderly husbands who are still abusing their elderly wives. On the other hand, the numbers of elderly men who are being abused by wives whom they previously abused when they were stronger and less vulnerable is also high. Given the graying of America and the rise in the numbers of the very old who need adequate care facilities, there is renewed interest in preventing elder abuse by exploitation, neglect, starvation, medical neglect and malpractice as well as physical maltreatment.

IMPACT FROM ABUSE

Child maltreatment has known detrimental effects on the physical, psychological, cognitive, and behavioral development of children that lasts long into adulthood. These consequences range from minor to severe and include physical injuries, brain damage, low self esteem, problems with attachment in relationships, developmental delays, learning disorders, mental illnesses, and aggressive behavior. Some of the mental illnesses associated with child abuse include Post-Traumatic Stress Disorder (PTSD), depression, and conduct and substance abuse disorders. In more serious cases of child sexual abuse, we have evidence of dissociative disorders and even schizophrenia spectrum disorders that have developed. Many physical illnesses have known association with childhood abuse including those that involve a breakdown of the immunological system such as Lupus, Fibromyalgia, and cancer. New studies demonstrate the impact of abuse on the brain development of children so that PTSD and other brain involvement may not be able to be prevented in those who have been exposed. This can impact on the child's educational and career aspirations. Not surprisingly, the percentages of people in prison for all types of crimes who were abused or maltreated as a child number close to 85%. It seems that putting some more money into prevention and early intervention programs might save us lots of money on the other side.

Costs of Maltreatment

Direct costs reflect the dollars spent by the child welfare, judicial, law enforcement, health, and mental health systems. In 1998, the federal government spent almost $5 billion dollars just on the child welfare system itself. States typically spend millions for protective services, foster care, health costs of low birth weight babies, medical treatment of injuries from abuse, special education costs, psychological care for maltreated children, juvenile justice system and correction services, and adult criminality. In addition, indirect costs of lost wages, lost sales tax from children's deaths, teen pregnancies, welfare dependents, domestic violence, and other problems bring the totals to unfathomable amounts of money that must be spent on what appears to be a cycle of abuse that continues to repeat itself. This does not include the money spent in child custody and visitation battles raised by domestic violence perpetrators who themselves had a high rate of exposure to child abuse. Various groups have tried to place dollar amounts on the cost of maltreatment as a way of influencing policy-makers to put more money in the front end to prevent or treat early abuse.

FOSTER CARE, ADOPTION, AND FITNESS TO PARENT

One remedy to stop child abuse by a parent is to remove the child from the parent's home and place the child in foster care. The state delegates the authority to CPS to take custody of the child and provide for his or her needs. The court oversees how CPS handles the case by demanding reviews on a regular basis after the initial treatment plan is approved. One problem that was raised in the earlier chapter on custody and visitation is the mandate for reunification of the family, in this case between the offending parent and the child. If the parent does not complete the reunification plan, for a variety of reasons, then the children may be placed for adoption.

Fitness for Adoption and Foster Parenting

A special area that differs some from custody determinations where one or both parents are the biological ones occurs when families are trying to raise children who are not related by blood ties. In many states, relatives who wish to care for a child can apply for 'kinship care'. Sometimes the state grants financial assistance to these relatives in order to promote the continuation of family ties. However, careful psychological evaluation of the best interests of the child rarely occur in these cases and social conditions that breed poverty and abuse may remain untouched.

In cases in which it is a non-biological and non-family person who wishes to raise a child, this usually occurs by foster parenting or adopting a child. If the foster care parent does not adopt the child, the state will continue to provide financial assistance to the parent while an adoption places the parent on his or her own, financially. Sometimes the question for the forensic evaluator is an easy one. This might be where the child is already flourishing in a foster home, the foster parents want to adopt the child and the biological parental ties have been broken. Here, the mental health professional must comment on the fitness of the foster family to meet the best interests of the child. These cases may be heard first in juvenile court where the state agency with responsibility for child protection has followed a permanency plan that resulted in the termination of the parental rights to the child. Family case workers following the standards outlined in Public Law 105-89, the *Adoption and Safe Families Act of 1989* may already be involved and the subsequent long term foster care or adoption proceedings are simply a pro forma continuation.

In some cases it gets more complicated, especially when there are mixed races between the prospective adoptive parents and the child or when gay or lesbian couples are the prospective adoptive parents. While it is possible to challenge outdated state laws on these issues with psychological data indicating that there is no psychological evidence that gay, lesbian, or bisexual birth or adoptive parents per se, have a negative impact on the children involved, heated emotions, religious concerns, and conservative ideology may be difficult if not impossible to overcome in some areas. A recent Florida decision to ban the adoption of one parent's biological child with her Lesbian partner, even though she had been co-parenting the child together with her partner, demonstrates the difficulty in getting the court to base such a decision on scientific data.

In performing an evaluation for adoption, it is also necessary to include information about the adoptive parents' reasons for wanting to adopt the child especially if it is not an infant. It may be important to know about their determination of infertility; ability to psychologically accept a non-biological child of a different age, race, religion or culture, and willingness to provide for a child with special needs, if that is relevant. Information about why a particular child is available for placement may also be relevant, such as kinship issues, financial difficulties of the birth parent, health of the mother, or other reasons for her unavailability, such as incarceration. Now that adoption records are more accessible to both birth parents and adult children, newer forms of adoption are available, such as leaving records open at the child's birth instead of sealing them, arranging for adoptive parents to have structured or flexible contact with the birth parent, or keeping contact with cultural or kinship ties in international or interracial and transracial adoptions.

Most adoptions are handled by private and public agencies. These agencies have the responsibility to perform evaluations of adoptive parents and available children. Usually the courts recognize the work of these agencies and finalize adoptions faster than if the evaluations are made through private attorneys and mental health professionals. Although the *U.S. Multiethnic Placement Act of 1994* prohibits adoption agencies from receiving federal funds if they use race as a sole criteria for adoption placements, psychological findings indicate that a connection to a child's racial and ethnic heritage is important to healthy development.

The laws covering state and international adoptions are quite complicated and require specialization. In the seven-year period between 1988 and 1995, in U.S. there were over 10,000 adoptions of poor, lower socioeconomic status, dark skin toddlers who did not speak English as their first language, many of whom came with health and malnutrition problems. Bureaucratic red tape snafus caused many of delays in bringing these children to their new homes, creating even more psychological and developmental problems. Although some religious groups did help these adoptive parents to anticipate dealing with these children, most were not prepared for the extent of difficulties they would experience. Today, 13 countries have adopted the rules proposed by the 1997 *Hague Private Law Convention on Protection of Children and Cooperation in Respect of International Adoption* and the 1989 *United Nations Convention on the Rights of the Child.* The United Nations has supported the development of children's legal rights around the world and serves as an important resource for those who work in this area.

INTERVENTION PROGRAMS

The most recent reports indicate that parents and other caretakers are the most likely people to abuse a child. As has been the case for years now, the majority of those reported to have maltreated a child are women (59%) with an average age of 31 years old as compared to 34 years old for the men. Over 80% of the children who were maltreated were abused by their mother and/or father with 41% of those abused by the mother and 19% abused by both parents. However it is important to remember that women spend more time with children than do men. Males are most likely to commit the serious, life-threatening physical and sexual abuse against children.

There are a variety of intervention programs for parents who are accused of abusing their children. The most common are the low cost educational 'parenting classes' that are usually run by local agencies who get referrals from the different branches of the court; in particular, the family and juvenile court systems. Treatment programs for parents who abuse children are much more expensive and difficult to find. If the abuse was caused by or related to a substance abuse problem that the parent has, there may be community programs in the substance abuse community. If domestic violence co-exists (there is a 60% overlap between child and woman abuse) battered women shelters and court ordered offender treatment programs may address the parenting concerns. But, if the abuse is because a parent is mentally incompetent to take care of their children, there are few programs available. We will discuss two model programs: the Ft. Lauderdale, Florida OPTIONS program for seriously mentally ill women who are involved with the criminal justice system and the Southern California PROTOTYPES program for substance abusing and mentally ill women.

PROGRAMS FOR THE ELDERLY

Although physical abuse is a problem with the elderly who are dependent upon caretakers who are untrained, unsupervised, or just worn out, it is neglect that poses the biggest challenge for communities today. The largest number of very elderly—over 80 years old—are women who live alone, are lonely, and do not have enough money to purchase sufficient food, medication, and other necessities of life. They are often unable to drive or to get around on their own as they approach 90 years old but if their minds are still active, they do not want to be sent off to assisted living centers. Few grown children are able to have parents or grandparents live in their homes, and many live too far away to provide much assistance. There are some community programs that provide meals to seniors, and other organizations and religious groups provide some small amounts of home care, but basically the elderly in the U.S. get little assistance as they age.

MENTALLY CHALLENGED ADULTS

Mentally challenged children are provided with special education programs until they turn 18 years old (in some communities the age is 21 years old) and then the state must take over providing them with services if the parents cannot do so. There are sheltered workshops and other vocational where they learn skills that may be helpful in the community, assisted living facilities and group homes, and residential centers for those who are too profoundly retarded to live by themselves in the community. The state does take responsibility for providing programs and protecting these citizens although most of the responsibility falls on the family.

PARENTING CLASSES FOR ABUSIVE PARENTS

The assumption is made that an abusive parent will commit abuse or fail to prevent it from occurring if that parent does not have knowledge of what to expect from a child developmentally or uses the child to make up for deficits in his or her own life history. In fact, a large number of child abusers do need education about children's needs, and, for them, parenting classes may be helpful. However, another group of parents, usually women, fail to protect their children because they cannot even protect themselves from violent and abusive partners. These protective mothers may be forced to co-parent their children by a family court that is insensitive to the danger both the mom and children are in when the dad is willing to abuse power to control them.

Parenting classes are not sufficient or helpful here, either for the dads who are court-ordered to attend or the moms. The dads need a more hands-on approach so that they can be told immediately when they are inappropriate or miss the signals their child is giving them. Many of them learn to repeat back in a rote manner what they are supposed to do but haven't a clue as to how to apply what they learn in real life. They need a step down series starting with didactic parenting classes, then supervised therapeutic visitation, then supervised visitation, and finally short periods of unsupervised visitation with monitored pick up and return of children.

PROTOTYPES: A PROGRAM FOR SUBSTANCE ABUSING WOMEN

Many moms are unable to properly care for their children because they have a substance abuse problem that needs treatment. PROTOTYPES provides a residential program where moms and their children can live together while she learns to stay sober, gets help for any mental health problems, learns how to stay out of domestic violence relationships, and how to parent her children. The children are placed in school and mental health programs that include establishing good peer relationships which many of them lack. Both moms and children have difficulty attaching and bonding to relationships, so the program focuses in these areas, too. This is also a step down series program with moms coming alone first after they detox and begin their substance abuse program. They add a domestic violence prevention component shortly after. If appropriate, they may be offered individual therapy in addition to the groups they attend. Women without vocational skills may also begin training programs once they are stable. A stepdown program reintegrating the mom and children together begins with supervised therapeutic visitation when the CPS caseworker brings the children to the PROTOTYPES center, increases to mom and children monitored in different activities, and finally, unsupervised or monitored time together when the children are returned to live with the mom at the PROTOTYPES residence. Once the women are discharged from the residential facility, they continue to participate with a caseworker and therapist where appropriate.

OPTIONS for Seriously Mentally Ill Women

The OPTIONS program was begun as a day treatment therapeutic community for seriously mentally ill women who were involved in the criminal justice system. The 69 women who were part of this intensive program had almost as many children together although some women had none and others had many. Most of their children were in the care of CPS or relatives, as these moms could not adequately care for them. As might be expected, most of these women had been abused as children or in their adult lives. Their diagnoses centered around schizophrenia spectrum disorders and bipolar and affective disorders in addition to PTSD. The women participated in a variety of group programs, including parenting modules, and those who had access to their children were encouraged to bring them in at specific times for hands on parent training.

Individual Psychotherapy and Case Management

Children who have been abused are often placed in individual therapy programs to heal from the abuse they have experienced. In the past twenty years, techniques to deal with specific problems commonly seen in abuse victims have been developed. They are too numerous to address here. However, it is important to note that like others who experience PTSD and associated disorders, these children need therapeutic assistance so that the adaptations and accommodations they made to protect themselves as best they could do not become part of their adult personality patterns. Mental health centers, schools, church groups, and trained private practitioners are available to provide such services.

It is more common for adults who were abused as children to wait until they begin to develop chronic or serious mental health symptoms as adults before they seek therapy for their problems. Women and men do not always experience the effects of abuse right away, and in fact they might be okay for many years, sometimes developing specific problems when they become parents themselves. Like the exposed children, adults also have a choice of different treatment modalities although those in rural areas often have more difficulty in finding trained clinicians.

We still don't know why some people develop certain symptoms and disorders and others develop different ones when they were all exposed to the same type of abuse. In fact, we do not know why different children in the same family develop differently. For example, five children in a family where the parents were alcoholic and neglected them can turn out differently with some becoming educated professionals and others unable to hold a job or stop their own substance abuse or domestic violence when adults. As we discussed in the chapter on interventions in forensic settings, theorists who work in the field of substance abuse differ in whether the problem is viewed as an addiction, a disease, or a behavior control problem.

Most studies find a definite gender difference in the impact of child abuse with boys more likely to use violence in their own lives and girls more likely to be the abuse victim. In one such study boys who were exposed to violence in their family were 700 times more likely to become abusers. If those same boys were also abused themselves, the risk of becoming abusive was raised to 1000 times children who were not abused. New brain imaging studies have found problems with dysregulation of emotions and other PTSD type of problems in children who have been exposed to abuse.

CIVIL LAWSUITS

In addition to treatment, some adults who were abused as children file lawsuits against their abusers. These cases are more successful when the defendant is not related to the plaintiff, such as the clergy, a teacher, or someone else with 'deep pockets'. If parents or other relatives are sued, it often causes serious splits in the family that make it difficult for the plaintiff to ever have a supportive relationship with some family members. If other children were also involved, it may give the plaintiff a natural support system. As difficult as these cases can be for the plaintiff, it also can be therapeutic to confront the abuser and force an apology. As we have stated in other chapters, a civil lawsuit can only give a plaintiff financial compensation for the damages he or she has experienced. Forensic psychological evaluations to document psychological damages are often required by attorneys who take these cases to trial.

SUMMARY

In this chapter, we reviewed the laws that have been passed to protect children, the elderly and others in protected classes who have special needs. The Child Protective Services agencies throughout the country have been under scrutiny for their inability to protect children. Reasons for the difficulties include the social mores that protect the family unity and ignore many reports because of poor investigations. The youngest and least experienced workers are assigned to protect children and while many are dedicated to their work, their caseloads are enormous and the resources to back them up are limited or non-existent. Children who are abused often give many clues but do not put it all together for the adults who could protect them. The relationships between them and their parents are complex and include both love and fear of further harm. They learn to accommodate to the situation, keeping the parent as calm as possible. Foster families are not a good solution for most of these children whose needs are great and resources are few. Adding support to the mother or natural family is another possible way of offering them some protection. Adoptions are often a good way to help children find a good family. International adoptions and those with hard-to-place children challenge the system but when they work out, everyone is happy. Interventions with abusive families involves long hard work and often requires protecting the child while the parent gets it together. Residential programs where mothers and children can come together to learn new ways of relating to each other seem to have good success rates. Battered women shelters, substance abuse treatment programs, and residential or day treatment programs for women with serious mental illness all help mothers deal with raising their children. Programs for men, however, are less successful, perhaps because there are so few with hands-on experiences as compared to programs for women. Programs for the protection of the elderly are more difficult to locate and fund but do exist in most communities. Other programs work with the mentally challenged and disabled populations that also need special protections.

14

Reproductive Rights and the Law

INTRODUCTION

The history of the control of women and children parallels the history of reproductive rights and the law. Many believe that the new women's movement really began when the rights of a woman to choose if and when she would bear a child became legal. There are some who believe that the institution of monogamous marriage itself was created by men who needed to know who their progeny were and only if they found a way to keep women monogamous would that be a certainty. This may make sense given the history of the marriage contract indicating that those who entered into marriage became one body and the governance of that body was by men who retained all the rights. For example, Susan Brownmiller, in her book, *Against Our Will: Men, Women and Rape* suggests that in olden days when we were a nomadic people, women married one man to keep from being raped by many men.

History tells us about cultures where one man was permitted to have many wives, certainly an arrangement that would help the man keep control over his own progeny. Ann Jones, wrote in her book, *Women Who Kill*, that men battered women for the same reasons. Jean Auel's anthropological novels about her character, Ayla beginning with *The Clan of the Cave Bear* traces some of this history. In any case, the issue of who fathered whose baby has dominated the structure of most societies in the world since we have historical records including the Bible. As a result, monogamous marriages became institutionalized and the decisions about whether or not to have a child supposedly resided within the marital couple. However, as we shall see, the state has a compelling interest at least in protecting women's health, which has permitted laws to be passed that limit women's reproductive and health rights and access to good health care.

Psychologists have become involved in these legal arguments in a variety of ways. They have offered testimony in class action lawsuits that deal with the constitutional issues around safety to health and especially the mental health of any woman to be forced to carry an unplanned pregnancy to term. Social, developmental, and clinical psychology research that has been provided to courts demonstrate that there are NO adverse psychological effects from an abortion by itself or from providing information about appropriate counseling techniques. Other research has dealt with the impact of consent laws on the psychological health of teens, about the incidence and prevalence of family violence (partner, child abuse, and incest) and its impact on consent laws, with the cognitive capacity of teens to make good health care decisions. In addition, mental health professionals have offered testimony on individual cases where mental health status is an issue. This can include cases where assessment of high risk health issues are at stake, where vulnerable psychological states of mind are at issue, or where parental fitness is needed for termination of parental rights, adoption of an infant, or participation in the new reproductive technologies.

RIGHTS TO USE CONTRACEPTION

We must remember that the legal rights that do exist today were won case by case over the past fifty years as not all individual rights were automatically abrogated by the marriage contract. In the mid 1960's in *Griswold v. State of Connecticut (1965)*, the court affirmed the rights of individuals to be free of government interference when choosing to use contraceptives.

The court based their decision on the privacy rights given in the 14th Amendment. Some states had adopted laws, supported by those with strong religious views that prohibited the use of contraception including condoms and intrauterine devices (IUD's and diaphragms with spermicidal jelly). In the early 1900's Margaret Sanger and other strong suffragettes founded clinics for poor women to distribute contraceptives so women could safely prevent and control their rate of pregnancies. Doctors, nurses, and other health workers and counselors who worked there were subjected to similar negative feelings and harassment as are workers in 'pro-choice' women's health centers today. These early clinics became the infrastructure for Planned Parenthood, the most widely organized centers for gynecological and reproductive health in the U.S. Today there are a number of organizations including the Center for Reproductive Law and Policy that are involved in the legislative, political, and legal arena to obtain access to good health care. They have websites that are available for information on a regular basis.

Regular and Emergency Contraception

Family planning and reproductive health centers around the world are modeled after these early courageous clinics. When the safe oral contraceptive ('the pill') was introduced in the early 1960's, many believed that the women's legal rights around reproductive choice would be won. A mostly safe, reversible, inexpensive and non-invasive process, the pill was hailed as a substitute for irreversible sterilization, vasectomies, or even abstinence. By 1973, when *Roe v. Wade*—the famous case that a 26-year-old Texas attorney, Sarah Weddington, argued before the U.S. Supreme Court—decided that women did have the constitutional right to control their own bodies even though the state did have an interest in protecting women's health, women's advocates believed the legal battles were over. As we will demonstrate below, this did not happen.

In a similar way, advocates had the expectations that *mifepristone*, the so-called 'morning after' pill, RU486, would eliminate the need for abortions and therefore, permit women the right to control their own reproductive needs. But, cases like *Planned Parenthood v. Danforth (1976)*, in which the court found that children's rights may supercede parents' rights have continued to be litigated in the courts. Many believe that emergency contraception should be available to women without needing to have a doctor prescribe it. As we will see in the later chapters on family law, children's rights really are not the issue here. Rather, the issue is who will have power and control of women's bodies to bear children. It is undeniable that birth control and abortion make it easier for women to venture outside the home, pursue an education, and realize career aspirations without having to be married.

CONTRACEPTIVE EQUITY

The legal battle for the right to use contraception other than abortion is far from over especially for those who use third party insurance to pay for their reproductive health. In the U.S., where health insurance is tied to the place of employment, rather than in other countries where the state provides health benefits for all its citizens, there are great disparities between health services for the poor versus those who can pay for their health services without relying on insurance benefits. Since 1999, there has been a movement within the U.S. for state legislatures to pass what is called, 'contraceptive equity bills' to force insurance companies that pay for Viagra (the drug that helps men overcome erectile dysfunction to reach and maintain erections so they can perform sexual intercourse) to also pay for birth control pills, IUD's, and emergency contraception regimes. A bill that would improve private insurance coverage for contraceptives and reproductive health, *Equity in Prescription Insurance and Contraceptive Coverage Act (EPIFCC)*, was introduced in Congress and signed by 123 co-sponsors, but by 1999 it had stalled in committee. In 2003, the Center for Reproductive Law and Policy found that one-half of the major health insurance companies still did not offer equity in access to contraception and other reproductive health needs.

A class action lawsuit filed by Planned Parenthood and others on behalf of all women in the state of Florida has been shuttled around to different legal forums for the past 7 years where it is alleged that there is a disparity of treatment for poor women in the state because men can obtain Viagra paid for by Medicaid while women cannot obtain contraception including abortions. If this bill reaches the state or U.S. Supreme Courts, it could have far reaching implications on not providing contraceptive equity for poor women. Obviously, these issues have political, legal, and psychological ramifications for society. As discussed below, the psychological consequences of being forced to bear an unwanted child are far greater than the psychological effects from any of these procedures.

Conscience Clauses

As a counter-measure in which insurance companies and states have granted contraceptive equity, doctors, counselors, nurses, and pharmacists are being permitted to 'opt out' of prescribing or otherwise fulfilling health-related duties around contraception if they claim that 'moral convictions' prevent them from doing so under new 'conscience clauses' that legislators have been introducing into law, sometimes in unrelated legislation, making it difficult to find. Language in a bill that was introduced in Congress but has not passed, the *Religious Liberty Protection Act*, could also be used to permit religious objections to any law to take precedence over women's reproductive and health rights.

RIGHTS OF A WOMAN TO CHOOSE AN ABORTION

In 1973, there were several cases that broadened the argument of whose legal rights should govern the procreation of children. Since then, over 20 cases dealing with different aspects of women's right to choose an abortion have reached the U.S. Supreme Court. In the now famous Texas case, *Roe v. Wade* (1973, 410 U.S. 113.) the decision of whether or not to abort a fetus was left to the woman and her physician, at least during the first trimester of pregnancy. Since that time, state legislatures under the influence of religious and politically conservative members, have attempted to place restrictions on the woman's right to choose to bear a child, the most recent being laws passed to prohibit second or third trimester abortions when the fetus might be viable. Currently, laws have been passed in twenty states that mandate that women be given specific written information prior to the procedure while thirteen states also mandate waiting periods that extend from one to 24-hours. There is some indication that states are looking to lengthen that waiting period to 48 hours or longer. Obviously, this places a greater hardship on women who must travel great distances to find a safe clinic to obtain an abortion. Although laws that mandated written permission to be obtained from a married woman's husband have failed to be upheld by the appellate courts, there are still attempts to require his notification. As we will see later, sometimes it is not in the best interests of the marriage or the woman's safety or health to force such notification, especially if he is not the co-conceiver or he has a history of aggressive and violent behavior towards the woman and other children.

ROE V. WADE

This well-known U.S. Supreme Court case actually was a challenge to Texas' statutes that made either participating in, or performing an abortion, a criminal act. The legal argument that won the case was that criminalizing women's health and reproductive rights was a violation of privacy and due process as given by the 14th Amendment of the U.S. Constitution. It was broadened to a 'class action' lawsuit using the argument that although this plaintiff was the individual currently involved, the laws could impact all women who could become pregnant and should have the choice of whether or not to terminate the pregnancy. Although the Texas criminal statute challenged had been passed in 1854 and like similar statutes in other states had not been widely used, it had never been repealed. The legal argument by Texas was that a state had the legitimate interest to protect the health of its citizens, including women and children and that superceded a woman's right to terminate pregnancy.

The 7 to 2 decision of the U.S. Supreme Court Justices (Blackmun, Brennan, Burger, Douglas, Marshall, Powell & Stewart in the majority and Rehnquist & White in the minority) gave a woman the right to make her own decisions about abortion together with her 'licensed' physician through the end of the first trimester of pregnancy. In the second trimester, usually 4 to 6 months of pregnancy, the decision stated that the government may regulate the procedure, but only for the women's health. Here, psychologists may become involved in rendering opinions on a woman's state of mind if necessary. The third trimester was where the state was granted the right to regulate or proscribe abortion in two conditions: 1) to promote interest in human life but only if does not interfere with, and 2) to preserve the health and life of the mother. Again, psychologists may be asked to render an opinion in this circumstance, especially if the pregnancy resulted from rape or incest. As we will see later, this is the area where new laws banning so-called 'partial birth' procedures or 'stem cell' research have occurred. The *Roe v. Wade* Justices did not deal with the particularly thorny issue of when life begins, leaving the door open to theologians and other moralists to continue the argument until today.

The *Roe v. Wade* decision immediately touched off a firestorm of controversy in the U.S. that still has not quieted down today. It divided people into polarized groups — religious people divided into the religious right vs. liberals, politicians divided into conservatives vs. liberals, gender groups into males vs. females, women's rights advocates vs. family rights advocates. Political groups vied for the popular names—pro-choice vs. anti-choice or pro-life vs. baby killers. Whether one was for or against women's right to choose to terminate a pregnancy became oversimplified into a political litmus test and was used to win arguments or to keep out those on the wrong side of whatever other issue was being decided. Women's groups became more politically active in electing legislators who passed their litmus test. So did the conservatives or those identifying with the religious right. However, the real money seemed to be provided by those who were much more invested in keeping control of women's bodies and health for whatever reasons. Obviously, this battle is far from resolved and as such, reproductive rights will continue to be a controversial area. Let's look at some more recent legal cases that involve psychology as an example.

In the 1990's, there were a number of cases attempting to define whether married women needed to obtain their husband's permission before choosing to abort a fetus (e.g., *Casey v. Planned Parenthood*), but so far the woman's right to control her own body was held to be a more compelling right.

Undue Burden Test *Casey v. Planned Parenthood (1992)*

Casey v. Planned Parenthood challenged the Pennsylvania Abortion Control Act that had been passed in 1982. The act was broad and included requiring: 1) informed consent from the woman seeking to terminate the pregnancy 24 hours prior to the abortion; 2) parental consent for a teen from one parent or a judicial-by-pass procedure (explained below); 3) spousal notice in which the married woman must sign a statement that she notified her husband of the intended abortion; 4) definition of what was a medical emergency that exempted compliance from this legislation; and 5) mandated reporting procedures for providers.

In this case, the Court affirmed *Roe v. Wade*, but modified it somewhat when it applied what is called the *undue burden* test and stated in its Opinion that is the rule to use in determining if a new law conforms to the requirements. In this case, the *Casey* Court found that: 1) before a fetus is viable, a woman can choose an abortion without state interference, but 2) once a fetus is viable, the state has the power to restrict abortions unless it endangers a woman's health, and 3) the state has a legitimate interest in the outcome of a pregnancy by protecting both the infant's and mother's health.

Family Violence, Notification, Informed Consent, and Gag Rules

Testimony from one of the authors (LW) in *Casey* gave data about the abuse of power and control by husbands who batter their wives and suggested that the largest number of married women who do not discuss their decision to get an abortion involved those married to batterers. Batterers as a group will insist on making the decision for the woman, so there can be no discussion and joint decision-making in these relationships. The *Casey* Court cited this as one of their reasons for striking down that provision of the Pennsylvania law. Obviously, another reason for holding the law unconstitutional is that it places a different burden on married women from unmarried women who were not required to obtain permission from the fetus's biological father or as some studies state, the 'co-conceiver'. Since then, no other state has been able to require such permission. However, notification laws have been passed, particularly in regulating adolescent's rights to abortion that will be discussed below.

In *Thornburgh v. the American College of Obstetricians and Gynecologists (1986, PA)* the U.S. Supreme Court began to deal with the issues of informed consent and gag rules among other issues. This case struck down a provision of the Pennsylvania law to give a pregnant woman seeking an abortion pictures of fetal development at different stages. However, it still permitted written information describing fetal development as well as information about prenatal care and adoption. Further, it permitted the state to set a waiting period after counseling and before the procedure would be performed. In *Casey*, which came down six years later, the court defined the informed consent piece to include a mandatory waiting period of 24 hours for the woman despite testimony that this time period may be unduly burdensome for women who had to travel long distances to obtain the procedure. *Casey* did make it illegal to require notification or consent from the husband or co-conceiver.

Partial Birth Legislation

The vacuum aspiration method of performing an abortion in the first trimester of pregnancy has been found to be even safer than childbirth itself for the woman's health. In the second and third trimester of pregnancy, different methods of terminating the pregnancy are used depending on the stage of fetal development, length of pregnancy, and health of the woman. These are medical decisions and should be made on a case by case basis rather than legislated by law. One method, known as partial birth as it requires dilation and extraction of a potentially viable fetus, has been banned in 24 states at this time, although some of these states have injunctions against the implementation of the law until reviewed by the appellate courts. These laws have been challenged as they do not protect the health of the woman. In some cases, when the fetus has died or was found to be deformed *in utero,* it is the only method to protect the woman's health. In other cases, it is a necessary method to use even with pre-viable fetuses so there would be contradiction between two laws governing the same issue. The laws are too vague to be of assistance and they do not permit a doctor to make the final decision based on the individual woman's health needs.

STEM CELL RESEARCH AND ABORTION

Research into genetic cures for some diseases has been done using stem cells that came from human embryos. This research has already pioneered some genetic alterations that may make spinal cord and other nerve cells regenerate themselves. This could mean new hope for some paraplegics to walk again or even for finding a cure for debilitating diseases such as Parkinson's disease, Multiple Sclerosis, or Muscular Dystrophy. Yet, laws forbidding such research using fetal tissue from abortions have slowed down or actually curtailed these important scientific advances. These laws also seem to have created a black market for fetal tissue driving up the price and supporting other unscrupulous practices.

PSYCHOLOGICAL RESEARCH ON IMPACT OF ABORTION

POST ABORTION SYNDROME DOES NOT EXIST

Defining women's health requirements is a complex and difficult task because each woman has individual requirements depending on her physical and mental health status prior to becoming pregnant. One of the arguments against freedom of a woman to choose whether or not to obtain an abortion is that it could cause her psychological harm either immediately or later in life, such as when she goes into menopause. Citing individual cases in which psychological problems did occur after an abortion or at menopause, the existence of a Post Abortion Syndrome that left women with unanticipated psychological problems was promulgated without any empirical evidence that such a syndrome actually occurred.

Several major research studies gave further information that negated the existence of such a syndrome. Of course, there are some women who have a negative reaction to an abortion, but these women either had emotional problems before they became pregnant that worsened or they were coerced into an abortion by others and really didn't want to terminate the pregnancy. Many of these individual women can be easily identified with pre-abortion counseling and often clinics will suggest further counseling before performing the procedure as a precaution. However, five states (Louisiana, Michigan, Missouri, North Dakota and Pennsylvania) have passed what are known as 'gag rules' forbidding state employees from counseling women about abortion. The federal government has also passed legislation forbidding family planning clinics that receive money from the U.S. and the U.N. to perform counseling about abortion, negatively impacting the health of women in poor, developing countries who receive our aid. This is further described below.

The data that counselors have and could present to women are very clear. The twenty or more decisions by the U.S. Supreme Court since *Roe v. Wade* have not removed the right of a woman to proper health services or the requirement that women give 'informed consent' to the procedure. Yet, these so-called gag rules appear to be mandating only a limited amount of information that does not reflect the state of knowledge in the field today. For example, when the data about mental health problems seen after an abortion were compared to the data of mental health problems seen after women give birth, including those who experience post partum depression after childbirth, it was found that there were significantly fewer emotional problems after an abortion than after childbirth. The American Psychological Association has published papers that present the available research and has testified and entered Amicus briefs in many of the landmark reproductive health cases during the past 35 years.

What Do We Know about Women who Obtain an Abortion

Statistics

Some statistics that are available suggest that there were 1.37 million abortions performed in the U.S. during 1996. This represents about one-quarter of all known pregnancies that year. This rate is actually decreasing in the U.S. since 1990. It probably would be even lower if long term and emergency contraception was easily available. The majority of women seeking abortion were young, with 54% under the age of 25, 22% who were teens, and 24% who were age 30 or older. Sixty-four percent (64%) were not married. Two-thirds of the women stated that they wanted more children in the future. Women who stated they have no affiliation with a religious ideology were four times as likely as religious women to obtain an abortion. Low income and women on Medicaid were twice as likely to abort as non-Medicaid recipients. This statistic may be misleading as women with private doctors may not have their procedures listed as abortions but rather other types of gynecological or obstetric care.

Who Do Women Talk To before an Abortion?

The research suggests that over 90% of married women do talk to their husbands before making the decision to obtain an abortion. Those who do not tell their husbands seem to have good reasons. The three most popular reasons in one study were 1) their husband was not the co-conceiver; 2) the couple was experiencing marital problems; and 3) the woman feared the husband's reaction. Interestingly, the research also found that over four-fifths (80%) of non-married women also consulted their co-conceivers. Two-thirds of the women (68%) surveyed said that they consulted their best girlfriends and half (50%) said they consulted their doctors. Only 3% said they consulted their religious clergy.

Reasons for Abortion

Most women state that they wanted an abortion because having a child at this time would negatively change their lives. Some reasons included inability to afford a baby, problems in their relationship, lack of readiness for the responsibility of raising a child, youth or immaturity, completion of their child-raising years, demands from their current children who need them, or knowledge of an incurable genetic defect in the fetus.

Psychological Effects of the Experience

Women surveyed stated that the experience of an unwanted or unplanned pregnancy and the decision to obtain an abortion is emotionally distressing, but it offers the possibility of being a positive emotional growth experience. Most women stated that they experienced positive emotions after the procedure especially if they had social support.

PARENTAL NOTIFICATION AND PERMISSION FOR TEENS

Another series of cases have been litigated to determine whether a teenage girl's rights superceded the rights of her parents if she chose to abort a fetus without their knowledge or permission. Currently, 16 states require a parent's consent for a minor to obtain an abortion and 14 states require parental notification. In these cases, a judicial by-pass procedure was put in place by the appellate courts for when an adolescent was unable or unwilling to go to one or both parents for permission. Testimony from psychologists about the cognitive and intellectual ability of adolescents to make similar competent decisions on their own and the impact of exposure to family violence on girls' ability and willingness to confide in parents was designed to help the courts make these decisions. In some cases, such as *Hodgson v. Minnesota (1990, 497 U.S. 417.)*, the American Psychological Association entered an Amicus Curiae brief to explain the state of psychological knowledge about such issues, as well as the data about the lack of psychological damage from abortion in most cases.

Pending federal legislation, the *Child Custody Protection Act* is an attempt to require that a teen may only obtain an out-of-state abortion if she is accompanied by a parent by imposing stiff penalties on any person, other than a parent, who 'knowingly transports' a woman under the age of 18 across a state line to obtain an abortion if she has not met the requirements for parental notification or consent in her state of residence. Parents whose daughters have abortions under such circumstances would have the right to initiate a civil action against such a person. Although this federal legislation has still not been passed, some states are considering similar legislation that will definitely challenge the previous decisions to protect adolescents from unnecessary state interference.

Why Teens Do Not Tell Parents

A remarkably small percentage of teenage girls who become pregnant refuse to tell at least one parent, usually because they fear the reaction of the parent. Many fear being forced into the parent's decision and thus, they would not have a choice of what to do. Of those who do not tell a parent, one-quarter (25%) disclosed they have histories of physical or sexual abuse. That percentage would be higher if exposure to parent's domestic violence were recorded. Many are financially independent and may live outside of the parents' home. Some stated that their families are unable to talk about any sexual information. Those who do not tell their parents often tell other adult family members, including aunts or grandmothers.

Who Do Teens Talk To?

Interestingly, teens find different people supportive at different stages of decision-making. Over half first talked to their co-conceiver when they first suspected they were pregnant and almost half talked to their friends.

But, if a pregnancy was confirmed, then over half talked to their parents. Approximately one-third of those who made the decision to obtain an abortion found their parents and their co-conceivers helpful in making the decision while only one-fifth found their friends helpful and less than 10% found a counselor helpful.

Reasons for Wanting an Abortion

Most teens have valid reasons for choosing not to have a child despite their sexual activity and resulting pregnancy. Reports from judges who hear judicial by-pass procedures indicate that they found most of the women who came before them to be thoughtful and mature in their reasoning skills. Psychologists who have testified in the class action lawsuits resulting in the judicial by-pass have presented arguments to indicate that sexually active teenage women usually have the cognitive ability to make good judgments about whether or not telling a parent will be helpful and supportive to their health needs.

Over three-quarters of girls who have been surveyed said they wanted an abortion because they were too young and not mature enough to raise a child. Over one-third said they wanted to finish their education first and over one-quarter said they couldn't afford to raise a child. Approximately one-half cited social disapproval or problems with their co-conceiver partners as a reason for terminating the pregnancy. A small number felt coerced by their parent to have an abortion. Approximately 10% learned the fetus had an irreversible genetic defect.

Surveys of teenage mothers who decide to keep their babies and raise them do not indicate such good judgment and emotional health and well-being. Many are survivors of child abuse and incest, while others grew up in homes where they felt unloved and unwanted themselves. Often they state that they want to have a baby in order to have someone love them. This attitude poses a high risk to become a child abuser. Funding for programs for teenage moms in the public schools is not easily available which forces most of these young women to drop out of school and not complete their education. This lack of social support only brings about a repeat of the vicious cycle of poverty, abuse, lack of education, mental and physical disability, and incomplete participation in society.

ACTIONS AGAINST ABORTION PROVIDERS AND CLINICS

Family planning and women's health clinics have provided simple and inexpensive abortions as it became clear that the access to good reproductive health care was going to remain difficult regardless of the law. These clinics have been picketed by protesters making it difficult for women to enter them safely, doctors have been personally harassed and abused, a few clinics and doctor's homes have been bombed, and public funding has been withdrawn or was never accessible.

Hyde Amendment and Global Gag Rules

Unfortunately, people's personal views have been codified into legislation such as the so-called Hyde Amendment that was attached to the Health and Human Services funding bill in 1977 and continues each year making it difficult for anyone to provide or receive adequate reproductive health services. Under the Bush government, recent legislation supported what is called a 'global gag rule' where international family planning and reproductive health clinics are unable to utilize U.N. funding if they provide abortions or other services on the prohibited list. Since the major funding support of these clinics in developing nations provide many other services in addition to abortions (which are now legal in over 75% of the countries of the world), this rule has virtually shut down women's education programs funded by our government. These programs also provide education about democratic ways of life that are vital to our national interest in promoting democracy around the world.

TRAP Laws

Today, the local reproductive health clinics are also undergoing challenges posed by new laws, often called TRAP laws that stands for Targeted Regulation of Abortion Providers. These laws, now passed by 25 states, often single out health centers that provide abortions and require that they meet regulations that are different and more stringent than other comparable medical centers. In some states, such as South Carolina, even the privacy of women who seek services in these clinics is violated by permitting state inspectors to copy their medical records without the woman's permission or even stating a reason why medical confidentiality can be violated. In its 2003 term, the U.S. Supreme Court permitted an appellate court decision to stand without reviewing the constitutionality of this law despite the fact that it appears to violate the *Roe v. Wade* decision that during the first trimester a decision to terminate the pregnancy should be made by the individual woman and her licensed physician. In other states, such as Arizona, similar regulations have been overturned by the courts.

ACCESS TO GOOD REPRODUCTIVE HEALTH CARE

The politicalization of women's reproductive health care has made it difficult for all women to get adequate medical care because of limited access to well-trained caregivers. Poor women who must rely on government services under Medicaid have restrictions on what providers they can see and what services are allowed. Although these restrictions have been challenged on a number of grounds including 'disparate treatment' under the law, many have remained stalled in various legal forums. Whether or not it is illegal has yet to be clearly ruled on by the Courts as each term Congress passes new legislation (sometimes adding it on to completely unrelated bills so it does not draw attention). One area to watch in the future is the criminalization of Female Genital Mutilation (FGM) in various countries of the world where it was practiced. A large number of African countries that had tolerated if not actually approved of the practice, which essentially excises a woman's clitoris and renders her unable to experience physiological sexual pleasure, have now declared the practice illegal. However, not being 'circumcised' as the practice is sometimes benignly called, may make a woman unmarriageable, which can doom her to a life of prostitution or servitude.

Migration to the U.S. has brought many immigrants who still believe in the practice and have attempted to genitally mutilate young girls so they can be promised in marriage. As might be expected, they are subjected to criminal penalties for engaging in a practice that might be culturally relevant but against the law.

RIGHT TO HAVE A CHILD

The government is not only interested in a woman not having a child, such as regulation of abortion clinics and contraceptives, but also in the ability of pregnant women to seek proper medical treatment during the pregnancy. At a 1998 conference on reproductive health held in Moscow, Russia, sponsored by the World Health Organization, researchers from around the world presented data that suggested deteriorating conditions for women's health since the U.N. International Conference on Population and Family Planning held in Cairo in 1994, just four years earlier. Among the data presented were statistics indicating an increase in the number of miscarriages, infertility, death from infectious diseases, pregnancy anemia, and other complications that threatened the health of women who worked outside of the home. Although some of these conditions were seen as due to the HIV/AIDS pandemic around the world and some were concerned with toxic substances in the workplace, others were believed to be caused by the lack of priority given to women's reproductive health needs.

PUNISHING SUBSTANCE ABUSING PREGNANT WOMEN

Women who do not practice proper health care of themselves and their fetuses during pregnancy, such as those who continue to use sufficient quantities of alcohol and drugs that are toxic to the fetus (called a 'tetrogenic effect') can be punished by the U.S. criminal and civil law. Here psychologists may be called upon to evaluate the woman's potential to change her problematic behavior or the woman may be incarcerated until delivery and/or the infant may be removed by social services with the court's permission from the mother immediately upon birth.

While this may sound like a reasonable public policy plan to protect the infant, in fact, it is usually against the infant's best interests in the long term. First, the legal and human rights of the woman are violated and can cause or exacerbate psychological trauma. This is of particular concern since many of these cases involve sexually and physically battered women who are in danger of being further abused or developing even more serious post-traumatic stress disorder symptomology. It is common for victims of sexual assault and domestic violence to use alcohol and other drugs as a form of self-medication to keep the psychological symptomology under manageable control. Second, few jails or prisons have the resources to provide good prenatal care for a pregnant woman that would include proper nutrition, adequate rest, appropriate exercise and good medical care. Third, and perhaps most important, is that the infant is not really protected by what appears to be punishment to the mother. One of the major areas of damage that can occur with fetal alcohol syndrome and drug-exposed fetuses is the subsequent inability of these infants and children to emotionally connect and attach to others. By placing these sometimes fragile infants into foster care programs that may not have stability, it almost guarantees later psychological problems in interpersonal relationships. Many of these infants have great difficulty in being soothed so they constantly cry and are fretful even when being held, something research suggests they need. To avoid developmental problems, the best solution is to add one or more additional helpers to the home who can assist the mother in providing for the infant's and the mother's needs. Thus, adding support services to the mother, rather than isolating and punishing her, appears to be the most helpful long term solution to a difficult problem.

ASSISTED REPRODUCTIVE TECHNOLOGIES

Reproductive rights cases continue to fascinate the general public and the judiciary, especially those that deal with helping infertile couples to become parents. Recently there have been a number of cases that dealt with the impact of the assisted reproductive technologies (ART) on family law. For example, if a couple who wants a child cannot conceive or carry a fetus to term, there are a number of technologies including removal of sperm and eggs for in-vitro fertilization (IVF) and replanting the resulting embryo in that woman's or another surrogate's uterus. These embryos or gametes can also be frozen and implanted at another time. Psychologists are often called upon to evaluate the parties to see if they can handle the stress of the medical procedures and the subsequent child raising or termination issues. Let's look at the following case:

> Jana, a 36-year-old woman, with a great position in one of the major stock brokerage houses on Wall Street in NYC woke up one morning realizing that she was getting older and that meant she'd better decide whether or not she would have babies. Bill, her equally ambitious husband, had brought up the topic several times during the ten years they had been married, but Jana was too busy building her career to think about building her home and family also. Besides, women of her generation were told that they could have babies whenever they wanted to — after all, there were all kinds of new technologies that extended the possibility of motherhood well into a woman's forties.
>
> That night she and Bill had a long talk about whether or not they really wanted a baby now and both decided this was as good a time as any to begin. However, six months later, when Jana still hadn't gotten pregnant, they had to review their decision to have a family and make a different kind of commitment to the long and sometimes embarrassing process that has developed with using the new reproductive technologies.
>
> Did they really want a baby so much that they would be willing to enter The IVF program, as the in vitro fertilization program is often called?
>
> First screened by a psychologist to see if this couple could withstand the difficult and invasive medical procedures, Jana and Bill were accepted into the program. It involved Jana taking hormones to stimulate the production of more ova, surgically removing several ova from Jana's ovaries, fertilizing them with Bill's sperm in a petrie dish in the laboratory, and then implanting the embryos in Jana's body. Several ova are taken at a time in the hopes that at

*least one IVF procedure will be successful. Since the procedure is so invasive,
it is also common for several groups of ova to be removed, fertilized, frozen,
and then stored for later use either because the first try didn't succeed or in
the hopes of having a second child in this way. Jana and Bill opted for the
procedure and decided to freeze several sets of fertilized ovum in the hopes of
having another child to complete their family.*

*Two years after their daughter was born, Jana and Bill's marriage fell
apart and they decided to get a divorce. Now, forty years old, Jana wanted
custody of the fertilized ova they had frozen with the intention of using for
such a purpose. But Bill, perhaps understanding he would have the financial
responsibilities of raising another child, wanted the embryos destroyed. Unable
to resolve this issue on their own, Jana and Bill went to the courts to settle
the question for them. Recognizing the precedent it was setting, the court
decided that in this case, it would be unlikely for Jana to obtain new 'good'
eggs because of her age and history, so he gave her their custody to either use
them to become pregnant or destroy them, as she decided.*

*What do you think is the right decision? What if Bill insisted that Jana
become impregnated with the ovum and she refused? What if the man had
testicular cancer and he no longer had his own sperm to fertilize other ovum?*

WHO OWNS THE FERTILIZED OVUM?

More recent cases have helped couples decide who owns fertilized
eggs that were frozen after their marriages were terminated. In a Tennessee
decision *(Davis v. Davis, 842 S.W.2d 588, Tenn. 1992)* that first brought national attention to this problem, the Court set the rules for other cases
to follow. In what is considered a three-part decision, the Court stated a
divorce court should first look to the parties wishes about ownership of
the cycro-preserved embryos. If they can't resolve the dispute themselves
then the court would go to the second step, which is to look to prior agreements between the parties. Third, absent some current or prior agreement,
the party choosing to avoid procreation should prevail unless the other
party does not have a reasonable possibility of achieving parenthood by
some other means.

In the Davis case, although Ms. Davis originally wanted to use the
frozen embryos to have a child, by the time the divorce was final, she
wanted to donate them to another woman who had infertility problems to
save her the medical ordeal she experienced. Here the court said that the
father's right not to procreate was stronger than her right to donate the
embryos to a third party although had she wanted them for herself, that
right would probably have been greater than Mr. Davis' rights not to be a

father because of her infertility problems. Thus, she could have implanted the embryos or 'gametic material' had she not changed her mind about their disposition.

Interestingly, in a subsequent California case (*Hecht v. Superior Court*) a California man made several deposits of sperm that were frozen in a sperm bank prior to committing suicide. He signed an agreement that if anything should happen to him, he wanted the sperm to go to his girlfriend. His grown children filed a lawsuit to stop the transfer of their father's sperm as they had an interest in protecting their inheritance rights by no further progeny from their now deceased father. The court ruled that his testamentary gift to his girlfriend was valid and gave the ownership of the sperm to her. Other cases have been resolved, usually in favor of the party who does not want parenthood. Some suggest that this decision prevents women from having their full reproductive rights to their fertilized embryos as they would if the conception took place naturally in their bodies. The argument suggests that it is a violation of *Roe v. Wade* and *Casey* not to give the woman full rights over the gamete as the sperm donor has already made a commitment to procreate by becoming a co-conceiver.

What if a storage company makes a mistake and gives or sells your gametes to another couple who implant your genetic material in a surrogate? Is that theft, negligence, or some other tort action? What if you decide to genetically clone yourself using new DNA techniques that are available in the laboratory? These are fascinating questions that have yet to be answered in the law.

Surrogacy

Legal issues around the validity of surrogate contracts especially when disputes arise have made headlines such as in the *Baby M* case in New Jersey when a surrogate mother decided to keep the child and not turn her over to the biological father and his wife [*In re Baby M*, 525, A.2d 1128 (NJ Super. Ct. Ch. Div. 1987; In re Baby M*, 537 A.2d. 1227 (NJ 1988)]. Using similar technology as in the ART programs, a surrogate (usually a woman) agrees to carry the fetus to term and delivery and then relinquish the child to the biological father and his partner. Media report cases where mothers or other family help a daughter or sister to have a child by being a surrogate for their fertilized embryos. Drugs permit once incompatible parents and blood types to successful bear babies in this way. Although some states have created special contracts in the law to protect surrogates and biological and adoptive parents, other states have declared such contracts are illegal and cannot be enforced. Laws have been promulgated to prevent babies from being sold or women from being exploited and used as 'incubators' or 'baby-hatchers'. Science fiction stories are based on these possible scenarios.

Finally, what about men who want to become surrogates? Some scientists suggest that it is possible to fertilize an embryo outside of the uterus, build a synthetic uterus, implant it in the abdominal cavity of a man, implant the embryo in the synthetic uterus using drugs to enhance both the implantation process and nutrient delivery system to the growing fetus, and then deliver a healthy baby by Caesarean surgery. The question is whether the man would be the child's legal father or mother?

MOVING TO THE HEAD OF THE RIVER

We're swimming in a river of change...
We've spent the last decade standing on the river bank,
Recuing women who are drowning.
In the next decade,
Some of us have to go to the head of the river
To keep women from falling in.
GLORIA STEINEM

V

Juvenile Justice

The Juvenile Justice system was originally set up with a rehabilitative, instead of a punishment model, when adolescents break the law. Interventions were to be based on the youth's needs, rather than on the nature of the crime. In practice, however, these courts became quite punitive and by the late 1960's, the U.S. Supreme Court declared they were "Kangaroo Courts" and recognized the need for juveniles to have due process and other legal rights when in the juvenile system. Juveniles continue to be waived into adult court, particularly if the nature of their alleged criminal acts are egregious. We look at the questionable intervention programs that fail to take account of significant abuse histories in the background of many juveniles in the detention centers. Even so, only around 20% of those arrested for delinquency go on to becoming what is called, 'career criminals' when they get older. The constitutional issues regarding Miranda waivers, competency, insanity, and the death penalty for juveniles are examined here.

School violence is a highly publicized area of violence that is increasing while other areas of violent behavior in juveniles has decreased. We look at warning signs that have been found to be high risk for a school violence incident, compare it to other forms of workplace violence, and suggest some prevention programs that have been designed and implemented by psychologists. Finally, we will consider the uneven manner in which children's rights have been handled in the courts. On the one hand, the state assumes that parents always act in the best interests of their children and therefore, giving children NO civil or legal rights. On the other hand, we will look at some cases to see where children have been given some legal rights to sue their parents because the parents have not acted in their best interests. We predict that this area of the law will continue to develop and have a profound impact on how juveniles will be treated in the justice system.

15

Delinquency

Alisha was just hanging out with her other 15-year-old friends in the parking lot of the local fast food hamburger place. It was after 10 pm, earlier than her curfew. She knew she could get up to go to school the next morning so she was pretty unconcerned about the hour. All of a sudden, it seemed without any warning, she and her friends were surrounded by the local police. She watched them hassle a few of the guys for a few minutes and then, she and some of the others started yelling at the police to stop mishandling their friends.

"We ain't done nothin' wrong. Why 're you hurtin' them? Leave us alone."

These were some of the comments Alisha can remember making. Before she knew it, the police were all over her too.

"Don't touch me. Don't touch me!"

She remembers screaming at them while grabbing for her backpack to hold up as a shield. One officer grabbed her backpack away and began rifling through Alisha's stuff, letting her brand new $15.00 lipstick fall to the ground and crack open. The $20 bill she had persuaded her mother to give her before she left home that evening lay next to the lipstick, ready to be blown away by the wind. Alisha said was 'freakin' out' as the police officer started to pat her down. Without thinking, she started fighting back, hitting and kicking, all the *while screaming, 'don't touch me!' Satisfied Alisha did not have any weapons on her, she was handcuffed and placed in the back of the police car. Finally, she was taken to the police station along with several other teens.*

Alisha was luckier than some of the others. Her mother was at home and came down to the station to bring her home that night. Several of the other teens spent the night at the detention center and some never got to go home when the next day the juvenile court sentenced them to a youth facility after being charged with unlawful loitering and battery on a law enforcement officer.

Was Alisha a delinquent minor? Should she have been arrested? Could this whole incident have been prevented? Of course, she was not behaving in the true spirit of delinquency as it was conceived. The facts were pretty clear. The officers did not have any reason to hassle the teens. The owners of the hamburger joint had never told the teens to move on. This was a pretty popular hangout and everyone knew it. The teens were angered by the mishandling of several of their friends who turned out to have been previously known to the police who were just stopping in for a snack anyhow. Unknown to the police, Alisha had been sexually assaulted less than one year earlier. Touching her brought back all those memories of her abuse in a flashback and in her mind she was fighting back against her rapist and no longer even realized the police were present. Had the police used a more sensitive approach with all of the youth there, this entire incident probably could have been prevented.

HISTORY OF JUVENILE JUSTICE SYSTEM

The history of the juvenile justice system began in 1899 with the first court that was especially designed for juveniles established in Cook County (Chicago) Illinois. Within 30 years, all states had followed Chicago's lead and enacted laws and special rehabilitation services for responding to the needs in youth. It must be recognized that it wasn't until the late 19th century that we began to see youth as different from miniature adults. Until then, minors who got in trouble with the law were treated as adults with the same penalties. Children under the age of seven were considered to be in their infancy and that was an absolute defense. From ages 7 to 14, there was a presumption that a youth had the mental capacity to form intent to commit a crime which could be rebutted by a showing of immaturity, similar to the competency standards in use today. Otherwise, a child was treated as an adult.

As we began to develop a comprehensive mandatory public education system, instituted child labor laws, and began a child welfare system, we accepted the state's responsibility for protecting youth. Children, especially adolescents, began to be seen as still in their formative years where personality could be more easily changed and shaped than when they became adults. Thus, their misconduct did not have to demonstrate that they would become hardened or career criminals as adults to be eligible for delinquency court. In fact, today we have data that suggest that less than 20% of those arrested as youth will go on to become 'career criminals'. This is amazing given the poor track record that we have in adequately providing for the needs of these youth. Unfortunately, Alisha's story is not unusual, even 100 years after we openly recognized the need to treat adolescents differently from adults.

BALANCING REHABILITATION WITH PUBLIC SAFETY

Rise of the Rehabilitation Model

In the beginning of the 20th century, juvenile courts were by definition set up to be rehabilitative, not punitive or retributive. They were supposed to operate under the doctrine of *Parens Patriae* which, as we discussed in an earlier chapter, is Latin for a wise and merciful 'substitute parent'. The guiding rule was that adolescence was the transition period between childhood and adulthood. Some children needed more guidance and help in making this transition. Juvenile court was designed to help 'delinquent or wayward' children become responsible adults. Rehabilitation in the juvenile court meant procedures were supposed to be informal, closed to the public, and dispositions were individualized to the child's needs. To do this, it became important to use mental health workers to gain an understanding of the child and what we today call his or her biopsychosocial needs. Then, mental health workers, usually social workers, were supposed to educate the court.

Rehabilitative decisions were to be made on the basis of what the child needed, not based on what acts the child had done to get arrested. Thus, the 'sentencing decisions' for a runaway girl (technically a status crime) might be the same as for a girl who was shoplifting or stealing a car (delinquent crime) if their needs were the same. A status crime involves an act or acts that would not be considered criminal except for the status or age of the child. Examples of status offenses include truancy from school, running away from home, and incorrigibility or inability of a parent to properly supervise the child. A separate juvenile court category for children in need of supervision developed to deal with some of these cases now mostly being handled in the dependency and neglect courts as described earlier in Chapter 13.

By the middle of the 20th century, it became clear that the rehabilitation model was not working well in juvenile courts. First of all, the court system has always had difficulty in moving away from a punishment model as we saw earlier in Chapter 8 when we discussed psychological interventions in forensic settings. The law has a way of defining someone as the act he or she has committed, rather than dealing with who he or she really is. Secondly, the juvenile courts became overcrowded and resources to understand and treat youth became scarce. Rarely were these adolescents placed in good treatment programs even though reports of outstanding programs made it seem like they were the norm. Reports of abuse in the programs that did exist became widely known and much like in the criminal system, the public lost confidence in the possibility of rehabilitation. Besides, the laws were all stacked against children's rights and in the favor of parent's ability to best care for their children despite the evidence that was emerging about the impact of abuse on these families. This is further discussed when we raise the issue of children's rights in Chapter 17.

Thirdly, the violent crimes committed by some youth began to take center stage and the type of crime rather than the needs of the child became more of the court's focus. Although violent crimes committed by juveniles actually have been decreasing over the second half of the 20th century, the general public believes that adolescents are very violent and are afraid of them. Short term public safety needs began to outweigh the long term need to rehabilitate the youth. The recent publicity given to school violence shootings has reinforced the message that violent teenagers are not easy to differentiate from normal teenagers prior to their committing violent behavior as we describe in Chapter 16.

MOVEMENT AWAY FROM THE REHABILITATION MODEL

By the middle of the 1960's there were two U.S. Supreme Court cases that are credited with recognizing the juvenile courts had defacto changed from rehabilitation and back to a quasi-punishment model. By this time there was ample evidence for the U.S. Supreme Court to believe that many juvenile courts around the nation were really punitive despite the law, and so they decided that juveniles needed the due process protections as well as other legal rights.

In the first case, *Kent v. United States*, 383 U.S. 541 (1966), the Court found that juveniles were entitled to procedural due process because children in juvenile court received "the worst of both worlds". By this statement, the court meant that neither the procedural protections of adult court nor the proper care or treatment of children were actually being practiced in juvenile courts despite their mission. One year later, in the second case, *In re Gault*, 387, U.S. 1 (1967), the Court went further and actually described juvenile courts as "kangaroo court[s]" and reiterated its belief that children deserved the protection of due process and procedural rights by stating, "neither the Fourteenth Amendment nor the Bill of Rights is for adults alone." Thus, the U.S. Supreme Court ruled that the juvenile courts had failed to live up to their rehabilitation promise. Had they done so, it would not have required so many legal protections as the U.S. Supreme Court were now granting to juveniles. Interestingly, neither of these cases would have better protected Alisha or her friends, in the story recited above, from the attitudes of the police although, we cannot be sure she would have been able to tell her story without the court being required to listen to her defense had she not had those legal rights.

The rights that the U.S. Supreme Court cases *Kent* and *in re Gault* mandated for juveniles included the same rights of others who are arrested and brought into criminal court on the same charges. This includes the right to have an attorney represent them, the right to know what the charges against them are, the right not to incriminate themselves, the right not to be charged more than once for the same act (double-jeopardy), and other adult rights except for the right to a jury trial in front of the public. Their age was considered a sufficient reason to protect them against loss of confidentiality in a public trial or in open records. In addition, the state was required to meet a burden of proof in juvenile court cases which had not been required previously as cases were disposed of, rather than adjudicated. But, dispositional evaluations, as the forensic psychosocial histories and reports had begun to be called, were still admitted in the post *Kent* and *in re Gault* cases as judges retained great discretion and latitude in final dispositions of cases.

Further drawing the juvenile court away from the rehabilitation model was the American Bar Association's Juvenile Justice Standards Project rejection of treatment in favor of what are sometimes called the five D's:

1. due process;
2. desserts (punishment based on blameworthiness);
3. diversion (when punishment and juvenile court jurisdiction isn't necessary);
4. deinstitutionalization (preference for community placement); and
5. decriminalization (of minor crimes, status crimes, and incorrigibility).

In the past ten years, there has been a further movement away from a rehabilitation model by states making the juvenile codes more stringent and emphasizing the role of the courts to protect public safety rather than guiding youth into adulthood. In many jurisdictions the age for judicial waiver or transfer into adult court has been lowered. In most courts it is now 16, rather than 18, years old. During the same period of time, the U.S. Supreme Court also ruled that it is permissible to execute youth over the age of 16. It is also now permissible to transfer a case to adult court at age 13, rather than at age 14, as it used to be and for a wider variety of charges such as possession of a handgun and sexual assault on a minor. In some states it is even mandatory to transfer to adult court when a serious violent offense is charged no matter what the child's age. The issue of waiver will be further discussed in Chapter 17. However, the juvenile court still remains a separate part of the judicial system in most jurisdictions and an attempt to follow the rehabilitation model or at least give it lip service remains.

WHAT DO WE KNOW ABOUT JUVENILE CRIME?

In 1994, a Gallup poll indicated that Americans sampled believed that 43% of crime is due to juveniles while in fact only 13% of all crime is due to youth. However, although the number of juvenile crimes has decreased in general, the number of youth using guns to commit crimes doubled in the five-year period between 1987 and 1992, and the number of violent crimes against persons by youth also increased by 56% during that time. So, although the overall crime rate is down, the violence used in crimes appears to be increasing. Even so, the number of teens murdered by adults is much higher than teens doing the killing. For example, six times as many teens are murdered by their parents than are parents murdered by teens. Over 70% of all teens who are killed are murdered by adults, not other youth. Obviously, the numbers of adults and teens killed during the rise in school violence in middle-class areas is also of concern although school violence has been noted in inner city schools for decades now. We shall discuss school violence in the next chapter.

GENDER AND VIOLENCE

Offenses against other persons by teens occur as much in a gendered role as they do in adults. In 1992, four out of every five violent offenses against other persons were committed by males. Only 6% of violent offenses were reported committed by girls in 1992. Newer data from the

Office of Juvenile Justice suggest that there is an increase in use of violence by girls at an even younger age. However, girls are more likely to engage in relational violence, while boys are more likely to engage in gang violence, homicides, and sexual offenses. Girls are more likely to be arrested for status crimes, which are defined by the age at which they occur, such as running away from home, truancy, and inability to be supervised by a parent. They are less likely to have arrests for antisocial behavior and crimes of violence than are boys.

Although antisocial and aggressive behavior can be noted at any age developmentally, the earlier it develops, the more likely it will have persistence across the life span. Thus, in one study 75% of those with a first arrest from 7 to 11 years old were found to be more likely to continue 'life persistent' use of violence and antisocial behavior. In fact, most of those children retrospectively were found to have conduct disorders as young as three years old. In comparison, only 25% of those youth who were arrested from ages 11 to 15 were found to continue their antisocial behavior through their life cycle. As most of these studies dealt with boys, it is difficult to understand the specific issues that are raised with girls who do use violence. Interestingly, 80% of all youth in the juvenile justice system have no further arrests after age 21 and therefore, are assumed to have stopped their antisocial and aggressive behavior. However, many undoubtedly continue to physically or sexually abuse women and children in their families without being arrested.

Psychopathic Traits

Youth who end up using predatory violence (searching for victims outside of their homes) have certain characteristics consistent with later development of psychopathic behavior as adults. This includes poor peer attachments and lack of empathy for the pain or other feelings of others. They are more prone to mood disorders, Attention Deficit and Attention Deficit Hyperactivity Disorders (ADD & ADHD), Post-Traumatic Stress Disorders (PTSD), oppositional and conduct disorders as children and neurological problems. Some symptoms of early onset schizophrenia may occur as early as 15 to 16 years old and these youth are prone to using drugs to self-medicate against the symptomology that they cannot control in any other way. Often, these youth are rejected by peers as young as by the age of 6. They have numerous school problems and their ability to learn particularly in an educational setting suffers. Again boys are more likely to fall in this category than are girls.

CHILD ABUSE

If these youth experienced child abuse in their home, at least one study found that they are at a 40% higher risk to use violence. In another study, boys who are exposed to violence in their homes are 700 times more likely to commit violence themselves and if they are also abused, that raises their risk to 1000 times those who have not been so exposed. Girls who are found to use violence are even more likely to have been exposed to violence in their homes, especially early sexual victimization. In a recent study of girls arrested and brought to the detention center, it was found that over 85% of them had experienced abuse at some time prior to the arrest. Yet, nowhere in the supposedly rehabilitative programs' curricula are there issues addressing the impact of physical and sexual abuse and psychological maltreatment at home or in other parts of their lives.

INTERPERSONAL RELATIONSHIP DIFFICULTIES

Interestingly, youth who are more likely to become career criminals are more likely to misperceive intentions of other youth towards them and in particular, they believe that people are being negative towards them more often than is factually accurate. In addition to misperceiving aggressive intent, they are more likely to have problems in solving interpersonal conflict situations than others their age. This may be because of or a result of the social rejection they experience as they are growing up. It is of critical importance to provide more corrective socialization experiences for at risk youth in order to prevent some of these lasting conditions. In fact, the studies that look at abused youth who overcome the obstacles and are successful find that the single most important factor is the ability to affiliate and get along with peers.

ROLE OF COGNITIVE, EMOTIONAL, AND NEUROPSYCHOLOGICAL DEFICITS

Those who are mentally retarded also make up a large proportion of the adult criminal population even though they are not as large a group arrested as youth. In some rare cases, mentally disabled youth are manipulated and used by other delinquent youth in the community to commit crimes for the benefit of those delinquents, not the retarded youth who was trying to please and make friends. There are a number who are just in the wrong place at the wrong time and then are coerced into confessing to crimes that they did not commit, although they may have seen what happened. Let's look at the case of Tim.

> Tim was a large, African American 15-year-old when he was passing by an all night convenience store on his bicycle one night. Although tests indicated his cognitive abilities were around an IQ of 54, he had never been placed in special education program by the schools he attended. No one seemed to care whether he attended school or not, so obviously he rarely showed up as he got older and was less able to follow the lessons being taught. He was held over twice and then continued to be promoted for social reasons. He grew up in a family where his father abused his mother, Tim and the other children who lived there. The abuse was quite severe especially when his father was high on crack cocaine, and included the use of weapons.

> When Tim was 12, his mother was arrested for shooting at his father but charges were dropped when she proved that her actions were in self-defense and in defense of Tim. His parents then divorced. Two years later, his father was shot and killed by his then current partner who interestingly enough was never prosecuted for the shooting. By then, Tim had been arrested several times for loitering, shoplifting, and car theft. Each time he was held in the detention center or sent to a juvenile correction facility, and each time he came out without receiving any psychological treatment.

> On the night in question, twelve years ago, when Tim was only 15, he witnessed the shooting of a police officer sitting in his car in front of the convenience store, working on writing up his reports for the night. Tim was so high on drugs when he was questioned, that he was released and back on the streets soon afterwards. But, seven months later, the murder was still unsolved and police again picked him up. This time without giving him access to his mother or an attorney, denying him due process, he was questioned throughout the night. He says he was beaten up by the police. Of course, they deny it. But, by the end of the questioning period, Tim had confessed to the murder of the police officer. He had denied having anything to do with the murder before and after that fateful night of questioning. He was automatically waived into adult court without a hearing, as is possible in the state of Florida simply upon the request of the state attorney, tried and convicted by a jury, and by the time he was 16 years old, he was incarcerated for the rest of his life in adult prison and labeled a murderer.

> Tim's mother never believed that he had killed that police officer. She knew it was his right as a juvenile to have her present and to have an attorney present during the questioning and that denial of his rights resulted in a false confession. She knew her son was mentally retarded, although those words were never directly spoken. She didn't believe he could read or understood Miranda rights. For 12 long years, she faithfully visited Tim and promised to find a way to get him out of prison. Finally, the opportunity she had prayed for

happened. Another police officer confessed to killing his colleague. But, he both confessed and then recanted his confession confusing the police department that did not want to believe the scandal that was buried with the death of the first officer. The governor appointed a special investigation team to try to learn the true details, but they too were unable to come to any conclusions about who really murdered the officer.

Whose confession was more reliable and valid? A 15-year-old, mentally retarded youth or a former police officer? Despite local and state investigations, no one except Tim's mother, his lawyers, and his psychologists believed in his innocence. After all, he already had a juvenile record.

None of the state appellate courts wanted to hear the case, so it was taken to Federal court on a writ of Habeas. The Federal court Judge who heard Tim's appeal, listened to the testimony of psychologists who explained in detail what mental retardation meant in terms of what Tim could and couldn't understand during the police questioning. For example, the Miranda statement asked Tim to remember about seven items in sequence, something impossible for someone with an IQ of 54 to do. Finally, in a 90-page opinion, the judge ruled that the confession was not properly obtained and returned the case to state prosecutors with instructions to decide whether to retry him without the statement within 90 days. Tim was released on bond from prison fully expecting the state not to retry the case without any evidence of Tim's involvement in this homicide without the improperly obtained confession.

As we will see later, the procedural unfolding of Tim's case is similar to what has occurred in death penalty cases in which new technology such as genetic DNA testing has freed so many who have been charged and convicted of murders they did not commit.

NEUROPSYCHOLOGICAL DEFICITS

In one case in which both authors were involved, a 17-year-old youth killed two older neighbors. Despite the fact that records documented his brain damage at birth, placement in classes for the educable and emotionally disturbed, and prior hospitalizations for psychotic and violent behavior, the state waived this young man into adult court where he was charged with a capital crime. Much to our surprise, an adult court judge declared him competent to proceed to trial with the state asking for the death penalty. Eventually, they dropped the death penalty and the now 20-year-old man pled guilty to first degree murder and was sentenced to spend the rest of his life in prison. Would sentencing him to a mental hospital for the rest of his life been a better outcome? This was the only other option if he were found not guilty by reason of insanity.

It is important to remember that mental retardation and neuropsychological problems have many causes. Many of these individuals who end up in juvenile court cognitively and emotionally react much younger than their chronological age even though they may be committing actions similar to other adults. In fact, they may even look like adults because of their size and appearance but interviewing techniques need to be tailored to their level of understanding. This is also true for those who because of severe emotional problems are not competent to understand what has happened or what will happen to them after an arrest. The number of youth who are arrested today who are not competent seems to be growing. Considering the number of television programs that deal with crime these days we would expect them to understand that they do not have to give up their rights not to talk to detectives without a lawyer present. Like their adult counterparts who are arrested, one only has to go into the juvenile detention center on any day to find more mentally disabled youth than in a mental hospital.

FORENSIC EVALUATIONS OF JUVENILES

Until the recent reforms making juvenile courts more a part of the criminal system than following the earlier rehabilitation model, clinical evaluations of the youth usually by psychologists, psychiatrists, and social workers were sufficient for the court. The court was interested in making proper placements of the youth to dispose of the cases and forensic issues were not as relevant. That has now changed given the court's changing role and today, a more forensic-oriented evaluation needs to be done by those clinicians who practice in juvenile court. This includes assessment of the youth's competence to waive Miranda rights at the time of arrest, ability and competency to proceed to trial, violence risk assessment to determine public safety issues, necessity for detainment of the juvenile and waiver to adult court for trial, amenability to treatment—rather than incarceration—as punishment, and what if any role the juvenile's family should play in the rehabilitation process. Let's take a look at each of these questions.

COMPETENCY TO WAIVE MIRANDA

As we have seen before, 'Miranda rights' is the term given for mandating law enforcement to recite a suspect's legal rights, especially the right to remain silent and not be interrogated until a lawyer is present. The U.S. Supreme Court granted these rights under the constitution to anyone who was suspected of committing a crime in a case called *Miranda vs. Arizona (1966)*. In addition to having the right to have an attorney present while being questioned, juveniles also have the right to have a parent present if they choose. Let's take a look at Tim whose experience with the legal system is summarized above. He had been questioned and arrested several times prior to being questioned about the murder of the police officer. At each arrest, his mother was present during the questioning by the police. He never went to trial, as the court disposed of his cases usually by sending him to juvenile facilities for rehabilitation. However, he never received therapy or other psychological intervention.

Tim spent a few months at each facility every time and was returned home to the same situation he had been in before his arrest. At the time of this last arrest for murder, he was at home awaiting placement in a higher level locked facility. Being out on the streets while awaiting incarceration in a locked facility doesn't make sense for public safety or rehabilitation, does it? But, the juvenile facilities were too crowded to accept him right away. His reading scores from school records and achievement tests indicate that he couldn't read above a second grade level. His comprehension was even lower. Yet, on each of the Miranda warning statements that obviously were above 5th or 6th grade reading level, he initialed and signed that he read and understood each of those rights. Twelve years later, he learned in prison to read and understand what the rights were that he didn't know he had but gave up then. Tim claimed the detectives beat him up and forced him to sign the Miranda waiver. His mother testified that she saw the bruises several days later when they finally let her see her son.

Grisso has developed a standard protocol to test to see if someone can understand their legal procedural rights. He suggests that it is critical for law enforcement to develop and carry cards with the legal rights written in simple language. For those who appear to be cognitively impaired, it is important to explain the Miranda rights in a simple enough way to match their developmental level of understanding. Is it possible for law enforcement to be trained to know what appropriate levels of understanding at different ages are? It seems that at a minimum, juvenile detectives must have this information if the minor's Miranda rights are to be respected.

Competency to Stand Trial

Legal Competency vs Competency to Consent to Treatment

Psychologist Thomas Grisso has also developed a psychological assessment instrument to measure legal competency in youth that is consistent with most of the statutes on competency in effect today. Grisso's research parallels the research funded by the MacArthur Foundation that assesses for competency in adults and youth. This covers the following areas:

Understanding of charges and potential consequences

1. ability to understand and appreciate the charges and their seriousness;
2. ability to understand possible dispositional consequences of guilty, not guilty, and not guilty by reason of insanity;
3. ability to realistically appraise the likely outcomes;

Understanding of the trial process

4. ability to understand, without significant distortion, the roles of participants in the trial process (ie: judge, defense attorney, witness, jury);
5. ability to understand the process and potential consequences of pleading and plea bargaining;
6. ability to grasp the general sequence of pretrial and trial events;

Capacity to Participate with Attorney in a Defense

7. ability to adequately trust or work collaboratively with attorney;
8. ability to disclose to attorney reasonably coherent description of facts pertaining to charges, as perceived by the defendant;
9. ability to reason about available options by weighing their consequences, without significant distortion;

Potential for Courtroom Participation

10. ability to testify coherently, if testimony is needed;
11. ability to control own behavior during trial proceedings;
12. ability to manage the stress of trial.

Competency to consent to treatment is measured differently. Here we are interested in the youth's cognitive, affective, and emotional functioning. Any mental disorders are assessed and the youth's capacity to weigh the risks and benefits from treatment is estimated. These results are used to create treatment plans and find appropriate placement for the child should home not be an appropriate setting.

Violence Risk Assessment

Assessing the risk of further violence of a juvenile presents even more difficulties than assessing an adults' risk of further violence. As was stated earlier, only 20% of those youth who commit a crime and are arrested for delinquency go on to become career criminals as adults. Figuring out which youth are in that 20% is complicated. Researchers have tried to adapt some of the actuarial tests used on adult violent offenders and sexual offenders to juveniles without much success. The MacArthur variables used to measure risk of further adult violence are also not easily adapted for juveniles. One reason is the incomplete brain development of a youth especially in the frontal areas of the brain that control impulsivity. At the same time, studies of those adults who have committed violent crimes indicated that the highest risk is for those who have been abused themselves or exposed to abuse as a child and those who have had serious school problems throughout most of their childhood.

Assessment of Mental Health Issues

Those with active psychotic symptoms of a paranoid nature are the most likely to be violent especially if they are experiencing delusions or hallucinations. It is important for law enforcement to understand that if they are approaching a teen who may be in a psychotic or drug-induced psychoticlike state, they must use non-aggressive and carefully chosen means of making contact with the youth so as to avoid setting off a violent incident. If these youth are more likely to misperceive aggressive intent on the part of a law enforcement officer, it may also be a good idea to approach in an overly friendly manner so that their intentions are made very clear from the outset. This is often counter-intuitive as many believe that it is important to establish who is 'boss' right from the start. However, there are many techniques that can be used to remain firm but friendly and non-aggressive to avoid any misperceptions and unnecessary force when dealing with these youth.

Substance Abuse Issues

Substance abuse in teens represents both normal experimentation and a desperate attempt to moderate emotions otherwise difficult to do or even block out symptoms of mental illness, especially depression and thought disorders. Only a small percentage of those teens who experiment with alcohol and other drugs go on to a life history of substance abuse. However, it is difficult to pick out those who will do so except for the complex histories with other forms of dysfunction. It is also important to note that the most serious violent crimes are committed by youth under the influence of alcohol or other drugs. So, this is a serious problem in the juvenile community.

INTERVENTION STRATEGIES

PRETRIAL DETENTION CENTERS

It is common for youth who are arrested to be taken to the police station, booked, and sent over to the main detention center for youth in that community. Once in the detention center, a hearing must be held to determine if there is probable cause to hold the juvenile on particular charges. In some communities children have a lawyer assigned to represent them, but it is not a uniform practice, especially if they cannot afford to pay for an attorney themselves, which covers most juveniles unless the parents can afford to hire an attorney to represent the child and choose to do so. About half of the children who are charged are sent home to await further court proceedings while the other half remain in the juvenile detention center for a specified length of time, usually up to 30 days. The Juvenile Justice case manager must find a residential placement for the child that is appropriate to his or her needs. Rarely do youth who are held in the detention center receive psychological services although it would be a good time to provide crisis counseling, intervention for abuse and trauma including reduction of PTSD symptoms, and psychotherapy for depression or other diagnosed mental disorders.

JUVENILE FACILITIES AND BOOT CAMPS

Adjudicated youth can be sentenced to juvenile facilities that function more like prisons than detention centers or other holding areas depending on the level of seriousness of their crime or how many prior arrests had occurred. The facilities are rated by levels of security needed and each level has more restrictions with a locked facility similar to a prison at the highest level. A newer concept that has been introduced in juvenile justice has been the 'boot camp' modeled after the strict adherence to following rules that occurs in the military induction camps. Instructors are very strict, sometimes even punitive, especially when the rules are broken. No excuses are accepted. The goal is to intentionally break the youth's spirit so that it can be rebuilt in a more pro-social way. Obviously, the definition of what is pro-social is up to the individual program. While this type of program has gained popularity with the general public and legislatures, the research studies indicate very mixed results.

Let's look at two major psychological issues that may make rehabilitation difficult if not impossible under these conditions: 1) moral development in juveniles and 2) social modeling in adolescents.

Moral Development

Psychologists who have looked at the moral development in children believe that the highest level of moral judgment is reached by early or mid adolescence even though there is some controversy about what constitutes this highest moral level. One school of psychology, represented by Kohlberg found that the highest level of moral judgment is to understand the rules and apply them appropriately. Another school of psychology, represented by Gilligan found that for girls, the highest level of morality is to know the rules and apply them with compassion. Psychologists studying gender issues with males and females tend to find that compassion in following the rules and applying them to justice is more likely to be found in a gender-sensitive person. Police and other law enforcement officers, particularly those who are comfortable in using a military style training program, are rarely gender-sensitive people. Gender sensitivity tends to be more likely associated with non-violence while military programs are used to train people to use violence in the military setting. Boot camp programs probably do not pay attention to these subtle but important differences.

Social Modeling in Adolescents

Child development specialists who believe that adolescents are still developing in cognitive, emotional and behavioral ways suggest that the strongest influence on the youth's behavior is identification and modeling with other peers. If adolescents who get in trouble with the law are placed in facilities with other youth who commit offenses, they will not have social models appropriate for pro-social development. The psychological data suggest that they will learn how to behave from their peers. If all their peers are acting-out and committing anti-social acts, will they learn how to behave as better criminals? Psychological theory would suggest that they need to be in a mixed school environment where both prosocial and acting out youth are present, not in locked facilities with other delinquents.

CRISIS INTERVENTION AND PTSD SYMPTOM REDUCTION

As was discussed in the earlier chapters abuse victims can be expected to have some or all the symptoms of PTSD. Untreated, these symptoms will create many of the problems that juveniles who are placed in detention exhibit. They are more anxious, have a lower threshold for impulsively acting out their feelings, and demonstrate hyperarousal when feeling threatened. They may also have sleep and eating disorders. They will have difficulty with interpersonal relationships and try to control their environment through manipulation and other indirect techniques. They may be depressed, dissociate, deny, and repress their feelings until they explode or they become non-functional. They will respond to intrusive memories especially if in a situation which reminds them of the abuse they experienced. Without treatment or medication, they may try to self-medicate or use other dysfunctional ways to deal with the painful symptoms. Severe criticisms and being yelled at will invoke memories of their past experiences and their responses will be mixed with fear for their own safety. Substance abuse treatment is important for those who have abused alcohol and other drugs, or they will go back to using as soon as the substances are available to them.

Methods for dealing with stress and other crisis intervention techniques can help this population better deal with their PTSD symptoms. Talking about problems in group settings can be therapeutic as long as precautions are taken to avoid challenges to confidentiality. Earlier treatment methods suggested group therapy as a means of improving self-esteem but research generally does not show that this approach is as effective as is cognitive behavioral treatment. Teaching juveniles problem-solving techniques, relaxation training techniques, and ways to cognitively restructure negative thoughts can help reduce the impulsivity and acting-out that get these youth into more difficulties. Most successful juvenile programs are direct and confront the youth with a step-by-step way to think through avoiding trouble and prevent relapses. An environment that stresses the positive strengths of these youth, rather than concentrating on their deficits, will teach them what is acceptable behavior, rather than focus, on what not to do in different situations. Adolescents need to associate with positive energy peers, as well as non-critical adults whom they respect. Fostering this kind of atmosphere will help keep youth out of further trouble.

SUMMARY

In summary, youth who are arrested and adjudicated as delinquent are sent into a special juvenile justice system to be rehabilitated unless their crime is adjudged to be so dangerous as to warrant being 'waived' into adult court. The history of how the juvenile justice system moved from being punitive to being rehabilitative and back now to a quasi-punitive and quasi-rehabilitation model is discussed in this chapter. Although the general public believes that adolescent crime is rampant, the statistics from the Office on Juvenile Justice make it clear that only a small percentage of crimes are committed by teenage youth. It is also important to recognize that only 20% of adolescents adjudicated as delinquent will go on to criminal behavior as adults. Girls tend to be arrested more for status crimes, which are those that an adult would not be arrested for, such as being truant or a runaway from home. The high number of teens adjudicated as delinquent who have been abused is alarmingly high and intervention programs must take into account PTSD symptoms, as well as other causes of crime.

16

School Violence

INTRODUCTION

Although the actual rate of serious youth violence appears to be decreasing, there are two types of violent behavior by teens that appear to be on the increase. First is the violence committed by girls, which is discussed in an earlier chapter. Second, are the mass killings that occur in or out of school by boys, sometimes acting alone and sometimes acting together with others. The shootings that occurred at Columbine High School in Englewood, Colorado in April 1999, described above, is a good example of how two teenage youth who committed such mayhem were able to escape detection and intervention by parents, school authorities, law enforcement, peers, and the community. It is difficult to understand how the massive amounts of ammunition, bombs, and even a video outlining violent plans, could not trigger concern on the part of adults who had to have known that this behavior is not normal for most teens. Only when we understand how to recognize both the clues our children give us and listen to what they actually tell us, will we be able to prevent these kinds of incidents from happening in the future. In this chapter we will examine the

Columbine High School

On April 20, 1999 at exactly 11:19 a.m. in the morning, two Columbine High School students, Eric Harris and Dylan Klebold began a 16-minute shooting rampage that left 15 people including themselves dead and 21 wounded. Two 20-pound propane bombs that Harris and Klebold are believed to have put in the cafeteria that morning could have killed all 488 students and teachers who were there had it detonated as it was supposed to have done. The Littleton, Colorado shooting was the worst incident of school violence in the history of the United States; far worse than Kip Kinkel's killing his parents and two students and wounding 25 others at Thurston High School in Springfield, Oregon one year earlier in May 1998. Or, the shooting and killing of four students and one teacher and injuring 10 others by 13-year old Andrew Golden and 15-year old Mitchell Johnson at West Side Middle School in Jonesboro, Arkansas in March 1998. West Padukah, Kentucky, Santee, California—these are all cities or towns where nice middle-class people live. Had urban shootings finally come to suburbia, the media pundits wondered? "What has gone wrong with our youth?", is the question they all ask. Standard answers that included poor parenting, school difficulties, poverty, divorce, violence on television, mental illness, too much sex, too much spoiling . . . all were raised but the question still goes unanswered even though these two young men put out many messages that they were about to explode for at least one year prior to the 1999 killings. In fact, they had made a video for a class the previous semester that detailed the Columbine High shootings as well as even more violent plans afterwards. Their teachers corrected the video's technology but did nothing about the disturbing violent images they viewed in the content of the videos. Their parents have had to live through the tragedy of that day's violence and lawsuits filed against them for failure to properly supervise their children (there was enough ammunition and explosives found in one boy's garage to blow up the entire school).

The Columbine investigation took several years to complete with 4400 leads followed up by 80 investigators. The original response to the tragedy involved over 1000 first responders such as law enforcement, fire rescue, medical and psychological service providers, and clergy from nearby Denver and its surrounding suburbs. Filmmaker Michael Moore made a movie, *Bowling for Columbine* asking the same question; what could have led these two young men into committing such mayhem? All of the recent school shootings have been done by boys, most of whom have given signs that they were in deep emotional trouble. But, these signs were either missed by the adults who could have gotten them help ignored and treated as if they were not serious, or were recognized as desperate attempts to get help that was not available. The facts are clear—there are fewer and fewer mental health services for our youth, especially those that they can get to on their own or at a cost they can afford. The stories of all these boys suggest we could have prevented this needless violence with more attention to the psychological health of all students but especially boys. In this chapter we discuss ways for schools to recognize those students who are at highest risk to explode into violence and intervene to prevent it.

typical clues that we must look for and discuss some possible interventions to avoid further escalation of violent incidents.

The murders in Columbine High School are not the first school shooting events to come to our attention. However, the majority of prior attacks were in schools located in poor neighborhoods filled with minority youth who were expected to use violence in poor urban communities that are known for the inability to protect residents. People live there because economically they cannot afford decent housing or better schools for their children, not because they like the violence they are exposed to on a daily basis.

STATISTICS

Statistics tell us that mass murders in schools have increased from the period of 1992 to 1998 with 75% of the deaths caused by gunshot wounds. Less than 1% of children die from murder so these attacks are quite limited despite the high levels of publicity they receive and fear they instill in people. Non-fatal violence with bullying behavior and fights among peers are the most frequently reported incidents in school although teacher victimization is also being reported. Teachers report both threats and actual physical attacks towards themselves. The prototypical violent youth is a male who attends public, not private, schools. Interestingly, 75% of the attackers who do commit murder also threaten suicide which is an important clue to rate the seriousness of all the violence threats. The line between suicide and homicide is a very thin one and as we saw in the chapter that discussed police psychology, the skills needed in successful hostage negotiations are also important when working with someone who is determined to cause his own destruction and/or violence towards others.

Bullying behavior tends to be most commonly experienced at the elementary school level, with physical fighting increasing as the youth gets older. The recent shooters appear to have been both the victims and aggressors of bullying behavior at different times of their lives. Researchers suggest that the probability of a child becoming a victim of a threat of or injury from violence depends on whether or not weapons are available to the aggressor. Probabilities are stated in population-type statistics. An elementary school child has a 13 in 100,000 chance of becoming a victim of an injurious attack by other school child (ren), a middle school child has a 93 in 100,000 chance and a high school student has a 103 out of 100,000 chance. These rates increase in larger schools in urban areas.

CLASSIFICATION OF SCHOOL VIOLENCE

WHAT DO WE KNOW ABOUT THE DYNAMICS OF VIOLENCE

We know from our studies of different types of violent acts, that there are multiple pathways to the use of violence. Violence is generally organized, fixated, and focused behavior on a specific target. Violent actions almost always seem to legitimize violent problem solving. So if someone thinks about violence and comes up with a plan, it is more likely than not that they will carry it out. There is usually a sense of urgency or at least a specific time frame for violent actions. Sometimes this timetable makes no sense while other times it is critical to the success of the operation.

Kris Mohandie and the late Chris Hatcher, psychologists at the National Threat Assessment Center in California have done the major psychological studies on school violence in the U.S. They have divided the events into three classifications:

Type I Events include violence by a perpetrator who has no relationship in the school. An example of a Type I event would be the shooter at a Jewish Community Center preschool in the Los Angeles area.

Type II Events include violence by a perpetrator who is a service recipient or customer of the school. This can include parents or guardians, students, or someone who is related to either group. Columbine students and other youth who killed teachers and/or students in the school would be an example of this group.

Type III Events include violence by a perpetrator who has or had an employment relationship with the school. An example might be a school janitor who held a child hostage.

THREAT ASSESSMENT

According to Mohandie, there are definite warning signs that include verbal statements and threats, bizarre thoughts, physical and behavioral signs, and obsessions that those who committed school violence demonstrated before the shooting events. The FBI, National Threat Assessment Center and others suggest paying serious attention to the following warning signs:

Warning Signs — Verbal

- Direct and indirect threats
- Verbalizing a violent plan
- Recurrent suicide threats and statements
- Child expresses a wish to kill, a wish to be killed, or a wish to die.
- Threatens or brags about bringing a weapon to school
- Threatening or harassing phone calls or emails
- Hopeless statements
- Bragging about violent behavior or fantasies
- Excessive profanity in an inappropriate context
- Challenging or intimidating statements
- Name calling or abusive language

Warning Signs — Bizarre Thoughts

- Persecutory ideas with self as victim
- Paranoid ideation
- Delusions in general or specific delusional ideas
- Command hallucinations
- Grandiose delusions involving power, control and destruction
- Significantly deteriorating thought processes

Warning Signs — Physical and Behavioral

- Physical altercations with another person
- Frequent fights
- Inappropriate weapons use or possession
- Drawings or other creative outlets with persistent violent themes
- Attire associated with violence (camouflage fatigues, violent messages on t-shirts)
- Physically intimidates peers or young children
- Following or surveillance of target individuals
- Short fused, loss of emotional control
- Destruction of property
- Bullying or victim of bullying
- Deteriorating physical appearance
- Violent literature and hate group materials

- Inappropriate displays of emotion such as anger, hate, rage and depression
- Isolating and withdrawn behavior
- Signs or history of substance use, abuse or dependency
- Rebellion against school authority
- Identifiable violent tattoos

WARNING SIGNS—OBSESSIONS

- Self as a victim of a particular person
- Grudges and deep resentments
- Particular object of desire (unrequited love turned to hate, shame, rage etc)
- Perceived injustices, humiliation, and disrespect
- Thoughts of death and violence
- Narrow focus—belief there is no way out type or tunnel vision
- Immersion in aggression (themes are consistent)
- Sequence specific stimulation of repeated aggression ideology
- Publicized acts of violence
- Interest in historically violent figures (Hitler, Nazi literature)
- Violent music and other media
- Weapons of destruction
- Stalking (simple obsessional, love obsessional, and erotomania)

Experts agree that it will take more than just a few of these warning signs to trigger a further inquiry. But, it is important to recognize these signs when they appear in children or are reported by others. In the Columbine tragedy, it appears that police and other students had observed some of these warning signs at least one year before the massacre. Peers found the two youth to be unusual and weird, teachers had viewed the violent video they made for a class assignment and graded it for technological skill, ignoring its prescient violence, and others stayed away from them, isolating and ignoring their behavior. Apparently they had been stockpiling bombs and other explosive devices and weapons of destruction for a period of time before the incident, hiding them in one boy's family garage. It is difficult to know who knew what before the incident occurred because of the spate of civil lawsuits that have been filed against different players, each lawsuit insisting that their defendant's duty to warn and duty to protect were not met causing compensable injury and death to many. It is still too early to know how these lawsuits will fare. We may not ever know the outcome should the parties enter into confidential settlements.

STABILIZATION AND PREVENTION

Is it possible to prevent violence from erupting in youth who have a vested interest in disguising their anguish and thoughts of violence as well as in those who display at least some of the warning signs? Mohandie suggests that every school should put a school safety plan into effect, much like the protective plans that employers put into effect to try to prevent workplace violence or sexual harassment. A typical school safety plan is discussed below. In addition, it is important to assess school violence and other criminal acts in the school carefully and accurately. Too many school administrators try to bury violent incidents either by minimizing their significance or failing to report their occurrence to the district. It is difficult to create penalties and stick to them without the impetus from laws that regulate behavior.

Laws for Schools

In 1994 Congress passed the *Gun Free Schools Act* that mandated a minimum of a one-year expulsion from school for any youth bringing a gun to school. Federal funding such as money received under the *Elementary and Secondary Education Act (ESEA)* where Title IX and other funding originate from can be withdrawn if the school does not follow this policy. Some states have made it even more stringent, mandating immediate expulsion, not suspension for anyone with a gun in the school. The only exception to this strict policy on a federal level is if the youth has a disability that is related to his or her bringing the gun to school. If the youth meets the definition under the *Individuals with Disabilities Education Act of 1999 (IDEA)*, then an alternative program can be implemented. Obviously, students who are found to be mentally retarded or seriously emotionally disturbed would fit into the exception category.

How would someone know that a student has a gun or other weapon if he doesn't show it? The Fourth Amendment to the U.S. Constitution, dealing with search and seizure limitations makes it clear that a student's locker, school bag, or person cannot be searched without probable cause and proper search warrants being issued. Schools often bypass these legal necessities thinking they are simply not important and then they cannot make the legal case against a dangerous student, resulting in everyone being in jeopardy. The Fifth Amendment to the U.S. Constitution guarantees a student the right to remain silent and not incriminate himself. This is where the issue of whether a juvenile understands the Miranda rights that should be read to him and the inability of authorities to question a student without a parent or attorney present becomes central. While the student may waive the right to request the presence of a lawyer or a parent, it is important to demonstrate the youth's competence to waive these rights. Psychological methods for assessing Miranda and Competency issues were discussed in Chapter 15 on juvenile delinquency.

To complicate matters even further, the *Family Education Rights and Privacy Act* makes it clear that records of any discipline of a student issued by the school must be kept confidential. Each state has laws regulating the disclosure of information related to juveniles. Federal and state *Occupational Safety and Health Act* (OSHA) requirements mandate safe work environments with stiff fines issued for any violations. So, ignoring a threat of violence by a student could trigger an investigation of the possible lack of compliance with OSHA standards. At the same time, the school has a duty to a mentally ill or cognitively impaired youth under the IDEA or even the Americans with Disabilities Act. If the youth threatens or disrupts the safety of another student, it may trigger the threshold for a child abuse report to the local child protection agency or police.

Individual school districts should put campus safety regulations in place whether or not there is legislation mandating it. This should be done in conjunction with reviewing other local and educational codes for a safe entrance and departure from the school. School rules about discipline and any dress codes must be explicit and known to all the students. If there are known problems with gang membership in the community, it will also impact on the school culture. Only when all of these areas are understood, can new strategies and programs be put in place to carry out the school policies.

REVIEW SCHOOL WARNING SIGNS

Review all hiring, supervision, retention of personnel, wrongful termination and violations of student rights that might have occurred and be sure to take cautionary steps if found to be a problem. Let parents know that they may have civil liability for foreseeable youth violence (know or should have known is the usual standard) that they could have prevented. Areas of liability here might be awareness of the youth's access to guns or other weapons including those of mass destruction and failure to stop it, negligent supervision of a child (in some jurisdictions it is against the law to leave a child under twelve unsupervised), failure to get therapy or take some other action when aware of a youth's emotional problems and failure to notify others of the danger posed by a youth who is demonstrating a sufficient number of warning signs to be of concern. Schools may also have liability if they report danger inappropriately. If students or employees fail to readjust after a school violence incident has occurred and the school did not provide any services to help the readjustment, there may also be some civil liability. Administrators must walk a very fine line between preventing a violent incident and avoiding liability.

WHEN TO USE CIVIL COMMITMENT LAWS

If it is decided that the risk of violence is too high for everyone's comfort, there are a number of things that a school psychologist or other mental health professional can begin to do. First, civil commitment laws can be used by the school in order to meet its duty to prevent harm to those in the school. Youth can be involuntarily hospitalized by the school or parents who go to the Court to get the youth declared mentally ill and dangerous to himself and others. Secondly, school and family stabilizers can be recommended and help in implementing them will lessen liability issues should they arise later if unsuccessful.

STABILIZERS

The school is an organization that has its own culture that can be utilized as a stable influence on minimizing the risk of violence on its campus. It is important to provide assurances of safety to students so that they know that everything is being done to protect them and prevent violence from occurring. This may include the presence of campus safety officers (usually unarmed) who are visible to students although there are some who believe that the physical presence of such officers are viewed as a challenge to some violent youth. Some urban schools use trained off-duty police officers as safety guards while others prefer to have officers with less of a law enforcement profile.

Many schools have set clear rules and boundaries including no weapon rules. As was mentioned previously, it is important to follow up and hold students responsible for obeying the rules or they will not have the meaning that is intended. For example, if there is a mandatory dress code then those students who do not follow the dress code, for whatever reason, must change their clothes or cannot attend class. Resources need to be available for all to access in the school. For example, if lighting in the building is dimmed because of financial reasons, all students, staff and faculty will not feel safe. Most important, there needs to be a cultural attitude that makes it easy for students, staff and faculty to talk to each other about disturbing signs that something is not okay. Fear of consequences of bringing up the topic must be alleviated and students must actually be encouraged to talk about the classmates whose behavior or conversation frightens them. School guidance counselors and school psychologists often can keep such information confidential unless they gain knowledge of specific threats against specific people. At that point, the community police must be brought in if this has not been done earlier.

In addition to school stabilizers, there are also steps that families can take to reduce the likelihood that a member would become involved in violent crime, although it is clear that most of the teenage shooters did not label their behavior as criminal. Rather, they saw it as justified, a way to teach people who had hurt them. Family stabilizers include trying to help the family behave in more responsible and less dysfunctional modes of behavior. This may be less obvious in intact families than in those where parents do not live together. Presence of step parents in the home can be destabilizing although in some homes, the presence of a strong male figure that is not punitive may be helpful in setting boundaries and following rules. It is important to get the family caregivers to become involved, notice problems, and demonstrate positive rather than punitive interest in the youth. Often violent youth come from homes where harsh punishment was the discipline utilized and there were no other effective coping strategies to be modeled. Corrective methods for youth with problems in controlling their violent behavior often are multidetermined and a variety of resources are necessary for its success. Families need support while trying to assist the identified youth in controlling his hostile feelings and aggressive impulses. School personnel who take the extra step to assist families in following through with referrals often find that they are more likely to utilize and benefit from other services.

HATCHER/MOHANDIE RISK INVESTIGATION MODEL

THREAT ASSESSMENT TEAMS

One of the new models for prevention of school violence is for a school to create its own Threat Assessment Team (TAT) and give support including investigatory powers to its members. Members on the TAT are usually multidisciplinary and include the principal and other administrators, teachers, mental health consultants, and security and legal representatives, together with student representatives. The size of the TAT varies according to the size of the school. In large school districts, there may be a school-wide team that meets on a regular basis with the in-school team members. In smaller schools, the individual teams may be small but meet with a larger system-wide group regularly.

The TAT members become first responders in the school, convening as soon as safety concerns arise. The TAT team is responsible for disseminating accurate information to administrators, staff, faculty, and students when safety concerns arise, attempting to keep everyone calm and well informed. TAT teams also develop a school-wide anti-violence campaign that advertises the school's policies including 'zero tolerance for violence' while still encouraging students and teachers to make reports when there is suspicion that a student is having some difficulties with some of the earlier mentioned warning signs. These teams must have the support of the school administration so that there is a clear policy about who makes decisions, what the policy is regarding the making and documentation of reports.

RISK INVESTIGATION MODEL

Hatcher and Mohandie suggest that when a report is made and investigated there are five different categories in which it can be placed.

1. *High violence potential.* This qualifies *for immediate hospitalization or arrest of the student.* There is an *imminent risk of harm* to someone in a category 1 incident.
2. *High violence potential but it does not qualify for immediate hospitalization or arrest of the student.* However some immediate action must be taken. There is a *high risk for harm* in a category 2 incident and there are enough warning signs to require other services.
3. *Insufficient evidence of violence potential but with evidence of repetitive and intentional emotional distress.* There is a *moderate risk for harm* in a category 3 incident and some stabilizing factors need to be instituted immediately.
4. *Insufficient evidence of violence potential but there is evidence of unintentional emotional distress.* There is a *minor risk for harm* with a category 4 classified incident but there is some insensitivity and some warning signs so stabilizing efforts should be started.

5. *Insufficient evidence of violence potential and insufficient evidence of emotional distress.* There is *low or no risk of harm* in a category 5 incident that appears to be misunderstandings, peer trouble and poor judgment.

POSSIBLE FALSE REPORTS

Although only small in number, there may be false reports of incidents that do not have any further violence risk. These reports often can be identified. Some of the reasons for them include: bragging or talking about false claims to make themselves look 'tough', wanting attention, revenge, reconciliation, or even an alibi for an otherwise embarrassing event. These reports may be identified by inconclusive or inconsistent forensic evidence, stories with conflicting statements or even preposterous or outrageous stories. Sometimes the victim doesn't behave as expected and often there is a big drama in the retelling. There may also be a history of misperception of events or even outright lying that requires careful scrutiny. In many of these cases there is an intuitive or 'gut' feeling that something is not true or at least being grossly exaggerated. On the other hand, it is important not to dismiss a suspicious claim too quickly as many youth scenarios for violence appear to be improbable to adults who are not familiar with the fantasies of those who have been abused or exposed to abuse and violence.

WHAT IF WORKPLACE VIOLENCE IN THE SCHOOL IS THREATENED

The school is a workplace for many people and violence can be threatened and can occur by strangers who have no relationship with those in the school (random drive-by shootings, a police chase that ends up in the school parking lot, or a sex offender who impulsively wanders into the bathroom when he sees children on the playground. These events are random and cannot be predicted although precautions can be taken. Still they may cause emotional distress and psychological harm to those who work in the school as well as the children. Often, when we think about school violence, we do not think of the impact on school staff as we pay so much attention to the children. Violence can also be threatened or committed by those who have had an employment relationship with the school and are disgruntled—similar to what has received high publicity in post offices by dissatisfied employees.

Types of Workplace Violence

Workplace violence may take different forms including threats, vandalism, equipment sabotage, and personal conflict with other employees. Threats often include angry letters (signed and anonymous), telephone calls and verbal arguments. Vandalism may occur in the school offices, in the building, in bathrooms, or in the parking lots. The most common equipment to be sabotaged are computers although this may also occur in schools that have expensive equipment for the vocational training programs. Fights with co-workers can escalate out of control especially if there are grudges held, romantic liaisons that are broken, or even unrequited love by those with what Dr. Reid Meloy calls, erotomanic obsessions, and delusions. Employees who have been fired, have had their jobs reclassified, have lost benefits, or were given negative performance evaluations may become so enraged that they commit serious violence towards the person(s) responsible. In some cases they have taken an office filled with workers hostage in order to retaliate for what they believe is unfair treatment. One of the most common types of workplace violence involves a perpetrator of domestic violence who stalks and comes looking for his partner and then shoots and kills her when he finds her at work. Homicides and suicides are not uncommon in these situations. Innocent workers or children can be injured in a school setting especially since there is so much movement in the building between classes in middle, junior high and high schools.

Workplace Preparation

Although it is not possible to predict an incident of violence in the school, it is possible to prepare a policy in the likelihood that it should occur. All employees should be trained to cope with threats. The suggested routine to cope with threats is to stay calm, maintain eye contact with the attacker, be courteous, get someone else to go for help using a prearranged signal, be patient while stalling for time, keep talking but do not risk harm to self or others—especially children—if they are present. If it is possible, get a witness on the extension when talking to someone who is making threats on the telephone. Keep the person talking by asking him to repeat the message and write it down. Try to listen for background noises or clues while getting more information such as where the person is calling from, how to return the call, etc.

It is also suggested that special plans be developed and implemented for high risk situations such as domestic violence. Many workers do not reveal that they are in a domestic violence relationship to co-workers but there are suspicions anyhow. Workplace policies that treat domestic violence as confidential as other medical or substance abuse problems often have advance warning that a batterer may be escalating violent behavior. As was described in the earlier chapter on syndromes, the most dangerous time for a batterer to stalk and kill a battered women is when they separate. If there is a specific crisis plan and a high alert occurs, all employees should have instructions not to disclose the woman's whereabouts or put telephone calls through to her. The TAT team or a designated employee safety leader should be notified immediately. Perhaps the woman's work schedule can be modified to avoid detection. Any crisis plan should be rehearsed and updated as needed.

WHAT IF SCHOOL VIOLENCE OCCURS

Crisis intervention plans as described in Chapter 8 are often the most useful intervention immediately after a violent incident has occurred in the school. Many different professionals are trained in using crisis intervention including those in the community called 'first responders' who are often police, fire workers, social workers, counselors, and other volunteers. The Red Cross, Sheriff's Departments and other community groups often advertise for volunteers when they conduct training programs. However, in addition to the outside assistance that may be available, it is important for the school officials and TAT members to debrief the staff and students.

DEBRIEFING

To debrief after an incident really means to control the information flow immediately to avoid rumors, inaccurate information being disseminated, or speculation that raises anxiety in those inside and outside of the school. Media usually are at the site of a violent incident immediately, sometimes even before the first responders get there! It is important to have a policy in place about who will speak to the media and what information can be released. This often must be coordinated with law enforcement so their investigation is not compromised. Obviously, the most important information is about the safety of the children and staff in the building. If there are injuries, information about where they are and their condition would also be important to release with warnings for non-relatives not to try to go to hospitals or where ever they are taken. Depending on the numbers of people impacted, it may be appropriate to set up a debriefing station in a place away from the school building. A designated spokesperson needs to provide updated and accurate information as it is available as well as responding to questions that arise. Obviously, that spokesperson should know what can and cannot be released to those inside the building and those outsiders who want and need information.

Return to Normal Quickly

It is important for all to return to the business of school as soon as possible after an incident. Work is therapeutic. So is going about one's daily business. Quick and thoughtful interventions can mitigate the traumatic stress reactions. Debriefings, informal discussions, individual support, and follow-up services all may need to continue for awhile after school is resumed. It may also be important to give extra support for those who were caregivers, as well as those who were victims to prevent secondary victimization that can occur when there is a major traumatic event. This may involve special groups to talk about the experience or individual counseling. The aftermath of a school violence incident may be long lasting, especially if there were significant injuries and deaths. Lawsuits that are filed by different parties will keep the traumatic memories alive and re-experiencing the trauma will occur if there is participation in depositions and trials. With good preparation and significant support services, the psychological impact from disaster incidents such as school violence, can be minimized even when they can't be prevented.

SUMMARY

In summary, the shocking reports of teens who bring guns and other weapons to school and go on a shooting spree have prompted research into the psychological signs and predispositions that these youth may have demonstrated before they explode with violent behavior. All of the recent spate of school violence incidents were committed by boys, not girls. All displayed some of the symptoms that have been categorized as verbal, physical and behavioral, bizarre thoughts, and obsessions. Most had paranoid disorders with delusions and PTSD and some also used alcohol and other drugs, perhaps as a way to treat their mental disorder symptoms. There are a number of new laws passed within the past ten years that guide schools as they restructure the safety within their buildings. No weapon policies are mandated now. Threat Assessment Teams and crisis intervention policies must be put into effect prior to experiencing an incident. Employees can also trigger a workplace violence problem at schools, which are also workplaces for them. It is important that other employees have had training to deal with any crisis or hostage situations that arise.

17

Legal Rights of Children

WHAT LEGAL RIGHTS DO CHILDREN HAVE?

Historically, children were considered the property of their fathers and had no legal rights themselves. All decisions that affected their lives were made by their fathers. All earnings they might have, belonged to their fathers. If they needed discipline, then it was the fathers' responsibility and corporal punishment was allowed. These rights were accorded to the father, under the law, using the same philosophical belief that we discussed in the earlier chapters on marriage and families: parents will act in the best interests of their child. However, as we saw in the chapter on protecting abused family members, this does not always happen. Despite the Ninth Amendment to the U.S. Constitution that recognizes certain basic personal rights for everyone, the law has always tolerated a certain amount of physical discipline and abuse from parent to child. It was not until the early 1970's that corporal punishment of a child was outlawed in the U.S. except what is regulated in schools and at home, and criminal statutes against family violence were not enforced until the mid 1980's. In many countries around the world, children still do not have the right not to be abused by a parent.

The social milieu today is more permissive towards children's rights to express feelings, thoughts, needs, and their opinions in families than it was before World War II. This milieu has resulted in a modification of the law towards giving children more legal rights. Despite the state's reluctance to make decisions against what parents want for their children, there has been a steady increase in the legal rights being accorded to children.

Let's take a look at a 1904 case called *Rule v. Geddes.* Here, a daughter requested a hearing before the court because her father demanded that she be sent to reform school. In this case the Court opined that she had no right to control her own actions or select her own course in life and refused to acknowledge her request for a formal hearing. Courts continued to permit parents to make decisions impacting their minor children's rights until quite recently. For example, in another case, *Katz v. U.S. (1967)*, the Court reaffirmed the personal privacy of a parent except in what they called 'dire' circumstances. But, by 1971, in *Gibson v. Gibson*, a California Court struck down the doctrine of 'parental immunity' and substituted the 'reasonable prudent parent' standard to be used to decide if a parent's decision about a child was appropriate. As cases appeared that challenged the age and standards by which a child could be considered competent to testify, the presumption that no child was competent was changed to all children are competent unless they don't know what is happening in the courtroom, cannot recite the facts of what happened to them, or do not know the consequences of taking an oath (or can't tell the difference between truth and fantasy). In most jurisdictions, the child may be protected from testifying if a mental health expert testifies that he or she would be harmed by the experience or 'medically unavailable' in some laws.

CHILDREN'S PRESENCE IN THE COURTS

Granting children legal rights remains a controversial area today with some psychologists and jurists believing that doing so will destroy the family. Others believe that it is necessary to give children the legal right to contest decisions that will harm them as protection against child abuse. Still others believe that criminalizing child abuse laws that permit children to testify against a parent is particularly destructive to the family unit. Others believe that it is the abuse itself that is destructive to both the child and the family unit. Obviously, there is not an easy answer to this issue.

In the 1990's, a movement towards greater empowerment of children and a change in focus to children's rights and needs became an important reform in all areas of the legal system including divorce, child welfare, delinquency, and criminal cases. However, the acceptance of what types of rights and when they can be granted is still not settled. Legal case decisions such as *in re Gault (1967)* gave juveniles more rights in delinquency courts, *Craig v. MD (1990)* permitted special arrangements in the courtroom for reliability of children's testimony, and guardians-ad-litems (GAL) and children's attorneys were given standing in cases involving minors other cases. However, other cases such as *Bellotti v. Baird (1979)* and *Parham v. J.R. (1979)* suggested that adolescents had fewer legal rights than did adults primarily because they were less competent to make informed judgments about many decisions especially those involving medical treatment. We saw in Chapter 14 on Reproductive Rights how many states were willing to exercise their special powers over adolescent girls by refusing to permit them to decide whether or not to obtain an abortion without a parent's or judge's consent.

Lawsuits that involved children became popular in a number of different areas including disputes over property, family business controversies, disagreements over inheritances, disputes over child support, assault and battery cases involving damages from incest and abuse, kidnapping and deprogramming from cults, children suing to divorce their parents or terminate parental rights, and cases involving injuries sustained where parents may be covered by insurance (such as car accidents). Let's look at a few of these areas.

Cases involving parents *who take children's property* and refuse to return it have received some publicity on the so-called 'reality television shows' recently. Can a child sue a parent for refusing to return property such as gifts given to the child or even property purchased by the child and left in the home when the child goes off to school? In some courts, when the child is emancipated (usually at age 18 but sometimes earlier depending on circumstances), he or she can file such a lawsuit. Rarely can it be filed when the child is still a minor unless it is a *dispute over child support* that is sent by one parent for the child but spent by the other parent. Those who favor a more therapeutic and healing role for the courts believe that this type of a lawsuit should be settled in mediation. However, the belief that the parents always make the right decisions for their children is simply a myth as we have shown in families where mental illness, other incapacity or abuse is prevalent.

Family business controversies carry this illusion even further. Historically, the oldest male inherited the father's property including the businesses. Today most families share their wealth equally. But, what if one child is better at running the business than the others? What if the father and the other children do not get along? Or, the father doesn't like the child who could keep the family business profitable? Generally fought out in family court, unless a parent dies and children take the battle to probate court, arguments about who inherits the family business may cause even further dissension among family members. *Challenges to inheritances* by one child against one or more other children, or a subsequent wife may also be resolved in court rather than within the family.

Cases in criminal court often involve a parent who is accused of abusing a child, usually sexual abuse. Several of the cases cited above are in relation to the issues raised by child abuse cases. Usually the child is represented by his or her own attorney who has responsibility only to the child or by the Court's appointment of a GAL who has more responsibility to look out for the best interests of the child and report to the Court. The issue raised by those opposed to minor children testifying against a parent is whether the child's testimony will render his or her role in the family as irreparable. This is especially difficult when the child's other parent is supporting the accused parent and not the child. Research on abused children generally finds that different types of relationships between the alleged abuser and the child may be established after the legal proceedings are over. Some studies have found that some sexually abused children are able to forgive their abusive fathers for their abusive acts before they can forgive their mothers for 'failing to protect' them, even when they never told their mother what occurred. There has been little research to understand whether the parental bond is irretrievably broken when the child provides testimony in open court or what relationship a child and parent can have after that parent is sent to prison on the basis of the child's testimony. These are interesting areas that need to be studied.

Civil court personal injury cases may be filed by an emancipated child or adult against a parent for damages from child abuse. There is usually a statute of limitations about how long after the child becomes an adult that the lawsuit can be filed but this statute can be 'tolled'—the term for beginning to count the time period from the time that the person 'knows' that he or she was hurt and harmed by the parent's actions. It is not uncommon for adult children in their 30's to go into therapy, discover they have been harmed by the parent's abuse (in some rare cases, even gain total recall that the abuse occurred while in therapy) and file a lawsuit against the parent many years after the statute expired. However, proof that he or she didn't know that he or she was harmed, even if some aspects of the abuse were never repressed, may permit the lawsuit to stand.

Lawsuits against therapists for 'implanting false memories' of abuse have been instituted with accused parents using information obtained from a group called the False Memory Syndrome Foundation as help in initiating these lawsuits. Interestingly, this organization was founded by two psychologists whose own daughter, also a noted psychologist, accused them of abusing her. Although the parents' denied the abuse, in fact, their daughter has publicly stated that she always remembered the abuse and thus, whatever arguments about memory that were raised by this group should not be applied to her.

Jennifer Freyd has written extensively on the betrayal that is experienced by an abused child that disrupts the parental relationship and extends to other relationships also. The issue of recovered memories has been a controversial one in psychology and will not be discussed in depth here. However, it is important to understand that human memories can be stored in the cortex or cognitive area of the brain or in the midbrain structures such as the thalamus, hypothalamus, and amygdala within the emotional areas of the brain. As they are easier to retrieve when processed and stored in the cortex, we know more about them but newer research on emotional memories and emotional intelligence have helped understand the clinicians argument about trauma and abuse memories.

The case of *Ramona*, a California case that was heard in the 1990's put therapists on notice that improper assessment or treatment methods could cause a client to develop a memory of abuse that had not occurred. In this case, the client, *Ramona*, had been given sodium pentothal and supposedly remembered an incident where her father sexually abused her. The father did have a known history of inappropriate sexual behavior that came out during the trials. She confronted her father who filed a lawsuit against the therapist and psychiatrist who gave her the sodium pentothal for implanting false memories. Ramona denied that the memories were false and did not join in the lawsuit. There were several novel legal issues that this lawsuit raised. The most important one was whether the father had standing in the court to file a lawsuit against his daughter's therapists. The court ruled that he was an interested party since the therapist had a joint session with the father and his daughter and permitted the lawsuit to go forward. Eventually, the father prevailed which frightened therapists who worked in this area.

Another area that further clarified the legal rights of children occurred when *children who joined a cult* tried to sue parents for hiring detectives to find, kidnap, and deprogram their children who were living in a cult or cult-like group. These cults and pseudo-religious groups were popular from the 1960's to the 1980's. They used brainwashing techniques to get youth to join and stay with them. These brainwashing techniques included repeated lectures, immersion in a new culture, isolation in retreats, and concepts such as 'heavenly deception' and 'love bombing' to persuade members to engage in risk-taking activities. When several of these charismatic cult leaders led their followers to commit suicide, many parents got worried and hired these deprogrammers who reverse-brainwashed them into their families of origin. Interestingly, some adult children went right back to the cult and sued their parents for breaching their privacy rights and freedom of religion. The lawsuits had mixed results. Kaslow, who has been studying the impact of cults on families found three common areas of vulnerability for a child to join a cult: 1) there was an external locus of control and a ready submission to authority figures; 2) there was a prior weakness in their relationship with their own father; and 3) something emotional or spiritual was missing from the family of origin.

Children suing a parent for divorce or termination of parental rights. It was unheard of for a child to obtain legal standing in the court to sue a parent for divorce or termination until the Florida case of *Gregory K* that occurred in 1992. Gregory K was an 11-year-old foster child who was under the care of the state having been placed there voluntarily by his mother who could not care for him. He hired his own attorney and sued his birth parents for divorce demanding his constitutional and other legal rights in order to be adopted by his foster parents. Evidence suggested that the child had never formed an attachment to his birth parents. His mother had substance abuse problems and originally placed Gregory and his siblings in the custody of the state child protection agency (CPS) foster care voluntarily. She rarely visited him and one time she took him home to live with her for several months but again placed him back with CPS who returned him to his foster family.

In 1991, the court ordered termination of his mother's and father's parental rights and his foster family made plans to adopt him. Six weeks later, the court reversed itself and CPS began reunification plans with his mother. Although the court had appointed a GAL to represent Gregory, this person never met with him during the two years in which the case was pending. Gregory hired his own lawyer and fought for standing in the court to present his case. The court entered an order that affirmed

Gregory's legal rights, stating that minors have the same rights as adults to due process; equal protection; privacy; access to the courts; and the right to defend life, liberty, and pursue happiness.

Although the appellate courts later reversed the trial court's decision, recent cases suggest that the law may well be moving in the direction of giving children greater legal rights even to choose new parents when the old ones are inadequate. *Gregory K* set an important precedent that raises some important questions. Do children have the same legal rights as do adults? Will the granting of legal rights to children destroy the family as we know it or will it strengthen it? Obviously, families that do not fulfill their responsibilities to their children and meet whatever threshold the state sets for its interference already can lose their rights to privacy under the child abuse laws as we saw in Chapter 13. But, what about non-abusive parents like Gregory K's mother who placed him in the state's care because she knew she could not care for him properly? Do Gregory K's rights to have parents who can help him reach his full potential take precedence over his mother's rights to reunification with her son. Should reunification be the goal in these cases? Does reunification meet the legal standard of 'the best interests of the child'? Finally, can psychologists determine that a non-genetic parent will be better than the biological parent in promoting the best interests of the child?

Assessing Children's Competency

The issue of children's competency to testify in court has changed from the presumption that no minor is competent to the presumption that all children are competent. This means that a child can be compelled to testify whether voluntarily or not. The burden of proof is on the child to prove that he or she is not mentally competent by 1) establishing that the minor does not have the requisite cognitive abilities to understand the case and all of its consequences; 2) cannot behave appropriately in the courtroom; and 3) cannot tell the difference between fact and fantasy. These requirements are similar to those that the courts require in criminal cases as we discussed in Chapter 5.

Cognitive development of children has been studied by various psychologists over time with new theories expanding and replacing older ones, just as we would expect in science. One of the major theories about how children develop their abilities to think and solve problems was found in the ideas put forward by a French psychologist, Jean Piaget and his followers. Piaget conceptualized children's mental development as occurring in stages with the final stage of formal operations beginning at around 11 or 12 years old. Children in that formal operations stage were thought to be able to generate many solutions to a problem, think about each one, antic- ipate their consequences, and weigh each factor in coming to their conclu- sion. Surely a child who could reliably think in this way would meet even the most stringent legal test for competency. However, most researchers found that there was a significant difference between the cognitive abili- ties of younger adolescents and those who were 16 or older with the older cohort being more likely to think in a manner more similar to adults than the younger ones. The issue is whether the younger adolescents are legally competent also.

Newer child development researchers suggest that adolescents are more variable in their capability to make cognitive judgments similar to adults, as skill development occurs continuously, rather than in stages, such as suggested by Piaget. Nonetheless, the research seems quite clear that in most areas of decision-making, adolescents are capable of using salient knowledge and applying good reasoning skills to reach a judgment. Ob- viously, when under stress, it is probable that adolescents may be subject to influences from their own emotions and pressures from others includ- ing parents. But, isn't this true for adults also? We all make better, more thoughtful decisions when we are not under extreme emotional stress.

The courts are still inconsistent about what level of cognitive ability is needed to make what kinds of decisions. For example, in child abuse cases, children as young as 3 to 5 years old are presumed competent to tes- tify about some issues but not competent to testify about where they want to live if the abusive parents divorce. Adolescents are considered compe- tent to be granted medical authority over their health issues including the right to choose their own psychotherapist, but cannot make the decision of whether to have an abortion. A pregnant adolescent has the right to marry without parental permission in some states. We grant adolescents the right to drive a car at the age of 16 in many places even though a car can be used as a deadly weapon. Recently, the trend in criminal courts has been to waive minors who commit serious crimes into adult court rather than remaining in juvenile court, based on the premise that if they commit an adult crime, they should be judged and punished as an adult.

Cognitive Competency and Execution

The issue of whether or not to execute a juvenile who is convicted of a capital crime in adult court has been of interest to the U.S. Supreme

Court in several important cases. The leading case, *Thompson v. OK* (1989), resulted in an opinion that the state could not execute an individual who was younger than 16 years old at the time of the crime. This was based on the U.S. Supreme Court's reasoning that a juvenile had limited intellectual and moral development. Thus, the juvenile should not be regarded as blameworthy as an adult. Interestingly, at the same time that *Thompson* was heard, another case was before the U.S. Supreme Court dealing with the same issue but in a mentally retarded defendant rather than a juvenile. In this Texas case, *Penry v. Lynaugh* (1989), the defendant was found to be mentally retarded at the time of the crime which of course implies that he did not have the same intellectual and moral development of an adult. In *Penry*, the Court did not ban execution of mentally retarded defendants per se but did indicate that a state must consider mental retardation as a mitigating factor. However, Texas did not have any mitigators specified in the instructions to the jury although it did list three aggravators that it considered to be special issues: 1) whether the criminal act was deliberate; 2) whether the defendant would be violent in the future; and 3) whether the defendant's criminal behavior was unreasonable in response to the provocation.

The U.S. Supreme Court sent *Penry* back to Texas with the instruction to consider mental retardation as a mitigating factor. As we discussed in Chapter 7, juries must consider both mitigators and aggravators before sentencing a defendant to death. In the retrial of *Penry*, the jury instructions remained the same, but the judge did admonish the jury to "give effect to the mitigating evidence". Penry was convicted a second time and again the case went back to the U.S. Supreme Court in 2002. By this time, 13 years later, 18 other states had banned the execution of people with mental retardation and the U.S. Supreme Court decided to reconsider the issue with two other cases, *McCarver v. North Carolina* and *Atkins v. Virginia*. While the McCarver case was pending the state of North Carolina passed a law banning such executions. Using the *Atkins* case the U.S. Supreme Court considered whether there was an emerging national consensus against the execution of a mentally retarded defendant and in 2002 found such a consensus existed and ruled that it was unconstitutional to execute the mentally retarded.

WAIVER INTO ADULT COURT

The headlines screamed from the newsstands as I (LW) walked into the courthouse that morning, "nine-year-old girl shoots brother while fighting over a Nintendo game". I was asked to go to the juvenile detention center to see

Tiesha as soon as I arrived. When I got there, I found a tiny scared nine-year-old with neat pigtails who was wearing a sweat suit that was at least three times as big as she, was but it was all that they had to give her. She took out a crumbled piece of paper from inside her pocket that she said her lawyer gave her. On it was written the words, "I cannot speak to you without my lawyer". I explained that I was a psychologist who was sent by her lawyer and showed her my ID without much hope that she really believed me or even understood what a psychologist did. Together we called her parents (who expected the call) and they told her it was all right if she talked with me since they couldn't be with her. They were at her $2^1/_2$ year-old-brother's bedside in the nearby hospital where he was recovering from the gunshot wound that luckily just grazed his head and left a surface wound.

Tiesha told me that she and her brother were not fighting over the Nintendo game, but rather they were playing cooperatively until he noticed the box where the gun was kept sticking out from under the dresser. Curious as one might expect a two-year-old to be, her brother took the box out and they both saw the gun when it was opened. Tiesha, who had seen her Dad teaching her older brothers how to shoot, wanted a closer look, and picked it up. She didn't know what happened to make the gun go off but it did and her brother lay on the floor crying and bleeding. Tiesha called for help immediately. It was clear from my interview with this child that she was not a tough street kid, but rather a curious young girl who should not have been left alone with a two-year-old, nor should a loaded gun have been left in the house.

I then went to the hospital to interview the brother and parents as requested by Tiesha's attorney. Her brother was doing well and was able to support what Tiesha had told me. Tiesha and he didn't fight. They both were looking at the gun together.

Lesson #1—Do not believe sensational media headlines too quickly!

The parents told of having recently moved into the neighborhood, wanting the children to feel safer than in their old neighborhood where crime was rampant. They were both working in order to support their family. The mother had left for her night job and the father left the children alone for a short time to help a neighbor fix the car. He thought older children were also at home and could watch Tiesha and her brother. He insisted that he didn't know that the gun had been removed from the closet where he kept it hidden.

Lesson #2—good intentions can be damaged by a lapse in judgment.

In other words, in trying to improve their economic and social situation and bring better safety to their family, the parents neglected to protect the children adequately for that split second when a tragedy could have occurred.

Was this a criminal case that deserved prosecution? In Florida, the prosecutor has the legal right to waive a case where one youth shoots someone with a gun into adult court without a transfer hearing. Fortunately, the prosecutor used his judgment and did not do so. This was a case that appeared to be able to benefit from rehabilitation, not punishment. Based on the psychological evaluation, done immediately after the incident with a child-centered interview technique that avoided getting stuck with an inaccurate version of the incident, the child's lawyer was able to successfully argue dismissal of the criminal case. Arrested for a crime, this nine-year-old had the same legal procedural rights as did an adult as the U.S. Supreme Court determined in 1967 *in re Gault*. The two-year-old victim had the same rights as would be accorded an adult victim of a similar crime. Even so, when the criminal case was dismissed, the state referred the family to the state agency responsible for protecting children and they put the family under their supervision for several months to make sure all the children were properly protected.

Cases where the crime committed by a juvenile resulted in someone's death usually get handled differently by prosecutors. As we described above, since the *Thompson* decision, the law now forbids the execution of juveniles under the age of 16. But there is a growing trend for these juveniles to be tried as adults and sentenced to life in prison with other adult offenders rather than seeking a plan for possible rehabilitation. We described the case of Tim in Chapter 15 who was both under the age of 16 and mentally retarded, yet he was tried and convicted of first degree murder and sentenced to adult prison for the rest of his life for a crime he steadfastly denies ever committing. We know that this has happened with other individuals that attorney Barry Scheck and his Innocence Project have freed from prison with newly analyzed DNA evidence proving their innocence.

WAIVER OF JUVENILES INTO ADULT COURT

There are three major ways that youth may be diverted from the juvenile system: dismissal of the charges if already charged, civil commitment to psychiatric care, and automatic waiver to adult criminal court. In most states, a hearing to waive a juvenile into criminal court may be requested for certain serious crimes usually if the youth is over 14 years old. In some states, such as Oregon, the law permits youth under the age of 14 to also be transferred to adult court if certain criteria specified in the law are met. Florida, interestingly, has no requirement for a hearing. Rather, any youth can be charged with a serious crime by the prosecutor. Neither the judge or defense attorneys can present evidence to persuade otherwise. Judges in adult court are permitted to take the youth's age into account, but they are not required to do so.

Two recent cases have attracted national attention to Florida in this area: Broward County's Lionel Tate who admitted killing the six-year-old girl whom his mother was babysitting by wrestling with her when he was 12 years old and Nathaniel Brazil, the 14-year-old West Palm Beach youth who shot and killed his middle school teacher after being sent home from school. Both were featured in the media and both prosecutors immediately waived them into adult court for adjudication. Tate's mother turned down a three-year sentence offered in a plea agreement before the trial and he was convicted and sentenced to spend the rest of his life in prison. The legal arguments have dealt with the contradiction here: how can he be considered cognitively capable of using adult-like reasoning to commit a crime, but not cognitively capable of making a decision to accept a plea different from his mother's decision? Brazil was found guilty of manslaughter and received a much lighter sentence than would an adult. Why the differences? One reason might have been the discrepant opinions offered by psychologists on the witness stand about the mental competency at different developmental ages. Another possible reason might have been Tate's behavior—he had a long history of aggressive behavior and was noted to be a violent and disturbed child at an early age. We may never know for sure but these two cases point up both the difficulties in assessing and evaluating juvenile's intellectual and cognitive abilities and moral development and the utilization of these evaluations in the search for justice.

EMPOWERMENT OF CHILDREN

Psychological studies of youth who have been arrested for delinquency indicate that they have many needs that are not being met by either parents or the child protection system. Areas that have been found to be predictors of youth crime include teen pregnancy, family abuse, school problems, poor peer relationships, and violent community lifestyles. Once a youth is arrested and held in a juvenile detention facility, it is important to assess for these factors and begin interventions that will give the juvenile more power over his or her own life. How can a juvenile who does not have full civil rights be empowered legally? This was an interesting question for a new experimental program that is funded by the Legal Aid Foundation and being implemented in Broward County, Florida as well as several other communities.

TeamChild

Broward County Legal Aid, Nova Southeastern University Center for Psychological Studies and the Broward County Public Defenders' Juvenile Division have been involved in a project called TeamChild to identify and offer legal assistance to girls who have been arrested for delinquency or status crimes. Girls were selected because there were reports that their arrests were increasing in numbers and in the seriousness of their charges. The goal of the program was for each girl who participated to be assigned an attorney who could assess for and educate the girl about her legal and civil rights and represent her in court to obtain them. The legal aid attorney did not take the place of her criminal defense attorney and the two attorneys often worked cooperatively along with the case manager from the Office of Juvenile Justice. In the two years of the project, over 150 girls were represented by an attorney who helped stop the school neglect they faced, helped them get appropriate school placements, advocated for their medical and psychological needs, helped them get away from abusive parents even petitioning the court for emancipation in some cases, and taught them to use the courts to fight for their rights rather than battle it out on the streets.

> Janie was referred to TeamChild after her fourth arrest for running away and fighting with her teacher. Janie had a long history of school failures and although she was 13 years old and in 7th grade, she still couldn't read very well. The psychological screening found that she had been physically abused by her mother and sexually abused by several of her mother's boyfriends during her young life. Her family did not have many resources and when her eye glasses were broken in a fight, no one thought to get them replaced. The school failed to even notice that one reason for her poor performance in reading and other classwork was that she couldn't see without glasses! The juvenile courts failed to note the importance of protecting her from further abuse during her previous appearances. TeamChild got her accepted into a good residential school, got her health services through Medicaid, and managed to get her new glasses; Janie is on her way to a non-criminal lifestyle.

Not all cases are as relatively easy as Janie's. Nor do they all have such successful outcomes. But, teaching juveniles how to use the system to help themselves can prevent turning towards alcohol and other drugs for comfort. Calling a lawyer at night is better than getting into an argument that results in a violent encounter. Schools are more interested in juveniles who have someone advocating for them. It is better to have someone who will listen to a complaint about the unfair practices of a teacher and teach the child how to formalize the complaint if it is legitimate than to go home, become so emotionally distraught that he comes back to school with a gun and shoots the teacher as Nathaniel Brazil did. The girls that are part of the TeamChild program have become empowered. Their number of rearrests have dropped significantly. Their success stories have multiplied. A new program for boys who have been arrested based on the same empowerment model also has now been implemented. Again, the goal is to prevent these youth from turning to a life of crime by providing them with models about how to obtain their legal rights in a socially approved manner.

SUMMARY

In summary, the trend is towards giving children the same legal rights as are given to adults in criminal, juvenile, family, and other courts. There is still much controversy about the competency for children in different settings with their being waived up to adult court if they commit a crime while being forced to remain in family court to get permission to have an abortion. Children's moral development is explored with the conclusion that unless there is a serious mental illness or mental retardation, most children are competent to make thoughtful and intelligent decisions.

TABLE 17-1. CHILDREN'S LEGAL RIGHTS CASES

Rule v. Geddes (1904)	Court refused daughter's request for hearing and reaffirmed father's right to make decisions about her course in life.
Katz v. U.S. (1967)	Reaffirmed parents' right to privacy and doctrine of 'parental immunity' except in 'dire' circumstances
Gibson v. Gibson (1971) '	Reasonable prudent parent' standard to judge parental decisions
In re Gault (1967)	Gave juveniles due process and other legal rights
Craig v. MD (1990)	Permitted special arrangements in courtrooms to create reliable testimony from a child.
Bellotti v. Baird (1979)	Adolescents were less competent than adults
Parham v. J.R. (1979)	Adolescents were less competent than adults
In re Ramona	Case that lasted several years alleging therapists implanted memories in client's minds.
Gregory K	Child divorced his parents so he could be adopted by his foster parents.
Thompson v. OK (1989)	Cannot execute someone under 16 years old when crime was committed
Perry v. Lynaugh (1989)	Mental retardation must be considered as a mitigation factor in death penalty cases.
McCarver v. N.C.	State of N.C. banned executing people with mental retardation
Atkins v VA(2002)	U.S. Supreme Court banned execution of mentally retarded.

VI

Legal Consultation Based on Social Psychology

Social psychology or the study of how humans behave in groups provides the empirical research that provides the foundation for cases that deal with discrimination and civil rights, reliability and validity of eye-witness testimony, and jury selection and other trial consultation. Clinical psychology is also utilized in these cases, particularly when there are damages that arise from other people's discriminatory behavior. Deprivation of civil rights is a serious matter in a democracy and our laws provide a process for recognizing when it occurs and ways to redress the wrongs that are based on such discrimination. In this section, we look at the federal anti-discrimination laws, including those that address racial and sex discrimination and sexual harassment. In the federal law, it is only necessary to prove that a pattern of discrimination occurred as such behavior is already considered harmful. However, in some cases, the plaintiff chooses to quantify the damages which may also be useful if state discrimination charges are also pending. However, it is important to recognize that when psychological injuries are claimed, the plaintiff opens her or himself up to having their mental health in their whole life examined.

In determining the reliability of an eye witness whose testimony may well resolve a case either for or against the plaintiff or defendant, it is important to remember that research that is conducted in the experimenter's laboratory is presented and then generalized to the real world. Sometimes the findings are the same when both types of studies are completed, but sometimes they are not. The issue of how prejudice and other attitudes impact on what a person remembers is an important lesson in social psychology. This is also true for other lessons learned about how juries make decisions. The impact that different kinds of evidence has on an individual is profound and we give examples of how jury selection was the important trial strategies an attorney made in these trials. In addition, we also look at the various methods of studying community attitudes that might influence all members of the jury pool and how to handle situations where a person cannot get a jury of his or her own peers—the fundamental right of every citizen in a democracy such as ours. Using scientific methods such as focus groups, scientifically-crafted surveys, mock trials, shadow trials, and other trial consultation can help attorneys determine the way evidence should be presented to give their clients the best chance at being fairly judged.

18

Discrimination and Sexual Harassment

HOW DO WE KNOW IF DISCRIMINATION STILL EXISTS IN THE U.S.?

In 1991, an African-American man named Rodney King was stopped by four Los Angeles police officers and beaten mercilessly. Luckily for him, the beating was captured on a home video camera and subsequently played for the entire world to see his non-violent response to these police officers. Would he have been so seriously beaten if he had been White? Was he discriminated against by the Los Angeles police department and if so, was it a systematic policy or simply widespread discrimination of Blacks by police officers there? These were interesting questions that were put to the test by taking the case to the jury. The four officers were charged and prosecuted under the state law in a county that had mostly White people in the jury pool. They found the officers not guilty and riots broke out in downtown Los Angeles. Civil rights attorneys decided to take the case to Federal Court and they filed complaints against the police officers using the theory that they violated the constitutional rights of Rodney King by using uncalled for violence during their arrest. Although widely criticized for violating the police officer's rights against 'double jeopardy' or being tried twice for the same act, two of the officers were found guilty by a jury more racially reflective of the city of Los Angeles.

The 1994 trial of O.J. Simpson, as described later in Chapter 20 on Jury Selection, occurred after the Rodney King publicity and many suggest that the ease with which African-American jurors believed that Detective Furhman and his colleagues were racist had much to do with the climate of distrust created by the earlier Los Angeles trials. In fact, the then District Attorney, Gil Garcetti, stated that he filed the case against O.J. in downtown Los Angeles, rather than in suburban Santa Monica courts where Brentwood criminal cases were more typically filed precisely because he wanted to avoid the allegations of discrimination that followed the Rodney King affair.

Los Angeles is not the only city that needed to look at the existence of racial discrimination in its government and service workers. In February 1999, an immigrant to New York City from the African country of Guinea, Amadou Diallo, was shot and killed by four white police officers as he left his building in the Bronx to get something to eat. These plainclothes officers, searching for a serial rapist they believed to be in the neighborhood shot Diallo over 40 times. One year later, after the trial was moved to upstate Albany, NY where few immigrants live, the four officers were found not guilty as were the officers who beat up Rodney King on the other side of the country. At the same time, several New York City police officers were found guilty of brutalizing a Haitian immigrant, Abner Louima in the New York City courts with a jury composed of the racial mix found in NYC.

The question for psychology to answer is "Were these acts evidence of racial discrimination and if so, can it be proven using psychological research?"

WHAT DOES SOCIAL PSYCHOLOGY HAVE TO SAY ABOUT DISCRIMINATION?

Social psychology is the branch of psychology that studies the attitudes and thoughts that are motivation for the behavior of people in groups. So obviously, the study of discrimination is an area for social psychologists to study. People naturally put other people and things into categories so that they can better understand their world. 'Prejudice' is the internal feeling that ascribes attributes to people who belong to a particular group without having sufficient information about the entire group. People who are said to be prejudiced often use a bias that comes from using a few characteristics or membership in a particular group, to view everyone as the same if they belong to that group.

STEREOTYPES AND DISCRIMINATION

'Stereotypes' are the over-generalized attitudes that categorize a particular group. Prejudice, which is often said to influence the development of a stereotype that can create discrimination, is the internal attitude while 'discrimination' is the behavior that results. Prejudice can be a negative or positive bias although we usually focus on the negative ones when studying the effects of these attitudes on stereotypical and discriminatory behavior. Once a person is identified as part of a group it is more difficult for that person to be classified on the person's own unique characteristics. People expect members of a group to be more alike than different.

Overt and Covert Discrimination

When studying discrimination we look for both overt and covert negative behavior. Overt discrimination can include violence, aggression and hostility while covert discrimination can be patterns of withdrawal, isolation and avoidance of a particular class of people. 'Racism' is considered to be a form of discrimination where the behavior expresses hatred towards all members of the group. In the King and Diallo cases, it was said that the police used more force than necessary because of their internalized hatred of African Americans. Certain groups are more likely to experience discrimination than others because of the historically marginalized position in a particular society. In the U.S. the groups that are most likely to experience discrimination are by race, ethnicity, color, religion, national origin, gender, age, sexual orientation and those with physical and mental disability.

Sometimes these groups change with events of a major social magnitude. Arab Americans, for example, have claimed to feel prejudicial attitudes against them in the U.S., perhaps because their different customs and dress cause them to stand out. But, it was not until the terrorist events of September 11, 2001—led by members of the Al Quaeda, a terrorist organization with training camps all over the world preaching hatred of Americans, using the Muslim religion as an excuse—did the fear that

TABLE 18-1. COMMON RATIONALE FOR
DISCRIMINATION

1. Race, ethnicity, color, religion, or national origin
2. Gender
3. Sexual Orientation
4. Age
5. Psychological & Physical Disability

the prejudice would turn into hostile discriminatory acts surface as legitimate by non-Arabs. Reports that pilots and passengers refused to fly on airplanes together with suspicious Arab-looking passengers is an example of how these stereotyped attitudes can affect daily life. Detention of Arab-American citizens under the newly expanded war powers given by Congress in what is often referred to as the Patriot Act of 2001 is another example. The impact of a clash of different stereotyped attitudes was observed on television with Iraqi citizens demonstrating against American soldiers, calling them invaders, during the 2003 war in Iraq despite the American attitudes that they would be well received as they were rescuing the Iraqi people from a cruel dictator.

SEXISM AND SEX STEREOTYPING

'Sexism' or the application of prejudicial attitudes towards women because of their gender, is considered to be a similar process and includes behavior common to racism by social psychology and the civil rights laws. Psychological research on sex stereotyping indicates that they are not any more inaccurate than are other kinds of generalizations but nonetheless, they do lead to either intended or unintended discrimination against women which then leads to feelings of inferiority, low self-esteem, and difficulty in trying to function up to one's full potential in many areas such as education, social relationships, and business. As with racial prejudice, over-generalizations about gender are often either inaccurate or do not apply to an individual within a group. So, women are less likely to be seen for their own individual characteristics than if they are part of the group.

The expectations that are created when people are over-generalized into a group can lead to distorted judgments about that person and about the group as a whole. This faulty reasoning then leads to more biased feelings about individuals and then are applied to the entire group which further disadvantages them, not because of who they are or what they do but because of the group they belong to. People in the 'in-group' get

Box 18-1   CASE OF *HOPKINS V. PRICE WATERHOUSE*

Ann Hopkins was an account executive with Price Waterhouse, a large accounting firm with offices all over the United States. She worked in the Washington, D.C. office. She brought in over $400,000 worth of business to the firm, well over the expectations set for most of the male partners in the firm. To be eligible for senior status and a share in the company earnings, associates strive to become partners by doing the things required of them including working many long hours, servicing clients of the partners they are assigned to work for, and bringing in sufficient revenues and cases to build one's own group of clients. Law firms function in this manner as do most large national and international accounting firms.

Ann Hopkins brought a federal sexual discrimination lawsuit against Price Waterhouse when they passed over her and did not offer her partner status despite the fact that other men who completed exactly the same steps as she did but brought in even less business revenues were made partner. Luckily for her, at the partner meeting where her status as partner was discussed, one senior level partner's comments that she was too loud, pushy, and aggressive to become a partner and recommendations that she attend a 'charm school' for her 'finishing' were recorded. She was denied her partnership.

The American Psychological Association submitted an Amicus Brief in this case citing the work of social psychologists, particularly Susan Fiske, showing that sex role stereotyping behavior results in the discrimination that Ann Hopkins experienced. As a woman, she was expected to be demure, charming and passive while men who exhibited aggressive behavior were rewarded for it. The U.S. Supreme Court ruled in her favor and cited the influence of the social science data in their brief.

preferential treatment while those not in that group, do not. In work and in some fields in higher education, men are the 'in-group' and women are not. Therefore, men are more likely to get the benefits including promotions and plum appointments while women are less likely to do so.

Studies have been conducted on the attitudes and biases that men and women have about women in general and in the workplace particularly. These attributes are often based on typical behavior thought to be stereotypes of women. These sex role stereotypes have been found to cause discrimination against women. In particular, they are based on faulty descriptive beliefs about women and how closely women behave in this manner. The case of *Hopkins v. Price Waterhouse* is a good example of this process in operation.

Ann Hopkins had worked in a large accounting firm as described in Box 18-1. She was denied partner status after doing all the same things her male counterparts had accomplished. In her file were the remarks made by one partner who criticized her for her loud and aggressive verbal behavior. He suggested that she attend a 'charm school' before she apply for partner status and wrote down this recommendation and placed it in her file. The American Psychological Association (APA) submitted an Amicus brief in this case that apparently influenced the justices in their decision as it was cited in their final opinion that found in the favor of Ms. Hopkins. Psychologist Susan Fiske's research on sex role stereotypical processes was an important part of that brief.

ARE WOMEN DISCRIMINATED AGAINST FOR BEHAVIOR PRAISED IN MEN?

In an earlier 1972 study of attitudes towards the behaviors that lead to good mental health of men, women and people in general, Psychologist, Inge Braverman and her colleagues found that gender bias existed here too. They gave a list of adjectives that described women's and men's behavior and asked people to check off what behaviors were important to each group's mental health. Mentally healthy men were seen as having the same attributes as mentally health people but mentally healthy women were not. Like the senior partner in *Price Waterhouse*, this study demonstrated that mentally healthy women were expected to be passive rather than active, non-assertive, non-aggressive, more introspective and less physically strong than men or people in general. Obviously, this study underscored the bind for women—if they were seen as mentally healthy for women, they were not seen as a mentally healthy person. Lest we think that these attitudes have sufficiently changed to claim that gender discrimination is no longer operative or powerful, in 1985 Braverman reported at an APA meeting on a replication of her earlier study and the results were not very different. In fact, in a recent class project in 2003 in one author's (LW) Nova Southeastern University's graduate class in feminist therapy, the Braverman study was replicated with results that showed some liberalization of attitudes, but not as much as might be expected after 30 years of fighting for equal rights.

Research continues to confirm that non-feminine women are less popular and more poorly adjusted than are those who conform to the stereotype. Just like the data that show that people in the in-group get preferential treatment, women who behave according to expectations are preferred over women who do not. This may be a contributory reason to why women are less likely to do well in upper level managerial jobs than are men. Recent research published in the Harvard Law Review demonstrates that women who are part of the corporate culture can get ahead until they reach what is called the 'glass ceiling' where it appears that they should be promoted to the next level, but like Ann Hopkins, are passed over in favor of the man who may have the same characteristics needed for the job. However, in the woman, these characteristics are not viewed as gender-appropriate even if she would get the job done.

WOMEN AND MANAGEMENT STYLE

Other research shows a different type of discrimination in effect in some cases where women have a distinctly different managerial style that may be incompatible with the male-dominated corporate culture. Often described as horizontal or vertical management, women are less comfortable with the vertical, hierarchical, or authoritarian style and do better with a more egalitarian, inclusive, and high contact with people style of management. So, in a military or paramilitary (e.g., law enforcement) command, women in general might be less comfortable, especially in management positions. But, what about the individual woman who likes the hierarchical work environment and is as effective as a man in an upper management position there? Would she have the basis for a Title VII Sex Discrimination lawsuit here if she were passed over for promotion?

COMMON WORKSITES WHERE DISCRIMINATION EXISTS

There is research that has found that certain types of work environments do promote discrimination against women because of sex role stereotyping. The most important contributory condition here is where the group from which the individual comes is rarely found in the work setting. If less than 15% of the work force is female, the woman is considered to have 'solo status' and if there are fewer than 25% females in the pool from which they are to be selected, the less likely a woman will be preferentially selected. In most discrimination cases, the so-called 'tipping balance' is around one-third of the group. This percentage was actually set forth in cases that dealt with racial discrimination and the quality of education in the schools but has been found to apply in sex discrimination cases also.

Anti-Sex Harassment Policies and Interventions

Work environments can put forth certain policies to try to minimize the impact from any kind of discrimination. Not only would such actions place the company in a favorable position should an employee file a lawsuit

TABLE 18-2. POLICIES AGAINST DISCRIMINATION

Psychologists can consult with organizations to develop policies and procedures that
will discourage discrimination of marginalized groups such as:
1. Create heightened awareness about possibilities of overgeneralization.
2. Provide accurate information about groups likely to be discriminated.
3. Encourage self-examination and correction of biased attitudes.
4. Make it clear there is consensus for disapproval of prejudicial attitudes,
    statements and discriminatory behavior.
5. Give motivational incentives for collaboration including team projects that
    include members from groups where there is a high risk for discrimination.
6. Create a culture where each person's talents are displayed and necessary for
    successful completion of team programs.
7. Encourage specific performance criteria for evaluating job competency.
8. Use company newsletters and other media to educate all employees about the
    negative impact from discrimination of any kind.
9. Encourage anti-racism and anti-sexism company training programs.
10. Prepare company procedure manuals that stress no discrimination.

for discrimination, but it also makes good business sense. A list of these
policies can be found in Table 18-2.

Companies can recognize the natural tendency for people to categorize and the subsequent links that occur between such categorization and
bias. Of course, it is important to openly discourage any kind of bias in the
workplace. People often can resist that link between categorization, prejudice and stereotypy by gaining more information about people who are
different from them. They are then more likely to correct their errors. Motivational incentives that support increased attention to the problem and
consensual disapproval of stereotyping and discriminatory behavior can
also be instituted. An example of this occurred when President Bush used
the media to urge Americans not to give in to the temptation to stereotype
all Muslim Arabs in the United States after the attacks on the World Trade
Center and Pentagon on '9-11'.

Encouraging teamwork to solve problems with people from different
groups may be important over the independent work atmosphere. Creating
a culture of 'interdependence' in which people have different competencies
to create the whole project is another way to encourage getting to know
the individual talents of people. The more objective and well defined the
criteria for judging the efficacy of a person's efforts, the less likely performance will be misjudged because of distorted attributions. More information rather than limited, ambiguous, performance criteria are important
here.

MEN AND WOMEN'S ATTITUDES TOWARDS HARASSMENT

Sexual harassment is considered a form of sexual or gender discrimination. Sexual harassment is similar to other forms of violence against women in that it is usually committed by men who abuse the power they have over women in order to control the women. The general public gained a greater awareness of sexual harassment in 1991 during the Senate confirmation hearings for U.S. Supreme Court Justice Clarence Thomas. His former staff member, attorney Anita Hill, testified about unwanted sexual advances that her then supervisor Thomas made towards her. She did not report his behavior nor did it stop her from following him to the EEOC when he was offered that position. In fact, she did not come forward to offer the testimony herself; it was discovered while Thomas was being investigated for the position on the Supreme Court.

Interestingly, women were far more likely than men to believe that Hill's testimony was credible and had a ring of truth to it despite Thomas' denials. Opinion polls taken by several reputable social science research organizations found that close to 90% of women surveyed at that time had observed or experienced unwanted sexually harassing attention in school or at their workplace while less than 1% of men surveyed either had the same experiences as women described or defined similar behaviors as either unwanted or harassing. Although Justice Thomas was eventually confirmed, Hill's testimony may well be considered a watershed for recognition of sexual harassment. Indeed, the following year, Congress passed legislation strengthening the issue of sexual harassment being a violation of women's civil rights and added more penalties to the sexual harassment actions under the Civil Rights Title VII Act making it easier for women to bring lawsuits into Federal court to seek remedies.

PSYCHOLOGICAL IMPACT FROM SEXUAL HARASSMENT

The impact of the experience of sexual harassment on the victim, unlike that of most other forms of abuse, seems to have wide variation, with the most overt and egregious misconduct having, predictably, the most negative effects. Often the victim never tells anyone; sometimes she is able to talk about what happened many years later, especially if others have also accused the man. It is not clear why some women appear to have less psychological distress on exposure to behavior that seriously traumatizes other women. Some women and most men still do not take most forms of sexual harassment seriously. Often the victim is blamed for seductive behavior or past problems when she reacts with major psychological stress, although there is more understanding when the most egregious forms of sexual touching occur. In fact, difficulties in defining what behaviors constitute sexual harassment has been a problem in recognizing its negative effects in those who present for clinical treatment, as well as in conducting empirically based research.

SEXUAL HARASSMENT LAWSUITS

Under Title VII of the Federal Civil Rights Act of 1964 (42 U.S.S.C. 2000 3), it is possible to file a sexual harassment lawsuit if first the harassment is reported to the company's Equal Employment Opportunity officer so that the company has an opportunity to investigate and make substantial changes to remedy the situation. If that is insufficient, then the employee has the opportunity to file a complaint with the U.S. Equal Employment Opportunity Commission (EEOC) requesting that they investigate and obtain remedies. If that fails, then the EEOC issues what is called a 'right-to-sue' letter which gives the employee the opportunity to file a Title VII Civil Rights complaint in Federal court. The employee then becomes the Plaintiff and the company is the Defendant who must defend against the employee's claims. The Plaintiff has the burden-of-proof which is at the clear and convincing evidence level. To prove the claim it is often necessary not just to demonstrate that the offensive behavior occurred, but also to prove that the alleged behavior actually constituted sexual harassment. Psychologists are often called upon to provide this expert testimony.

DEFINITIONS OF SEXUAL HARASSMENT

The most commonly accepted definition of sexual harassment is cited in the U.S. Equal Employment Opportunity Commission (EEOC) (CFR Ch. XIV, 7-1-90 edition, p. 1604.11), which states:

> "unwelcome sexual advances, requests for sexual favors, and other verbal or physical conduct of a sexual nature constitute sexual harassment when (1) submission to such conduct is made either explicitly or implicitly a term or condition of an individual's employment, (2) submission to or rejection of such conduct by an individual is used as the basis for employment decisions affecting such individual, or (3) such conduct has the purpose or effect of unreasonably interfering with an individual's work performance or creating an intimidating, hostile or offensive working environment."

Furthermore, such actions must be considered in the context of the entire working conditions as stated:

> "In determining whether alleged conduct constitutes sexual harassment, the Commission will look at the record as a whole and at the totality of the circumstances, such as the nature of the sexual advances and the context in which the alleged incidents occurred. The determination of the legality of a particular action will be made from the facts, on a case by case basis."

And to make sure that other civil rights violations that might simultaneously occur are not overlooked, the rules further state that:

> "Harassment on the basis of sex is a violation of SEC 703 of Title VII (The Principles involved here continue to apply to race, color, religion or national origin)."

The connection between other forms of discrimination in the workplace and sexual harassment is clear. Often it is the woman of color, the woman who has a physical disability, or the lesbian woman who is more likely to be picked on or sexually harassed, especially if she also appears to be vulnerable for some other reason. As might be expected, the workplace atmosphere has much to do with individual workers' behaviors. Those sites where diversity is accepted are less likely to have reported sexual harassment complaints.

ADA AND VAW CIVIL RIGHTS LAWS

For example, the *1990 Americans with Disabilities Act (ADA)*, with most provisions having gone into effect by 1992, is now being used in conjunction with other civil rights protection, including the Civil Rights Act's provisions enacted by Congress in 1991 and signed by President Bush to enforce equitable treatment of women at worksites. The ADA is discussed further later in this chapter. As women's civil rights are being violated not only by sex discrimination and harassment, but also by use of violence against them, in 1992 the U.S. Congress passed the *Violence Against Women Act* which declares use of gender-based violence against a woman can be remedied by civil rights law. This law provides for recovery of compensatory and punitive damages as well as an injunction against the offending party to prevent future damage and retaliation. Perhaps the most interesting part of the VAW is the denial of a gun permit to anyone who has been convicted of domestic violence. This provision was bitterly contested during the renewal of the VAW legislation because it had a major impact on

TABLE 18-3. IMPORTANT SEXUAL HARASSMENT CASES

- *Rogers v. EEOC, 454 F2d,234, 238 (5th Cir. 1971)*
- *Bundy v. Jackson, 641,F.2d,934, 944, (DC cir. 1981)*
- *Rabidue v. Osceola Refining Co, 805 F.2d 611, 619-20, (6th Cir 1986)*
- *Meritor Savings Bank,FSB v. Vinson, 477 US 57, 65-67, (1986)*
- *Scott v. Sears Roebuck, 798F2d 210, 213 (7th Cir 1986)*
- *Price Waterhouse v. Hopkins, 490 US 228 (1989)*
- *Harris v. Forklift Systems, 510 U.S. 17.114 S.CT. 367, 63 FEP (1993)*
- *Clark Cty School v. Breeden (1994)*
- *Ellison v. Brady, 924, F2d 872, 880 n 15 (9th Cir, 1991)*
- *Oncale v. Sundowner Offshore Oil, 83F. 3d 118, 70 FEP (1998)*
- *Faragher v. Boca Raton, 110 s.ct. 2275, (1998)*
- *Davis for Lashonda v. Monroe County B of Ed (1999)*
- *Pollard v. duPont (2001)*
- *Neal v. Ferguson Constr,237F.3d 1248, 1253 (CA10 2001)*

police and law enforcement officers who could no longer serve in that occupation, having been found guilty of domestic violence at home and now forbidden by the law to carry a gun, which was required on the job. As the provisions are still quite controversial, it has been difficult for anyone to successfully recover under this law.

Psychologists and other mental health professionals are being called on by the courts to help determine the extent of damage that comes from oppression because of gender, racial or ethnic group, sexual orientation, and disability. Presentation of social psychology research on the negative psychological effects of discrimination in general (cf. *Price-Waterhouse* and *Harris v. Forklift* cases, in which the American Psychological Association submitted Amicus Briefs), as well as the clinician's assessment of specific damages to a particular individual, have been important in federal lawsuits. See Table 18-3 for a list of the important cases.

SUBTLE HARASSMENT

Obviously, there is a line between behavior that is clearly considered sexual harassment and that which is considered normal bantering between males and females in the work setting. Women often define the line at the point at which they are uncomfortable enough about the behavior for it to continue to bother them, even if they cover up their feelings of discomfort by pretending to ignore it or even talking back to the males.

Sometimes the same behaviors are classified differently depending on the status of the initiator in relation to the victim and the explicitness of the behavior. Gutek et al. (1983) found that some behaviors might be tolerated from a peer while viewed as harassing from a supervisor. Sexual harassment differs from "flirting" by the uninvited, invasive, and often embarrassing behaviors that persist despite the woman's obvious displeasure or lack of interest. Other terms used to describe this behavior include "seductive behavior," "sexual bribery," "sexual coercion," and "sexual assault." Sometimes sexual harassment is contained under the legal term of "sexual discrimination."

The differences in male and female views of sexual harassment are important to understand when designing a treatment plan to assist the woman in recovery. Most victim advocates would put theoretical understanding of sexual harassment at a place similar to that of rape in our culture twenty years ago. Some attitudes toward rape find their counterparts in sexual harassment. Psychologist Ken Pope has found that sexual harassment and exploitation produces similar negative psychological impact to rape. Psychiatrist, Judith Herman in 1992 found that men's definition of what constitutes rape does not appear to be based on women's experience of violation but rather, just slightly above the slightly higher level of coercion that is acceptable to men. MacKinnon in 1983 indicted society for not stopping or preventing all sexual assaults against women. She claimed that rape, from women's point of view, is regulated and gives many examples of how this occurs. Since most women who have experienced sexual harassment are aware that their experience of what happened to them is different from the experience of the men who committed the acts, and that other people are more likely to view the behavior from the male cultural standard than from the victim's own personal experience despite the law, women are less likely to report such harassment or even pay much attention to it until it becomes emotionally impossible not to deal with its effects. There have been attempts to debunk the myth that women cannot effectively persuade some men to stop rape or sexual harassment, by describing many different types of attempts made by women, some of which may be successful in limiting the harm they experience. These data also support the validity of the individual woman's perceptions of danger while in the middle of the attack.

TYPES OF SEXUAL HARASSMENT BEHAVIORS

The most commonly reported modes of harassment are verbal comments about the woman's body, jokes about sex, sexual innuendos, and invitations, which persist for a long period of time, regardless of the woman's response. In some studies more than one-half of the women report also being subjected to repeated physical advances which include touching and kissing. Sexual parts of the woman's body are fondled or grabbed without her consent (usually breasts, buttocks, and crotch areas), and it is not uncommon for the offender/harasser to restrain the woman with some kind of physical force such as putting his arms around her or backing her up against a wall or furniture.

The American Psychological Association brochure on sexual harassment suggests that although there are many different types of behavior that constitute sexual harassment, the defining characteristic is that it is *"unwanted."* The brochure lists the following broad categories, the first two being considered the most common:

1) generalized sexist statements and behavior that convey insulting or degrading attitudes about women. Examples include insulting remarks, offensive graffiti, obscene jokes or humor about sex or women in general, and the display of graphic materials of a sexual nature.

2) unwanted, inappropriate or offensive social invitations, sexual overtures, or advances. Examples here include unwanted letters or phone calls of a personal nature, insistent requests for social contacts (drinks, dinners, dates), and repeated unwanted requests for sexual contact.

3) the subtle or overt solicitation of a personal relationship or sexual activity by promising benefits—for example, a promotion or a pay raise.

4) coercion of social contact or sexual activity by threat of negative consequences. For example, a negative performance evaluation, withholding of promotion, or threat of termination.

5) unwanted physical contact, including touching, feeling, pinching, grabbing, or kissing.

6) threats of physical or coerced sexual activity.

7) sexual assault (APA, 1993, pp. 1–2).

CLARIFYING DEFINITIONS OF SEXUALLY HARASSING BEHAVIOR

Definitions of sexual harassment have also been used in training companies to prevent such behavior and thereby used to limit their liability in potentially expensive litigation. One such program suggests to employers that there are three parts to a common-sense definition of sexual harassment: First, that the behavior doesn't necessarily mean that the perpetrator's intent is to have sex. Rather, the entire continuum of sexual behavior is included "ranging from the least severe end—sexual jokes, innuendos, flirting, asking someone for a date—to the most serious end—forced fondling, attempted or actual rape, sexual assault." *Sex-based* behavior is defined as "negative behavior that is directed at, or has an impact on, only one gender. Negative gender-related behavior can include men putting down women or women making negative remarks about men—in other words, a serious battle of the sexes at the job." It is suggested that where this sex-based behavior occurs, the more serious forms of sexual harassment are not too far behind.

The second part of this definition of sexual harassment is that *"the behavior has to be deliberate and/or repeated."* This stresses that some forms of the behavior are so offensive that the first time they occur they are considered deliberate, hurtful, wrong, and maybe even illegal. For example, forcing a woman to have oral sex, pushing one's clothed genital area against the woman while making writhing movements and suggestive sounds, forced intercourse, or grabbing a woman's breasts and fondling them, all would be considered deliberate behavior by most people. Definitions become less clear where the behavior is more common, such as patting the woman's behind, running one's hand seductively up and down the woman's back under her sweater while she is pinned against the wall, breathing heavily at her desk or whispering in her ear about how sexually aroused she makes him feel.

While some jokes may be sexually offensive to some women immediately, other women may find them funny at first. Sometimes it is the repeated nature of the joking that wears the woman down until it ceases to be funny anymore. Even if the individual behavior is not considered illegal, exposure to it day after day can wear women down, sometimes coming up to the standard of a *'hostile work environment'*. Those companies with a history of discrimination against women in their employment practices, which often includes jobs that are traditionally male, often have such negative attitudes towards the first women hired that the behavior needs less repetition to cause the same effects as the more serious harassment and abuse. It is suggested that "the more severe the behavior is, the fewer times it needs to be repeated before reasonable people define it as harassment; the less severe it is, the more times it needs to be repeated." We would also add that the more negative the attitudes towards women in general in the workplace, the less repetition is needed to produce severe psychological effects.

The third part of this definition of sexual harassment is that *"sexual harassment is not welcome, not asked for, and not returned."* This does not mean women should be considered as accepting the behavior directed toward them when they do not take strong action to try to stop it because of fear of reprisals. Some women may try to make a joke of it while giving the message that such attention is unwanted. Behavior that might not be defined as harassment when it is mutually acceptable outside of the work environment is often unwanted within it. Even mutually desired behavior by two people may be considered unacceptable if it promotes a "hostile work environment" that appears to facilitate or even just tolerate other men's sexual behavior towards other women in the same environment. On the university campus or in small offices with civil service career workers, this is a particularly difficult problem. Obviously, if one woman is perceived as gaining advancement through sexual behavior, this creates an environment that is perceived as having barriers to equality for women who refuse to sexually submit.

Perhaps the most critical factor in defining sexual harassment is that the issue of mutuality or consent cannot exist when there is an unequal power distribution between the man and the woman involved. Thus, although the woman may believe that she willingly engaged in a sexually intimate relationship with a male in a supervisory or power role, in fact, the power differential makes equality, and therefore mutual consent, impossible, and the exchange includes more than sexual affection. Legal scholars often call this *quid pro quo*, or an exchange of "this for that"— that is, an exchange of sexual favors for better work conditions or job advancement. In typical *quid pro quo* cases the woman is approached by a more senior level male with direct or indirect ability to affect her career and is asked to provide sexual favors (sometimes presented in more affectionate terms) in return for job benefits (sometimes using a less direct promise.)

Perception of particular sexual incidents as harassment has been found to be influenced by several factors—including gender, severity or explicitness of the incident, and behavior of the woman, according to psychologist Louise Fitzgerald whose trail-blazing studies have resulted in most college and university campuses adopting anti-sexual harassment policies. Although universities tried to use 'consent' between adults as defense against allegations of sexual discrimination and harassment lawsuits, the issue of how the unequal power difference created a hostile work environment for everyone in that workplace overcame the attempt to prove consent was willful and totally voluntary. Further, it gave an unfair disadvantage to those women who were submitting to sexual demands and unfairly punished those women who did not by preventing advancement in their careers.

MacKinnon (1979) makes a distinction now commonly in use between two main forms of behavior constituting sexual harassment, which has been used in the courts. She calls the *quid pro quo*, in which sexual compliance is exchanged or proposed to be exchanged, for an employment opportunity; and sexual harassment as a 'persistent condition of work'.

> "In the *quid pro quo*, the coercion behind the advances is clarified by the reprisals that follow a refusal to comply. Less clear, and undoubtedly more pervasive, is the situation in which sexual harassment simply makes the work environment unbearable. Unwanted sexual advances . . . can be a daily part of a woman's life [even though] she is never promised or denied anything explicitly connected with her job." (p. 40)

RACIAL, ETHNIC, AND CULTURAL ISSUES

As we have seen, women from racial, ethnic, and cultural minorities (and those with other kinds of minority status as well) are even more likely to experience sexual harassment, especially if they also appear vulnerable for some other reason. At the same time, they are less likely to report such behavior, fearful that it will only add to society's negative attitudes toward their minority group.

CAN A MAN BE SEXUALLY DISCRIMINATED AGAINST?

Interestingly, the issue of sexual harassment of a man by another man was raised in a lawsuit, *Oncale v. Sundowner Offshore Services (1998)*. In this case, a male co-worker physically assaulted a male co-worker in what was claimed to be a sexual manner. The man who performed the alleged assault claimed it could not be litigated under the sex discrimination civil rights laws because his behavior was not sexually motivated. The U.S. Supreme Court found that Title VII applied to the same kinds of sexual harassment in both men and women. Further, the Justices found that sexual harassment does not have to be motivated by sexual desire but has to constitute discrimination or creation of a hostile work environment because of sex and not just some simple sexual teasing and roughhousing.

EMPLOYMENT DISCRIMINATION LAWSUITS

DISCRIMINATION LAWS

Most employment discrimination lawsuits are based upon the civil rights law. As we discussed earlier, *Title VII of the Federal Civil Rights Act of 1964* prohibits discrimination by private and public employers, and by labor organizations and employment agencies, with respect to hiring, classifying, promoting, demoting, firing, pay, or other employment conditions. *Title VI of the Federal Civil Rights Act of 1964* provides that no individual on the basis of race, be excluded from participation in, denied the benefits of, or subjected to, any discrimination under any program or activity receiving federal financial assistance. Title VI does not apply to religious discrimination although it does apply to race, color and national origin.

The Civil Rights Act of 1991 expanded the 1964 Act in a number of different ways. Most importantly, it granted certain relief such as back pay, rescission of discipline in retaliation cases, injunctions, reinstatement of a job, seniority, benefits and the like. The 1991 Act also provided for *compensatory damages* in cases where 'intentional discrimination' occurred or the employer's conduct caused 'pecuniary' and 'non-pecuniary' losses but not to 'disparate impact', 'disability', 'age-based' claims. Pecuniary losses are out of pocket expenses to be incurred in the future such as medical or psychotherapy costs while non-pecuniary expenses are those losses associated with emotional harm and intangible injuries. All of this relief is subject to reasonable caps on the amount to be recovered depending upon the number of employees in a firm with $300,000 set as the maximum compensatory damages to be covered. In some cases, where 'malice or reckless indifference to civil rights' can be proven, punitive damages may be ordered. However, federal employees are not eligible for punitive damages in these cases. There are other federal and state laws that also apply to fair employment practices including the education and civil rights laws. The first amendment to the constitution sometimes is applied to discrimination cases by arguing for freedom of religion as well as freedom of speech.

Worker's Compensation cases that deal with specific injuries to employees while on the job are separate cases and usually are not part of a civil rights complaint. This system was designed to efficiently deal with workplace injuries by having a hearing officer determine equitable solutions after hearing the facts presented by employers and employees. Many workplaces have contracts that govern the relationship between the worker and the employer. Sometimes the contract rules are written and other times they are implied in employee manuals and handbooks. Many employers have instituted an informal and formal employment equity office to handle complaints before they are submitted to the nearest federal Equal Employment Opportunity Commission (EEOC) office. After the EEOC reviews the case (which can take a long time), they may issue findings that support the claim to discrimination. In these cases, the employer usually negotiates a settlement that is favorable to the plaintiff. If the EEOC does not make such a finding, they may issue what is called a 'right to sue' letter which then must be filed together with the lawsuit in Federal court.

RACIAL DISCRIMINATION LAWSUITS

As described above, *The Civil Rights Act of 1964* that was amended by Congress in 1991, as well as both federal and state case law, have provisions for compensation if it can be proven by clear and convincing evidence that racial discrimination took place in a private or public workplace. Under the law, it is not necessary to prove that the company intended to discriminate. Rather, like in sex discrimination cases, a pattern of discrimination is sufficient proof in most cases. As in sexual harassment discussed above, it is possible to file a civil rights complaint in state court; as well as in Federal court. However, in state court, it is usually necessary to prove both that the discrimination occurred and caused specific damages. In Federal court, it is only necessary to prove that discrimination occurred as the question of damage when someone's civil rights are violated is already accepted. One reason for this difference is that the Federal statutes are designed to discourage further discrimination rather than simply compensate an individual for what happened to him or her. However it is important to note that once the issue of emotional damages is raised separately in a federal lawsuit, it is possible to put the individual's entire mental health history at issue, rather than limit it to the discrimination complaint. To avoid opening this issue, psychologists will often review records and give an opinion on whether or not the behaviors specified are consistent with harassment and discrimination, but do not examine the plaintiff for mental health damages.

AMERICANS WITH DISABILITIES ACT (ADA) LAWSUITS

The ADA (1990, 42 U.S.C.$ 12101) goes further than the civil rights legislation and not only prohibits employment discrimination or harassment, but also requires the employer to make 'reasonable accommodation' for the employee's disabilities. Employers with more than 15 persons in their company are prohibited from discriminating against a qualified person with a disability in hiring, advancement, discharge, compensation, training, and benefits. The definition of a qualified person with a disability is that with or without reasonable accommodation, the person can perform the essential functions of a particular job. A two-step process is required to determine if the employee meets these qualifications: 1) Does the person meet the requisite skill level, experience, education, or other job-related requirements? and 2) Can the person perform the job whether or not it is with some difficulty but without major health risks? For example, in one case, the employer was ordered to make reasonable accommodation for a woman who developed cancer and needed time off for treatments two days per month. In another case, the ADA was found not to apply when an employee with diabetes developed diabetic retinopathy and could no longer work at the computer, an essential requirement of the job.

Defining what constitutes a disability under the ADA has been a subject of concern since its inception. At this time there is a three-pronged definition including: 1) physical or mental impairment that substantially limits one or more life activities; 2) records that such an impairment actually exists; and 3) the person is known to have the impairment. Impairments can affect the neurological, muscular-skeletal, sensory, respiratory, cardio-vascular, reproductive, digestive, genital, urinary, endocrine, and blood and lymphatic systems, as well as the skin and any mental or psycholog-ical disorder such as mental retardation, organic brain injury, emotional or mental illness, and specific learning disabilities. Obesity, advanced age, pregnancy, and personality traits that are not part of a mental disorder are not covered under the ADA definitions of disability.

Although most mental diagnoses that appear in the DSM-IV are cov-ered, there appears to be some conflicting case law about conduct and disruptive behavioral disorders. Many of the other specific requirements for invoking the ADA legislation are clearly defined in the act which is different from other civil rights legislation that relies on case by case argu-ments. This is because the legislation was intended to prevent stereotyping of individuals due to misperceptions of what limitations are caused by a disability. However, definitions of what is a 'reasonable accommodation' by an employer is decided on a case by case basis. Unfortunately, unlike the civil rights laws, the ADA does not specify the relief to be granted should an employer be found to have discriminated against a person be-cause of disability. Some employment discrimination scholars suggest that it is impossible to make a disabled person 'whole' which is the concept of relief under the civil rights act. Others suggest that the law was too new to really grasp what kinds of relief would be appropriate in these cases.

SUMMARY

The anti-discrimination laws that have been adopted by Congress arise from the civil rights that are given to every citizen by the U.S. Constitution. Evidence of the psychological harm from stereotyping, harassment and discrimination was part of the evidence that persuaded Congress and the Courts that laws were necessary to prevent further damage. Although the civil rights laws have been amended from time to time and the court's interpretations vary depending upon the political climate in the nation, it is still clear that employers cannot discriminate or retaliate against people who challenge their behavior.

19

Eyewitness Identification

INTRODUCTION

In the minds of most laypersons, the most devastating thing that can occur to a defendant in a criminal trial, who has pled not guilty, is to have an eyewitness state that she or he was indeed the perpetrator of the crime. Lay people think of eyewitness identification as highly accurate and reliable. Studies of juries have shown that it is the single most important factor responsible for convicting a defendant. However, as you shall see in this chapter, eyewitness errors are the cause, in many cases of wrongful convictions. In many recent cases, in which convicted defendants were later exonerated on the basis of DNA evidence, it was found that one or more eyewitnesses falsely identified the innocent person. Experimental psychology has demonstrated for many years that eyewitness identification is not as accurate as lay people would believe because of the witnesses' problems in retrieving accurate memory of events.

In eyewitness memory cases, the psychologist plays a very different role than has been discussed in many of the preceding chapters. In earlier chapters, a psychologist with clinical training examines an individual (most often the defendant in criminal trials or the plaintiff in civil trials) and attempts to answer certain legal questions about the person's state of mind, such as whether or not she or he has the mental capability of assisting an attorney in preparing a defense or whether the psychological condition from which the person suffers could be attributed to a certain trauma, accident, or injury. In eyewitness identification cases, the psychologist is usually an experimental researcher who does not examine the person involved in the court proceedings. Instead, the psychologist presents information to a judge or jury regarding experimental studies that demonstrate the unreliability of eyewitness identification. On occasion, these experimental presentations may be coupled with clinical testimony (usually of another psychologist), when there are questions regarding the ability of a specific witness to recall matters (e.g., if that witness may be neurologically impaired).

There are a number of factors that a psychologist called upon to testify about the reliability of eyewitness testimony will assess. These include the nature of memory as we know it today, the factors that influence a person's suggestibility, and the techniques that a detective can use to enhance memory or actually contaminate the memory of a witness. Recent controversies over the nature of memories of personal trauma are included here because they involve differences of opinion between some experimental psychologists studying cognitive memory and clinical psychologists who specialize in understanding the impact of emotion on memory.

COGNITIVE AND EMOTIONAL MEMORIES

One of the basic concepts that is central to the studies of the reliability of eyewitness testimony, and has been documented for at least seventy years, is that cognitive memory is reconstructed. Cognitive memory is not like a photograph and when you recall what you remember, it may not accurately describe what actually happened. This is because we do not remember everything we experience but rather, we only remember details that are meaningful to us. Cognitive memory is stored in special sections of our brain in the cortex and is retrieved from there using appropriate cues. We must reconstruct events using the limited details that we do remember. This is what is called reconstructive memory. People may forget details that seemed unimportant to them at the time or add in details that really didn't occur for various reasons. So, human memory becomes a mixture of what really happened, with what a person has heard about the event, feels must have happened, or whatever other information the person uses to "fill in the gaps."

This reconstructive view of human memory has gained general acceptance in the scientific community. However, the clinical psychology community has challenged some of the cognitive psychology research especially when trauma memory is involved. Cognitive psychologists suggest that all memory gets processed in the same way and stored in the memory areas of the cortex part of the brain. Clinicians have found that clients who are in psychotherapy have other ways of dealing with memories that are loaded with emotional content. Research in what is called 'psychoneuroimmunology' or PNI now demonstrates that these emotional memories are stored in the midbrain area—probably in the hypothalamus, amygdala, adrenalin, and pituitary axis—regulated by hormones and neurotransmitters, and they are not easily accessed because they have not been verbally processed. The midbrain area of the brain is different from the cortex which is where cognitive memories that have been verbally processed are thought to be stored. Emotional memories especially when they are of very strong feelings that get stored in the midbrain area actually influence our emotional state of being because they regulate the autonomic nervous system. This is one of the ways stress has been found to impact our physiological and mental well-being.

Many clinicians believe that verbal psychotherapy is successful in helping people deal with strong emotional experiences because it helps retrieve these emotional memories out of the midbrain centers, processes them in therapy sessions, and then the person is able to store them in the memory centers of the cortex. The person is then able to retrieve the memories without being flooded by overwhelming emotions. Cognitive psychologists question the accuracy of these memories given what they know about the reconstructive memory process. They suggest that there are many places along the way that memory can be altered, sometimes purposefully and sometimes because of the process itself. Clinical researchers do not disagree that the memories can be altered intentionally by unscrupulous people or even unintentionally, but believe this is only temporary. For example, prospective studies of women who were sexually abused as children found that there were periods of time that the women remembered certain details and forgot others, but despite this variability of memory, what was remembered was usually accurate.

RECONSTRUCTIVE MEMORY

The reconstructive memory approach divides memory into three stages: acquisition, retention, and retrieval. The first stage, acquisition, has to do with the encoding of stimuli (events, information, encounters, conversations, situations) into memory. Retention refers to how this information is stored over time. Finally, retrieval refers to the ability to find what has been stored. Different factors impact on each of these stages and therefore can have an effect on the accuracy of recall. Complete and accurate memories of complex events are highly unlikely, because people cannot pay attention to all the things going on at the same time. During acquisition they tend to form general impressions and focus on what seems most important at that time. Expectations of what *should be* in a given circumstance, may well distort what is actually there. During retention, details may be distorted, changed, or forgotten. If outside sources talk to the person about the event, the memory of it may change and incorporate these outside sources. This is one reason why clinicians examining witnesses are cautioned not to use leading questions. One frequent technique in a criminal trial is to cast doubt on the accuracy of a defendant's statement by implying that the police 'planted seeds' which distorted the witness's actual memory. A particularly controversial area which led to many debates in the recent past was whether therapists could 'implant' in people's memories false recollections of abuse while helping the client to process emotional memories and store them in the cognitive areas of the brain. In the final stage, retrieval, the conditions under which the recollection is retrieved (sometimes called cues) may influence what is remembered.

ACQUISITION PHASE

Let us now look at some of the factors that can influence the first stage, acquisition. In the acquisition phase, the time factor can influence the accuracy of a witness's ability to encode the event. The longer a witness views an event, the more accurate the encoding usually is. How frequently the event occurs is another important factor, but, of course, most crimes that an observer is seeing are one time events. In non-criminal legal cases, it is possible that memory can be impacted by witnessing scenes repeatedly, such as friends who witness behavior between a husband and wife who are claiming duress in a marital case or co-workers in an office where there are allegations of sexual harassment. However, since eyewitness testimony has been studied mostly in the context of criminal investigations, we will use those examples here.

Encoding Core and Peripheral Events

People tend to be more accurate when they encode what is called *core* as opposed to *peripheral* events. This is sometimes problematic in eyewitness testimony because a peripheral event might be the major identifier in a case and the memory of the clothing a shooter was wearing is less reliable than other factors such as actually seeing where the shooting event occurred. What the person may have been wearing, however, may be important in terms of proper and accurate identification. The complexity of the scene being observed can detract from accurate identification as well. If some item draws the observer's attention away from the core event, it can result in less accurate identification. Expectations of what a situation *may* have been like can distort the accurate encoding of what it actually had been. In other words, if a witness is accustomed to see certain things regularly in a scene, the witness may state that he or she recalls those things being present, even if they were not at the time of a particular incident.

Think about a shooting that occurs in the driveway of the house across the street from you. You see the person's car parked in the driveway every day. The day of the shooting the car was not there. However, you may describe the scene with the car where it is always parked because your memory encoded both the shooting event and your memory of the car together. Merging these details may or may not make your memory of who did the shooting less reliable but on the witness stand, the jury will have more trouble believing your eyewitness identification than if you had a clear, photographic memory of the event.

Inaccuracies can also occur if the event is viewed under unclear or rapidly moving circumstances. When a witness says to a police officer, "It all happened so fast, I really can't remember," she or he is giving an example of this finding. Lawyers often will try to demonstrate that the witness is not credible because he or she cannot remember certain peripheral details about a crime that were proven by pictures of the crime scene. If the witness says, "I can't remember" or gives an inaccurate fact, then it can be assumed that whatever the person can remember is not reliable either.

Stressful Incidents

The relationship between stress and the accuracy of memory is complex, with some studies suggesting that stress enhances accurate memory and others suggesting that it detracts. Many researchers view the level or intensity of the stress to be the important factor: moderate levels increase accuracy, while high levels decrease it. For example, if an individual was witness to a crime that took place a distance from the observer and there was little likelihood that the observer would be hurt by that activity, it could be considered medium stress. On the other hand, if the incident occurred closer to the witness and his or her safety might have been in jeopardy that could be considered high stress. Therefore, it would be expected, if all other factors were equal, the witness' memory would be more accurate for the incident that took place further away. However, other factors could influence the accuracy of memory including the fact that the person needs eyeglasses for distance viewing and he or she didn't have them on that day.

On the other hand, brain researchers are finding that memories of events that are perceived as traumatic do not get processed right away. First, they are encoded directly into the areas of the brain that regulate emotions. So far, the research suggests that these memories are recorded as they actually occurred which may be partially responsible for the reexperiencing of all or parts of the memories of the traumatic events along with the emotions experienced at the time in survivors with Post-Traumatic Stress Disorder (PTSD). If the process of retrieving these emotional memories is protected from outside contamination, the reconstructive memories that finally get stored in the cognitive memory area might even be more accurate than those that are processed immediately.

RETENTION OR STORAGE

The second stage of cognitive memory is retention or storage. A number of factors that occur in this stage may also influence the reconstructive memory. For example, the longer the time between the observation of an event and when it is reported, the greater the likelihood of its being forgotten or reported inaccurately. Sometimes, additional information obtained during retention can detract from the accuracy of reporting. For example, a 5-year-old child who witnesses the shooting death of his mother may be interviewed by several different people about the event. During these interviews, the child may learn new information from the questions being asked and encode and store that information along with the original memories. Or, the child may recall the emotional memories from the experience of fear and trauma and process them into the cognitive memory including some inaccurate information either intentionally or unintentionally provided by the interviewer. The next time that memory is reconstructed, it may contain the new information mixed together with the original scene, confusing everyone. Interviewers asking witnesses to retrieve stored memories must be careful not to taint them while reconstruction is taking place. Even subtle cues such as smiling when the child is saying certain things and repeating certain questions when the child says other things will influence what the child reports.

Forgetting Information

Generally, the tendency to forget information increases with time, but this varies with a number of factors. One factor is how familiar the information may be to the witness. If the witness is unfamiliar with a particular person or place, she or he may forget more about the details over time than if the witness was more familiar with it. Another factor is the length of the time between the observation and its report. Research shows that the longer the time interval, the greater the likelihood that the individual's recognition of an event will be incorrect. However, clinical conditions can alter this finding. For example, an individual who already has PTSD and is under stress during an event may fill in gaps of memory with similarly perceived trauma events that are recalled mentally at the time the actual incident is occurring. So, police officers must be very careful when interviewing witnesses right after an event to clarify what was actually occurring and what was being reexperienced mentally.

Sometimes cues presented may assist with accurate retrieval and reconstruction of memory. Other times, if subtle pieces of incorrect information are embedded in the cues, it can result in even more memory distortions. The more often the person repeats an incorrect recognition, the more likely each time the memory is reconstructed, it will not be accurate. Thus, repeated questioning can result in even poorer reconstructive memory. Some researchers addressed whether the increased tendency towards incorrect recognition was observed in adults as well as children. Most studies have found that children are similar to adults in that regard.

A variety of techniques have been found to increase such inaccuracies. If, for instance, the interrogator used complex rather than simple questions, the potential for inaccurate identification increases. If an interrogator were to use strong, as opposed to weak, verbs in describing behavior (such as he attacked the man rather than he hit the man) inaccuracies of reconstructive memory also are more likely to occur. However, if the interviewer uses cues such as props to aid in recall, it may enhance the person's memory, especially with young children.

Source of Information

The source of the information can have a major effect on the accuracy of the memory retention. Two factors seem to be operative here: the status of the individual providing the information and whether or not the person is perceived as unbiased or without self-interest in the issue. If the source is perceived as high status and unbiased, then that person may have a profound impact on altering memories. Since police are often perceived as having high status and are thought to be unbiased by jurors, attorneys may cross-examine them vigorously to try to uncover any bias that might have influenced their witness interviews or when they obtain confessions from defendants during the interrogation. This is what happened in the O.J. Simpson trial. Although, the defense attorneys were accused of playing the 'race card', in fact, uncovering the racial bias of detective Mark Furhman demonstrated the unreliability of his testimony at the trial. For the same reason, therapists and parents who uncover child sexual abuse are held to a different standard in order to demonstrate that any bias they might have towards protection of the child, did not unduly influence their interviews to persuade the child to say what they knew the therapist or parent wanted them to say, if it was not the truth.

Many such different mechanisms seem to be involved in the distortion of memory and, most often, inaccuracies are due to the joint effect of several of these mechanisms interacting together. Thus, both forgetting and contamination by material presented after the actual event can result in inaccuracies in memory during the retention phase.

RETRIEVAL

The final stage in reconstructive memory is called retrieval. During this stage, information that was encoded and retained is brought back to consciousness. Witnesses may make a police report, be asked to identify suspects from a police lineup, and ultimately testify in court. Many interviews with eyewitnesses may be conducted under poor conditions; witnesses may be injured, psychologically upset, distracted, or confused. Police may form premature conclusions about what happened and intentionally or unintentionally bias the witness. Sometimes these premature conclusions can lead the detective to ask leading questions, and construct biased line-ups or photo arrays that aid in identifying the individual whom they already suspect. Given the previously noted status of police officers including both respect and fear that some minority groups may have, these interview techniques can profoundly influence the accuracy of eyewitness identification.

Many police employ artists who try to draw a composite sketch of a suspect from verbal or visual memories of witnesses. These sketches are then used as props both to choose photos to go into a photo line up and to enhance the witnesses memory prior to showing him or her the photo line up. The closer the photo is to the composite sketch that has been seen by the witness, the more likely he or she will compare the photos to the sketch rather than his or her memory of the actual scene. This can result in choosing an inaccurate person from the photo line up. However, it will be difficult to change the person's opinion as he or she is certain having seen the sketch a few minutes before the line up. It has been found that putting several pictures of people who resemble the suspect together will result in more confusion than just one mixed in with several dissimilar pictures. This is also true for a live line-up used for identification purposes.

In general, when testimony is given in court, it will be more accurate if fewer details are required to be remembered. Here too, attorney's questions can have a substantial impact on what is remembered. A witness's testimony is usually most accurate if first, the person's free recall is obtained. Afterwards, it is okay to use open-ended questions and eventually it is okay to ask more specific questions. However, it is best to avoid misleading questions and multiple-choice options as they can confuse the person and memory retrieval will be less accurate. The most accurate eyewitness reports have been found to be obtained by first asking the witness to give a narrative of what was observed at the scene. Then, they should ask simple, brief, and direct questions that are designed to elicit direct responses. Finally, they should make a broad request for any additional information.

As might be expected, police and attorneys have been made aware of the extensive literature regarding these effects and attempts to help them formulate better questions is an important trial consultation strategy. Even so, the legal and psychological literature are replete with stories about the poorly constructed questions asked of eyewitnesses right after a crime scene and in follow up interviews and depositions. Sometimes police are unable to prevent one witness from hearing the information provided by another witness, further contaminating the individual's memory. They may take poor notes, forget to turn on the tape recorder or even destroy recordings so that neither the complete questions nor answers are available for analysis. When unedited reports are available, analysis sometimes reveals frequent interruptions by police during the witnesses narrative preventing a full and complete response. They also found police ask too many questions requiring just a yes or no answer without letting the witness put the events in his or her own words. These questions give away the answer that the police want and so, really do not measure the witness's own observations. Asking too many compound questions results in a lack of clarity as to which part of the question the response addresses as does asking too many questions with inappropriate sequences that witnesses do not get a chance to correct. When training police in interview techniques, they are encouraged to slow down their pace of questions and design each question taking into account the particular person being interviewed and the specifics of the previous answers rather than using generic questions from a list that have not been rephrased or put into their own language.

Trauma Memory Retrieval

One of the controversial, and not yet satisfactorily answered questions regards the timing of an interview of a witness to a traumatic event. Some studies suggest that deferring interviewing until the stress subsides yields more accurate results, while other studies suggest more accuracy in reporting before some of the factors enumerated above have had a chance to intervene. As was discussed earlier, trauma memories are not always processed in the cognitive areas of the brain although they remain in the midbrain area where emotional memories are stored. Retrieval from the emotional memory area is like retrieving a lost document on the computer before it has been saved into hard drive memory. You know it is still there someplace because every now and then, parts of the emotional memory pop up just like parts of the unsaved document pop up in RAM memory, but then disappear again before it can be properly labeled and saved.

People experience their emotions differently so retrieval of emotional memories would be expected to differ depending on how much control a person has been able to exercise over his or her emotions. For example, someone whose emotions are still on a roller coaster might be less accurate depending on where they were in their emotional cycle when an event occurred while someone who keeps their emotions under very rigid control might be more accurate. On the other hand, so much of the processing of emotional experiences occurs automatically and involves the secretion of hormones and neurotransmitters that are difficult to consciously control or measure, that it may be difficult to know the impact on someone's cognitive recall and retrieval. Psychologist Daniel Goleman has written about this area of study in his popular book, *Emotional Intelligence.*

Enhancing Retrieval of Memory

Other issues that come into the retrieval stage deal with various techniques used to enhance the retrieval of memory. Some of these are hypnosis, guided memory, and what has been called the cognitive interview. While these techniques may, on the one hand, enhance the retrieval, some critics suggest that they may influence and distort the accuracy of the memory.

Hypnosis that is recorded by audio or video means may be permitted as reliable evidence in some courts but if the suggestions are likely to alter the memory, then the witness may not be permitted to testify. Guided memory or imagery is a techniques often used by interviewers to relax the person so they can more easily access memories. The cognitive interview is a technique that police may use to instruct the witness to recreate the crime scene in his or her mind before the police begin asking questions. Witnesses are instructed to focus on sensory recollections, such as how things appeared or what smells or sounds are recalled. The police may also ask questions to stimulate recall of what he or she was doing, feeling, or focusing attention on at the time.

RELIABILITY OF EYEWITNESS IDENTIFICATION

A number of intriguing issues have emerged from the basic premise regarding the unreliability of eyewitness identification. One of these is cross-racial identification. Generally, people are more accurate in identifying people of the same race than those of different races. It also appears that the difficulty in cross-racial identification increases as the potential witness grows older. This is an area that needs further study. One hypothesis to consider is whether those who live in areas where there are many different cultures can more reliably identify differences within groups than those who live in more homogeneous areas. The old popular saying, "People from another ethnic group all look alike" may have more to do with memory processes and identification than the racist meaning that has been attributed to it.

Another area of study by experimental researchers dealt with whether intelligence positively correlates with greater accuracy in eyewitness testimony. While it makes some intuitive sense that the two *should* be related, there does not appear to be any consistent evidence that they, in fact, *are* related. Similarly, there have been suggestions that lower intelligence would correlate positively with greater suggestibility. Again, no consistent relationship has been demonstrated with the exception of individuals who are performing significantly below average intelligence (e.g., in the borderline or mentally retarded range). Courts have accepted research on the limited resources that individuals with low intelligence have when responding to police questioning. For example, a person with an IQ of 55 would not be expected to be able to remember a question with 4 or 5 parts in it. This is also true when questioning those who are mentally challenged or even those with Attention Deficit Disorders (ADD or ADHD) who cannot be expected to remember more than one or two things in a sequence. We discussed this in an earlier chapter on children's rights and Miranda questioning. Reliability of responses from mentally challenged adults may be enhanced by using appropriate language, unbiased cues and props similar to what is recommended with children.

In a similar manner, personality characteristics and cognitive styles that one would intuitively believe to be correlated with higher accuracy in eyewitness identification, in fact have not demonstrated any consistent relationship. Thus, the belief that someone who was an independent thinker and less dependent on cues from the environment to make decisions, would be a more accurate witness has not been verified consistently in the laboratory. In a similar manner, attempts to predict eyewitness accuracy based on such measures as introversion–extroversion or reflection–impulsivity have been equally unsuccessful. As a general rule there are no consistent data regarding gender differences in eyewitness accuracy but this has not been well studied by those psychologists who have expertise in gender issues.

Estimator and System Variables Impacting Accuracy

Estimator Variables

Many experiments regarding eyewitness accuracy are carried out in laboratory settings. The two major types of variables are estimator and system variables. Estimator variables refer to those that influence reconstructive memory because of the individual's tendency to estimate the scene from memory. They deal with various environmental and personality factors that influence accuracy of acquisition, retention and retrieval of memories. For the most part these variables are not under the control of the criminal justice system although interviewers must pay attention to them so as not to manipulate the witness.

Among some of the variables impacting accuracy are:

1. age of the witness (less accuracy in children and in the elderly);
2. unusual aspects of the person being observed;
3. seeing the face at a different angle than originally viewed;
4. change of context (less accuracy if seen in a different setting);
5. intoxication of the witness; and
6. the degree of violence (more accurate memory if event is non-violent).

In addition to these variables, perceptual salience, or something the defendant did that involved drawing attention to him or herself or somehow cause him or her to stand out, may increase accuracy. Global impressions are generally more accurately recalled than specific features. However, despite the success in the laboratory in finding factors that increase reliability, concerns have been raised regarding the applicability of these variables in the real world due largely to complex interactions of variables that have not (or cannot) be tested in the laboratory. In other words, the findings that emerge from research are based on holding certain factors constant in the laboratory, factors which, in the real world, occur in a context that might further influence the witnesses' memory.

System Variables

System variables refer to the type of police procedures used that can negatively impact on the reliability of a witness' memory. Police can be trained to use appropriate interview techniques to avoid many of these pitfalls. The degree of accuracy of eyewitness identification, in other words, can be influenced by the procedures used. These procedures include the type of questioning done by the police, the nature of the lineup or photographs shown to the potential witness, and whether or not the procedures have been videotaped. Further, there is a subtle interaction between the personality of the potential eyewitness and the police. Such dimensions as the witness's reasoning processes, suggestibility, self-confidence, authoritarian submission, and conformity, can all influence what is presented as eyewitness testimony.

The dynamics of the interview situation itself can reflect on the accuracy of the recall of memories. The witness often looks for verification or confirmation of what he or she remembers and can interpret a nod of the head or some other unintentional movement as a signal. Witnesses may feel under pressure to give the right answer or at least not to appear ignorant when being questioned by authority figures. This is called the 'demand characteristics' of the situation and are cues as to what the witness is expected to respond. If a witness did not notice the color of someone's shirt and yet is asked that question during questioning, he or she may make up an answer rather than appear stupid. Leading questions by the police can impact the witness's memory but to date there are no studies in which actual interrogation techniques have been studied outside of the laboratory. If a witness is shown a picture of a suspect more than once, such as in two different interviews separated by a period of time, this can increases the likelihood that the wrong picture will be identified. If the same question is asked repeatedly during an interview, it may influence the witness's response, perhaps causing him or her to change the answer believing the first one given was not acceptable to the interviewer.

FRYE AND DAUBERT STANDARDS AND FEDERAL RULES ON ADMISSIBILITY OF EVIDENCE

Given all of the above cited research, does the scientific knowledge about reliability and validity of eyewitness testimony meet the legal standards for admissibility of this testimony in court today? Remember, earlier discussions that the Frye standard calls for a 'general acceptance within the relevant scientific community' while Daubert and the Federal Rules also require a judge's determination about the reliability and validity of the scientific basis upon which the testimony will rest. Let's take a look at what this research says:

1. Testimony of an eyewitness can be significantly impacted by the way the questions are worded.
2. The instructions that police give to a witness viewing a line up can affect both the witness's willingness to identify someone and the probability of identifying a particular person.
3. Testimony of eyewitnesses can be impacted by information obtained after the actual event.
4. The degree of confidence an eyewitness has in her or his own accuracy does not correlate well with actual accuracy.
5. Attitudes and expectations of an eyewitness may have an impact on his or her perception or memory of an event.
6. The less time that a witness observes an event, the less accurate the memory.
7. Witnesses may 'transfer' identification; in other words, they identify someone as a perpetrator whom they have seen before in a different context.
8. Misidentification is more likely if a witness is shown one individual rather than a full line up.
9. Most forgetting occurs immediately after the event and levels off subsequently unless trauma memories are involved.
10. Caucasians tend to identify other Caucasians more accurately than they can identify other racial groups such as African Americans.

11. The likelihood of accurate identification in a line up increases the more the members of the line up resemble the subject.
12. Eyewitnesses tend to overestimate the length of time an event takes to occur.
13. High levels of stress negatively impact on accurate identification while moderate levels of stress enhance it.

Finally, the important question to be raised is the relevancy of this information to judges and jurors who must make decisions about guilt or innocence of defendants of crimes. The rules of evidence that govern testimony suggest that there should be different standards for what is admissible and how its credibility is weighted by the finders of fact. Some suggest that the laboratory research on factors that influence acquisition, retention and retrieval of memory in general are well enough known by the average person so that it is no longer necessary to have expert witness testimony to explain the possible contamination to memory. Those who take this position believe that jurors can sort it out themselves. Others believe that the weight given to the credibility of a witness may be so skewed by the status or confidence with which a witness testifies, that expert testimony is necessary to avoid mistakes being made. You decide for yourself!

20

Jury Selection and Trial Consultation

PSYCHOLOGY OF THE TRIAL

The area of trial consultation including selecting juries is one that has developed over the past 30 years into an important area of forensic psychology. This has occurred despite the skepticism that occurred because of the possibility for unscrupulous attorneys or psychologists to overstep the boundaries of ethical and moral behavior as was portrayed in the *Runaway Jury* by John Grisham. Everyone likes to think that psychologists can see into people's minds and use what they learn to be manipulative. While that occasionally can and does happen, in fact, most trial consultants use perfectly acceptable research methods to obtain important information that lawyers can then choose to use or discard.

One of the most celebrated cases in which one side took advantage of the knowledge that trial consultants offered and the other side ignored it was the O.J. Simpson criminal trial. In her 1997 book, *Without a Doubt*, prosecutor Marcia Clark said she was offered the services of a trial consultant,

Donald Vinson, 'pro bono' or at no cost, but rejected the advice he gave her because she was personally offended by his attitude. The defense team hired Jo Ellen Dimetri, a well-known and respected trial consultant who worked with them as part of the so-called 'dream team' throughout the trial. Through the use of scientific methods, both consultants concluded that African-American women were more likely to be sympathetic towards Simpson than towards Brown. However, Clark believed that she could persuade these women to sympathize with the victim, using her theory that unchecked domestic violence led to Brown's death, ignoring the racial issues raised in this case. Author LW, who was a consultant to the defense, remembers Johnnie Cochran's excited telephone call to her when they had selected the final 12-person jury that had eight African-American women and one African-American man. Based on the research he had obtained, he was sure that the prosecution had made a terrible mistake that would favor his client. Social psychology data clearly suggested that the identification with racial discrimination was stronger for African-American women than their identification with gender.

Interestingly, there are those who suggest that the prosecution lost that trial when they filed the case in the downtown Los Angeles courthouse, rather than at the suburban Santa Monica site. Since the deaths of Nicole Brown and Ron Goldman occurred in the wealthy suburb of Brentwood, the usual filing would have been in Santa Monica where the juror pool would better represent those who live in the more affluent neighborhoods than downtown Los Angeles. However, Gil Garcetti, the L.A. District Attorney at that time, believed that managing the media would be a major issue for the city and preferred to hold the trial in the larger and more accessible courthouse. Sometimes hard decisions must be made when two conflicting issues are raised such as in this case.

WHAT RESEARCH METHODS CAN BE USED?

Social science provides us with many different ways to collect information about jurors that will allow attorneys to learn about their general attitudes and biases for and against specific clients. For example, conducting a 'public opinion poll' using a sample of people who live in the area from which jurors will be selected can help attorneys learn what potential jurors know about the case, whether pre-trial publicity has caused them to favor one side or the other, if there are certain specific facts that might be more troublesome than others, and if it is impossible for the client to obtain a fair trial in that jurisdiction. Sometimes the media publicize a case without all the facts or even using facts that might later prove to be erroneous, which make it difficult for anyone who has been exposed to those facts to forget them. This can cause bias that negatively influences that person's ability to listen to the facts presented at trial. Systematically collecting this information using scientific methods can produce the evidence to persuade a judge to move the trial to another community where jurors have not been exposed to the detrimental information.

Sometimes the community as a whole has certain attitudes and beliefs that would make it difficult for members to serve fairly as a juror on a particular case. This is particularly true for attitudes about racial and gender bias. A U.S. Supreme Court case, *Batson v. Kentucky, 106 S. Ct. 1712 (1989)*, found that jury selection could not be based on racial prejudices. In other words, a defendant is entitled to have members of his or her own racial group on the jury and they cannot be excluded on the basis of race. In *J.E.B. v. Alabama,114 S.Ct. 1419, 62 U.S.L.W. 4219 (1994)* the Court decided that one gender cannot be systematically removed from the jury. One of the tenets of the jury system is that a person can be judged by other people who are similar to them—'a jury of their peers'. If you are a dark-skinned woman who grew up in San Juan, Puerto Rico, you speak Spanish as your first language and you are on trial in a small farming town in Iowa, the chances of finding a jury of your peers is quite remote. However, if you were to be on trial in the Bronx, New York, you may well be judged by others who understand how your culture impacts on your behavior.

Some attitudes and prejudices are more subtle to discover so trial consultants may conduct 'community surveys' to try to find out what people think about these issues prior to trial. Using a random system of selection, a trial consultant may distribute a survey designed to collect information about certain attitudes in the community. The results of both the Public Opinion Poll and the Community Survey may be attached to a 'Motion for Change of Venue' and used to try to persuade the judge to move the trial somewhere else. Sometimes the trial consultant is called to testify at such a hearing while other times the court makes the decision based on written documents. The downside in filing for a change in venue is that the new community selected by the court might hold even more unsympathetic attitudes towards the client than the original one.

JUROR SELECTION OR DESELECTION

Many people believe that selecting jurors is not fair. They believe that psychologists are hand-picking the right people to unfairly decide a case.

Although they fear that psychology can really help select the best juror to determine the outcome of the trial in favor of their client, in fact, what psychological research is best at doing is predicting who would not be good on a particular jury. Thus, we should call it juror deselection rather than jury selection, since we are trying to learn who should be sent home because they will not be able to be fair and impartial on a particular case.

Focus Groups

Once the decision is made about where a trial will be held, the jury pool can be studied even further using social science methods to determine what information would a typical juror need to come to a decision favorable to one side or the other. This can be determined by creating small groups of perhaps eight to ten members called a 'focus group' and presenting the facts of the case to these people. After the case is presented, they are encouraged to discuss the case amongst themselves and determine their opinion based on the information presented so far and what additional information might persuade them otherwise. These groups are particularly helpful in focusing on one or two aspects of the case rather than on all the facts at the same time. Using a scientific method rather than relying only on an attorney's intuition helps remove some of the guesswork from the trial outcome. The results can give attorneys a better understanding of who might be sympathetic to their client and who might not be.

So, for example, in the O.J. Simpson trial, if the attorney wanted to know the sympathies of African-American women, a focus group of a variety of different African-American women would be selected and the facts to be studied would be placed before them in a systematic manner. Different issues could be varied so that Marcia Clark's belief that identification with the feminist issue of domestic violence could be tested to see if it would be more persuasive than identification with being an African-American man in a racist culture who was framed by the police. Different focus groups could study different sides of this issue including identification with being an African-American man who was rich and made it in the 'white man's world', sympathy for a white woman in an interracial marriage, disgust for a racist police officer who may have manipulated evidence, lack of credibility for the proper preservation of scientific evidence and other facts upon which a case is decided. Jo Ellen Dimetri chose various focus groups to study the answers to these questions. This guided the attorneys in their selection of jurors chosen. While the evidence was being presented, a 'shadow jury'composed of people similar to the real jury, was also getting the evidence to help the attorneys decide the best way to present the facts so they could be understood. In the end, the O.J. Simpson jurors were able to identify with the belief that some police officers could lie and manipulate especially in a case against an African-American man, even one who was more identified with rich white men, and that the medical examiner's office could destroy evidence either by sloppy procedures or by deliberately following the detective's orders to ignore chain-of-command in collecting such evidence.

Mock Trial

Another technique that is popular with trial consultants is to hold a 'mock trial' before the actual trial occurs and actually present the elements of a trial to a 'focus group' who have been selected as comparable to the population from which the actual jury will be selected. Here the attorneys put together an opening statement representing the best version of their case, the facts in a particularly chosen order, and a closing statement. Presenting the best version of the opposing side's facts for the client or the worst version, depending on what information is desired by the attorney, can vary the presentation. Using this method, attorneys can learn which jurors would be most sympathetic to which facts. Mock trials are also used as a way to gather information about trial strategies such as which order would be best for a particular set of facts, which facts should be emphasized, which should be minimized, and how much information about a particular issue a jury can remember. If only parts of the trial strategy need to be tested, a focus group can be used instead of the entire case being presented at a mock trial.

Analogue Jury Studies

Mock trials are often used as research methodology for professors to study problems that seem important to social science and psychology, in general as well as in a particular litigated case. One of the most important studies of how different jurors might be impacted by new information was done by psychologist, Regina Schueller, in Ontario, Canada. Schueller took groups of college students and presented different case studies of battered women who killed their partners to them changing the facts slightly and varying the composition of the group so she could study general attitudes to specific fact patterns in what is called an 'analogue' study. The outcome or criterion measure was whether the mock juror would vote for first degree murder, manslaughter, or not guilty by reason of self-defense.

Schueller looked at variables such as whether being a man or a woman would impact the mock juror's verdict, the age of the mock juror, factors from the mock juror's background that might influence the vote, and the amount of information about the abuse that was necessary to change from murder to self-defense. Then, she put the mock jurors together in a room to deliberate with each other. This is a time when each juror's individual opinion can be impacted by another juror's point-of-view. Obviously, if you think jurors are leaning in your favor, you want some jurors on that panel who will be persuaded by the strong majority. But, if you have bad facts or think that the jury is leaning against your client, you want a few individualists on the jury to try to persuade the others or at the worst, hold out for a mistrial because they couldn't come to agreement.

In Schueller's experiments she found that women were the most sympathetic to battered women who claimed to have killed their abusive partner in self-defense. Although this seems like it would be consistent with public opinion, in fact, earlier jury studies about the credibility of rape victims showed that women were often less likely to believe the victim was raped. Psychologists interpreted this finding as evidence that women who identified with the woman as a victim first had to accept that they were vulnerable to attack, too. If they blamed the victim for going out late at night, going into a 'bad' neighborhood, wearing a seductive outfit or whatever, then they were more likely to falsely believe they had control over their own vulnerability—if they didn't do those things, then they wouldn't be raped.

Another interesting fact that Schueller found in her experiments was that jurors are more likely to acquit a battered woman because of self-defense if there is direct evidence about the psychological state of mind of that particular woman introduced at trial. An argument in psychology in these cases suggested that a social scientist could testify effectively about the dynamics of domestic violence and expect the jurors to generalize from the expert witness testimony about all battered women to fit the facts of the particular victim who was on trial. Schueller presented the same set of facts to her mock jury using three conditions: 1) information given through general fact witnesses; 2) information given through a social psychologist who had not examined the woman on trial; and 3) information given through an expert witness who had examined the woman and testified as to her specific state of mind. As we saw in Chapter 6 on syndrome testimony, the standard for a not-guilty by reason of self-defense verdict is that the person had a reasonable belief of imminent danger usually proved by her terrifying fear that she would be seriously hurt or killed at or around that time. Schueller's research found that no expert witness testimony resulted in the highest number of convictions of first degree murder, testimony by a general expert witness resulted in a higher number of manslaughter convictions and testimony by an expert witness specific to the defendant on trial resulted in the highest number of acquittals. This research can be introduced in admissibility arguments or for post-conviction relief to demonstrate that a woman didn't get a fair trial if she didn't have the opportunity to introduce specific expert witness testimony on her behalf.

Non-Sexist Language

Research has also demonstrated that to be fair, jurors need to have their jury instructions given in the same gender as the person on trial, not using only male pronouns to imply both male and female or even the newer generic language emphasizing plurals. This means that all pronouns need to be female for a woman litigant. Thus the statement written above about the elements of self-defense should be stated, "If you believe that this woman had a reasonable belief that she was about to be killed or seriously injured by the batterer, then she had the legal right (in some places, legal duty) to defend herself using deadly force, and you should find her not guilty."

WHAT IS THE PROCESS OF 'VOIR DIRE' FOR A JURY?

Armed with all this research, it is now time for the attorneys, sometimes with the trial consultant, to enter the courtroom. In some places, prospective jurors are given written questionnaires to fill out when they enter the jury room. This usually includes general questions such as name, age, county of residence, driver's license, citizenship, magazines and newspapers read, favorite television programs, education, occupation, marital status, number and age of children, partner's occupation, last vacation taken, and the like. Responses to these questions will give the consultant information to make some inferences about the likes and dislikes of jurors and some potential biases.

In some cases, attorneys want more specific information about prospective jurors especially since this is probably the last time they can legally ask their questions directly. Specific questions that are often developed by the litigation consultant especially for this case include those about possible bias because of exposure to media reports of the case, opinions about some of the facts in the case and sometimes personal facts that might influence the ability to be objective and fair. For example, in one case where a man shot and killed his former wife in the cemetery while visiting the grave of their daughter, the television reporter who had told the man about where his ex-wife was filmed the entire incident and parts of it were frequently broadcast on television. Specific questions about what the prospective juror who saw the newsclips remembers from when it was viewed can help determine the degree of potential bias for that particular person.

PEREMPTORY CHALLENGES AND CHALLENGES FOR CAUSE

Jurors are selected in a particular way right before the trial begins. Each side in a case can request a certain number of jurors to be dismissed for no particular reason. This is called a 'peremptory challenge'. Other jurors can be 'dismissed for cause' if the judge can be persuaded that they cannot listen to all the evidence and make a fair and impartial decision. It is important to save as many peremptory challenges as possible so they are not all used up in the beginning leaving the attorney with no recourse to someone who has a known bias but is able to persuade the judge that he or she can listen to all the evidence and make a fair and impartial decision afterwards. Those potential jurors who have special needs or cannot serve in a particular type of case may be excused before they even get into a jury pool for a specific trial. This may include people who cannot sit through a long trial because of physical health problems, cannot understand the English language or have special duties like health or child care. Others may not be able to sit on a jury because of religious reasons or moral opposition to the death sentence. However, there are still other reasons that may make it important for the judge to excuse someone for good cause, rather than expect the attorney to utilize a peremptory challenge, although that is always an option until there are no more left.

METHODS OF CONDUCTING VOIR DIRE

Usually the attorney walks into the courtroom to do the voir dire (Latin for 'tell the truth') for jury selection with several sheets of paper that list the potential jurors who will be in the first jury pool. If a 12-person jury is to be selected, usually 30 to 50 prospective jurors will be sent to the courtroom for questioning. Individual judges usually determine how much verbal questioning the attorney can do with each juror. In cases in Federal court, it is common for the judge and not the attorney to do the voir dire. Judges will sometimes ask attorneys to submit written questions for them to consider or sometimes just ask attorneys to submit areas in which they wish to gather information. If potential bias is an issue, it is possible to scan written responses that were done earlier or perhaps written questionnaires are distributed before verbal questioning begins. Once the responses are reviewed, it is common for trial consultants to confer with the litigant and the attorneys, perhaps even sitting at the same table in the courtroom. If there is time, information collected earlier on each of the prospective jurors is in front of the selectors. Rounds of questions begin, not only to learn new information about each potential juror, but also to impart information to everyone sitting in the room.

Good attorneys use this period of voir dire to educate the potential jury members by the questions they ask others as well as that particular person. For example, if the case is about a juvenile, it may be helpful to ask a mother about the different abilities of children who are the same age as the juvenile in question. Further questions can be asked if it appears that that woman can do a good job of educating the jury pool members to better help those who might eventually be selected decide the case. If the case is about a big business company, it may be helpful to ask about attitudes towards business and find someone who is a stockholder or someone who knows someone who was harmed by a similar company, depending on what information would be helpful for jurors to have.

In some cases, such as those involving such personal issues as abuse, mental illness or other potentially embarrassing facts, these questions may be asked of individual prospective jurors in the judge's chambers. While this does save the potential juror from embarrassment, it may cause the attorney to lose a potentially important period of education of the jury panel itself. Another danger to asking about specific instances of abuse, for example, in a battered woman or rape case, is that the other side can use its peremptory challenges to get rid of the juror if the court won't do so for cause.

It is important for attorneys to remember that jurors make decisions using a variety of variables that include general group variables such as gender, race, culture, community norms, educational level, and experience. Individual personality characteristics and attitudes are also important. For example, it is thought that the more authoritarian someone may be, the more likely that person will be conviction-prone in a criminal case. The opposite is also thought to be true, the more egalitarian attitudes a person might hold, the more likely that person might favor the defense. However, in a justification defense case, sometimes a person with more authoritarian attitudes better understands the need to carry a gun and use it to protect oneself than someone with more liberal views who does not believe in guns for personal use. All kinds of other factors will also influence jurors in addition to the variables they bring to the jury room. The strength of the evidence, who gets chosen as foreperson, how well the jurors get along with each other and unpredictable things that happened during the trial may also influence how their final decisions get made.

PSYCHOLOGICAL TESTS

Social psychological tests may also be helpful to gather information about attitudes and decision-making in prospective jurors. Basic social psychology research indicates that people with different attitudes may look at the same data and make different inferences. These different attitudes can be measured by psychological tests given to prospective jurors. The *Juror Bias Scale* (Kasin & Wrightsman, 1983) and the *Legal Attitudes Questionnaire* (Kravitz, Cutler, & Brock, 1993) are two popular measures that have good predictive validity of who would be more likely to vote with the prosecution and defense in criminal trials. However, these tests have been validated using college students and videos of simulated trials and have not been validated using real-life jurors. Tests like these that measure general attitudes are probably better than guessing or using intuition alone, but their predictive accuracy is low when it comes to verdicts by actual jurors.

Biases that occur in civil trials have not been as easily identified as attitudes that impact on verdicts in criminal cases. For example, how people feel about the amount of risk someone takes when using a product later found to cause injury, such as cigarette smoking and cancer, automobile defects and accidents, and the famous lawsuit against MacDonald's restaurant for serving a woman a cup of coffee hot enough to burn her, can all impact on a civil product liability verdict. Assessment tools are being researched on people's attitudes about cases against third parties who fail to properly protect consumers, doctors who harm patients, people who file too many lawsuits, and corporations who ignore warnings and pollute the environment or fail to provide worker safety. To date, there are no assessment tools to measure attitudes towards cases that involve civil rights, discrimination, harassment, or violence against women, although many jury consultants utilize the general stereotypes described in the previous chapter to assist in choosing sympathetic pro-plaintiff or unsympathetic pro-defense jurors.

RESEARCH TO ASSIST THE ATTORNEY IN TRIAL PREPARATION

Trial consultants may also be asked to conduct research for the attorney during the pendency of the trial. Sometimes this occurs when an unexpected witness or previously undiscovered evidence becomes available and the attorney wants to have an idea how it might affect the sitting jurors. In these cases, other methods will have to be used rather than directly questioning jurors themselves. It is not possible to question jurors once they have been selected. This may be called 'jury tampering' and it has been outlawed by the courts in several important cases. In *Kelly v. U.S., 1918*, as reported in Wrightsman (2001), the court found that a person can be held in contempt of court for trying to communicate with jurors even if it is not clear that the person was trying to influence the jurors. In *Sinclair v. U.S., 1929*, a defendant was held in contempt of court for hiring a detective agency to follow jurors during a trial, similar to the description in *The Runaway Juror* (Grisham, 1996), even though no jurors became aware of their surveillance. It seems likely that should there be such surveillance of jurors who have already been 'empanelled', rather than prospective jurors, even in today's more liberal acceptance of psychology in the courtroom, it would still be held as overstepping the boundaries and limits. Thus, analogue studies such as the ones conducted by Schueller on battered women syndrome defenses or focus groups that are selected to match current juror characteristics might be utilized to experiment with different outcomes.

PSYCHOLOGICAL CONSULTATION ON TRIAL STRATEGIES

Another popular area for behavioral trial consultation today is assisting the attorney in planning trial strategies. This includes deciding on the theme of the case, what facts to emphasize, which ones to downplay, how to get the jurors' attention, and how to persuade them to see things from the client's perspective. Lawyers who may be good at collecting relevant data for a case may not have any idea how to best organize it. This is like planning for any other type of activity that needs organization. For example, you might be wonderful at picking out just the right shoes to go with a particular outfit, but if your closet is a disorganized mess, you may never be able to match those shoes with the intended outfit. The same is true for a trial. Not all facts have the same amount of importance in a case, nor should they. Rather, some are more important to emphasize while others have little or no real meaning even though they might be relevant enough to leave in. Just as you might hire someone to clean out and organize your closet, so might an attorney hire a behavioral trial consultant to help organize the case so that the jurors remember what the litigant wants them to know to make a decision in his or her favor.

Litigation consultants can use psychology to assist in figuring out how to emphasize the best features of a case. Often visual aids are used in the courtroom such as charts and graphs that help explain complicated figures or theories. Graphics presented in an interesting and attractive way can enhance the credibility of the material as well as assure that the jurors understand what the facts actually mean. Although chalkboards and poster boards are still used by witnesses in some cases, others may hire graphic designers to create their visual aids.

PREPARING WITNESSES

Trial consultants may use knowledge gained in social psychology to help prepare witnesses to testify at trial. Social psychology experiments that deal with the influence of attractiveness and appearance of confidence on the credibility of information given by someone have helped consultants prepare witnesses so that what they have to say will really be heard by jurors. Pleasant facial expressions, color and style of clothing that blends with the community, upbeat attitudes when discussing important information, and more serene attitudes when discussing problems are all part of the consultants' package. People can't look too slick, sound too rehearsed, sound too unprepared, demonstrate mental instability, talk too much, giggle, get angry or display a whole host of other behaviors that can detract from the credibility of what they testify to.

Cases have been lost when witnesses laugh too much in the bathroom even though they might demonstrate a serious demeanor in the courtroom. Sitting on the witness stand is a daunting task for many people, even professionals who must testify. If a witness's words are mumbled or garbled, if the witness doesn't look the jurors in the eye, if the witness's behavior does not match the expected emotions for what he or she is testifying to, if there is too much squirming on the witness stand, if the witness doesn't answer the question asked or other observable behaviors are demonstrated, the chances are that witness's information may not be remembered although the person's demeanor might be.

Trial consultants are often hired to work with witnesses to help improve the delivery of their testimony. In some cases, attorneys hire actors to assist witnesses in speaking, as if they have a particular role in the theater to prepare for. After all, many believe that the courtroom is theater, where both sides have the opportunity to play act what they believe is their truth.

TENSIONS RAISED BY RELATIONSHIPS BETWEEN PSYCHOLOGISTS AND ATTORNEYS

As might be expected, many attorneys believe that they are best at jury selection, figuring out the best trial strategy for a particular case, and presenting their case to a jury. Often that is true for experienced trial attorneys who have learned to sharpen their intuitive skills. However, adding the rigor that science provides can prevent disasters that can occur when an attorney gets too sure of his or her ability to persuade a group of people about his or her client's version of truth. In the O.J. Simpson case, Marcia Clark believed she was capable of persuading the jurors that her version of the truth was correct without understanding the complexities of the impact of race, gender, and culture on how people make these decisions. But, she didn't like the trial consultant's attitude and rejected his advice even though it was probably accurate.

It is not unusual for trial attorneys to complain that consultants take too much control over the decision-making role in their trials while consultants complain that attorneys do not follow their advice, even when they pay for it. It is most helpful when all professionals who work on a case are thought of as a team with the attorney and sometimes the client in-charge of making the final decisions. Smart attorneys and clients permit the professionals they hire to make the decisions appropriate to their expertise. But, it is the attorney and client who must adopt a master plan to strategize a case and all the other professionals must fit into their goals. That is truly the role of a consultant who gets paid to give away knowledge and advice. In the end, it is the client and sometimes the attorney who must live with the consequences while the trial consultant goes on to the next case.

SUMMARY

Jurors make decisions based on many different factors as is suggested in the preceding chapter on social psychology and attitude formation. In this chapter, we reviewed the common psychological methods used by trial consultants to gather scientifically systematic information about prospective jurors before they are selected to participate in the voir dire and after they are empanelled. Community surveys, public opinion polls, and demographic data collected from a representative community sample can yield information about the types of people who may be found in the large jury pool. If pretrial publicity or special characteristics of the community appear to make it difficult to find jurors who can give a litigant a fair trial, then these research data can be used to accompany a Motion for a Change of Venue which, if successful, would move the trial to a new location. Once a pool of prospective jurors are sent to a courtroom, written or verbal questions can be used to gather information about the individual's habits, lifestyle, personality style, or other factors that might help predict how a person might decide facts of a particular case. Mock trials and focus groups may also be used to gather information about how someone with similar characteristics and attitudes might listen to and decide a case. Psychological assessment inventories may provide information about general attitudes held by prospective jurors that help predict where their sympathies lie. A jury deselection process where prospective jurors are questioned and dismissed on the basis of cause, or by an attorney using a preemptory challenge, then occurs.

Trial consultation also includes gathering information about how to organize the information for the trial. Opening and closing arguments, selection, timing, and sequencing of witnesses may be tested and the best way to present the evidence decided by scientific data gathering rather than intuition or the attorney's beliefs. How to present facts and preparation of visual aids might also be an area for psychological consultation. Preparing witnesses to testify, especially if their testimony is critical to the theory of the case, may also be part of the trial consultant's work. Although many people have questions about the ethics of trial consultation and jury selection, in fact research suggests that this may be the fairest way to obtain a jury that can carefully listen to all the testimony, ascertain the facts, and make a decision based on the facts of the case and not be influenced by other known and unknown factors. It is important for both consultant and attorney not to overstep their roles and carefully collect only those data that are needed to come to appropriate decisions.

VII

Practical Tips for Forensic Psychology Experts

Our last section gives some important practical hints on how to organize the data gathered by the forensic expert and communicate it effectively to attorneys, judges, and juries at trial. We discuss ways for psychologists to think about the information they now possess and find ways to help attorneys understand and properly use the findings. Once the case proceeds to trial, we assist the forensic expert in presenting the testimony effectively. Since an effective cross-examination can win or lose a trial, we discuss ways for a psychologist to handle a good, vigorous cross-examination and still remain a credible witness. We call this the 'nuts and bolts' section because we designed this section to be of practical assistance. Finally, we look at ways that a psychologist can reduce the risk and behave in a manner in accordance with the ethics code. As many other mental health professions utilize all or part of the psychology ethics standards, this chapter is intended to be useful to all.

21

Forensic Experts and Attorneys: Communication Process

As we have seen in this book, mental health professionals speak different languages and approach situations differently from attorneys and judges. As we have written this book from the perspective of both the forensic expert and the lawyer, we need to spend some time learning how to communicate effectively with each other. In this chapter we begin by suggesting a communication strategy that begins at the time the contract to perform services begins and goes up through the expert submitting a report and testifying in a legal proceeding. We summarize the steps in Table 21-1 and provide some description in the text that follows. In the second section of the chapter, we present discussion of practical solutions to difficulties when an expert and attorney work together during the actual testimony itself.

TABLE 21-1. STEPS IN THE COMMUNICATION PROCESS
BETWEEN ATTORNEY AND EXPERT

Step 1	Clarify the referral question
Step 2	Obtain appropriate collateral materials
Step 3	Perform an initial assessment
Step 4	Expert and attorney consult about initial findings
Step 5	Complete the forensic evaluation
Step 6	Integrate Findings
Step 7	Expert and attorney discuss findings orally
Step 8	Additional agreement to further consult on case
Step 9	Prepare written report
Step 10	Prepare for trial or deposition
Step 11	Immediately before testimony
Step 12	Confer after trial testimony is completed

Step 1. Clarify the Referral Question

It is important for both the forensic expert and the retaining attorney or court to be clear on what is (are) the referral question (s). If each party understands the role he or she must play together, it will make the final product more useful than if the expert doesn't understand the law or the lawyers don't understand the limits of the examination. Check out admissibility issues to determine what may need to be done. Make sure important court dates are clearly understood so that deadlines are not missed. Sometimes putting the referral question in a written contract letter can focus everyone on the same issues.

Step 2. Obtain Appropriate Collateral Materials

It is important for the attorney to forward any materials that the expert will need for corroboration of the forensic issues in a timely manner to the expert. Often the attorney will ask the expert to specify what is needed. It is suggested that all pleadings filed, hospital, employment, and school records, police records and discovery including witness statements be obtained. Sometimes the expert will ask the attorney for additional information based on the first reading of the documents provided or during the evaluation period. It can be quite damaging to a case if an expert has not been provided with materials on which he or she will be cross-examined at deposition or trial.

Step 3. Perform an Initial Assessment

It is often helpful for both the attorney and the expert to be present when the client is introduced. Sometimes this is not possible due to distance or schedules. However, the attorney must give the client or defendant information concerning the reason for the evaluation and why it is important to cooperate. Permission must also be given to defendants to discuss the criminal act in sufficient detail if the expert is asked to determine his or her state of mind at that time. If the contract specifies that the expert will work under the attorney's privilege which is essential in a criminal case and preferred in other cases, then the information is kept privileged until such time as the expert is disclosed as a witness. The attorney can leave once the clinical interview or testing begins. Generally preliminary data are obtained at this first meeting unless scheduling requires all psychological data be collected at one time.

Step 4. Expert and Attorney Consult about Initial Findings

Attorney and expert discuss the initial findings and psychologist puts together the plan for further evaluation. Records that were not provided initially should be requested at this time. For example, if there is question about an earlier head trauma, it is important to try to find any records that would clarify if there were any injuries at that time. If there are other people who could give information about the person's history, decide who will interview them and when. If there is need for referral to another specialist, such as a neurologist or neuropsychologist, discuss who might be a referral source.

Step 5. Complete the Forensic Evaluation

This will consist of detailed clinical interviewing and gathering of important histories such as childhood, school, relationship, and work history from the client. Also obtain information relevant to the client's state of mind at the time in question. Administer, score, and interpret any psychological tests or review other expert's test results so they can be integrated into the findings. Conduct collateral interviews or review depositions or investigator interviews.

Step 6. Integrate Findings

The expert needs to integrate all the information gathered during the examination, collateral sources, and records reviews and provide him or herself with a summary of the key findings. Consult with peers or other professionals involved in the case at this time. It is important to organize and catalogue the file so that all materials are carefully labeled and easily found should a particular point or issue need to be verified.

Step 7. Expert and Attorneys Discuss Findings Orally

The expert and the retaining attorney discuss the findings from the evaluation. At this point the initial contract is complete if the referral questions are answered. It is important to record the date and substance of the conversation in the expert's file so that it is clear that the findings were indeed reported. If the findings are not helpful to the attorney's or client's case strategy, then this will terminate the expert's work on the case. Although it may be required to put findings in written format in some limited areas, unless agreed upon by the retaining attorney, it is usually best not to do so or the collaborative process will be disrupted. On the other hand, it is also important to retain the integrity of each professional and not compromise an objective examination in any way.

Step 8. Additional Agreement to Further Consult on Case

At this point, if the attorney, expert, and client decide that the expert's testimony will be helpful to the case, a second retention occurs for this part of the consultation. Here the attorney and expert work closely on fashioning what the expert testimony will cover. Findings are usually put in written format although in some cases, attorneys prefer not to have written reports until closer to trial. In cases where sworn depositions are taken, preparation for the expert's testimony in deposition will begin.

Step 9. Prepare Written Report

The written report needs to be short and to the point while still disclosing the data on which the expert's opinion is based. Sometimes a draft of the report is reviewed collaboratively and changes are made for factual accuracy and clarity in communicating findings to legal questions. The expert's opinions are not changed unless new data is obtained. The outline of a report should include the following sections: Reason for referral, Procedure (i.e.: time, date, and procedure used at what location, documents reviewed, collateral materials and interviews used), Brief Relevant History (Integrate materials obtained from various histories, reports, and collaterals), Findings (These are the expert's findings and the basis upon which they are based. Test and clinical findings may be compared to the known literature.), Conclusions (repeat the legal conclusions using 'in my professional psychological/medical etc opinion . . .' to introduce each of the findings that answer the legal questions, and Recommendations (usually in a list that makes it easy to read).

Step 10. Prepare for Trial or Deposition

The expert and the attorney, together with the client where ever possible, need to carefully analyze the strong and weak points of the findings. Begin to strategize questions for the direct examination and how to handle the areas that may pose some difficulties. The attorney may request your assistance in preparing questions for other experts' or witness's depositions especially if your findings will be strengthened by what they can confirm. If during deposition, it is discovered that further information is needed, make arrangements to obtain the information before the next testimony is given. Be sure to review the file prior to deposition testimony and bring the entire file including materials requested in subpoena unless otherwise directed. Make sure not to waive reading of the deposition and submit errata sheets if necessary.

Step 11. Shortly before Trial Testimony Is Scheduled

Schedule sufficient time to review the entire file so that all the information is reviewed, the file is in order with no extraneous papers in any folder, and the contents catalogued so they can be found easily if necessary during testimony. Bring the entire file to the courtroom and be prepared to look up information that may not be easily remembered to avoid giving erroneous information. Try to know the information in the report and deposition so well that it is not necessary to refer to notes unless a question requires a precise and detailed answer. Remember that the role of the expert is to educate the triers of fact, so the presentation has to convey the expert's findings in a way that both the jury and judge can understand.

Schedule sufficient time for rest so that the expert and attorney are alert and ready for the trial. Dress professionally in the proper courtroom attire for the community and observe courtroom protocol. That includes that there should be no talking about the case until outside the building. Be respectful of any jurors who happen to be in the same place and leave as quickly as possible. If the expert has to fly in to testify, make arrangements to review testimony with the attorney prior to taking the witness stand. Make sure all the rules of the particular court are known to the expert to avoid unnecessarily upsetting the judge. For example, in some jurisdictions, it is not permissible for the attorney and expert to confer once testimony has begun. In others, the attorney and expert may confer but no other witnesses may be present.

Step 12. Confer after Trial Testimony Is Completed

In addition to sharing the outcome of the trial, it is also important for the expert and the attorney to get together afterwards to review their work together. This permits each party to learn from the experience, both the positive and negative issues that arose during the entire process. Sometimes experts and attorneys cannot work together because they approach the trial with different styles. Other times each can respect the other's process and actually learn how to complement the other. Of course, if the outcome of the trial is success for the client, at a minimum everyone deserves to be pleased.

NUTS AND BOLTS OF EXPERT TESTIMONY

When mental health professionals, academic professors, or experimental psychologists leave the security of their offices and laboratories to enter the courtroom, they encounter an atmosphere which can be both challenging and intimidating. A first time expert will find that the preparation of a forensic report and testimony regarding a case involved new ways of gathering the data, interpreting it, and distinctly different ways of presenting one's conclusions. Most importantly, the forensic expert cannot merely say in a declaratory way whatever she or thinks is relevant about a particular topic to educate the judge or jury, but must figure out (hopefully, with the attorney) how to present the opinions in response to questions posed by an attorney.

QUALIFICATION OF THE EXPERT

The process of rendering expert testimony proceeds in phases. In the first phase, the attorney who has retained the expert will attempt to qualify him or her in front of the judge which is called 'voir dire'. It is the judge who determines whether a particular individual will be allowed to testify as an expert and give opinion testimony. Recall our discussion in Chapter 3 where the Federal Rules of Evidence defined an expert as someone who has the knowledge, skill, education, experience, and training to render an opinion. Questions will therefore be asked of the proposed expert regarding his or her educational background, training, and what experience he/she has had in dealing with the particular kind of issue being adjudicated in this case (e.g. competency, custody). This may be relatively brief or very extended, given the strategy that the attorney chooses to use. Usually the attorney wants to impress the jury with an expert's credentials to enhance credibility of the opinions to be offered. Opposing counsel will then have the opportunity to also voir dire the expert, to challenge the expert on her or his degree of experience, expertise, or training. Challenges to the expert opinions will come during cross-examination, after the direct examination rather than during the voir dire. At times, the opposing attorney will defer the examination of the proposed expert's credentials to later in the proceeding during cross-examination. This happens when the opposing attorney understands that the judge will admit the testimony so any challenges to credibility of the expert will occur during the cross examination phase. The retaining attorney will then "proffer" the individual as an expert in a particular area.

DIRECT TESTIMONY

Once the judge accepts the individual as an expert, the direct testimony is then presented. Direct testimony will cover the methodology used by the expert, the conclusions reached, and opinions regarding the legal issue(s) at hand. Depending on the criteria for admissibility in a particular jurisdiction (e.g., Frye or Daubert), the expert may also be asked how widely accepted the methodology is or the degree of scientific research behind the theories utilized. (In some cases, there may, in fact, be a separate admissibility hearing to determine these issues, even prior to the qualifications of the expert.) The questions asked during direct examination usually have to follow the format that the rules of the court require. In some jurisdictions this means a question and short answer colloquy is acceptable while in other jurisdictions, the expert's answers can be much longer. It is important to organize the testimony so it has some rhythm to it so it holds the interest of the jury. If demonstrative evidence such as charts and drawings can illustrate the points to be made, it is advisable to use them, especially if the testimony is expected to be longer than one hour and on complex information for the layperson. For example, when giving the results of the MMPI-2, it is helpful to have a chart of the graph to explain the scores to the jury. Or, if a diagnosis is made using the DSM-IV criteria, a chart that already has the criteria listed can help the jury follow along and make the diagnosis with the expert. These decisions should be made well in advance of the testimony so materials can be prepared and ready to be used. It can be a nightmare if there is no easel or place to hang a chart or the marker pen runs out of ink in the middle of direct testimony. In traveling to unfamiliar areas, it is often helpful for the expert to carry his or her own marker pens.

CROSS EXAMINATION

The direct testimony is followed by the cross-examination in which opposing counsel may try to undermine the witness's credibility or the basis for her or his opinion. We discuss ways to handle typical cross examination questions below. However, the best cross-examination is one where the expert listens carefully to the question and provides as short an answer as possible to answer the question. Less is better here. Smart attorneys do not keep an expert on the witness stand any longer than is necessary to make a few points, usually raising questions about what the expert did not do whether or not that was necessary to arrive at an opinion. It is rare that an attorney knows as much psychology as does the expert, so it is not usually a good idea to keep on asking questions. Attorneys who do that often permit the jury to hear the expert's opinions over and over again. As we shall discuss later, it is best not to fight with the attorney while on the witness stand; nor is it appropriate to give an inaccurate response to a question.

REDIRECT EXAMINATION

Retaining counsel may then utilize redirect examination to clear up any inconsistencies that were raised during the cross-examination or provide additional information that the opposing attorney would not let the witness testify to. For example, the opposing attorney may have asked the witness to read a sentence from a paragraph in a book which when taken out of context had a different meaning than when put in its proper context. If it is important, the retaining attorney may ask the expert to read the whole paragraph at this time. In some cases there is time between cross examination and redirect for the expert and retaining attorney to prepare some questions. However, most of the time the attorney needs to rely on the earlier preparation to decide what is and is not important to go back over. New areas cannot be raised during redirect so it is usually kept fairly short.

RE-CROSS EXAMINATION

If any inconsistencies were raised during redirect, the opposing attorney may ask one or two questions to be sure the expert's answers are clear.

The judge may also ask questions of the expert at this time to help him or her better understand the testimony of the expert.

PREPARATION FOR TESTIMONY

Careful preparation is the key word in any forensic evaluation. This involves preparing not only one's opinion, but preparing an attorney with the proper questions in order to best elicit the opinion. This requires a somewhat more proactive stance than traditionally trained clinicians generally take. It involves not only analyzing and interpreting one's own data, but also anticipating the challenges to one's opinion that may come from rigorous cross-examination. It is suggested therefore, that the expert not wait until cross-examination to deal with these challenges; rather one should present and try to defuse attacks in advance during the direct examination.

If this strategy is followed, the retaining attorney should ask as many questions as possible during direct testimony that may come up as subsequent challenges. On occasion, especially when working with an attorney who is not familiar with the particular area of testimony, the expert may actually have to prepare written questions for the attorney to ask.

An example follows:

A defendant had been charged with a violent offense during which he had apparently suffered a brief psychotic episode. By the time the defendant was being evaluated at the hospital forensic unit, he had gone into remission and did not appear to be overtly psychotic in his behavior on the ward. Since the daily nursing notes are always important to review as a source of data, the clinician could anticipate that this relatively normal behavior would be brought up as a challenge to the opinion about a psychotic episode. Therefore, during direct examination, the clinician prepared the attorney to ask what a brief psychotic episode was, how long the symptoms might be expected to last, whether they might not be obvious in surface behavior, and whether the clinician would have to look for more subtle signs, such as responses on projective tests (where, in fact, the psychotic thinking did emerge). In this way, the drama was taken out of the cross-examination when the challenge to the psychotic symptoms occurred. As a strategic matter, it also demonstrates to the trier of fact the degree of careful preparation by the expert. The expert would be well advised, before consulting with the retaining counsel, and certainly before coming to court, to cross-examine herself or himself, frankly examining both the weak and strong points of the proposed testimony.

The most common methodology in cross-examination is to highlight the areas which the expert overlooked or did not consider sufficiently. The above strategy will help to defuse this line of cross-examination.

Is it Possible That?

It is, of course, impossible to anticipate all possible grounds of cross-examination. The challenge to the clinician's opinion will frequently come in the form of "Dr., would it change your opinion if I told you...?" This question is really a legal trap. One should not answer the question either "yes" or "no." If one answers the question "yes," then the entire opinion immediately becomes suspect because the judge or jury may believe the witness is willing to change an opinion based on very little evidence, i.e. one question. If the expert were to answer the question "no," the opposing attorney would keep asking questions to which the expert would answer "no"; the expert comes to be perceived as a rigid, dogmatic fool, unwilling to change an opinion under any circumstances. In fact, the most appropriate response would be: "I don't know whether it would change my opinion or not; I would be glad to re-examine the client in light of the information you are presenting." The attorney may well respond that since trial proceedings are ongoing, they cannot be interrupted in order for the defendant to be re-examined, and could the expert speculate on whether or not her or his opinion might change? This becomes an excellent opportunity for a response indicating that one cannot speculate, because ethically one can only base an opinion on data sufficient to substantiate the opinion, not on speculation.

RESPONDING TO OTHER ATTACKS

While considering this line of cross-examination, we should also consider what is sometimes referred to as the double bind or "dammed if you do and damned if you don't" question. Any answer the expert gives will be attacked. An example would be "Have you reviewed records prior to examining the defendant (or plaintiff)?" If the expert answers "yes," then an attack follows about being biased by the records and not reaching a truly independent opinion. If the expert answers "no," then an attack follows about not being thorough or not doing a complete job. A suggested response utilizes what is called the 'precedent dependent clause'. When asked one of these 'double bind' questions, the expert responds, "If what you are asking me is ___, then I would answer ___, but if what you are asking me is ___, I would answer ___. The expert is essentially unraveling the bind deliberately created by the opposing attorney. For example, in the above scenario, the expert would answer, "If what you're asking me is whether record review is an essential part of a forensic assessment, the answer is, of course yes; because we are constantly generating and checking our hypotheses, confirming some, rejecting others, we are not being biased by any particular piece of data that we may have."

THREE LEVELS OF CROSS-EXAMINATION

Experts frequently become very anxious when confronted by personalized accusations on cross-examination. In fact, such personal attacks are really not so destructive. Attorneys learn to attack first the witness's credentials, secondly the witness's opinion, and only if the opinions and credentials are on solid ground, then to attack the witness personally. Therefore, far from being intimidated by such an attack, the expert should feel quite confident that the attack really is an acknowledgement of how solid the credentials and opinion are; the attorney is attacking the expert with the only material available.

What is an example of a personal attack? Implying that the expert is a "hired gun," or that the opinion can be "bought" is a frequent attack. The cross examiner may ask, for instance, how much one is being paid for one's opinion. One needs to listen carefully to the question, for it clearly implies that one will say anything if the price is right. An appropriate response would be, "I am not being paid for my opinion; I am being paid for my time." If the cross-examination persists, and one is asked how much one is being paid for one's time, the expert may respond, "that all depends on how much you cross-examine me . . . "

One of the authors (DS) had done work in a particular jurisdiction for both the Public Defender and the United States Attorney's office. In this particular case, he had testified for the government and was being cross-examined by defense counsel about his fee. Upon eliciting the amount of the fee, defense counsel shook his head in amazement and stated, "No further questions." On redirect, the United States Attorney elicited testimony that DS had also done work for the defense attorney, and, in fact, had charged him a higher fee than the present fee in the last case he had done for the defense attorney.

ATTACKS ON PSYCHOLOGICAL TESTING

When experts, especially psychologists, testify, with their findings based, in part on psychological testing, they may be subject to a variety of attacks. An attorney will often attack the validity and reliability of testing. The best defense against this attack is to understand fully the tests one is using, and the fact that the tests are only one part of a comprehensive forensic examination. Experts make serious errors when they try to make too many inferences from the testing, rather than using the tests in the same manner as any other data point in a forensic examination; they yield a hypothesis that is subject to confirmation or disconfirmation by other sources of data. It should be stressed in direct examination just what the forensic methodology is, and how it depends on the integration of, and consistency across, multiple sources of data. Then, when an attorney on cross-examination tries to isolate out a particular finding from one test, the response would be: "As I stated in direct examination, that score is only one part of a comprehensive methodology, and I did not rely exclusively on that particular score or test." One may then add, the additional data that is consistent with that particular test finding (i.e., results from other tests, documented behavior, prior records, etc.). If an attorney seeks to ask questions about the validity or reliability of a given test, one should indicate that the question cannot be answered in such a simplistic manner, that there are many kinds of validity and reliability, and that the attorney would have to define her/his terms more precisely.

One of the authors (DS) was confronted with the following line of cross-examination:

ATTY: Now Doctor, you used the MMPI-2 as part of your examination, is that not true?

D.S.:   That is correct.

ATTY: Now, isn't it true, Doctor, that research has shown that the MMPI-2 is not valid for this population?

D.S.:   Could you please define what you mean by validity?

ATTY: Come now, Doctor, you're a psychologist, don't you know what validity is?

D.S.:   Of course, counselor, but there is face validity, construct validity, and predictive validity. You will have to give a more precise definition before I can respond accurately to your question.

ATTY: I withdraw the question.

Note here, that there was a trap that the author could have fallen into, when the attorney spoke of the test not being valid "for this population." Had the author asked "What population," then the attorney would have the upper hand. In focusing instead on the issue of validity, the author was able to demonstrate that the question really was a smokescreen, an attempt to "throw the witness off balance."

The expert will inevitably be challenged regarding whether or not a defendant is malingering or faking symptoms. One should be able to counter this by utilizing and being familiar with the many available assessment instruments for malingering now on the market. As noted in the chapter on Clinical Assessment, there are a number of well-validated assessment instruments designed to detect malingering, available from companies that publish psychological tests. The *Structured Interview of Reported Symptoms* (S.I.R.S.) is a highly valid instrument for the detection of malingering of psychiatric symptoms. The V.I.P. (Validity Indicator Profile) is an excellent instrument to use for evaluating malingering of cognitive impairment, and the Test of Memory Malingering (T.O.M.M.) for the evaluation of feigned memory deficits. On occasion, questions based on malingering in a clinical population will be asked to demonstrate that clinicians generally cannot tell the differences between a faked psychosis and a genuine one. It needs to be pointed out that in clinical settings one rarely checks for malingering because one assumes that a person is presenting herself/himself for treatment because of distress or dysfunction. In a forensic setting, on the other hand, the assessment of malingering is an integral part of the examination. In other words, to critique a forensic assessment based on findings from clinical work is really mixing apples and oranges.

A frequent line of such attack is seen in the use of Rosenhan's classic study *On Being Sane in Insane Places*. Rosenhan had several of his graduate students present themselves for admission to a psychiatric hospital claiming that they were experiencing auditory hallucinations. All were admitted. When they informed the staff, several days later, that they really were not mentally ill, that their being there was part of a class project, progress notes reflected their "delusional thinking." As noted above, when this study is used to cast doubt on one's forensic conclusions, one needs to point out the fact that this was a clinical, as opposed to a forensic, setting; within a clinical setting, there is no reason to assess for malingering, while in forensic evaluations, it is a question we always consider.

THE LEARNED TREATISE ATTACK

A frequent cross-examination question appears to begin in a rather benign manner. The expert is asked if she/he recognizes a particular work or author as authoritative in a particular field. This is an important question, with far reaching implications, because once the expert acknowledges something as an authoritative reference, then the expert can be cross-examined using it. If one is not familiar with, or disagrees with substantial portions of a particular work, one should not acknowledge it as authoritative. Be prepared to resist sarcastic comments such as "How can you, supposedly a trained psychologist, not be familiar with Dr. Zippendorfer's famous theory of motivation?" Of course, even if one acknowledges a particular work as authoritative, it does not necessarily mean that one agrees with everything in the work, and this needs to be made clear. Of course, if one is unfamiliar with the work, do not pretend that one is familiar with it. This is a mistake that a number of experts make, fearing that if she/he says they are unfamiliar with a particular work, it would appear to diminish her/his credibility.

Preparation with Relevant Case Law

The forensic expert needs to be aware of important case law that deals with expert testimony and work with the retaining attorney, preparing her/him for issues that may arise. For instance, attorneys may argue on cross-examination that because someone is not a medical doctor, that she/he is not qualified to render an expert opinion. Knowledge of case law will enable the expert to prepare the attorney to handle this, noting several decisions in which courts have ruled that the degree which a proposed expert has is not as important as the extent of qualifications, as determined by the individual trial judge. This was demonstrated quite strongly in a 1962 case, Jenkins v. U.S. 307F. 2d637 (1962). In addition, the Insanity Defense Reform Act of 1984 established total parity between psychologists and psychiatrists in federal law (and, by implication, in the state law of all states that revised their statutes to reflect federal law). Where the old law spoke of *psychiatric* evaluation, report, and testimony, the new law spoke of psychiatric or psychological evaluations, report, and testimony. If an attorney tries to "sandbag" an expert by demanding that the expert answer a question with a simple "yes" or "no," it would be helpful if the expert were aware of, and told the retaining attorney ahead of time, about a variety of cases in which the expert is either encouraged or required to give the bases for her/his opinions. Experts are sometimes instructed to give their testimony in the kind of detail that one might expect from a doctor trying to explain to a family about the nature of an illness that a family member has. This is more detailed in the "Instructions to Expert Witnesses," part of the case of *Washington v. U.S. (1967)* as was discussed in Chapter 4. This case states explicitly that the expert need not be restricted to a yes or no answer. Of course, the judge is (or should be) aware of the fact that an expert is not required to answer questions "yes" or "no." If an attorney is demanding a "yes" or "no" answer, it is often effective for the expert to turn to the judge and say something like "Your Honor", I cannot answer that question with a simple "yes" or "no"; may I be permitted to expand upon my answer?" It is a rare to nonexistent occasion when the judge refuses to allow such explanations.

The Hypothetical Question

A technique that may be well be used in cross-examination is the hypothetical question. An expert may be asked to assume, for the sake of the hypothetical, that various facts are in evidence, and then, if it is assumed that those facts are true, would it be a fair statement that ___, and the attorney will then ask a question of the expert. The expert must listen, very carefully, to the "facts" being presented in the hypothetical, because they are, very often, the exact opposite of observations reached by the expert. For instance, the expert may have reached a conclusion that a defendant (or plaintiff) may be of average intelligence, shows no signs of central nervous system impairment, and shows no signs of psychosis. The hypothetical, on cross-examination may well be, "Please assume that the defendant is mentally retarded, and shows signs of brain damage and psychosis, would it be a fair statement that ___?" The expert is advised to respond to such a question by saying: "I cannot answer that question the way it is asked because you have asked me to assume a variety of conclusions which are the opposite of the data I have gathered. I can only ethically respond to questions when I have data to support my conclusions." The attorney doing the cross-examination will, at that point, usually ask the judge to instruct the expert to respond to the questions, since experts are allowed to respond to hypotheticals. The judge will then ask the witness whether she/he can respond to the hypothetical; if the witness responds that she/he cannot, for the same reasons articulated above, this line of cross-examination will usually stop at this point. This is, of course, a similar response to that noted earlier, citing ethical constraints, when answering the "would it change your opinion" kind of question.

STAYING CLOSE TO THE DATA

A final caution should be noted. Do not speculate; render conclusions only when there is data adequate to support conclusions. Whatever conclusions are offered need to be supported with empirical or clinical data. If one is concluding that a defendant (or plaintiff) is depressed, one needs to indicate precisely what the indications of depression are; if one has concluded that there is evidence of psychotic thinking, what precisely are some examples of the distorted thinking? More importantly, how do these clinical findings lead to the forensic conclusions? Do not over reach in an attempt to make the clinical conclusions fit the forensic questions. For example, a conclusion that a person is mentally retarded, or organically impaired does not necessarily mean that the person is not, for instance, criminally responsible. One would have to demonstrate how the psychosis would interfere with the ability to appreciate wrongfulness or the ability to control one's behavior.

The fact that even well qualified experts sometimes lose sight of the difference between clinical data and the forensic conclusions is illustrated

TABLE 21-2. GUIDELINES FOR EXPERT TESTIMONY

1 Preparation.
2 Anticipate attack.
3 Present cross during direct.
4 Is it possible that?...Don't answer!
5 Beware of Double Binds—Learn to unravel them.
6 Three levels of cross-examination: Listen carefully and relax.
7 Psychological testing within Hypothesis Generating Model.
8 Consider and deal with malingering.
9 Beware of the "Learned Treatise" attack.
10 Prepare with Relevant Case Law.
11 Hypothetical questions: listen carefully—respond only with conclusions from available data.
12 Do not over generalize from data.

in the following example. A very bizarre series of homicides were committed by a defendant. His defense, not surprisingly, was not guilty by reason of insanity. There was conflicting expert testimony from many well qualified experts. When the jury convicted the defendant, rejecting the insanity defense, one of the defense experts expressed amazement that the jury felt that this very disturbed defendant was "completely normal." Of course, the jury was not indicating that the defendant was normal, but rather that, despite his serious psychopathology, he did not meet the legal criteria for insanity.

One must also be on the alert for words that may have very specific meanings in legal settings, that are different from the clinical usage which experts may use. We may opine, for instance on the basis of certain psychological tests, that an individual has difficulty anticipating the consequences of what they do, or has difficulty tolerating stress, or is impulsive. This may lead to an attorney's asking whether or not this individual could plan, deliberate, form intent, etc. It is best *not* to translate the clinical finding into a legal conclusion, unless there is other data present that supports it.

22

Risk Management in Forensic Psychology Practice

The mental health professional who goes into the courtroom faces an environment which is often different and challenging. Sometimes it can get hostile, so the wise forensic expert should take precautions to manage the risk by making sure he or she practices in an ethical manner. All of the mental health professions (e.g., psychology, psychiatry, social work, nursing, counseling) have their own codes of ethics. In reviewing these ethical issues, we will be referring to two documents, *The Ethical Principles of Psychologists and Code of Conduct* (1992, 2002) and *The Specialty Guidelines for Forensic Psychologists* (1991). Sometimes these codes deal explicitly with forensic issues and at other times, these issues are incorporated into more generic statements, applicable to professional practice as a whole. For example, some major issues that need to be addressed are:

1. **Who is the client?**
   In traditional counseling and psychotherapy relationships, the answer is simple: the client is the person, family, or group seeking

your professional assistance. In forensic settings, it is more complex, since the referral is usually from a third party, such as an attorney or the court. Some forensic professionals regard only the referral source as the client, while others maintain that in forensic settings, one has two clients—the referral source and the person being evaluated.

2. **What are the issues regarding confidentiality?**

In clinical settings, the issue is more clear-cut—the patient or client can expect confidentiality except under very unusual circumstances (child abuse reporting, protection of endangered parties). In forensic settings, we also encounter what is called attorney-client privilege. This privilege overlaps with, but is broader than, the psychologist's confidentiality mandate. Therefore, when a mental health professional works for an attorney, it must be decided if he or she follows the attorney-client privilege, or the therapist-patient confidentiality rules? Some experts try to blend the two together.

3. **Boundaries of competence.**

All professions urge practitioners to not practice out of the bounds of their competence. What does this mean within a forensic setting? Is general training in forensic assessment enough, or does the professional have to have specific expertise in the background presented by a particular client? Psychologists are required to make these decisions for themselves but be prepared to support whatever choice is made.

4. **Multiple Relations.**

In a counseling or therapy relationship, a therapist is careful not to engage in any multiple relationship that might lead to loss of objectivity or effectiveness and cause harm or exploitation to the client. This usually means that the therapist does not engage in romantic, sexual, or financial dealings with a client outside the therapy hours. Some forensic experts question the objectivity of a therapist who also testifies in a forensic setting. Some therapists question the ability of a forensic evaluator to present the complete picture of the client. Whatever choice the expert makes, it is important to carefully think through all the issues.

5. **Practice only in areas in which you are competent.**

Competence is defined as practicing in a particular area only if you have appropriate and sufficient education, training and experience. Within a forensic setting, where there is often a 'battle of the experts', and a temptation to exaggerate credentials, the expert must exercise some restraint, presenting only the education, training, and experience earned. For instance, someone who has been trained in adult personality and psychopathology would probably *not* have the competence to answer questions that would arise in a child custody situation, such as given a particular child's developmental needs, what parental arrangement would be in the best interest of the child? The expert must be prepared to present to the court the reasons why one's training is relevant to the specific matters being decided. The judge makes the final determination. The forensic professional also has to have a basic knowledge of the legal and professional standards governing his or her participation in a legal proceeding. If, for instance, the expert is practicing in a state where admissibility is determined by the scientific validity of one's opinions (Daubert), it is necessary to be prepared to present reasons why the material is scientifically acceptable. It is also important to understand the civil rights of parties in a legal proceeding and be aware of the legal basis, for instance, of a defendant's refusal, in a criminal case, to participate in an examination and avoid using any techniques that might threaten those civil rights.

Competence also refers to having enough continuing education to be aware of current developments in forensic assessment instruments, normative data regarding the applications of psychological testing in forensic settings, and the manner in which a competent forensic assessment is performed. For example, there has been a profusion of research and writing in the field of neuropsychological assessment. A psychologist, for instance, who is asked to address a neuropsychological issue, fails to utilize current assessment instruments and relies on outmoded screening instruments to answer these questions, could be found to not be practicing according to community standard.

Those presenting themselves as forensic experts have an affirmative obligation to present to the court and to attorneys their own areas of competence, and the relevance of their training to the issues at hand. If asked a question, which one cannot answer due to the limited scientific or professional knowledge on the topic, the expert must inform the court or the attorney that the question cannot be answered for those reasons.

6. **Informed Consent.**

The necessity for informed consent in a forensic evaluation has a lengthy judicial history going back at least twenty years. For instance, in a criminal case, it is necessary to inform the defendant of the nature of the evaluation, the lack of confidentiality in the evaluation, and to whom the results of the evaluation will be disclosed. In some states, if an expert is retained by a defense attorney, and reaches a conclusion that is not beneficial to that attorney, the negative opinion need not be revealed to the prosecutor. On the other hand, in several other states, once a mental health defense is raised, the defendant has essentially waived attorney-client privilege and the results of the evaluation are available to the government. It is therefore important for the expert to be familiar with the law in the state in which she or he practices, in order to properly word the disclosure statement. If the expert is retained by the government, any material that would be of assistance to the defense must be revealed. If the evaluation is court-ordered, no privilege exists and the report needs to be turned over to all concerned parties.

The expert needs to consider the defendant's capacity to render informed consent. While, in a court ordered evaluation consent is not technically required (though it would be advisable), an evaluation on behalf of either a defense attorney or prosecutor requires that the defendant be competent to render informed consent to the procedure. If the consent cannot be obtained, it is appropriate to notify the attorney or obtain a court order before proceeding.

7. **Use up-to-date assessment techniques.**
Mental health professionals need to be aware of the proper applications and uses of the techniques that they use and are sensitive to situations in which particular techniques or norms may not be applicable, for instance, in a forensic setting. Given the recognition that scores may mean different things in forensic settings than in clinical settings, clinicians must make qualifying statements about the degree of certainty with which diagnoses, judgments or predictions can be made about individuals.

Certain tests now have normative data based on forensic and correctional populations. The clinician doing a forensic assessment should attempt, whenever possible, to utilize these forensic, rather than clinical, norms. If using a test that does not have such norms, then the clinician must speak to the limitations of the validity and reliability of the conclusions or recommendations, since the population being tested is different from the population on which the test was normed.

Example

A psychologist within a correctional facility was evaluating inmates regarding whether or not they could be transferred to a less secure facility. The psychologist used an MMPI-2 normed on a clinical population, and concluded, based on the test results, that the defendant was defensive, out of touch with his hostile impulses, and therefore not appropriate for transfer to a less secure facility. This psychologist failed to factor in the situational or contextual variables. Any inmate being evaluated for a less secure environment would appear defensive on a test that had clinically generated norms.

There is now research detailing the patterns obtained on the psychological test results of victims of domestic violence. These often differ from the interpretive statements in various computer programs such as the MMPI-2. To interpret such profiles without consideration of the fact that the group under consideration (battered women) differs significantly from the group on which the test was originally normed (clinical outpatients) would certainly be a deviation from accepted practice, and has the potential for resulting in serious harm.

8. **Be accurate in describing your credentials.**

When an expert testifies in court, there is frequently an attempt to make her or him look more qualified than she or he really is. Generally, experts will not blatantly misrepresent credentials, but an attorney, trying to cast her or his expert in the best possible light, may exaggerate the expert's qualifications. If the expert is aware of this attempt to exaggerate the qualifications, he or she should take steps to correct the impressions.

Example

A psychologist, who did not have a doctorate, sent out announcements describing herself as being an "M.S., A.B.D., Forensic Consultant." A.B.D. usually stands for "all but dissertation," but, placed on a business announcement, implies that it is some kind of credential qualifying her to be a forensic consultant. The relevant ethical standard has to do with not misrepresenting one's credentials, either through commission or through omission.

9. **Avoid the misuse of your data or your influence.**

While the caution to 'do no harm' seems straightforward, many professionals do not perceive or think through the potential harm in their forensic activities. For example, should we do evaluations to determine competency for execution? If an individual is found incompetent for execution, should we participate in treatment programs to restore that individual to competency to be executed?

In a similar manner, many professionals are now participating in "sexual predator" evaluations to determine whether or not an individual is prone to act in a violent sexually predatory manner in the future. Before undertaking such an evaluation, it is important to be familiar with the available literature regarding prediction of sexual recidivism. Then, only if the expert decides if he or she is comfortable making predictive statements under the circumstances of rather limited research, should she or he proceed with such evaluations.

10. **Be certain you have sufficient data to back up your conclusions.**

    Example

    A patient who had suffered a closed head injury and was undergoing cognitive rehabilitation was referred to a psychologist for an IME (independent medical evaluation). The psychologist did not review any records, nor did he administer any psychological tests; instead, concluding, based on a brief clinical interview, that the patient was malingering. He contended that he could not have used any of these other sources of data because they would have "biased" his conclusions.

    This is clearly an inadequate basis for a conclusion of this magnitude since, of course, we are dealing with an apparent neuropsychological impairment and this psychologist did no neuropsychological assessment. In addition, there are many well-validated tests for malingering, none of which this psychologist relied upon in rendering his conclusion that this patient was malingering.

11. **Carefully document your records.**

    Documentation in forensic cases must be exact and comprehensive, anticipating that at some point, an attorney or judge may be looking at the record. The manner in which one reaches conclusions, in other words, how one gets from the data to the opinion needs to be specified. Merely to state that one reached an opinion because of thirty years experience is not acceptable. Making a diagnosis takes more than an intuitive "feeling". Adhere to standard procedures, for instance, in administering and interpreting tests. If a different or idiosyncratic approach to the assessment is used, document the reasons for the change, and specify that it is not the standard methodology.

12. **Personally examine the client unless special circumstances prohibit it.**

    Clinical forensic evaluations usually require a personal examination to come to an opinion about the client. There are certain circumstances in which this cannot be done. When, for whatever reason (e.g., an attorney objecting, a client being unavailable), the client cannot be personally seen, the conclusions in the report must be qualified in terms of the missing data. For instance, one may qualify the degree of certainty in one's conclusions by noting that the person could not be personally examined.

13. **Take steps to protect your data and your records.**
Sometimes, ethics and the law do collide (though not as often as people believe). The ethical obligation, under these circumstances, is to make known to the judge or attorney what the code of ethics requires and try to work out the situation responsibly. An area is which this occurs quite frequently is a demand for discovery of records. While the expert must be concerned about the preservation of the confidentiality of the records, under certain circumstances—for example, when a patient sues for mental or emotional damages—the privilege attached to those records may have been waived. Responsible steps would include notification of the legal authority involved about the ethical dilemma involved, and an attempt to work the matter out informally. This may require the judge to redact certain non-relevant parts of a therapy record or it may involve providing the records to another mental health professional who has been trained in their interpretation. On those occasions when this is not effective, the professional may have to file a 'Motion to Quash' or 'Motion for a Protective Order', explaining to the court, in a more formal manner, the same issues previously discussed informally. If the court orders the records to be released anyhow, it is permissible to do so under the court order, making appropriate documentation. Reasonable steps may also include obtaining consultation from fellow forensic professionals or obtaining the advice of an attorney.

SUMMARY

We have attempted to discuss some of the areas where forensic experts need to be sensitive to the ethical implications that can arise. In each case, it is important to understand the issues, clarify your own role, and make appropriate decisions based on your interpretation of the issues. Peer and expert consultation can support the fact that you have been thoughtful before you took whatever steps you choose. Always remember to document important issues in your records leaving a paper trail for anyone who questions your professional judgment.

Case Citations

Addington v. Texas 441 U.S. 368-376, 418-33 (1979)

Atkins v. Virginia 122 S. Ct. 2242 (2002)

Batson v. Kentucky 106 S. Ct. 1712 (1989)

Belloti v. Baird (1979) 443 U.S. 622

Brown v. Board of Education of Topeka 74 S Ct. 686 (1954)

Bundy v. Jackson, 641, F.2d, 934, 944, (DC cir. 1981)

Casey v. Planned Parenthood No. 93-1503, No. 93-1504 U.S. Court of Appeals for Third Circuit, 14 F.3d 848 (1993)

Clark City School v. Breeden (1994) No. 00-866 Supreme Court of U.S., 532 U.S. 268

Craig v. Maryland (1990) No. 63 Sept. Term, 1990 Court of Appeals of Maryland, 322 Md. 418.

Christy Bros. Circus v. Turnage 144 S.E. 68 (1928).

Cook v. Cook 912 P. 2d-264 (Nevada) 1996

Crane v. Kansas (SCUS) 534 U.S. 407 (2002).

Daubert v. Merrell Dow Pharmaceuticals Inc. 509 U.S. 579, 113 S. Ct. 2786 (1993).

Davis for Lashonda v. Monroe County B of Ed (1999)?

Davis v. Davis 842 S.W. 2d 588 Tennessee 1992

Dobi v. Marisoff

Donaldson v. O'Connor 493 F.2d 507, 518-522 (5th Circuit, 1974).

Ellison v. Brady, 924, F2d 872, 880 n 15 (9th Cir, 1991)

Equal Employment Opportunity Commission?

Faragher v. Boca Raton, 110 s.ct. 2275, (1998)

Gibson v. Gibson (1971), 3 Cal. 3d 914, 92 Cal Rptr. 288, 479 P.2d 648

Giovine v. Giovine (1995) 284 N.J. Super. 3; 663 A.2d 109

Griswold v. Connecticut (1965), 85 S. Ct 1678, 381 U.S. 479.

Harris v. Forklift Systems, 510 U.S. 17.114 S.CT. 367, 63 FEP (1993)

Hecht v. Superior Court (California) California Ct. of Appeals, 2nd Appel-
    lant Dist. Division 2, 192 Cal. App. 3d 560.

Heller v. Doe (1993), 113 S. Ct. 2637

Hodgson v. Minnesota 497 U.S. 417 1990

Hopkins v. Price Waterhouse USSC, U.S. District Ct. for D.C. 618 F. Supp.
    1109; 1985 U.S. Dist.

In re Baby M 537 A. 2d. 1227 (N.J. 1988)

In re Gault 387 U.S. 1 (1967)

In re Ramona (See Ramona v. Superior Court (1997)

Insanity Defense Reform Act of 1984, P. Law 98-473, 18 U.S.C. $ 17.

Jackson v. Indiana 406 U.S. 715-738 (1972).

JEB v. Alabama 114 S. Ct. 1419, 62 U.S.L.W 4219 (1994)

Jenkins v. U.S. 307 F. 2 d 637 (1962)

Kansas v. Hendricks 117 S. Ct. 2072-89 (1997)

Katz v. Katz (1967)

Kelly v. U.S. (1918)

Kent v. U.S. 383 U.S. 541 1966

Lessard v. Schmidt 379 F. Supp. 1376, 1379 (E.D. WIS-1974).

McCarver v. North Carolina 548 S.E. 2d 522 (N.C. 2001) cert. granted, 121
    S. Ct. 1401 (2001), cert. dismissed 122 S. Ct. 22 (2001).

Meritor Savings Bank, FSB v. Vinson, 477 US 57, 65-67, (1986)

Meyer v. Nebraska 262 U.S. 390 (1923).

Miranda v. Arizona 384 U.S. 436 (1966).

Neal v. Ferguson Constr, 237F.3d 1248, 1253 (CA10 2001)

Norris v. Norris (1979). D.C., 459 A 2d 952.

Oncale v. Sundowner Offshore Oil, 83F. 3d 118, 70 FEP (1998)

Parham v. J.R. (1979), 442 U.S. 584

Pablano v. Pablano (1980), California Ct. Supp., 1st District, July 9, 6 F.L.R.
    2753

Penry v. Lynaugh U.S. 492 U.S. 1 (1989).

Pierce v. Society of Sisters (1925), 45 S. Ct. 571, 268 U.S. 510.

Planned Parenthood v. Danforth (1976), 96 S.Ct. 2831, 428 U.S. 52.

Pollard v. duPont (2001)—Pollard v. E.I. duPont de Nemours & Co. 532 U.S. 956

Popham v. Duncan 87 Colo. 149, 285 p. 757, 70 A.L.R. 824 (1930).

Price Waterhouse v. Hopkins, 490 US 228 (1989)

Rabidue v. Osceola Refining Co, 805 F.2d 611, 619-20, (6th Cir 1986)

Ramona v. Superior Court (1997), 57 Cal App. 4th 107, 66 Cal Rptr. 2d 766. (2nd District)

Reynolds v. U.S.- U.S. Ct. of Appeals for 11th Cir. 209 F.3d 722; 2000 U.S. App Lexis 9356

Rennie v. Klein—Supreme Court of the United States 458 U.S. 1119; 102 S. Ct. 3506

Roe v. Wade (1973) 410 U.S. 113

Rogers v. EEOC, 454 F2d, 234, 238 (5th Cir.) (1971)

Rogers v. Okin 634 F.2d 650 (1st Cir.) (1980).

Romer v. Evans (1996), 116 S. Ct. 1620.

Rouse v. Cameron 373 F. 2d 451 (D.C. Cir. 1966).

Rule v. Geddes (1904), 23 App #D.C. 31.

Scott v. Sears Roebuck, 798F2d 210, 213 (7th Cir 1986)

Sieg v. Sieg?

Sinclair v. U.S. 1929?

Skinner v. Oklahoma (1942), 62 S. Ct. 1110, 316 U.S. 535.

Thompson v. Kowalsky?

Thompson v. Okalhoma US (1988) 487 U.S. 815; 108 S. Ct. 2687

Thornberg v. American College of Obstetricians & Gynecologists (1986), 476 U.S. 747.

Title VII of the Civil Rights Act of 1964, 42 usc 2000e et seq (1982).

Washington v. Harper (1990) 494 U.S. 210

Wyatt v. Stickney (1972). 344 F. Supp. 387 (M.D. Ala. 1972).

Youngberg v. Romeo 457 U.S. 307 (1982).

Selected Readings

Chapter 1

Goldstein, A.M. (Ed.) (2003). *Forensic psychology. Volume 11 in the Handbook of Psychology.* New York: Wiley.

Hess, A. & Weiner, I. (Eds.) (1999). *Handbook of forensic psychology, 2nd edition.* New York: Wiley.

Melton, G., Poythress, N., Petrila, J. & Slobogin, C. (1997). *Psychological evaluations for the courts: 2nd Edition.* New York: Guilford.

Munsterberg, H. (1907). *On the witness stand.* New York: Doubleday, Page, & Company.

Wrightsman, L. (2001). *Forensic psychology.* Cambridge, MA: Wadsworth

Chapter 2

Melton, G., Poythress, N., Petrila, J. & Slobogin, C. (1997). *Psychological evaluations for the courts: 2nd Edition.* New York: Guilford.

Wrightsman, L. (2001). *Forensic psychology.* Cambridge, MA: Wadsworth

Chapter 3

Goldstein, A.M. (Ed.) (2003). *Forensic psychology. Volume 11 in the Handbook of Psychology.* New York: Wiley.

Perlin, M. (1999). *Mental disability law.* Durham N.C.: Carolina Academic Press.

Chapter 4

Perlin, M. (2001). *Mental disability on trial.* Washington, D.C.: American Psychological Association.

Perlin, M. (1999). *Mental disability law.* Durham N.C.: Carolina Academic Press.

Perlin, M. (1994). *The jurisprudence of the insanity defense.* Durham N.C.: Carolina Academic Press.

Shapiro, D.L. (2001). *Criminal responsibility.* Sarasota, FL: Professional Resources Press.

Chapter 5

Grisso, T. (1988). *Competency to stand trial: A manual for practice.* Sarasota, FL: Professional Resources Press.

Grisso, T. (1998). *Instruments for Understanding & Appreciation of MIRANDA Rights.* Professional Resources Press: Sarasota, FL.

Grisso, T. & Borum, R. (2002). *Evaluating Competencies: Forensic Assessments and Instruments.* New York: Kluwer Academic Publishers.

Hoge, S.K., Bonnie, R.J., Poythress, N.G., Monahan, J. (1997). *MacArthur Competency Assessment Tool for Criminal Adjudication (MacCAT-CA).* Lutz, Florida: Psychological Assessment Resources, Inc.

Monahan, J. (1981). *The Clinical Prediction of Violent Behavior.* Washington DC: Government Printing office.

Perlin, M. (2001). *Mental disability on trial.* Washington, D.C.: American Psychological Association.

Perlin, M. (1999). *Mental disability law.* Durham N.C.: Carolina Academic Press.

Chapter 6

Browne, A. (1986). *When battered women kill.* New York: Free Press.

Dershowitz, A. (1994). *The abuse excuse.* New York: Little, Brown, and Company.

Ewing, C. (1988). *Battered women who kill.* Cambridge, Lexington Press.

Hagen, M.A. (1997). *Whores of the court: The fraud of psychiatric testimony and the rape of American justice.* New York: HarperCollins.

Walker, L.E.A. (1989). *Terrifying love: Why battered women kill and how society responds. NY:* HarperCollins.

Walker, L.E.A. (1994). *Abused women and survivor therapy: A practical guide for the psychotherapist.* Washington, D.C.: American Psychological Association.

Walker, L.E.A. (2000). *The battered woman syndrome: 2nd Edition.* NY: Springer.

Chapter 7

Frederick, R. (1997). *The validity indicator profile: Professional manual.* Minnesota: National Computer Systems/Pearson.

Grisso, T. (1997). *Instruments for understanding and assessing comprehension of Miranda rights: Professional manual.* Florida: Professional Resource Press.

Heilbrun, K. (2002). *Forensic mental health assessment.* New York: Kluwer Academic/Plenum Publishers.

Hoge, S.K., Bonnie, R.J., Poythress, N.G., Monahan, J. (1997). *MacArthur Competency Assessment Tool for Criminal Adjudication (MacCAT-CA)*. Lutz, Florida: Psychological Assessment Resources, Inc.

Rogers, R. (1992). *Structured Interview of Reported Symptoms (SIRS): Professional manual*. Lutz, Florida: Psychological Assessment Resources.

Shapiro, D.L. (2001). *Criminal responsibility*. Sarasota, FL: Professional Resources Press.

Shapiro, D.L. (1990). *Forensic psychological assessment*. Boston: Allyn & Bacon.

Tombaugh, T.N. (1996) *Test of Memory Malingering (TOMM): Professional manual*. Toronto, Ontario: Multi-Health Systems.

Chapter 8

Hare, R. (1993). *Without conscience: The disturbing world of the psychopaths among us*. New York: Guilford Press.

Harris, J. (1988). *They always called us ladies*. New York: MacMillan Publishing Co.

Linehan, M. (1993). *Cognitive-behavioral treatment of borderline personality disorder*. New York: Guilford Press.

Wettstein, R. (Ed.) (1998). *Treatment of offenders with mental disorders*. New York: Guilford Press.

Yochelson, S. & Samenow, S. (1975). *The Criminal Personality*. New York: Jason Aronson.

Chapter 9

Goldstein, A.M. (Ed.) (2003). *Forensic psychology. Volume 11 in the Handbook of Psychology*. New York: Wiley.

Melton, G., Poythress, N., Petrila, J. & Slobogin, C. (1997). *Psychological evaluations for the Courts: 2nd Edition*. New York: Guilford.

Chapter 10

Annon, J. (1996). *Assessment Scale for Potential Violence*. Available from author.

Hare, R. (1993). *Without conscience: The disturbing world of the psychopaths among us*. New York: Guilford.

Link, B. & Stueve, A. (1994). Psychotic Symptoms and The Violent/Illegal Behavior of Mental Patients compared to Community Controls in Monahan (Ed.) *Violence and mental disorder*. University of Chicago Press, 137–159.

Monahan, J. (1981). *The clinical prediction of violent behavior*. Washington DC: Government Printing office.

Meloy, J.R. (2000). *Violence risk and threat assessment*. San Diego, CA: Specialized Training Services.

Perlin, M. (2001). *Mental disability on trial*. Washington, D.C.: American Psychological Association.

Perry, G.P. & Orchard, J. (1992). *Assessment & treatment of adolescent sex offenders*. Professional Resource Press: Sarasota, FL.

Quincey, V., Harris, G., Rice, M., & Cormier, C. (1998). *Violent offenders*. Washington DC: American Psychological Association.

Webster, C., Douglas, K., Eaves, D., & Hart, S. (1997). *HCR-20 Assessing Risk For Violence*. Mental Health, Law, and Policy Institute.

Chapter 11

Gottman, J. (1999). *The marriage clinic: A scientifically based marital therapy*. NY: W.W Norton.
Kaslow, F. (Ed.) (2000). *Handbook of couple and family forensics*. NY: Wiley.

Chapter 12

Gould, J.W. (1998). *Scientifically crafted child custody evaluations*. California: Sage.
Holden, Geffner, R., & Jouriles.(Eds.) (1998). *Children exposed to domestic violence*. Washington, D.C.: American Psychological Association.
Kuehnle, K. (1996). *Assessing allegations of child sexual abuse*. Sarasota, FL: Professional Resources Press.

Chapter 13

Ashford, J.B., Sales, B.D. & Reid, W.H. (Eds.) (2001). *Treating adult and Juvenile Offenders with special needs*. Washington, D.C.: American Psychological Association.
Courtois, C. (1999). *Recollections of sexual abuse: Treatment principles and guidelines*. New York: W.W. Norton.
Gold, S.N. (2000). *Not trauma alone: Treatment for child sexual abuse in family and social context*. N.Y.: W.W. Norton.
Walker, L.E.A. (2000). *The battered woman syndrome*. NY: Springer.

Chapter 14

Planned Parenthood website
Center for reproductive rights and NARAL websites

Chapter 15

Fagan, J. & F. Zimring (Eds.) (2000). *The changing borders of juvenile justice: Transfer of adolescents to the criminal court*. Chicago: University of Chicago Press.
Grisso, T. (1998) *Forensic evaluation of juveniles*. Sarasota FL: Professional Resources Press.
Grisso, T. & Schwartz, R. (Eds.) (2000).*Youth on trial: A developmental perspective on juvenile justice*. Chicago, Il.: University of Chicago Press.
Loeber, R. & Farrington, D. (Eds.) (1998). *Serious and violent juvenile offenders: Risk factors and successful interventions*. Thousand Oaks, CA: Sage.
Office of Juvenile Justice and Delinquency Prevention (OJJDP) in Washington DC website

Chapter 16

Meloy, J.R. (Ed.) (2000). *The psychology of stalking: Clinical and forensic perspectives*. NY: Academic Press.
Meloy, J.R. (2000). *Violence risk and threat assessment*. San Diego, CA: Specialized Training Services.
Mohandie, K. (2001). *School violence*. San Diego, CA: Specialized Training Services.

Chapter 17

Perlin, M.L. (2001). *Mental disability on trial*. Washington, D.C.: American Psychological Association.

Stolle, D.P., Wexler, D.B. & Winick, B.J. (Eds.) (2000). *Practicing therapeutic jurisprudence: Law as a helping profession*. Durham, N.C.: Carolina Academic Press.

Wexler, D.B. & Winick, B.J. (Eds.) (1996). *Law in a therapeutic key*. Durham, N.C.: Carolina Academic Press.

Winick, B.J. (1996). *The right to refuse mental health treatment*. Washington, D.C.: American Psychological Association.

Chapter 18

Gilbert, D.T., Fiske, S.T. & Lindsey, G. (Eds.) (1998). *The handbook of social psychology, 4th Ed*. New York: Oxford University Press.

Eberhardt, J.L. & Fiske, S.T. (Eds.) (1998). *Racism: the problem and the response*. Thousand Oaks, CA: Sage.

Fitzgerald, L.F. (1992). *Breaking silence: The harassment of women in academia and the Workplace*. Washington, D.C.: Federation of Cognitive, Psychological, & Behavioral Sciences.

Herman, J. (1992). *Trauma and recovery*. New York: Basic Books.

MacKinnon, C. (1979). *Sexual harassment of working women: A case of sex discrimination*. New Haven, CT: Yale University Press.

O'Donohue, W. (Ed.) (1997). *Sexual harassment: Theory, research and treatment*. Boston: Allyn & Bacon.

Walker, L.E.A. (1994). *Abused women and survivor therapy: A practical guide for the Psychotherapist*. Washington, D.C.: American Psychological Association.

Chapter 19

Goldstein, A.M. (Ed.) (2003). *Forensic Psychology, Vol 11. Handbook of Psychology*. New York: Wiley.

Wrightsman, L. (2001). *Forensic psychology*. Cambridge, MA: Wadsworth.

Chapter 20

Clark, M. & Carpenter, T. (1997). *Without a doubt*. New York: Viking

Grisham, J. (1996). *Runaway Jury*. New York: Doubleday Press.

Schiller, L. & Willworth, J. (1996). *An American Tragedy: The uncensored story of the Simpson defense*. New York: Random House.

Wrightsman, L. (2001). *Forensic psychology*. Cambridge, MA: Wadsworth.

Chapter 21

Shapiro, D.L. (1990). *Forensic psychological assessment*. Needham, MA: Allyn & Bacon.

Walker, L.E.A. (1989). *Terrifying love: why battered women kill and how society responds*. New York: HarperCollins.

Index